MW01627348

Martin O. Holoien
University of California, Santa Barbara

Ali Behforooz
Towson State University

FORTRAN 77
for Engineers and Scientists

Second Edition

Brooks/Cole Publishing Company
Pacific Grove, California

Brooks/Cole Publishing Company
A division of Wadsworth, Inc.

Sponsoring Editor: Michael J. Sugarman
Editorial Assistant: Lainie Giuliano
Production Services Managers: Joan Marsh, Sara Hunsaker
Production Service: InfoTech
Development: John Barnes, Paul Quin
Interior Design: Paul Quin
Cover Design: Sharon Kinghan, Paul Quin
Cover Photo: © R. Royer/Science Photo Library/Photo Researchers
Typesetting: Zetatype Desktop Publishers
Cover Printing: Phoenix Color Corp.
Printing and Binding: R.R. Donnelley/Crawfordsville

The first edition of this text was published under the title *Problem Solving and Structured Programming with ForTran 77*, by Martin O. Holoien and Ali Behforooz, © 1983 by Wadsworth, Inc.

Printed in the United States of America

10 9 8 7 6 5 4 3 2 1

Library of Congress Cataloging-in-Publication Data

Holoien, Martin O., [date]
FORTRAN 77 for Engineers and Scientists, Second Edition /
Martin O. Holoien, Ali Behforooz
462 p. cm.
Includes index.

ISBN 0-534-14166-8

1. Science—Data processing. 2. Engineering—Data processing.
3. FORTRAN (Computer program language) I. Behforooz, Ali, [date]
II. Title.

Q183.9.H64 1991
502.85'5133—dc20

To Edie — *M.H.*

To Farideh and Amir — *A.B.*

Preface

This book is written to meet specific needs of a FORTRAN course offered to engineering and science students. We include a number of features directed at these students:

- *A large number of **easy-to-follow examples**.*
- ***Problem solving techniques** that lead naturally to the development of FORTRAN programs.*
- *Syntax and FORTRAN technique introduced **as students can use it**, so they start programming quickly.*
- *Many scientific and engineering problems, **thoroughly worked out** through executable FORTRAN programs, to show the student why and how to use FORTRAN skills.*
- *A set of **organized exercises**, including programming exercises, at the end of each chapter.*

Our ***problem solving approach*** and the process of developing FORTRAN programs from algorithms is of particular interest. We find that most beginning students have trouble deciding how to start writing a program. They tend to want to launch right into code, but most of the work is actually done before any code is written—in defining the problem, assessing the facts, and analyzing the information to arrive at a solution.

In this book we stress a ***top down approach*** for solving problems. We start with a thorough process of analysis during which the student develops a set of abbreviated English statements, or ***pseudocode***, identifying the steps that must be completed to obtain the desired results. Successively more detailed steps are developed until each pseudocode step suggests one or two FORTRAN statements. This process makes the transition from English to FORTRAN easy even for the first-time programmer. Of course, in developing the pseudocode style and vocabulary, we keep one eye toward the eventual FORTRAN program, so the nature of this pseudocode has been influenced by FORTRAN style and syntax.

In the process of developing solutions, we teach how to break the steps up into subprograms and subroutines. There is specific discussion of designing and implementing ***modular programs***. We work step by step through many classic subroutines, from Euclid's algorithm to bubble sorts, and teach students how to incorporate borrowed subroutines into a program and how to guard against the problems that often arise.

The book is intended for a first computer science course in FORTRAN and problem solving. Students should have completed beginning college algebra. In later chapters, we introduce the most ***important computational techniques*** used in engineering and science—some of them fairly advanced, all of them highly useful. Topical organization allows the instructor to omit some of these advanced applications of the FORTRAN language if desired without destroying continuity.

While we emphasize FORTRAN 77, we realize that it will be unusual for a student to work in a scientific environment without encountering other versions of FORTRAN. In addition, a few aspects of FORTRAN have been used for many years in several versions, even though they are not in FORTRAN 77. So we include, and carefully note, some ***features of other FORTRAN versions***, even though FORTRAN 77 does not include them.

Each ***chapter summary*** provides a quick reference to the concepts in that chapter. The extensive ***index*** makes it easy to locate all places in the book where a given topic is treated.

The book has been ***carefully structured*** so that the skills and concepts we present build on each other. We suggest that you teach concepts in the order they appear, from Chapter 1 through Chapter 8. Should you desire a different sequence, we suggest that you at least complete Chapter 1 and explore the techniques of problem solving before going on to concepts in other chapters.

Acknowledgments. Many of our colleagues assisted us by reviewing the manuscript and providing suggestions and encouragement. The final product is, of course, ours, but we would like to thank those who helped us along the way:

- Professor James P. Bandstra, University of Pittsburgh at Johnstown
- Professor Robert E. Billups, Citrus College
- Dr. Victor Forsnes, Ricks College
- Professor H. George Friedman, University of Illinois
- Professor Judith Hankins, Middle Tennessee State University
- Dr. G.E. Hedrick, Oklahoma State University
- Professor R.G. Selfridge, University of Florida

Martin O. Holoien
Ali Behforooz

Contents

Chapter 1

Problem Solving with Algorithms

In this chapter we explore in some detail the concepts and skills that facilitate problem solving and the development of algorithms. It would be a mistake to underestimate the fundamental importance of these aspects. Once a proper foundation has been laid, you will see that learning a programming language is relatively easy. The remainder of the book is devoted to teaching FORTRAN programming language and its syntax, but without a strong basis in problem solving technique, the most assiduous student will get nowhere.

We often bring up matters of *programming style*. If you plan to become an effective computer user, pay special attention to developing a clear programming style. It can mean the difference between producing programs that are understandable and useful and ones that even you are unable to comprehend once they have become cold to the memory.

Solving Problems

Before we discuss the problem solving process more formally, let's consider some examples that give us some insight into how to be successful at problem solving.

Problem 1.1 Finding an Average

OBJECTIVE Develop a step-by-step procedure that will read a set of numbers and compute and report the average of those numbers.

SOLUTION The average of a set of numbers is obtained by adding the numbers, then dividing the sum by the number of numbers added. Let's derive a version of this definition that lends itself more directly to developing a step-by-step procedure.

Suppose there are two numbers, X1 and X2. Then the average is given by the equation AVERAGE = (X1 + X2)/2

If there are five numbers, X1, X2, X3, X4, and X5, their average is given by the equation AVERAGE = (X1 + X2 + X3 + X4 + X5)/5

In general, if there are N numbers (X1,X2, . . . ,XN) their average is computed by applying the equation AVERAGE = (X1 + X2 + . . . + XN)/N

All of these steps assume that the *values* of the numbers to be averaged are known as well as the *number* of those numbers.

All of the facts mentioned thus far lead us to the following procedure for solving the averaging problem:

1. Obtain the numbers to be averaged.
2. Count the numbers.
3. Compute their sum.
4. Compute the average by dividing their sum by their count.

As we analyze these steps, it becomes clear that more details must be known in order to carry out the actions:

1. ***How do we obtain the numbers?*** Obviously, they can be obtained in a variety of ways. Let's assume that they are written on a set of index cards, one number per card, and that the numbers are obtained by picking the top card and reading the number on it.
2. ***How are the numbers counted?*** One method is to count the cards before we start reading the numbers. This is fine unless we permit other people to add cards to the stack while we are reading the numbers. In that case, our original count will not be correct. Suppose we eliminate this possibility by deciding that as we read the number from the top card, we count that card and continue reading and counting from the top of the stack until there are no more cards.
3. ***How do we add the numbers?*** We could read all the cards first, write the numbers in a column, then add the column. Suppose we select another method, which is to add each number as it is read. As the second number is read it is added to the first number and the sum noted; as the third number is read, it is added to the sum of the previous two, and the new sum noted in the same place. This process continues until the last number is read and added to the accumulated sum, and the sum of all the numbers is available.
4. ***This last step is straightforward.*** Finally the average is computed by dividing the accumulated sum by the count of the numbers read.

Now we are ready to write a more detailed solution. Let's first assign names to specific items, then restate the solution steps.

X Next number to be read

SUM Sum of the numbers read so far

N Count of the numbers read so far

AVERAGE Average of all numbers read

1. Assign to SUM and N the value zero, since no numbers have been read or added.

2. Perform steps 3, 4, and 5 until there are no more numbers to read, then proceed to step 6.

3. Obtain a value for X.

4. Add the value of X to the value of SUM.

5. Add 1 to the value of N.

6. Assign to AVERAGE the quotient SUM/N.

7. Report the value of AVERAGE.

8. Terminate the process.

Notice that this procedure reads and computes the average of any set of numbers. It is thus a *general* solution, not specific to just one set of numbers. Let's see how this solution works in another circumstance.

Problem 1.2
Reporting Average Speed

SITUATION You work for a firm that operates an arc incinerator used to destroy very high risk toxic waste. In transporting the waste from large auto painting plants, byproducts that are both highly toxic and extremely explosive, it is vital to reduce the possibility of traffic accidents.

Federal hazardous waste regulations require your firm to keep records of each driver's speed as well as the average speed for each truckload of waste paint.

Drivers report their location at the beginning and end of each day. The time of the report is recorded automatically, and the mile marker the driver reports is converted into the position on the route in miles from the painting plant.

OBJECTIVE Develop a procedure to compile the speed records from the driver reports.

ANALYSIS Driver reports are recorded in columns for the day N, the number of MILES driven, and the TIME it took in hours. The average daily speed, of course, is simply MILES/TIME.

If all the auto plants were the same distance from the incinerator, the trucks would all take the same number of days to make the drive. If that were, say, 5 days, you could simply define the five daily speeds and the trip summary:

SPECIFIC SOLUTION

SPEED for day 1 = MILES for day 1 / TIME for day 1
SPEED for day 2 = MILES for day 2 / TIME for day 2
SPEED for day 3 = MILES for day 3 / TIME for day 3
SPEED for day 4 = MILES for day 4 / TIME for day 4
SPEED for day 5 = MILES for day 5 / TIME for day 5
AVERAGE of daily speeds = (SPEED for day 1 + SPEED for day 2
+ SPEED for day 3 + SPEED for day 4 + SPEED for day 5) / 5

But the plants are at varying distances, so the trucks take a varying number of days N to reach the incinerator. You can thus see the problem as two smaller problems:

For each day from 1 to N, define the average SPEEDI as MILESI / TIMEI and compute it.

To compute the summary AVERAGE add the values SPEED1 + SPEED2 + . . . + SPEEDN and divide this SPEED_SUM by N.

and define a general solution as follows:

GENERAL SOLUTION

1. Find I.
2. Compute SPEEDI = MILESI / TIMEI for each day I.
3. Compute the summary
   AVERAGE = (SPEED1 + SPEED2 + . . . + SPEEDN) / N.

One way to proceed is to first count the number of daily entries to find N. Then calculate the SPEED for each day. Then calculate the AVERAGE speed. But you'd be going all the way through the table three times. Moreover, if a driver were to report an additional trip during your lunch hour, after you had counted N but before you calculated SPEED, your results would be inconsistent.

PROCEDURE

It's better to accomplish everything in one pass. So from the general solution, we develop the following procedure:

1. Set N and SPEED_SUM to zero, meaning that no numbers have yet been entered in them. Doing this at the beginning means you don't have to worry whether any values are left from the last time you ran the program.
2. Perform steps 3 through 8 for each pair of numbers, then proceed to step 9.
3. Read the next entry for MILES.
4. Read the next entry for TIME.

5. Calculate SPEED = MILES / TIME.
6. Add 1 to N.
7. Report SPEED as the value of the speed for day N.
8. Add SPEED to SPEED_SUM.
9. Calculate AVERAGE = SPEED_SUM / N.
10. Report AVERAGE as the value of the average daily speed.
11. Terminate the process.

This procedure will now produce a correct report no matter how many days the trip takes or how fast it goes. Let's now look at a little more complex but still common problem with checking accounts.

Problem 1.3
Updating a Bank Balance

OBJECTIVE Develop a step-by-step procedure for maintaining a correct record of the balance in a checking account. To do this you need to know the initial amount placed in the account and information about every transaction, including the following:

1. Withdrawals
2. Deposits
3. Service charges
4. Interest earned

SOLUTION First, we assume the bank complies with these checking account ***rules***:

1. If at any time during the month the balance is less than $200, there is a monthly fee of $5 plus a service charge of $0.20 per check. These charges are automatically charged to the account.
2. If the balance remains greater than or equal to $200 and less than $1,000, no monthly fee is charged, nor are there any charges for writing checks.
3. If the balance is $1,000 or more, not only are no charges assessed but interest is paid at the rate of 0.5 percent per month on the balance over $200. This interest is automatically added to the account on the last day of the month.

Next we identify ***terms***:

INITBALANCE The initial balance in the account.

BALANCE The current balance in the account.

TRVALUE The amount of the transaction.

TRCODE A code for identifying the transaction: W for withdrawal, D for deposit, I for interest, and S for service charge.

DATE The date of the transaction.

Then we determine how the ***data*** are collected. For each deposit or withdrawal we read the transaction code TRCODE and the amount of the transaction TRVALUE from a notebook. To determine interest or service charge, we check the current balance at the end of each day and apply the rules.

Finally, we develop a ***procedure*** to be applied daily to give the correct checkbook balance.

1. Assign to BALANCE the value of INITBALANCE.

2. Perform steps 3, 4, and 5 until there are no more transactions; then proceed to step 6.

3. Read TRCODE and TRVALUE.

4. If TRCODE = W then

Assign to BALANCE the difference BALANCE – TRVALUE.

5. If TRCODE = D then

Assign to BALANCE the sum BALANCE + TRVALUE.

6. If BALANCE < 200 then

Assign to TRCODE the value S;

Assign to TRVALUE the product of the number of checks times .20; add 5.00 if this charge has not been added this month.

7. If BALANCE ≥ 1000 then

Assign to TRCODE the value I;

Assign to TRVALUE the product (BALANCE – 200) * 0.005.

8. If TRCODE = S then

Assign to BALANCE the difference BALANCE – TRVALUE.

9. If TRCODE = I then

Assign to BALANCE the sum BALANCE + TRVALUE.

10. Terminate all processing.

COMMENTS Upon checking this solution to our problem it becomes apparent that all is not well.

We need to know the *number* of withdrawals (checks written) so that the service charge can be computed if necessary.

If the balance drops below $200 we must know whether the $5 service charge has *already been added* to the account charges this month.

When the balance reached $1,000 or more, we need to know if it is the *last day of the month*, since we add interest only that day.

No provision has been made for *overdrafts*.

REVISION To revise our solution we introduce two new variable names:

WCOUNT Number of withdrawals.

ADDED Whether the monthly service charge has been added this month. At the start of each month initialize ADDED to NO and when adding the service charge set ADDED to YES.

Here is a revised procedure for maintaining a checkbook balance:

1. Assign to BALANCE the value of INITBALANCE.

2. Read the date and if it is the first of the month, assign to ADDED the value NO.

3. Assign to WCOUNT the value zero to indicate that no withdrawals have occurred yet.

4. Perform steps 5, 6, and 7 until there are no more transaction data; then proceed to step 8.

5. Read values for TRCODE and TRVALUE.

6. If TRCODE = W then

If BALANCE ≥ TRVALUE then

Assign to BALANCE the value BALANCE − TRVALUE.

Add 1 to WCOUNT

7. If TRCODE = D then

Assign to BALANCE the value BALANCE + TRVALUE.

8. If BALANCE < 200 then

Assign to TRCODE the value S.

Assign to TRVALUE the product WCOUNT * 0.20.

If ADDED = NO then

Add 5.00 to TRVALUE.

Assign to ADDED the value YES.

9. If BALANCE > 1000 and DATE is end of month then

Assign to TRCODE the value I.

Assign to TRVALUE the value (BALANCE – 200) * 0.005, the monthly interest.

10. If TRCODE = S then

Assign to BALANCE the difference BALANCE – TRVALUE.

11. If TRCODE = I then

Assign to BALANCE the sum BALANCE + TRVALUE.

12. Terminate all processing.

In the process of obtaining this solution, we begin to build good problem solving habits. We start with one procedure, see the fallacies, and modify it until the desired solution is obtained.

Now let us look at a problem of estimation: What is a practical response when asked to compute an infinite series?

Problem 1.4
Designing a Curved Surface

SITUATION Your firm manufactures a cam for use in highspeed machinery. Because the cam rotates so fast, any discontinuity in the derivative of the curve of its surface can cause it to be crushed by the tremendous forces of the moving rods and rollers around it. To avoid problems, your firm intends to make the cam in the shape of sine and cosine functions projected on polar coordinates. These functions are infinitely differentiable and all derivatives are continuous.

The smallest radius of the cam is to be 15 mm and the largest 35 mm. The largest error that will be tolerated on the surface is 10 micrometers. In order to design the cam, you need a way to compute a value of the function *sin*(*x*) correct to three significant digits.

OBJECTIVE The problem can be stated in general terms: Given a value of *x*, compute an approximate value for the function *sin*(*x*) correct to 3 significant digits. Use the following infinite series:

$$sin(x) = (x/1!) - (x^3/3!) + (x^5/5!) - (x^7/7!) + \ldots + (-1^{(n+1)}\,(x^{(2n-1)}/(2n-1)!))$$

for values such that $-3.14 \le x \le 3.14$

SOLUTION

1. Read a value for *x* and check that it is in the specified range.
2. If $|x| > 3.14$ we subtract 3.14 from $|x|$ as many times as necessary to make the result XNEW less than or equal to 3.14.
3. If $x < 0$ we note it so that *sin*(*x*) is made negative.

4. Let V1 be the value of XNEW, K be the value 3, and initialize N to 1.
5. Let V2 be the value V1 – ($XNEW^K/K!$).
6. If |V1 – V2| ≤ 0.0009 the program has achieved 3-digit accuracy; terminate the process with V2 equal to *sin*(*x*). After V2 has been given the correct sign from step 3, report it as the desired value for *sin*(*x*).
7. If |V1 – V2| > 0.0009 then let V1 be the value of V2 and increment K by 2 and N by 1.
8. Repeat the process from step 5.

Note that we can test for the requested 3-digit accuracy by checking that V1 and V2 are within 0.0009 of each other.

The Process of Program Design

From our experience with these specific problems we can develop some general principles for problem solving. For example, recall the solution presented earlier for the averaging problem. Notice that the final detailed procedure allows us to compute the average for any set of one or more numbers, not restricted to the particular circumstances with which we began. When we write a computer program from such a procedure, we have a program that we can use often, in any circumstance where we need to average numbers.

Problem solving in the context of a course in computer programming always has the final goal of developing a computer program. We need to state the problem and define a solution in such a way that we achieve a *useful* program. The process can be seen as a sequence of four major tasks: First, understand the problem; second, develop a solution; third, test the solution; and, finally, write the program. We'll look at these areas one by one.

Understand the problem. The key to programming success is actually the first phase, understanding the problem. It is absolutely essential to think about the problem carefully and come to understand its basic nature. Think of as many related ideas as you can that even possibly bear on the solution, and carefully evaluate the problem statement itself through input/output analysis.

Input/output analysis. Input and output are both important in developing an understanding of a problem. Unless we give adequate thought to these two elements, there is little likelihood that we will ever design an effective solution. Taken together, a study of these two aspects constitute what is sometimes called the *input/output analysis* of a problem.

First investigate carefully all the information provided, the *problem input*. Normally, the problem statement does not include all related definitions, formulas, restrictions, and the like. You'll need to clarify any uncertainties and find any missing information.

Next, equal care must be given to consideration of all aspects of the information expected from the solution, the *problem output*. A clear understanding of the results you want is a necessary prerequisite to developing a useful solution.

This next example illustrates the necessity of first understanding the problem statement in full detail.

Problem 1.5A
Planning a Purchase

SITUATION Your first job out of college is as a surveyor with a small firm. Because there are only six workers in the office, everyone winds up helping out with whatever needs to be done.

Until recently, the owner handled all sales calls. But today he calls you in to say that he's hired two new salespeople. He wants a system to track sales calls and followups, so he and the new salespeople don't cross paths unaware but can help each other out when necessary.

Since you studied computers in college, he wants you to recommend a software/hardware package he can buy for less than $12,000. And he needs the answer in two days.

As you leave his office, he says, "By the way, why don't you also check around the office to see if there are other uses for additional computing ability. We won't be using this computer full time for sales tracking, and I want to get maximum use out of the system."

OBJECTIVE Develop a procedure for finding in the next two days the best possible computer system for the job.

ANALYSIS In order to solve this problem we need to consider many questions before we even begin planning. Here are some of the questions that come to mind:

- *Do we need any specific reports printed, like a list of sales calls to be made?*
- *Does the $12k budget need to include a printer?*

- *Does the boss merely want to keep lists of sales activity, or does "tracking" include some cross-comparisons?*
- *Which of the possible options a sales tracking system might offer are vital, which are desirable, and which inconsequential?*
- *Are there others in the office with computing needs?*
- *How do these needs compare with the needs of the sales tracking system? With each others needs?*
- *What crucial points besides price will eliminate a system from consideration?*
- *Who are the possible suppliers? How many of them will want to bid on supplying the needed equipment?*
- *What sort of training will the salespeople need to operate the system?*

Only after we develop satisfactory and well defined answers to these and other questions can we begin the program design process.

Develop a solution. Once we complete a thorough input/output analysis, we are ready to develop a solution. It helps to approach building the solution in an organized and thorough manner, always keeping the goals of the problem clearly in mind.

Top down approach. Begin with a comprehensive statement of the problem. This is called the *top* of the problem. Subdivide the problem into tasks, each of which leads down to the next until a result is reached. This *top down* approach can be likened to a system of filtering layers, where the water has different impurities removed as it flows from one layer down to the next, each layer's output providing input for the layer below, until the result is crystal clear.

Modular thinking. Each of these tasks at each level of precision is referred to as a *module*. The goal of the *modular approach* is to formulate a connected series of limited problems, each of which is in itself so simple that the steps to its solution are virtually obvious. The output at each level provides the input for the next module down. The collection of all these partial solutions builds the solution for the original problem.

- *The top down modular process is the problem solving technique best suited to developing clear and productive computer program solutions. The rest of the book is spent in cultivating and refining its use.*

Let's consider an example.

Problem 1.6
Refining a Solution

SITUATION The following exercise involves finding a solution to a classic mathematical problem: Is a number a perfect number? In the process, you will see how a solution is developed and refined until it is clear and complete.

OBJECTIVE Determine whether a given integer is a perfect number. A positive integer is called a *perfect number* if it is equal to the sum of all its integer divisors, including 1. For instance, 6 is a perfect number because

$$6 = 1 + 2 + 3$$

where 1, 2 and 3 are all divisors of 6.

The next larger perfect number is 28.

ANALYSIS One way to solve this problem is to have a list of all perfect numbers. When an integer is given, check the list to see whether the given integer appears. If it does, the integer is a perfect number; otherwise, it is not. At first, this seems like an easy and obvious solution to the problem, but it is actually not even a possible solution. The list of perfect numbers has no known end, so it is not possible to list them all.

A second possible approach is to apply the definition of a perfect number to the given integer. This solution can be divided into the following steps:

1. Obtain a positive integer N.
2. Apply the definition of a perfect number to determine whether or not this integer is a perfect number.
3. Report the results.

The first and third steps are obvious and simple. The second step is clear in its intent, but the process is far from self-evident. It needs further *refinement*. Here is one possible refinement of step 2:

2.1 Find all the integer divisors of N.

2.2 Find the SUM of all the integer divisors of N, including 1 but excluding N.

2.3 Compare N to the SUM of its integer divisors. If they are equal, N is a perfect number; otherwise it is not.

Among these steps, the second and third are easily understood and performed. The first step still does not express its process clearly.

We need to figure out a way to approach step 2.1 itself in more refined steps.

Suppose we start by making a list of divisors of N. Of course, 1 is on this list; we can start with that. Then we can check the succeeding integers 2, 3, 4, and so on up to the integer that is nearest to one-half of N. An integer larger than N/2, except for N itself, cannot be a divisor of N, so we can stop there. Any integers that are divisors of N are put on the list. Here is a possible statement of that process:

2.1.1 Let D represent a potential divisor of N. Set D = 1, since 1 is the first such divisor.

2.1.2 Put 1 on a list called LIST_OF_DIVISORS.

2.1.3 As long as D is less than or equal to the integer part of N/2, perform the following three actions; otherwise proceed to step 2.2.

2.1.3.1 Add 1 to D.

2.1.3.2 Divide N by this new D.

2.1.3.3 If there is no remainder, add D to the LIST_OF_DIVISORS.

SOLUTION Having made these refinements, we now have a step-by-step procedure for solving the problem. Let's list the steps all in order, being particularly careful to state each one clearly.

1. Obtain a positive integer, N.

2.1.1 Let D represent a potential divisor of N. Set D = 1, since 1 is the first such divisor.

2.1.2 Put 1 on a list called LIST_OF_DIVISORS.

2.1.3 As long as D is less than or equal to the integer part of N/2, perform the following three actions; otherwise proceed to step 2.2.

2.1.3.1 Add 1 to D.

2.1.3.2 Divide N by this new D.

2.1.3.3 If there is no remainder, list D on the LIST_OF_DIVISORS.

2.2 Find the SUM of all members of LIST_OF_DIVISORS.

2.3 If SUM = N then

2.3.1 Report that N is a perfect number.

Otherwise

2.3.2 Report that N is not a perfect number.

The goal of refinement. This problem was simple enough that it did not take very long to go through the refinement process. We refined our original step; then one of the refined steps was itself refined, making two levels of refinement. But not all problems are so straightforward. The question keeps coming up:

- *When does a step need no further refinement?*

Unfortunately, there is no formula for determining when subdivision and reorganization should stop. It's a matter of personal taste and an understanding that comes with experience. You may have to go through the process many times before you feel comfortable with knowing when to stop simplifying. A level of refinement that satisfies one person may need further simplification to satisfy another.

It is helpful to keep in mind that the goal of this process is the computer program. When the steps are simple and clear enough that you can write the program with no difficulty, consider the solution complete. However, in a course like this your instructor may expect you to develop algorithms to a specified level of detail. This practice helps you build experience, an essential foundation if you are to become proficient in developing solutions that other people can readily understand.

Guidelines. Even from working through these few problems, we can set out three basic guidelines for formulating a modular solution:

1. ***Each module must be clearly understood.*** Make a thorough input/output analysis of each subtask just as you do for the problem as a whole, carefully considering what information comes in and what the module is expected to produce.
2. ***Study together all tasks with similar or related processes.*** Not only will you eliminate overlapping efforts, but coordinating the development of the modules may also result in simpler structures as you exploit underlying similarities.
3. ***Present all modules in a consistent manner.*** Consistency reduces confusion and keeps the flow of information clear and comprehensible. It also helps assure that when the modules are assembled, the final program produces the expected results.

Always begin by clearly understanding the problem through input/output analysis and then proceed to the construction of clear, self-evident modules. With this careful approach, the final result will be an understandable and effective computer program.

Test the solution. Testing is a continuous process throughout the development of a solution. As each module of the solution is developed, it should be tested in some way for correctness. Often you execute each module using some characteristic input data and then check the results. If each subproblem is verified for correctness, then the combined solution is also likely to be correct.

There remains, however, a phase at which the entire solution is tested to show that it produces correct results. The techniques we use in this final test can also be used during module development to test solutions to individual subproblems.

The most thorough method of demonstrating the correctness of a solution is to apply the techniques used in mathematics to prove a theorem. This way we could show that the solution is correct under any valid circumstances. Such formal proofs, however, are well beyond the level of computer science maturity assumed in this book.

Critical input data. There is a second method, in which we test the solution using several sets of *critical input data.* These data have three basic goals:

1. ***Cover the boundary points of the problem.*** At least one of the sets of input data includes the minimum and maximum values allowed by the solution. A good solution checks for input data beyond the allowable limits, so critical input data should include some data to test this checking mechanism. For instance, the solution for a perfect number needs to check whether the given integer is negative and reject a negative number as invalid input data.
2. ***Include special cases.*** The solution should satisfactorily handle the legitimate occurence of unusual input data not normally present. For example, if you are asked to develop a procedure to alphabetize a set of names, you need to be able to handle identical names that are presented differently, like *St. Paul* and *Saint Paul*, names longer than the maximum you have allowed, and names with an apostrophe, like *O'Connor.*
3. ***Include a completely representative case.*** Sample data needs to test all possible logic paths in the solution. For example, in the checking account balance problem, test the solution with data that result in more than one withdrawal even though the balance is less than $200, data that call for withdrawals greater than the balance, and so on.

As you can tell from these attributes, critical input data must cover all possible cases of the problem. Obviously, your solution cannot be tested for every set of valid data, but by paying attention to the three goals for test data, they can usually cover both the normal conditions and any unusual cases of the problem.

Producing satisfactory critical input data can be difficult. The annals of computer science contain numerous stories of computer programs that have been working correctly for a long time, sometimes years, and suddenly produce erroneous results. This knowledge reminds us that it is impossible to be overly careful when selecting critical input data. And, although testing with critical input data cannot guarantee correctness in the same way as a mathematical proof would, it is usually adequate. If your solution gives correct results using well selected critical input data, you can assume that it is correct for the kind of data it is expected to handle.

Write the program. After a solution has been developed and tested, the final step is to write the programming language statements corresponding to each of the steps. In the approach we have taken it is the detailed step-by-step procedure rather than the computer program that is the true solution for the problem. Once we have the procedure, we convert it into a program to take advantage of the computer's computational skill.

Of course, problems and solutions have been around much longer than computers. Problem solving is not a computer original, but the computer's tremendous speed and remarkable accuracy have created a strong interest in problem solving techniques. For example, scientists have known for years how to compute navigation tables and how to generate the list of prime numbers less than 10 billion. However, in the past, such computations have required years of effort by skilled mathematicians, and even then errors have inevitably crept in. With the computational power of modern computers, either of these tasks can be done in less than an hour, with the assurance that the results will be accurate.

The other chapters in this book introduce you to the basics of FORTRAN programming—the principal computer language of many scientists and engineers. Throughout, remember that problem solving is always the basis for good programming. Perfect syntax and excellent programming habits are of no avail if the solution you develop to start with is flawed. Build your programming technique on a firm basis of top down modular thinking.

Simple Solution Structures

We turn our attention now to some common techniques that are helpful patterns for developing solutions. The three principal types of process that we are likely to use can be categorized as sequential, selection, or iteration. Each process has a corresponding common solution structure.

Sequential structures. In *sequential structures*, actions are performed sequentially in order one after the other. The process is always clear and proceeds entirely on a single level of operation. For example, this short sequence:

EXAMPLE

1. Read the data.
2. Compute the sum of X and Y.
3. Divide the sum just computed by N.
4. Report the result.

Selection structures. *Selection structures* are decision elements in a solution that may alter the sequence of execution of the steps. Usually selection structures provide for the testing of a condition: If the condition is true, one set of actions is taken; if it is false, another set of actions is performed. In other words, a selection divides the sequential steps of a module into two or more possible sets of actions.

One of the simplest of selection structures is known as the *IF-THEN-ELSE structure*. The general form of this structure is as follows:

```
IF Condition is True THEN
      perform Statements T1, T2, . . . , TM;
ELSE
      perform Statements F1, F2, . . . , FN.
```

EXAMPLE

Here is a specific application:

```
IF it is raining THEN
      stay home;              True block
      watch TV;
ELSE
      plan a picnic;          False block
      play softball;
      lie in the sun.
```

If the condition is true (that is, it really is raining), then the actions taken are to stay home and watch TV.

If the condition is false (it is not raining), then the actions taken are to plan a picnic, play softball, and lie in the sun.

We refer to the first set of actions as the *true block* of actions and to the second set as the *false block* of actions.

The selection structure we have just demonstrated is known as the *two-way selection structure.* A special case of this structure is worth noting here: The situation that occurs when no actions are specified if the condition is false. Thus there exists no ELSE followed by subsequent actions. Here is an example:

EXAMPLE

```
IF you are sick THEN
       call the clinic;
       make an appointment with the doctor;
       see the doctor.
```

Nothing is said about what to do if you are *not* sick. The sequence assumes that if you are not sick, things will go on as normal. No special actions need to be specified.

As we proceed with problem solving, you will see a lot of two-way selection structures, both in the complete IF-THEN-ELSE form and the abbreviated IF-THEN form. You will also discover a broader application of this structure called the *multi-way* selection structure.

Iteration structures. In the third type of structure, a block of actions is executed repeatedly some controlled number of times. Each repetition is referred to as an *iteration*, and the structure called an *iteration structure.* Of the three types of solution structures, iteration structures seem to be the most used specifically for computer solutions. Maybe it's that people dislike tedious repetition, so that tasks with a lot of repetition are assigned to computers.

The block of statements that is repeatedly executed is called a *loop*, and the iteration structure a *loop structure* or *repetition structure.*

A key attribute of iteration structures is the control of the number of times they are repeated. Two basic factors control loop repetitions, counters and conditions.

Counter controlled loops. The *counter* in a repetition structure is set up to allow only a predetermined number of repeats. The form of the counter controlled loop structure is as follows:

```
repeat Steps M through N a total of K times.
       Step M;
       Step M + 1;
       .
       .
       .
       Step N;
leave this segment
```

This structure controls steps M through N, known as the *loop body*, by allowing them to be executed exactly K times. Here is a specific example:

EXAMPLE

```
perform the next two steps 100 times
      read X;
      add X to SUM;
leave this segment.
```

This loop structure causes the reading of 100 numbers, one at a time, and accumulates their sum, adding one number at a time to SUM. None of the steps interferes with the control condition of executing the loop 100 times.

This straightforwardly counted control mechanism is preferred to any in which an alternative exit control condition is given within the loop body. Departure from a counter controlled loop structure should be through the exit at the end of the loop. On certain occasions it is acceptable to add a conditional internal exit mechanism.

POOR EXAMPLE

Here's an example of a loop structure with a secondary internal exit. We use a counter controlled loop structure to read and accumulate the sum of up to 100 numbers. However, if a negative number is read, one of the steps within the loop body causes an immediate exit from the loop, whether or not 100 numbers have been processed.

```
perform the next three steps 100 times.
      read X;
      if X is negative, then exit from the loop;
      otherwise, add X to SUM:
leave this segment.
```

If you study this example, you will see that only if all numbers are non-negative will the loop be executed 100 times and use the normal exit.

Condition controlled loops. Instead of matching a predetermined count, a loop can be terminated when certain *conditions* are met. There are two general forms of the condition controlled loop structure. One tests the condition before the loop, the other after.

Form A tests the condition first:

FORM A

```
WHILE Condition is True perform the following N Steps
      Step 1;
      Step 2;
      .
      .
      .
      Step N;
leave this segment.
```

As long as the condition is true, all steps are executed, and the condition is again checked. The only way to leave the loop is when the condition is false. When that occurs, the normal exit at the end of the loop is used. Here is a specific example:

EXAMPLE A

```
WHILE no more than 100 numbers have been read,
and the number just read is positive,
perform the following steps;
       read X;
       add X to SUM;
leave this segment.
```

Compare the net effect of this example and that of the poor example given previously. The results are identical. We still have two conditions, no more than 100 numbers and no negative numbers. But here the only exit is through the condition by which the loop is controlled. A single conditional statement provides for both exit cases.

- *Structure each loop with only* ***one entry*** *and only* ***one exit.***

FORM B

In form B, the condition follows the loop:

```
repeat
       Step 1;
       Step 2;
        .
        .
        .
until Condition becomes True, then leave this segment.
```

Notice that when the condition follows the loop, satisfying the condition terminates it. In form A, the condition must be satisfied each time before entering the loop, and it is only when the condition can no longer be satisfied that the program exits.

As you work with the examples, you will develop a sense about which form to use in which circumstances. Always be very careful to notice when the condition is checked, and how it should be stated to trigger an exit at the proper time.

Problem 1.5B Selecting a System

SITUATION

Let's return to the problem of choosing a computer system to track sales calls. Since we last discussed the situation, you have been able to define the parameters of the problem, and have come up with a set of conditions. One of the important considerations is that you can stop evaluating a potential supplier when it has become clear that the system offered does not meet your needs.

SOLUTION

1. There are four possible suppliers. Each has available a system that is said to perform the needed functions for the price.
2. Each supplier is given a list of 60 requests for specific results from the system, including periodic reports, questions to which immediate answers are needed, and related queries.
3. All responses to each request are evaluated in relation to a preset appropriate response requirement before proceeding to the next request. A potential supplier is eliminated when no appropriate response is given to 10 requests.
4. The study terminates when there is only one supplier remaining or when responses to all 60 requests have been given by each potential supplier.
5. The supplier chosen is the single one remaining at the end of the study. If that condition does not occur, choose the supplier with the fewest null or inappropriate responses.

TERMS Assume the following abbreviations:

BADR1, BADR2, BADR3, BADR4 Null or inappropriate responses by suppliers 1 through 4, respectively; begin each at 0.

SUPL Suppliers currently in the contest; begin with 4 and reduces as potential suppliers are eliminated.

REQ Responses to requests evaluated; also begin at 0.

MODULES Divide the problem into the following subproblems:

1. Evaluate responses.
2. Keep track of REQ and BADR1, . . . , BADR4.
3. Keep track of SUPL.
4. Check for the chosen supplier.

Evaluate the responses following this specific sequence:

1.1 Read a request and its preordained range of appropriate responses.

1.2 Compare the response of supplier 1.

1.3 Compare the response of supplier 2.

1.4 Compare the response of supplier 3.

1.5 Compare the response of supplier 4.

Keep track of REQ and BADR1, . . . , BADR4 as follows:

2.1 For each request evaluated, add 1 to REQ.

2.2 Each time a potential supplier provides an inappropriate response, or no response at all, add 1 to the relevant BADRN, where N = 1, 2, 3, 4 for the 4 suppliers.

Keep track of SUPL as follows:

3.1 When BADRN becomes 10, supplier N is eliminated.

3.2 Then subtract 1 from SUPL.

Check for the winner using these steps:

4.1 If SUPL = 1, there is only one remaining potential supplier; award them the contract.

4.2 Otherwise, supplier N for whom BADRN is least wins the contract.

The solution to this problem is summarized as follows:

```
While SUPL>1 and REQ<60 perform the following:
       evaluate responses;
       keep track of REQ, BADR1, BADR2, BADR3, and BADR4;
       keep track of SUPL:
leave this segment;
check for the contract winner.
```

Exercises 1.1

1. Define *sentinel data* and give two synonyms for the phrase.

2. List and briefly describe each of the four problem solving phases.

3. What is meant by *problem input, problem output,* and *input/output analysis*?

4. Describe the *top down approach* to algorithm development.

5. In the solution testing phase, what is meant by *critical input data*?

6. Describe sequential, selection, and iteration structures.

7. Distinguish between counter controlled and condition controlled loop structures. Give an example of each.

8. Go through the first two problem solving steps to develop a solution algorithm for this problem: Given the required dimensions, compute the volume of a right circular cylinder and report as output its volume and dimensions.

▪ *For exercises 9–11, perform the analysis and discussion necessary in order to complete the first three tasks in the development of a solution.*

9. Knowing that January 1, 1989 fell on a Sunday, develop a solution for the problem of taking any four-digit year designation and reporting the day of the week on which January 1 of that year occurred.

10. Now we want to be able to accept as input data someone's birthday and determine the day of the week on which it occurred.

▪ *Keep in mind when you discuss and analyze exercises 9 and 10 that when the integer representing the year is divisible by 4 it is a leap year and February has 29 days.*

11. A person has a total of $100 and wants to spend it in such a way that their total satisfaction level is higher. This table shows three items that can be purchased, the cost for buying one unit of each, and the satisfaction level derived from each purchase.

Item	*Cost*	*Satisfaction level*
Sewing material	$15	4
Shoes	$30	6
Book	$10	3

Determine what purchases should be made in order to achieve the maximum satisfaction level, and not spend over $100.

Using Algorithms

A dictionary definition of *algorithm* goes something like this: "A step-by-step problem solving procedure, as with a computer." The word is derived from the name *al-Khowarizmi*, or, to be complete, Abu Ja'far Mohammad ibn Musa al-Khowarizmi, the famous Persian mathematician of the ninth century, best known for his work in algebra.[1]

Because of the importance of algorithms to computer science, many people in the field have devoted considerable effort to studying and analyzing them. The literature on the subject is vast, and the interested student can find many current books on the topic. Our discussion in this chapter is simple and introductory, and does not begin to explore the many complexities and uses of the algorithm. Nevertheless, this coverage will help you make good use of this important tool of computer scientists.

1. For further information about the origin of the word, see Knuth, Donald E., *The Art of Computer Programming,* 2nd Edition, v.1 (Reading, MA: Addison-Wesley, 1976)

Two Ancient Algorithms

Before we present a formal definition, let's consider two classic examples that will help us understand just what an algorithm does.

Euclid's algorithm. It is appropriate that the first algorithm we consider is *Euclid's algorithm,* a procedure used for centuries to find the greatest common divisor of two positive integers M and N.

The greatest common divisor is the largest integer D that divides both M and N, where M is greater than or equal to N. For example, the greatest common divisor of 12 and 8 is 4.

ALGORITHM

1. Divide M by N and call the remainder from this division R.
2. If R is not equal to zero, then set M = N and N = R and repeat from step 1.
3. If R = 0, then set D = N.
4. Report D as the greatest common divisor of M and N.
5. Terminate processing.

When a condition is true, as in step 2, an action is specified. When that same condition is false, the program moves to the next action immediately following, in this case step 3.

▪ *Unless specifically instructed, programs perform all steps in strict sequence.*

Let's apply this algorithm to some specific data so you can clearly understand its use.

EXAMPLE 1 *Euclid's algorithm: If M = 286 and N = 105*

Loop execution	*Value of M*	*Value of N*	*Value of R*
1	286	105	76
2	105	76	29
3	76	29	18
4	29	18	11
5	18	11	7
6	11	7	4
7	7	4	3
8	4	3	1
9	3	1	0

The ninth execution of the loop in algorithm steps 1, 2, and 3 yields R=0 and assigns D=1. At step 4, 1 is reported as the greatest common divisor of 286 and 105, and processing stops.

EXAMPLE 2 *Euclid's algorithm: If* M = *360 and* N = *135*

Loop execution	*Value of M*	*Value of N*	*Value of R*
1	360	135	90
2	135	90	45
3	90	45	0

The third time through the algorithm produces R=0, so step 3 results in the assignment D=45. At step 4 we report 45 as the greatest common divisor of 360 and 135.

ANALYSIS It is clear from these two examples that all the actions required are precisely defined in the algorithm. However, it is not clear from just reading the algorithm how it terminates. Only by testing the algorithm with data does it become clear that the algorithm does actually stop. As you now know, however, even the first set of data, in spite of the tedious calcualations it requires, finally results in the algorithm coming to a halt.

A simple mathematical proof shows that Euclid's algorithm eventually halts after a finite number of steps regardless of the values of M and N. This is not the place to seriously explore that aspect of algorithms; simply consider the number of times that we could possibly perform step 3. Because the divisor starts as M and is repeatedly changed to the reminder R, even if R is decrease by only 1 after each division, M can not be changed more than M–1 times before the remainder is zero, thus stopping any further processing. This analysis should help you believe that Euclid's algorithm really is finite.

The Sieve of Eratosthenes. Consider another example of an algorithm that we inherit from the ancient Greeks, this from an Alexandrian mathematician of the third century B.C. Mathematicians define a *prime number* as any positive integer greater than 1 that has no integer divisors except 1 and itself. Examples are 2, 3, 5, 7, 11, 13, 17, 19, and so on. The *Sieve of Eratosthenes* determines the prime numbers less than a given integer N.

ALGORITHM

1. Define the set of integers S = {2,3,4,5,6, . . . , N}.

2. While set S is not empty perform steps 2.1 and 2.2.

2.1 Report the first number of S as a prime number.

2.2 Delete all members of S that are divisible by the number just reported, including the number itself.

3. Stop processing.

EXAMPLE Let's apply the algorithm to the case of N = 30.

STEP 1 S = {2, 3, 4, 5, 6, . . . , 30}.

STEP 2.1 Reports 2 as a prime number.

STEP 2.2 S = {3, 5, 7, 11, 13, . . . , 29}.

STEP 2.1 Reports 3 as a prime number.

STEP 2.2 S = {5, 7, 11, 13, 17, . . . , 29}.

STEP 2.1 Reports 5 as a prime number.

STEP 2.2 S = {7, 11, 13, 17, 19, . . . , 29}.

STEP 2.1 Reports 7 as a prime number.

STEP 2.2 S = {11, 13, 17, 19, 23, 29}.

S is still not empty, so we repeat step 2.1 yet again.

STEP 2.1 Reports 11 as a prime number.

STEP 2.2 S = {13, 17, 19, 23, 29}.

As you can see, all these 5 remaining members of S are reported in turn as prime numbers and removed from the set, eventually resulting in S being empty. At that point the algorithm executes step 3 and comes to a stop. Step 3 is executed only when we leave the condition controlled loop initiated at step 2.

ANALYSIS In this algorithm it is again clear that every step is well defined, precisely specifying what conditions are to be checked and what actions are to be taken. It's finiteness is probably more apparent than that of Euclid's algorithm. In fact, given any positive integer N, where N is greater than or equal to 2, steps 2.1 and 2.2 can be performed a maximum of N – 1 times. Step 2.2 deletes at least one member of set S each time it is performed. Since step 1 defines set S such that there are at most N – 1 members, step 2.2 can not be executed more than N – 1 times—clearly a finite algorithm.

Properties of the Algorithm

An algorithm is a finite sequence of well defined and effectively performable actions or steps for solving a specific problem in a finite length of time. It is useful to keep in mind some of the properties that make algorithms so valuable in computer science and set them apart from procedures, processes, routines, or techniques. An algorithm is

1. ***Finite.*** An algorithm halts after executing one or more of its steps a finite number of times. Without this property, an algorithm could not be implemented by either a human or a machine.

2. ***Definite.*** Every step of an algorithm is precisely stated, unambiguous, and well defined. This is an important quality, and is physically and mathematically possible.
3. ***Effective.*** An algorithm specifies simple actions that can be effectively performed. This property guarantees that the steps of an algorithm can actually be executed.
4. ***Input driven.*** An algorithm has zero or more input data.
5. ***Output producing.*** An algorithm produces one or more results, called *output.*

Problem 1.7 Addressing Numerical Operations

In each of the following problems, we develop a solution algorithm and examine it for the presence of all five essential properties. These short algorithms address a variety of simple numerical operations that find a variety of uses in science and engineering.

PART 1 Numerical experiments that generate tables of results for a function being studied are an increasingly common scientific tool. These experiments are set up to optimize a situation, that is, to find the best or worst possible case, usually by finding the maximum or minimum of a particular variable. Here, we look for a maximum.

OBJECTIVE Given a set of N numbers X1, X2, . . . , XN, find the largest number in the set.

ALGORITHM

1. Read the numbers X1, X2 . . . , XN.
2. Assume X1 is the largest number in the set and assign its value to LARGE.
3. Compare LARGE to XI, for I = 2, 3, 4, . . . , N. In each comparison, if XI > LARGE, then assign to LARGE the value of XI.
4. Report LARGE as the largest of the numbers and stop processing.

EVALUATION *Finite:* Step 3 is executed N – 1 times, after which step 4 is performed and processing stops.

Definite: None of the steps is ambiguous.

Effective: All actions are simple ones that can easily be performed.

Input/output: There are N input data and one output datum.

PART 2 OBJECTIVE The general problem is to find the first 100 positive integers divisible by 7.

ALGORITHM 1

1. Set the number of integers divisible by 7, call this COUNT, to zero. Set NUMBER to 1.
2. Increase NUMBER by 1.

   If NUMBER is a multiple of 7, increase COUNT by 1 and report NUMBER as a number divisible by 7.
3. If COUNT < 100, repeat the process from step 2.
4. Stop processing.

ALGORITHM 2 Here's an alternative:

1. Set COUNT to 0 and NUMBER to 7.
2. Report NUMBER as a number divisible by 7.
3. Increase COUNT by 1 and NUMBER by 7.
4. If COUNT ≤ 100, repeat the process from step 2.
5. Stop processing.

EVALUATION A cursory review shows that both algorithms are *finite*, *definite*, and *effective*. Neither algorithm requires input data, but both have the set of all positive integers available, which in a sense is *input*. The *output* consists of the first 100 positive integers divisible by 7.

Although both algorithms have the five essential properties, a little analysis will disclose that algorithm B is at least seven times faster. Algorithm B starts the process with a number 7, known to be a multiple of 7. Since the next value of the number is obtained by adding 7, it also will be a multiple of 7. In algorithm A, the number is computed from a staring value of 1 in increments of 1, thus requiring more time to obtain and test 100 integers that are multiples of 7.

▪ *Many problems, like this one, can be solved by more than one technically correct algorithm. The objective is to find the one that is more efficient.*

PART 3 OBJECTIVE Develop an algorithm to find all positive integers divisible by 7.

ALGORITHM

1. Set NUMBER = 7.
2. Report NUMBER as in integer divisible by 7.
3. Assign to NUMBER the value NUMBER + 7.
4. Repeat the process from step 2.

EVALUATION It will not take you long to perceive that although this algorithm produces output consisting of positive integers that are divisible by 7, it will never come to a halt. Therefore, the algorithm is *not finite* and cannot be implemented on a computer.

Of course, the basic fault of this whole situation lies in the problem statement. There is no way to find *all* positive integers divisible by 7 because there are infinitely many of them. Consequently there does not exist a finite algorithm to solve this problem.

PART 4 For encryption and decryption of privileged information, most modern systems use a nonrepeating sequence of digits as a key. A good key is generated from a definition, rather than having to be physically transported from sender to receiver. This makes the transmission safer. A good key is the Jth root of a ratio of two prime numbers, where J is another prime number. In order to use this key, both sender and receiver need to be able to easily find prime numbers.

OBJECTIVE Develop an algorithm that reads a positive odd integer N, where N is greater than 3, and determines whether N is a prime number.

SOLUTION The solution to this problem begins with recognizing that N, since it is odd, has no even divisors. Also, no divisor can be greater than (N+1)/2.

Therefore, by searching the set

{3, 5, 9, . . . , K}

where K is the greatest odd integer less than or equal to (N+1)/2 for a divisor of N,

we will be able to determine whether N is prime. If a divisor is found among the numbers of that set, N is reported as a nonprime number; otherwise, N is reported as prime.

ALGORITHM IS-N-PRIME

1. Read a positive odd integer N.

2. Assign to divisor D the value 3 and compute K as the greatest odd integer greater than or equal to the value of (N+1)/2.

3. While D is less than or equal to K and N is not divisible by D, perform steps 3.1. and 3.2.

3.1 Increase D by 2.

3.2 Compute N/D.

4. If the final value of D is greater than K, then report that N is prime.

5. Else terminate processing.

EVALUATION Because the value of D in this algorithm controls the repetition process, it is easy to see that the algorithm is *finite*, with D having an initial value of 3 and not exceeding K.

All of the steps are unambiguous, so the algorithm is *definite*.

Every step requires a simple action that can be performed, so the algorithm is *effective*.

There is one *input* datum required, the value of N.

The *output* of the algorithm is either the statement "N is not prime" or "N is prime."

Therefore, all essential properties of algorithms are present. Although this algorithm is easy to understand it is not necessarily the most efficient. Later in this chapter we shall present a simpler algorithm and also explore an alternative that includes error-checking capability.

- *This algorithm is named Is-N-Prime. Try it with at least one prime number, as well as with one that you know is not prime.*

PART 5 The prime numbers in our key can be no larger than a fixed constant N. We want to develop now a table of such numbers, from which codes can be randomly chosen.

OBJECTIVE Develop an algorithm to find all prime numbers less than the given positive odd integer N, where N is greater than 3.

SOLUTION The *Sieve of Eratosthenes* actually can be used to produce our table. But there is a different algorithm, we shall call *Primes-Less-than-N* that accomplishes the same results.

We employ algorithm *Is-N-Prime* to determine whether the positive odd integers between 3 and N, each one denoted by NUM as it occurs, are prime. If a NUM is prime, we report it; otherwise we do not. In either case, the algorithm continues with another value for NUM until all positive odd integers less than N have been tested.

ALGORITHM PRIMES-LESS-THAN-N

1. Read a positive odd integer N ≥ 3.

2. Report 2 and 3 as the first two prime numbers, and assign the value 5 to NUM.

3. Perform steps 3.1 through 3.4 until NUM > N.

3.1 Assign to divisor D the value 3 and compute K as the greater integer less than or equal to the value of (NUM + 1)/2.

3.2 While D is less than or equal to K and NUM is not divisible by D, perform steps 3.2.1 and 3.2.2.

3.2.1. Increase D by 2.

3.2.2. Compute NUM/D.

3.3 If the final value of D is greater than K, then report that NUM is prime.

3.4 Increase NUM by 2.

4. Stop processing.

In this algorithm we first report the integers 2 and 3 as prime. This is valid because N is greater than 3.

Notice that we have lifted steps 3.1–3.3 above almost verbatim from steps 2–4 of the algorithm *Is-N-Prime*. Because of the different condition, though, this algorithm does not terminate as soon as it has determined whether a give number is prime; it continues until it has processed all the numbers less than N.

▪ *It is often possible when developing an algorithm to insert steps from an algorithm previously developed.*

PART 6 Suppose you are a professor of computer science who needs to create problems for quizzes, examinations,and homework. The problems must involve nothing more complicated than simple algebra, and must be solvable by a well-defined algorithm.

OBJECTIVE Develop an algorithm for creating such problems.

ALGORITHM

1. Select a mathematically well defined set of numbers, for instance all the positive integers or all rational numbers.
2. Select a property shared by some but not all members of the set that can be defined in precise mathematical terms, for instance being even or divisible by 7.
3. If the number of members in the set chosen in step 1 is finite, write the problem as follows and terminate processing:

   Devise a procedure to find the <SET FROM 1> *that are* <PROPERTY FROM 2>.
4. If the number of members in the set chosen in step 1 is infinite, create a limiting condition that will select a finite number of members of the set. The limiting condition should allow a mix of some numbers that have the property in step 2 and some that do not.

   Then write the problem as follows and terminate processing:

   Devise a procedure to find the <SET FROM 1> *that are* <PROPERTY FROM 2> *and* <LIMITING CONDITION FROM 4>.

EVALUATION If you review this algorithm, you will find that it is *finite* and *definite*—none of the steps is ambiguous.

It is *effective* in the sense that all actions are simple and can be easily accomplished. Of course, the nature of this problem is such that formal specification of the steps requires a high order of abstract mathematics, but informal explanations given in a few sentences of ordinary English are sufficient for most people to follow the steps.

Knowledge of the kinds of numbers there are and their properties is the necessary *input.*

Production of a problem solvable by an algorithm is the *output.*

How to Write an Algorithm

Skill in creating algorithms is so important to becoming a good programmer/analyst that some universities offer entire courses in the topic. Of course, we will not develop the concepts to those depths, nor will we appeal to very sophisticated techniques. This section helps you develop essential skills and feel comfortable with algorithms as the key to problem solving.

The problems above helped define algorithms and their five essential properties. We now proceed to the basic steps in developing an algorithm. The process is parallel to the process of program design discussed at the beginning of this chapter: First, plan and organize, then set standards, and finally test the algorithm. The same logic is expressed in all stages of problem solving, from design through algorithm to the writing of the final FORTRAN code.

Plan and organize. Getting started is often the biggest hurdle to beginning computer programmers. Four simple organizing steps can help you begin creating a suitable algorithm for a given problem.

1. ***Write a precise statement*** of the problem to be solved, including the input data provided and the output to be reported.
2. ***Confirm clear specification*** of input data and required output.
3. ***Identify and list steps*** that must be solved in order to obtain the desired results; these are the subproblems.
4. ***Identify and list actions*** that must be completed to solve each subproblem.

Set standards. Once the beginner has assessed the problem and created a list of subproblems to be solved, the next big hurdle is to find the correct solution to each of the problems. In order to do this, you first need to know that in most cases there is no one correct solution to any problem, and then to develop a set of personal standards that will help you choose among the possible solutions. The basic worth of your solution is based on the care with which you planned and organized the problem, but it is also important to develop solutions that result in computer code that is fast, memory efficient, and well structured.

Choosing a solution. Already you may have asked yourself this question:

- *Is there a **unique** algorithm for solving a given problem?*

The answer is ***no***, as you probably surmised when we introduced both the *Sieve of Eratosthenes* and the *Primes-Less-than-N* algorithms to solve a single problem.

Theoretically, there are as many different algorithms for solving a given problem as there are people who develop them. However, the various workable solutions for a single problem tend to differ insignificantly. This leads us to suspect that although there is never a unique correct algorithm, there is usually agreement on the basic ingredients of a solution to any given problem.

Because solutions vary, it will often be your job to choose among a group of algorithms proposed or available to solve a given problem. In such a situation, the first order of business is to ask,

- *Which algorithm correctly solves the problem?*

Choosing among several valid algorithms starts with correctness, but there are many other factors involved. You may be working in a situation where you have only a small amount of computer time available or are using a microcomputer with limited memory resources. You may have unlimited resources, but need to reach a conclusion on the problem very quickly without time to spend on elaborate programming. You may be addressing a very focused problem, using many algorithms together to build a modular solution, or you may be working yourself only on a module for another, larger program. The answers to these further questions will help you define your criteria:

- *Which algorithm takes the least amount of computer time?*
- *Which algorithm, when coded into a computer program, takes the least amount of computer storage?*
- *Which algorithm can be implemented most quickly and easily?*
- *Which algorithm is most general?*

We will discuss these issues in turn, using examples to help develop your skill in analyzing and solving simple problem modules. A complete presentation of program speed and memory use issues requires computer and mathematics knowledge beyond the scope of this book. But as you experiment with writing and evaluating algorithms, you will learn through example how to achieve fast, efficient, and logical solutions.

Speed. It's not easy to judge just how fast any solution will be to execute, but you can notice how many steps an action takes. If you are conservative about the number of operations needed to accomplish a solution, you will build algorithms with fewer steps that are in consequence relatively fast to execute. For example, remember the discussion on finding numbers divisible by 7; simply introducing a step that skipped to the next seventh number saved computations on six intermediate numbers that were worthless in solving our problem. Such directness makes a solution neater and faster.

Because it is virtually impossible to compute the exact time needed to execute a given algorithm is no reason to ignore speed considerations. Be aware of the importance of efficiency, and use that as a guide in judging a good algorithm. The following two problems demonstrate this point.

Problem 1.8
Constructing the Simpler Solution

OBJECTIVE Given two positive integers N and M, determine whether N is divisible by M.

ALGORITHM

1. Read N and M.
2. Compute K as the greatest integer less than or equal to N/M.
3. Compute I = (K*M) – N.
4. If I = 0, report that N is divisible by M.
5. If I is not zero, report that N is not divisible by M.
6. Terminate processing.

Note that the time required to execute this algorithm is independent of the input data. Whatever the values of N and M, there is one set of computations.

REVISED ALGORITHM Now consider a second algorithm that solves the same problem.

1. Read N and M.
2. Assign K the value of N.
3. Compute K = K – M.
4. If K > 0, repeat the process from step 3.
5. If K = 0, report that N is divisible by M and terminate processing.
6. If K < 0, report that N is not divisible by M and terminate processing.

Here, the number of operations is definitely dependent on the input data. The larger the value of N with respect to M, the greater the number of times step 3 is executed. Thus, the greater the difference between M and

N, the longer it will take to complete these computations. It is obvious, then, that the original algorithm is faster.

Problem 1.7.4B Simplifying Is-N-Prime

DISCUSSION In the algorithm *Is-N-Prime,* we use divisors that increase in value up to the greatest integer less than or equal to the value (N+1)/2. It is easy to see that a number half the size of N is the largest divisor—such a number would divide into N two times; a larger number would divide at best once.

It actually turns out, however, that the largest divisor we need to test is the square root of N. Consider the case of N = 150.

EXAMPLE 1

150 = 2 * 75 = 3 * 50 = 5 * 30 = 6 * 25 = 10 * 15
= 15 * 10 = 25 * 6 = 30 * 5 = 50 * 3 = 75 * 2

Notice that in the second line, the factors repeat from those in the first line, simply switching position. The 10 factors of 150 shown in the first line are a complete list.

Thus we notice that we can stop searching for factors once the first, or leftmost, factor reaches the square root of N.

EXAMPLE 2 Now consider N = 71. Assume that *p*1, *p*2, *p*3, and *p*4 are integers. We can describe the possibilities as follows:

71 = 2 * *p*1	*71 is not divisible by 2; there is no p1*
71 = 3 * *p*2	*71 is not divisible by 3; there is no p2*
71 = 5 * *p*3	*71 is not divisible by 5; there is no p3*
71 = 7 * *p*4	*71 is not divisible by 7; there is no p4*

Therefore, 71 is a prime number. We do not have to check further. The possible divisor of 71 next greater than 7 is 11, the next integer not divisible by 2, 3, or 5, all numbers that are themselves not divisors of 71. Now suppose

71 = 11 * *p*5

where *p*5 is an integer.

Since we have seen that no number smaller than 11 is a divisor of 71, *p*5 must be 11 or greater. But that is impossible because 11 * 11 = 121, more than 71. Therefore, *p*5 does not exist.

It was sufficient to test potential divisors only up to 8, the greatest integer less than the square root of 71. Because 8 = 2 * 4, neither of which is a divisor, it actually sufficed to test up to the greatest prime integer less than or equal to the square root of 71.

REVISED ALGORITHM IS-N-PRIME

We now present another algorithm for determining whether a number is prime, using the discovery that we need not search beyond the square root of N.

1. Read N.
2. If N ≤ 0, then report Bad Input Data and terminate processing.
3. If N = 2 or N = 3, then report N is prime and terminate processing.
4. If N is even, then report N is not prime and terminate processing.
5. Compute K = greatest integer less than or equal to the square root of N.
6. Assign D = 3.
7. While D ≤ K and N is not divisible by D, do steps 7.1 and 7.2.

   7.1 Increase D by 2.

   7.2 Compute N/D.
8. If D > K, then report that N is prime.
9. Stop processing.

There are two reasons that this algorithm requires fewer operations—and thus less time to compute—than the original *Is-N-Prime*:
Step 4 eliminates all even integers (except 2, which was eliminated in step 3), so we need to check divisibility of only odd integers, taking only half the iterations.
The algorithm stops when D equals the square root of N, a number usually much smaller than the previous limit of (N+1)/2.

Memory. The second standard for algorithms is that they lead to programs that are as conservative of computer memory as possible. In spite of modern developments in computer hardware, computer memory remains a relatively costly and limited resource.

Some confusion enters here, because the more you work with computer programs, the more you see that the speed with which a program executes is often inversely related to the amount of memory it uses. There is a tradeoff between the two resources, and which aspect to emphasize depends on the situation. For example, a navigation system for a manned space vehicle will disregard memory conservation principles in favor of speed: Human lives may depend on obtaining results quickly. On the other hand, a program that produces monthly checks for Social Security recipients is likely to conserve memory costs and run overnight so that checks are delivered on time.

Even when speed of computation is the highest goal, however, it is not necessary to waste memory. And reviewing your algorithms for memory conservation will often lead you to notice ways of writing more effective and faster running algorithms.

Structure. The logical and physical organization of an algorithm should be easily understandable. An algorithm that is organized in both physical and logical ways is called a *structured algorithm.* Like the solution logic that preceeds it, the algorithm is developed top down in modules. And like the computer program that follows, the layout and logic of the algorithm are both important.

Physical format. Algorithm format visually indicates the relationships among steps. The most common technique is *indentation.* Loops, the various parts of conditional structures, and other related sets of operations indent one level beyond the condition statement that introduces them. The writer or reviewer of the algorithm can then easily keep track of opening and closing statements and their respective operations, even in complex nested loop structures.

The other principal way of showing relationships is by using extra *line spaces* between modules—sometimes even adding titles. This keeps subdivisions clear and makes it easier to review and revise the algorithm. Related FORTRAN code issues are discussed in detail in Chapter 2.

Logical development. The flow of operations in an algorithm starts with the first step and moves more or less straightforwardly to the last step. Loop structures do not confuse this order, because they execute for a finite number of iterations and then pass the control on to the next executable step. Branching backward and forward, however, only introduces confusion. It is important to be easily able to follow the logic of the solution.

Writing structured algorithms requires practice. Some people look on problem solving as an art acquired only though experience; others think of it as a science that benefits from the study of rules. Everyone agrees that the more one does it, the better one gets. Take advantage of the exercises presented throughout this book to help you gain practice in solving problems through algorithm development.

Some people refer to the development phase just preceding the writing of program statements as the writing of *semicode* or *pseudocode.* At this stage the tasks are detailed enough that they can readily be coded directly from the abbreviated English of the algorithm into programming language statements. After we discuss the test phase of algorithm development, we present the practice and theory of using pseudocode.

Test. An algorithm is simply a formalized problem solution. In developing the algorithm, just as in exploring any sort of solution, testing is a continuing and important part of the process. It is not safe to assume that a sequence of simple actions that seems to solve a problem actually does so. While it is possible to proceed with the implementation of the computer program without testing the algorithm, the resulting frustration is so great that many beginning programmers give up hope of ever writing a correct program.

There are two types of common programming errors: *Logic errors*, or errors in the basic design of the solution, and grammatical errors, also known as *syntax errors*. Eliminating logic errors in the algorithm allows the programmer to deal separately with syntax errors in the final code.

Testing begins as soon as the solution for any module is complete. Check each subalgorithm for correctness before proceeding to the next one. Although the word *debugging* refers to finding and removing errors in computer programs, we use it also for related processes with algorithms. Algorithm debugging includes proving correctness, tracing, and running test data. The details of these processes, especially the construction of critical input data, are the same as for basic problem solutions, discussed above.

Proving correctness. The process of proving an algorithm correct is similar to proving a mathematical theorem true. There is a large and growing body of supporting theory, the discussion of which would lead us well beyond the level of computer science knowledge expected in this book. For our purposes, it is usually sufficient to evaluate the correctness of an algorithm by tracing or by running test data.

Interested readers may want to pursue the subject of formal proofs on their own.[2]

Tracing. The process of using pencil and paper to execute an algorithm step by step using critical input data is called *desk checking* or *tracing* the algorithm. Desk checking is time consuming, but it is often the only method available to explore the solution logic. Select your data with care, as in every test stage.

2. An excellent introductory paper is Meyer, Bertrand, *An Introduction to the Art of Writing Correct Programs* (University of California, Santa Barbara: Department of Computer Science. Technical Report TRCS 84-05), a copy of which may be obtained from the Department of Computer Science, UCSB, Santa Barbara, CA 93106. Another source of introductory information is Gries, David, *The Science of Programming* (Berlin: Springer Verlag, 1981).

Running test data. We do not recommend running a program implementation of an untested algorithm. Sometimes, however, the most pragmatic process for testing an algorithm may be to translate it into programming language statements and run the resulting program using several sets of critical data. As with desk checking an algorithm, the proper selection of critical data is essential if the program test is to be effective. We warn you again of the potential source of frustration inherent to this process: The presence of program syntax errors. You may spend so much of your energy on eliminating them that you have little left for finding and eliminating the logic errors made in developing the algorithm.

As practice in debugging an algorithm, let's turn back again to the algorithm *Primes-Less-than-N* and look at some new options.

Problem 1.7.4C
Checking Errors with Is-N-Prime

SITUATION For many encryption systems the key is changed daily or hourly. This is often done by using a procedure to generate the prime root of a prime number, each day using a new *seed* or starting number.

Your firm is generating each day's key using the square root of

```
OLDKEY * (YRDAYS - YRDATE) / (MODAYS - MODATE)
```

where YRDATE is the day of the year, and
MODATE is the day of the month, with
YRDAYS given as 365 and MODAYS for February always 28.

You then need to check for the nearest prime number before taking the square root. But in leap years, this number may twice become negative, and negative prime numbers are undefined. Revise the former solution for *Is-N-Prime* to handle negative numbers.

OBJECTIVE Given an integer N, determine whether it is prime.

SOLUTION Now it is possible to have a negative value for N, which would generate an error in the program. To correct this, our first inclination may be to proceed in a manner similar to that used in the original algorithm *Is-N-Prime*. You would come up with the following ***incorrect*** algorithm.

INCORRECT ALGORITHM

1. Read an integer N.
2. Assign to the divisor D the value 2 and compute K as the greatest integer less than or equal to the value (N+1)/2.
3. While D ≤ K and N is not divisible by D, perform steps 3.1 and 3.2.

3.1 Increase D by 1.

3.2 Compute N/D.

4. If D > K, then report that N is prime.

5. Terminate processing.

REVISION It is obvious by looking at this algorithm that it does not eliminate negative numbers from consideration. Because the definition of a prime number does not include negative numbers, any algorithm dealing with potential prime numbers must eliminate negative input. This error can be corrected by replacing the original step 1:

1. Read N. If N ≤ 0, then report an appropriate message and terminate processing.

TEST Now test the algorithm with N = 1. In this case, desk checking results in 1 being reported as prime. But the definition of a prime number does not include the possibility of 1.

REVISION Change the algorithm to exclude 1 as a prime number.

TEST It would seem that we now have an error-free algorithm. However, except for the integer 2, all prime numbers are odd. That makes 2 an excellent critical datum with which to test this algorithm. Let's try it.

The execution of the latest steps 1 and 2 proceeds without mishap using N = 2. At step 3, it is clear that 2 is divisible by 2, so the value of D is 2 and the value of K is 1. Thus, 2 is reported as prime.

Since there are no more potential critical data, test the algorithm one more time with any other integer. You will find that it now reports the correct results for whatever integer is read.

It may be interesting for you to revise this algorithm based on the speedier *Is-N-Prime* given in Problem 1.7.4B.

Using Pseudocode

Algorithm development is probably best done by constructing the algorithm in modular segments using abbreviated English statements to specify actions and conditions. One can, of course, use full English sentences to represent an algorithm. In that case, the final product reads much like paragraphs of prose: It is more readable but unnecessarily long, and the logic is more difficult to follow.

At the other, brief, extreme is the program language code itself, the step after the algorithm. Here it is the extremely telegraphic and highly structured style that obscures the logic, especially for anyone not familiar with the programming language used.

The compromise technique is the use of pseudocode statements, halfway from English to FORTRAN. This makes it easy to set forth the solution logic in a clear and concise manner, yet avoid getting into the potential syntax problems of writing executable FORTRAN code. The pseudocode actually enables us to take the solution into any computer language, not just FORTRAN, without having to rework our solution. Pseudocode is very close to English, and while it has fewer special syntax rules than do the programming languages, there are some important forms to learn. We begin with loop notation, perhaps the most complex aspect of pseudocode.

Representing loops. Iteration structures are a convenient problem solving technique, as we have shown by using them in English solution statements. The algorithmic representation of iterations follows certain rules that make the structure of the loop itself clear and easy to understand and keep the process of translating the algorithm into actual code as straightforward as possible. Here we restate what we know about counter and condition controlled loops in this new pseudocode terminology.

Counter controlled loops. Counter controlled loops generally take one of two forms, depending on the nature and location of the control statement. These are the same two forms discussed earlier, the simple counting model, where each iteration increases INDEX by 1, and the model controlled by the variable STEP_VALUE that provides more flexible options.

FORM A

```
For INDEX = INITIAL_VALUE to FINAL_VALUE Do
       Step 1
       Step 2
       .
       .
       .
       Step N
End-For
```

Steps 1 through N are executed M times, where M = FINAL_VALUE − INITIAL_VALUE + 1.

Every time the steps of the loop are executed, the value of INDEX is increased by 1, and a test is made to determine whether the steps have been performed M times. If not, they are repeated once more, as are the increase and the testing process.

This continues until the steps of the loop have been performed M times, when the step following the End-For is performed.

If FINAL_VALUE and INITIAL_VALUE are equal, the steps between For and End-For are executed once.

If M is less than or equal to zero, which occurs if FINAL_VALUE is less than INITIAL_VALUE, the steps of the loop are not executed at all.

FORM B

```
For INDEX = INITIAL_VALUE to FINAL_VALUE by STEP_VALUE Do
      Step 1
      Step 2
      .
      .
      .
      Step N
End-For
```

Steps 1 through N are executed M times, where
M = ((INITIAL_VALUE − FINAL_VALUE) / STEP_VALUE) + 1

and M is then made the greatest integer less than or equal to the value just computed.

Every time the steps of the loop are executed, the value of STEP_VALUE is added to the value of INDEX.

As in the case of form A, if M is less than or equal to zero, the steps of the loop are not executed even once.

Following are examples of counter controlled loops as presented in pseudocode algorithms:

ALGORITHM 1

1. Assign to X the value zero

2. For K = 1 to 100 Do

2.1 Add K to X

3. End-For

4. Report X

causes the computation of X as 1 + 2 + . . . + 100 and reports that sum.

ALGORITHM 2

1. Assign to Y the value of zero

2. For K = 100 to 1 by −1 Do

2.1 Add K to Y

3. End-For

4. Report Y

causes the computation of Y as 100 + 99 + 98 + . . . and reports the result.

Of course, the results are the same. The difference lies in the values assigned to K and used in the computation of the respective sums.

Note that at the third step of either loop, the current value of K is added to the current value of X or Y, as the case may be, and the new sum is called by the same name, X or Y, as it was before K was added. This accumulates a sum at the location X or Y as the loop is repeatedly executed.

ALGORITHM 3

1. Assign S the value zero
2. For K = 1 to 10 by 2 Do
2.1 Add K to S
3. End-For
4. Report S

computes and reports the sum 1 + 3 + 5 + . . . + 9.

Condition controlled loops. Two different forms of condition controlled loop structures result from the placement of the step that checks for the condition. In some loops this step is first:

FORM A: CONDITION BEFORE

```
While Condition is True Do
       Step 1
       Step 2
       .
       .
       .
       Step N
End-While
```

The presence of the condition is checked. If it is true, steps 1 through N are executed.

When End-While is encountered, the condition in While is checked again. As long as the condition is present, or is *true*, steps 1 through N are executed.

Whenever the condition is not present, or is *false*, the next step to be performed is the one immediately following the End-While.

Here are two algorithms using loops that test for the condition before executing the loop:

ALGORITHM 1

1. Assign to X and K the value zero
2. While K is less than 101 Do
2.1 Add 1 to K
2.2 Add K to X
3. End-While
4. Report X

At step 1, X and K are both initialized to 0.

Steps 2 through 3 constitute the loop, with the condition being tested for in the first step. The steps of the loop are repeated as long as the condition is true.

Since K is initialized to 0 and increased by 1 each time the steps of the loop are executed, the loop is performed exactly 100 times.

The value of X when exit from the loop occurs is the sum 1 + 2 + . . . + 100.

ALGORITHM 2
1. Assign to X the value zero and to K the value 1
2. While X is not equal to K * K Do
2.1 Add K to X
2.2 Add 1 to K
3. End-While
4. Report values of K and X

At step 1, X is initialized to 0 and K to 1.

At step 2, the condition is tested. As long as this condition is true, that is, as long the value of X is not equal to the square of the value of K, steps 2 through 3 are repeatedly performed.

You have probably noticed that the logic of this loop is such that the condition is always true, so the loop executes indefinitely. We call such a loop an *infinite* loop. Obviously, no infinite loop can actually be implemented on a computer.

- *Avoid constructing infinite loops. They cannot be implemented.*

It is also possible to construct a loop that is executed zero times, as in this algorithm:

ALGORITHM 3
1. Assign to X the value zero
2. While X is greater than 0 Do
2.1 Add 1 to X
3. End-While
4. Report X

At step 1, X is set to zero.

At step 2, the condition tested for is *X is greater than 0.* Since X = 0 has just been defined, the condition is false and the steps of the loop are not executed.

Instead, the program moves to the first step following the End-While statement. Step 4 is performed and reports the value of X as zero.

Thus, loops may be constructed to be executed *any* number of times, from zero to a theoretically infinite number—although no implementation can actually be done for the infinite case.

In the second form of the loop, the test for condition is in the last step. Here is the general form:

FORM B: CONDITION AFTER

```
Repeat
        Step 1
        Step 2
        .
        .
        .
        Step N
Until Condition is True
```

Steps 1 through N are performed once before the occurrence of the condition is even checked. Following is a specific example of this type of loop structure:

ALGORITHM 4

1. Assign to X and K the value zero

2. Repeat

2.1 Add 1 to K

2.2 Add K to X

3. Until K equals 100

4. Report X

As in previous examples, the action specified at step 2.1 causes 1 to be added to the current value of K and that sum again referred to as K.

Similarly, the action at step 2.2 caused the current value of K to be added to the current value of X and the sum again referred to as X. In both cases, then, there is an accumulation occurring in connection with K and X, respectively.

Note that this last loop computes and reports the sum 1 + 2 + 3 + . . . 100 just as certain other examples given previously.

Rules for writing pseudocode. So far in this book you may have recognized that we have not been completely consistent in our algorithm representations. Sometimes we use more or less complete sentences, at other times abbreviated ones. Sometimes we describe actions with symbols, at other times words. Sometimes each algorithm step contains only one action, at other times more.

These inconsistencies have not interfered with our introduction to problem solving processes. But now that we move closer to work with FORTRAN syntax, away from a completely English context, it is useful to formalize our use of pseudocode.

There is no generally accepted definition of *pseudocode*: Anything between programming language code and full English prose could qualify. In this book, we follow a few rules about pseudocode structure and terminology that help keep our results more consistent:

1. Each step in an algorithm requires ***at most two actions***.

2. The steps of an algorithm are performed ***sequentially***.

3. The word END is used to specify a ***halt in processing***; synonyms are words like STOP and TERMINATE.

4. Loops or ***iteration structures*** are specified in one of the following ways:

COUNTER CONTROLLED LOOP

```
For INDEX = INITIAL_VALUE to FINAL_VALUE by STEP_VALUE Do
    { Loop body }
End-For
```

where the counter C = ((FINAL_VALUE − INITIAL_VALUE) / STEP_VALUE) + 1. The actions in the loop body are performed exactly C times. When STEP_VALUE is not stated, its value is assumed to be 1.

CONDITION CONTROLLED LOOP/FORM A

```
While Condition Do
    { Loop body }
End-While
```

The actions in the loop body are performed repeatedly until the value of the condition is false.

FORM B

```
Repeat
    { Loop body }
Until Condition
```

The actions in the loop body are performed once, then the condition is evaluated.

As long as the value of the condition is false, the actions in the loop body continue to be performed and the condition evaluated at the end of each loop. This process continues until the value of the condition is true.

5. ***Selection structures*** are specified in one of the following ways:

SELECTION STRUCTURE FORM A

```
If Condition then
    { If block }
Else
    { Else block }
Endif
```

When the value of the condition is true, all actions specified in the If block are performed, then control transfers to the statement immediately following the Endif.

When the value of the condition is false, all actions specified in the Else block are performed, then control transfers to the statement immediately following the Endif.

SELECTION STRUCTURE FORM B

```
If Condition then
    { Action statements }
Endif
```

If the value of the condition is true, the action statements are performed and program control proceeds on to the statement following the Endif.

If the value of the condition is false, control proceeds immediately to the statement following the Endif.

6. The set of ***permissible actions*** includes the following:

   DECLARE VARIABLE NAMES identifies ***variable names*** and the ***type*** of value associated with them. Data types include INTEGER, REAL, CHARACTER, and so on.

   INITIALIZE assigns ***initial values*** to objects.

   Any form of ***computation*** is allowed. Arithmetic symbols are used for ADD (+), SUBTRACT (–), MULTIPLY (× or *), and DIVIDE (/). Parentheses specify the order of the operations, as in algebra.

   Symbols or words are used for LESS THAN (<), LESS THAN OR EQUAL TO (≤), GREATER THAN (>), GREATER THAN OR EQUAL TO (≥), EQUALS (=), and NOT EQUAL TO (≠). These are the ***relational operators***.

   READ specifies that ***data*** are provided to the algorithm; synonyms are INPUT and OBTAIN.

   PRINT or WRITE specifies that ***results*** are reported; synonyms are REPORT and OUTPUT.

7. Pseudocode has ***no specific syntax limitations***. There is no one specific combination of words and punctuation marks to convey a given concept. Although we tend to use certain phrases consistently, do not be concerned about using those same words. The object is to describe accurately, for yourself and for others, what actions are to be taken to accomplish the tasks you intend to accomplish.

Problem 1.9
Practicing Algorithm Techniques

PART 1 Given a set of numbers of which the last is 9999, find the largest number other than the last and report its value.

The 9999 is not a valid input number, but is added as a signal to specify the end of data. Such an input value is called a *sentinel datum* and is not to be processed like the data that precede it.

ALGORITHM A

1. Initialize I to 1
2. Read the Ith number, XI
3. While XI is not 9999 Do

   3.1 I ← I + 1

   3.2 Read XI
4. End-While

5. BIG ← X1
6. For J = 2 to I – 1 Do
6.1 If XJ > BIG, then BIG ← XJ
7. End-For
8. Print BIG
9. End

Satisfy yourself that this algorithm correctly solves the given problem.

In particular, note how the algorithm avoids processing the sentinel datum by using I – 1 as the final value in the loop at step 6 rather than the value I.

ANALYSIS This algorithm, though correct, is not efficient. It reads in all the data in the loop at step 3 before using a second loop at step 6 to compare numbers and find the largest.

An alternative method is to combine these steps, and find the largest number of the set *during* the process of reading the numbers. Assume the first number read is the largest number so far. Each time a new number is read, compare it to the value of the largest number so far. If the new number is larger, replace the old largest number with the new one. This process is shown in algorithm B:

ALGORITHM B
1. Read the first number X
2. Set BIG = X
3. While X is not 9999 Do
3.1 If BIG < X then set BIG ← X
3.2 Read the next number X
4. End-While
5. Print BIG
6. End

This algorithm uses one loop instead of two and has no need to use index I or the subscripted variables XI.

PART 2 Read a set of numbers ending with 9999. Then compute their average and report it.

ALGORITHM
1. Initialize I to 1
2. Read the Ith number XI
3. While XI is not equal to 9999 Do
3.1 Set I ← I + 1
3.2 Read the Ith number XI

4. End-While
5. Initialize SUM to 0
6. For J = 1 to I − 1 Do
6.1 Set SUM ← SUM + X_J
7. End-For
8. Set AVERAGE ← SUM/(I − 1)
9. Print AVERAGE
10. End

This is similar to algorithm A in Part 1. Both use one loop to enter all the data and a second loop for processing, with a final value of I − 1 to avoid processing the sentinel datum.

One hidden assumption in all these algorithms is that the set of numbers has at least one member. If that assumption is not valid, the algorithm does not handle the situation correctly.

You may want to modify these algorithms so that they will properly handle the special case where the input set is empty. Although it may seem to you that a case in which the set of numbers has zero members is nonsensical—Why would anyone talk about finding the average of a set of no numbers?—such a case may come about because of errors in entering input data, and a good algorithm should work correctly in spite of such errors.

Also as an exercise, rewrite this algorithm with one loop structure.

PART 3 Read a set of scores attained by students on a test in which a negative score (not a valid score) indicated the end of input data. Compute the average score and find the lowest and highest scores among the valid ones read. Report these three scores as the output of the algorithm.

ALGORITHM

1. Initialize I to 1 and SUM to 0
2. Read the first score SI
3. Set HIGH ← SI and LOW ← SI
4. While SI ≥ 0 Do
4.1 If HIGH < SI , then set HIGH ← SI
4.2 If Low > SI, then set LOW ← SI
4.3 Set SUM ← SUM + SI
4.4 Set I ← I + 1
4.5 Read the Ith score SI
5. End-While
6. If I > 1 then

6.1 Set AVERAGE ← SUM / (I – 1)

6.2 Print AVERAGE, LOW, and HIGH

7. Else print "No scores in this list."

8. Endif

9. Terminate processing

In this algorithm, one loop enters input data and finds the lowest and highest scores. The same loop also accumulates the sum of test scores, used later to compute the average score.

Summary

Algorithms form the heart of this chapter: What an algorithm is. What constitutes a ***good*** algorithm. How to ***develop*** and ***represent*** an algorithm. Numerous examples demonstrate these concepts.

It is always good practice to ***test*** an algorithm before it is implemented. By ***desk checking***, or testing an algorithm by hand using sample input data, one is able to discover and correct logic errors and make it possible to write a workable computer program.

Pseudocode is convenient for presenting algorithms; review the guidelines. Our conventions are useful for following the problems in this book, and will also help you develop a clear personal algorithm style.

End of Chapter Exercises

1. Answer the following questions related to algorithms:

a. What word is often used as a synonym for *algorithm?*

b. State the computer science definition for *algorithm.*

c. Distinguish between *theoretically finite* and *feasibly finite.*

d. What is meant by a *well defined process*?

e. What is meant by the *top down* approach to algorithm development?

f. What is the significance of *uniqueness* as related to algorithms?

g. What is meant by *pseudocode*? Where in the development of algorithms and computer programs should it be used?

h. How can the *validity* of an algorithm be assured?

2. In each of the following, a problem is stated and an algorithm is given. Determine which algorithms correctly solve the corresponding problems and which do not. Where you find an incorrect algorithm, modify or rewrite it to solve the problem correctly if possible.

a. PROBLEM: Given any two numbers, identify the larger one.

ALGORITHM
1. Read two numbers X and Y.
2. Compute the difference D = X − Y.
3. If D > 1, output "The first number is larger."; otherwise output "The second number is larger."

b. PROBLEM: Given seven objects that appear identical, although one of the objects weighs slightly less than the others, use a balance scale no more than twice to identify the object that weighs less.

ALGORITHM
1. Set N = 3.
2. Put N of the objects on each side of the balance scale.
3. If the scale does balance, the object not on the scale is the lighter one.

   If not, set N = 1 and repeat step 2 using the objects from the lighter side of the scale.

c. PROBLEM: Given any two positive integers, find their *modular quotient*, the remainder obtained when the larger is divided by the smaller. For example, the modular quotient of 7 and 3 is 1: When 7 is divided by 3 the remainder is 1.

ALGORITHM
1. Read two integers J and K.
2. Find the positive difference of J and K and call it D.
3. If D is less than either J or K, then output D and stop.
4. Replace the larger of J and K with D.
5. Repeat the process from step 2.

d. PROBLEM: We know that if the number designating a year is divisible by 4, the year is a leap year and February has 29 days. Given any year and the sequence number of any day in that year, identify the month and day of the month.

ALGORITHM
1. Read YEAR and DAY.
2. If YEAR is a leap year assign 29 to MONTH2.
3. Make the following assignments:

   MONTH1 = 31, MONTH3 = 31, MONTH4 = 30, MONTH5 = 31,
   MONTH6 = 30, MONTH7 = 31, MONTH8 = 31, MONTH9 = 30,
   MONTH10 = 31, MONTH11 = 30, MONTH12 = 31,
   NAME1 = "JAN", NAME2 = "FEB", NAME3 = "MAR", NAME4 = "APR",
   NAME5 = "MAY", NAME6 = "JUN", NAME7 = "JUL", NAME8 = "AUG",
   NAME9 = "SEP", NAME10 = "OCT", NAME11 = "NOV", NAME12 = "DEC".
4. Compute DIFF = DAY − (MONTH1 + MONTH2 + . . . + MONTHI) for whatever value of I is required to make DIFF negative.
5. Compute D = DIFF + MONTHI.
6. Report as output, "The given day is day " D " of " NAMEI.

e. PROBLEM: Given a positive integer N, compute N factorial.

ALGORITHM
1. Read N.
2. Assign 1 to FACTORIAL.
3. Assign to FACTORIAL the value K * FACTORIAL.

Continue for K = 2, 3, 4, . . . , N.

4. Report the value of FACTORIAL as N factorial.

3. Write an algorithm for each of the following problems:

a. Given three numbers A, B, and C, find the solution of the quadratic equation $Ax^2 + Bx + C = 0$.

b. Given three numbers A, B, and C, find the fourth number X such that A/B = C/X.

c. A *Pythagorean triple* is a set of three positive integers A, B, and C, such that $A^2 = B^2 + C^2$. (For example, 3, 4, and 5 form a Pythagorean triple because $5^2 = 4^2 + 3^2$.) Find 25 Pythagorean triples.

d. Two prime numbers are called *twin primes* if their difference is 2 (for example, 3 and 5). Find the first 10 twin primes.

e. Given a number in standard decimal notation, determine the exponential notation. For example, 3765.23 = 3.76523E3.

4. Expand Euclid's algorithm so that it will determine the greatest common factor of K positive integers.

5. Develop an algorithm to find the least common factor of two positive integers.

6. Develop an alternative algorithm for finding the set of all prime numbers less than a given integer N.

7. Develop an algorithm to find the *mode* of a set of numbers. The mode of N numbers is the number that occurs most frequently among them.

8. Develop an algorithm for starting a small engineering firm. Make appropriate assumptions to define the problem as clearly as you need. Be sure to write them down. For example, you will need to define *small* and assume a specialty in order to determine staff needs.

■ *Exercises 9 to 13 each contain an algorithm that is supposed to solve the accompanying problem. Study the algorithm carefully and determine whether it has all the properties of an algorithm. Indicate what essential properties are missing, if any.*

9. Determine whether you should take your baby brother to the doctor.

ALGORITHM

1. Observe your brother for 15 minutes.
2. If he is actively playing, then he is all right.
3. If he is not actively playing, then take his temperature.
4. If his temperature is high, take him to the doctor.
5. If his temperature is not high but he has some fever, give him some children's Tylenol.

10. Read an integer A and report all integers from A to 1.

ALGORITHM

1. Read A
2. While A ≥ 1 Do

2.1 Print A

```
2.2        Set A = A − 1
3.     End-While
4.     End
```

11. Read two integers and compute and report their product.

ALGORITHM

```
1.     Read M and N
2.     Assign the value of N to to S
3.     Perform the next step a total of M − 1 times
3.1        Set S = S + N
4.     Print S
5.     End
```

12. Read two integers M and N where M ≤ N, and compute the sum M + (M + 1) + (M + 2) + . . . + N.

ALGORITHM

```
1.     Read M and N
2.     Set SUM = 0
3.     For I assigned values from M to N Do
4.         Set SUM = SUM + I
5.     Endfor
6.     Print SUM
7.     End
```

13. Given two integers A and B, determine whether A + B is odd or even.

ALGORITHM

```
1.     Read A and B
2.     Compute the remainder R1 when A is divided by 2
3.     Compute the remainder R2 when B is divided by 2
4.     Compute R = R1 + R2
5.     If R = 1 then A + B is odd; otherwise, it is even.
```

■ *In exercises 14 to 16, develop an algorithm for each problem, test its correctness, and discuss its efficiency.*

14. Write an algorithm for playing tic-tac-toe. Assume that the squares of the tic-tac-toe board are numbered as follows:

1	2	3
4	5	6
7	8	9

Assume also that there are nine blocks in a bag, each block showing one of the numbers. Each player draws a block from the bag, places it on the square of the same number, and marks a score for the player. Your algorithm terminates when one player has a line of three blocks, and thus has won, or when all squares have blocks on them.

15. Determine how to place the integers 1 through 9 in a 3x3 matrix so that the sum of each row, each column, and each diagonal is 15. A matrix in which all these sums are equal is called a *magic square.*

16. Read the name of one of the following geometric figures:

a. square
b. parallelogram
c. triangle
d. rectangle
e. circle

Then request the necessary data to compute the area and the perimeter of the figure. Report the name of the figure and the two computed values.

▪ *In problems 17 to 20, determine what is being accomplished in each algorithm.*

ALGORITHM **17.**

```
read N
for I = 1 to N
   for J = 1 to N
      K = I * J
      write K
   end-for
end-for
end
```

ALGORITHM **18.**

```
read N
K = integer part of (N/2)
I = 0
S = 0
while I ≤ K do
   I = I + 1
   if N is divisible by I then
      S = S + I
end-while
if N = S then
   print N, " is perfect."
else
   print N, " is not perfect."
endif
end
```

ALGORITHM **19.**
```
read X
SMALL ← X
LARGE ← X
while X > 0 do
   read X
   if LARGE < X then
      LARGE ← X
   if SMALL > X then
      SMALL ← X
end-while
print LARGE, SMALL
end
```

ALGORITHM **20.**
```
read M, N
R1 ← N/M
R2 ← integer part of (N/M)
R3 ← N - M * R2
print R1, R2, R3
end
```

21. Develop an algorithm to compute the combined resistance of N resistors connected in parallel. The N resistors are designated R1, R2, . . . , RN and the formula for computing combined resistance CR is as follows:

CR = 1 / ((1/R1) + (1/R2) + . . . + (1/RN))

22. Develop an algorithm to read the coordinates of 3 points P1, P2, and P3 in 2-dimensional space, then determine which of the following are true:

a. P1, P2, and P3 form a right triangle.

b. P1, P2 and P3 do not form a triangle at all.

c. If P1, P2, and P3 form a triangle, compute its area.

HINT: If P1 has the coordinates (X1, Y1) and P2 has coordinates (X2, Y2) then the distance from P1 to P2 is given by the equation

$\text{DISTANCE} = \sqrt{(X2 - X1)^2 + (Y2 - Y1)^2}$

and the slope of the line joining P1 and P2 by the equation

SLOPE = (Y2 − Y1) / (X2 − X1)

23. Develop an algorithm to compute the numerical value of the derivative of x^n. Note that the derivative of x^n is given by the symbolic expression nx^{n-1} for any value of x and any value of n.

24. Suppose $z = x + iy$ is a complex number. Develop an algorithm to compute the following:

a. The pth root of z.

b. The pth power of z.

HINT: First find the polar representation of z where $z = re^{i\theta}$, $x = r\cos\theta$, and $y = r\sin\theta$.

Chapter 2

Introduction to the FORTRAN Language

When the average American mentions a *computer* today that person almost certainly means *digital computer*, where the adjective *digital* refers to the fact that information is stored and processed in the form of off/on electrical signals representing a finite number of discrete digits. The other way of storing information is in *analog* form, rather like old longplay records where there is a continuum of sound values.

Digital computers are generally expected to perform at least four different functions:

1. Arithmetic/logic calculations
2. Control
3. Memory or storage
4. Input/output

Arithmetic/logic functions perform basic arithmetic calculations, compare stored values, and respond to the results of such comparisons. The ***control*** function discerns among various electrical signals entering the computer and responds to those signals by performing an appropriate action. ***Memory,*** or ***storage,*** functions retain information either temporarily in primary memory when the computer is on or permanently in secondary storage devices.

Input/output consists of the two closely related processes of *receiving* and *sending* information. For example, it may accept signals from the keyboard, transform them into appropriate electrical signals, and store them—that's *input*—and then send this stored information to a device like your video monitor or a printer that presents it in usable form—that's *output.*

General purpose computers are available in a large range, from lightning-fast supercomputers and large mainframes to minicomputers and microcomputers. You're probably using either a microcomputer (an IBM PC or compatible, or a Macintosh) or a terminal on a minicomputer (a DEC VAX 780 or something similar). If you are using a microcomputer, chances are that your primary input device is the computer keyboard and your primary output device the computer video monitor, with the option of a connected printer. If you are using a minicomputer, your input and output device is likely to be a video terminal—perhaps not even in the same room as the computer. You probably also have access to a printer for output.

This book helps you learn how to communicate with whatever computer system you are using and get it to do the calculations and provide the output you want by using the high-level programming language called FORTRAN.

Communicating with the Computer

The set of conventions used to instruct a computer in its operations is called a *language*. Computers actually operate from digital command strings, the formats of which differ from one computer to another. In order to make it possible for engineers and other scientists to write instructions for their computers, the higher-level languages, more like natural language, were developed, including FORTRAN. These languages are then automatically translated, or compiled, into the appropriate machine language for use.

Machine Languages

Although you do not write instructions for your computer in its native language, each digital computer has one, referred to by computer scientists as its *machine language.*

Machine languages are, by far, the most difficult and time-consuming means of communicating with computers. Each make and model of computer system has its own unique machine language, always numeric in form. Furthermore, most computers are designed so that their machine language programs must be entered in binary numbers (ones and zeros) or some closely related number system like hexadecimals.

To help you understand how a machine language functions, let's invent a very simple machine language for a simple hypothetical computer and then use it to solve a trivial problem. Note that the language we develop is not associated with any known computer. It is hypothetical, intended only to serve as a learning aid in this book.

Suppose the computer on which we are to execute this machine language has memory locations (*words*) each of which can store sixteen binary digits *(bits)* of information. Suppose further that when the contents of a word are intended as an instruction, the leftmost six bits contain the code for the operation to be performed and the rightmost ten bits contain the address of the memory location from which data are to be used or the numeric code for the device to be used in executing the instruction (Figure 2.1).

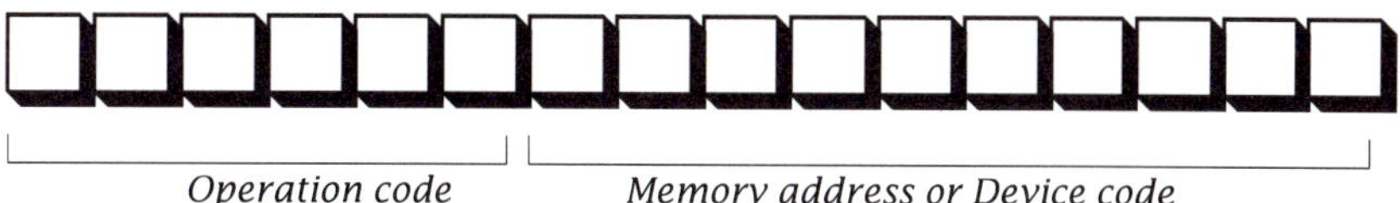

FIGURE 2.1 *Instruction format of hypothetical machine language.*

Assume that our hypothetical computer system has a video monitor, a printer, and a keyboard as input/output devices. Assume also that the only operations that can be performed are the following:

1. Store
2. Add
3. Input
4. Output

Here are the operation and device codes we use:

TABLE 2.1 *Machine language operation and device codes*

Operation	Code	Device	Code
Store	000010	Video monitor	0000001000
Add	000011	Printer	0000001100
Input	000100	Keyboard	0000001110
Output	000101		

Now let's use the machine language we have defined to accept three numbers, find their sum, and produce the sum as output on the printer. The *accumulator* is the device into which the Input operation places data and from which the Output operation extracts data. The Store operation extracts data from the accumulator and places it in the specified memory location. The Add operation requires that the accumulator have a stored number; the content of the specified memory location is then added to the number in the accumulator and the sum is stored back in the accumulator, all other numbers temporarily there having been erased.

Here is a machine language program that solves the problem:

MACHINE LANGUAGE PROGRAM

Instruction	***Comment***
0001000000001110	*Input first number from keyboard*
0000100001000000	*Store first number in location 0001000000*
0001000000001110	*Input second number from keyboard*
0000100001000001	*Store second number in location 0001000001*
0001000000001110	*Input third number from keyboard*
0000110001000001	*Add second number to third number*
0000110001000000	*Add first number to sum of the other two*
0001010000001100	*Output sum of all three numbers on printer*

Notice what a tedious task it is to write a machine-language program to solve even a trivial problem! Most of the tedium is caused by the need to get all the ones and zeros correctly written so that the right instruction is executed at the appropriate time and data are stored in and extracted from the correct memory locations. It should be clear why computer systems developers began early to think about easier ways to communicate with computers.

Assembly Languages

As pointed out in the previous section, the worst aspect of writing programs in machine language is the care that must be taken to use the right sequence of ones and zeros to get the desired operations correctly accomplished. Suppose we modify the operation and device codes:

TABLE 2.2 *Assembly language operation and device codes*

Operation	*Code*	*Device*	*Code*
Store	STO	Video Monitor	VM
Add	ADD	Printer	PR
Input	INP	Keyboard	KB
Output	OUT		

A computer language using abbreviated names of operations and devices is commonly called an *assembly language.* When designating memory locations in assembly language, it is customary to use a meaningful name made up of some combination of letters and numbers not to exceed a specified number, say six.

Now let's look at an assembly language program that solves our problem:

ASSEMBLY LANGUAGE PROGRAM

Instruction	***Comment***
`INP,KB`	*Input first number from keyboard*
`STO,N1`	*Store first number in location N1*
`INP,KB`	*Input second number from keyboard*
`STO,N2`	*Store second number in location N2*
`INP,KB`	*Input third number from keyboard*
`ADD,N2`	*Add second number to third number*
`ADD,N1`	*Add first number to the sum of the other two*
`OUT,PR`	*Output sum of three numbers on printer*

One thing you'll notice is that there is no reduction in the number of instructions needed to solve the problem. However, it is possible to look at this program and tell what is happening, or at least identify the operation and device codes, which remind us of the words for the operations and devices themselves. Such codes are called *mnemonic.*

Writing a computer program in assembly language is easier than in machine language primarily because we can use these more easily remembered mnemonic codes. However, assembly languages are still machine dependent, so the form of the language is specific to a given make and model of computer system and programs written for one system generally require rewriting before they can be executed on a different computer.

High-level Languages

Early programmers decided that it would be useful to have computer languages that are not machine dependent and that are more like human languages. But human language itself is ambiguous, and it is extremely difficult to be precise enough to tell a machine exactly what operations are to be performed and when to perform them.

As a compromise between human and machine languages, other computer languages have been developed that build on technical terminology and symbolism. For example, COBOL (COmmon Business-Oriented Language) was developed for use in business and commerce and FORTRAN was developed primarily for scientific and engineering applications.

There have been many such programming languages developed in the past. Besides COBOL and FORTRAN there are PL/I, ALGOL, APL, LISP, Pascal, BASIC, SNOBOL, PROLOG, Ada, C, Modula–2 and others. Since the vocabulary and structure of these languages are closer to those of human languages they are referred to as *high-level* languages. FORTRAN is properly called a high-level language.

Now, let's see the solution to our summing problem in FORTRAN:

FORTRAN PROGRAM

```
REAL N1,N2,N3
READ*,N1,N2,N3
SUM=N1+N2+N3
PRINT*,SUM
```

Not only is the FORTRAN program shorter than its assembly language counterpart, it is also much more readable. Even though you have yet learned very little about FORTRAN you can probably tell what most of the lines in the program accomplish.

History of FORTRAN

According to Jean Sammet,[1] the first document referring to FORTRAN, dated November 10, 1954, from the Applied Science Division of IBM, stated, "The IBM Mathematical Formula Translation System, or briefly

1. Sammet, J., *Programming Languages: History and Fundamentals* (Englewood Cliffs, NJ: Prentice-Hall, 1974).

FORTRAN, will comprise a large set of programs to enable the IBM 704 to accept a concise formulation of a problem in terms of a mathematical notation and to produce automatically a high-speed 704 program for the solution of the problem."

It took two and a half years to complete the project and in early 1957 the promised FORTRAN for the IBM 704 was released. It is interesting to note that customers were not willing to quickly accept this programming boon. A major objection seemed to be that the FORTRAN translating program could not produce as efficient a machine-language code as the customers' best programmers could—that is, programs resulting from FORTRAN translators took more computer time. Nothing was said about the greatly reduced development time.

In June 1958 a new version of FORTRAN was released, again for the IBM 704. This version was dubbed FORTRAN II. Later in 1958 FORTRAN systems were issued for the IBM 709 and 650 computers, and in 1960 for IBM 1620 and 7070. There is no record of a FORTRAN III, but in 1962 FORTRAN IV was issued for the IBM 7030, a very large scale computer used for scientific research.

It appears that the first non-IBM introduction of FORTRAN was in January 1961 by UNIVAC for its Solid State 80 computer. Records show that by 1963 virtually every computer manufacturer had provided or promised to provide a FORTRAN translating program for use with its equipment. How remarkable that in less than six years this programming language had such a significant impact on the world of computing! FORTRAN made it practical for engineers and scientists to actually program their own problems, and the similarity between their professional language and FORTRAN made it easy to learn.

Throughout the 1960s a myriad of FORTRAN compilers appeared with language differences not only among the various manufacturers but also among the models of any given manufacturer. It became apparent that some effort must be made to standardize the language. The first move in that direction was the calling of a meeting of Working Group X3.4.3 of the American Standards Association in August of 1962. After many meetings and considerable reactions from the computing community, two sets of FORTRAN standards were approved in March 1966, *FORTRAN* and *Basic FORTRAN*. In April 1978 the same organization, now named the American National Standards Institute, adopted specifications for FORTRAN 77. This book adheres to those standards unless otherwise stated.

Basic Conventions

Like any human language, FORTRAN has rules and conventions that make it work. These next two sections present basic conventions of structure, data types, and location names, and describe fundamental FORTRAN syntax. You will use this syntax to convert problem solutions, or *algorithms*, into actual FORTRAN programs that can be compiled and run on a computer.

Building Structures

The solution to a problem in FORTRAN uses three types of structures: *Sequential, selection,* and *iteration.*

Sequential structures. Structures that do not change the natural flow of performing actions are called *sequential structures.* Five types of statements qualify as FORTRAN sequential structures.

1. ***Declaration statements*** define the type and form of data used. Declaration statements are all *non-executable*—they do not result in any action by the computer. They do, however, affect the action resulting from executable statements.
2. ***Structural statements*** define the beginning or ending of a program or program segment. Some statements in this group are used to pass information back and forth among program segments.
3. ***Input and output statements*** provide a program with data for processing and produce results in usable form.
4. ***Initialization statements*** define initial values for variables at the beginning of a program.
5. ***Computational statements*** cause arithmetic operations to be performed.

In this chapter we discuss most of the sequential structures; some are left until later because of their special applications.

Selection structures. Structures that specifically alter the normal sequential execution of statements are called *selection structures.* Several types of selection structures are discussed in Chapter 3.

Iteration structures. Structures that result in the repetitive execution of a program segment are called *iteration structures.* Also called *loops* or *repetition* structures, they are discussed in Chapter 4.

Using Data Types

FORTRAN 77 provides for three data types: Numeric, character, and logical. Each type is handled in a unique way and needed in different circumstances.

Numeric data. Numeric data are subdivided into integer, real, and complex types, each of which has particular formats and uses.

Integer data. Recall from mathematics that any whole number (also called a *counting number*) or its negative is called an *integer.* For example, 2, –5, –7, –36, 1278961, and 0 are all integers. In FORTRAN any of these integer values could be the name—and contents—of an integer constant.

To denote a FORTRAN integer constant, simply write the integer value, being careful *not* to include a decimal point or any commas, even in large numbers when one might normally use them. Here are examples of integer constants that could appear in FORTRAN programs:

```
5            -15629       -8
89542        725          -16
```

Real data. Real data in FORTRAN appears in either *standard decimal form* or *exponential form.* The name *real* probably comes from the mathematics term *real number* and refers to a number that may have a fractional part.

Standard decimal form. In FORTRAN the standard decimal form of real data is simply the number written with a decimal point:

```
3.056        0.0165       -12.576
-46654.9     375.4        15.
```

Note that 15 is an integer, but when a decimal point is included, as in 15., it is stored as a real datum, not as an integer. This is an important distinction. It means that 15. (with a decimal) is stored in computer memory in an entirely different form that 15 (without the decimal). For further information on this topic, see the appendix.

Exponential form. When either very small or very large numbers are involved in computations, it is convenient to use a form of scientific notation called *exponential form.* For example, 0.0000000067 in scientific notation is 6.7×10^{-9}. Similarly, 30,000,000,000 is 3.0×10^{10}. Numbers of these magnitudes appear often in science and engineering.

FORTRAN provides an exponential form for real data, though it is not exactly the same as scientific notation. There are three parts to the exponential form of FORTRAN data:

1. The ***coefficient***, which looks exactly like the standard decimal form of a real constant.
2. The letter **E**.
3. The ***exponent***, which has the same form as an integer constant.

Table 2.3 shows FORTRAN exponential form compared with standard decimal notation and scientific notation. Although in scientific notation the coefficient is usually written as a number between 1 and 10, adjusting the exponent accordingly, in FORTRAN that standard does not hold. Therefore 6.67E–8, 66.7E–9, .667E–7, and 667.E–10 are all acceptable forms for 0.0000000667. Note that in both scientific notation and FORTRAN exponential form unsigned numbers are positive.

TABLE 2.3 *Comparison of scientific notation and* FORTRAN *exponential form*

Standard notation	*Scientific notation*	FORTRAN *exponential form*
0.0000000667	6.67×10^{-8}	6.67E–8
30000000000	3.0×10^{10}	3.0E10
0.0000589	5.89×10^{-5}	5.89E–5
983500000	9.835×10^{8}	9.835E8
–0.0000025	-2.5×10^{-6}	–2.5E–6

In summary, FORTRAN exponential form is related to scientific notation as follows:

`(Coefficient)E(Integer)` $= (\textit{Coefficient}) \times 10^{(\textit{Integer})}$

To obtain the FORTRAN exponential form from standard decimal form, carry out these steps:

1. Decide on the ***coefficient*** to be used and place the decimal point.
2. The integer ***exponent*** is equal to the number of positions through which the decimal point has been moved to form the coefficient. It is positive if the movement from the original decimal position has been to the left, negative if the movement has been to the right.

EXAMPLE Apply the rules to the number 37900000000. First, decide that the coefficient is 37.9. The decimal moves left 9 places, so the integer exponent is 9. Therefore, the FORTRAN exponential form is 37.9E9.

Complex data. Complex numbers are used mostly in engineering and physics. Mathematicians define complex numbers as numbers of the form $x + yi$ where x and y are real numbers and i is the square root of −1. Here are some complex numbers:

$2 + 3.21i \qquad 2.7 + i \qquad 0 + 2i$

In FORTRAN, complex numbers are written as a pair of real numbers enclosed in parentheses, so the same numbers are

```
(2,3.21)        (2.7,1)      (0,2)
```

Character data.

A set of acceptable characters—letters, digits, or punctuation marks—not intended for computation is called a *character constant, string constant,* or *literal.* There are two ways to denote character constants in FORTRAN: Defining a Hollerith constant and enclosing the constant in single quote marks.

Hollerith notation. This older method makes special use of the letter H. Immediately to the left of H an integer specifies the number of characters in the constant, and immediately to the right of H are the characters that form the constant. This method of defining character constants has been available for a long time, so although preferred methods are now available, we still include it. For example,

```
9HJOHN KNOX
```

where 9 specifies the number of characters in the Hollerith constant and the constant itself consists of the characters JOHN KNOX.

Note that the space between the first and last names is included in the count of 9.

Quotation. The second method, preferred by most computer professionals, denotes a string constant by enclosing the string within single quotation marks. Consider these examples:

```
'ABC'    'MARY AMES'    '5 162827 16'
```

The quotation marks both specify the boundaries of the string constant and enclose the characters of which it is to be composed.

Logical data.

In mathematical logic there are exactly two logical values, *true* and *false*. In FORTRAN these are written as

```
.TRUE.
.FALSE.
```

Naming Memory Locations

Any information to be processed by a computer must first be stored in the main memory of the computer. This implies that there must be a way to locate individual pieces of information within the memory. In FORTRAN, we do this by giving each memory location a unique name, or identifier, such as SALARY, SUM, NI, N2, and so forth. In addition to the rule that names in any given program must be unique, there are several other guidelines for naming constants and variables.

Naming constants. In the case of data that never change, called *constants*, such as 25, –10.6, and 'ROBERT BOE', the name is the same as the constant to be stored. Thus a memory location named 25 in a FORTRAN program contains the number 25. Similarly, a memory location named 'ROBERT BOE' contains the string ROBERT BOE.

Naming variables. Memory locations whose contents may change either during the execution of a given program or from one use of the program to another are given a *variable name,* often simply called a *variable*. There are three basic rules for variables:

1. The only characters permitted are letters A–Z and digits 0–9.
2. The first character must be a letter.
3. Use no more than 6 characters.

VALID NAMES

Here are some valid FORTRAN variable names:

```
JOHN
NAME
R7
J76
FORM21
```

INVALID NAMES

Here are some *invalid* FORTRAN variable names and the reasons why they are invalid:

FIRST NAME	*More than 6 characters*
3JOHNS	*First character not a letter*
K.ART	*Can't use decimal point*
R(	*Can't use parenthesis*
F-3	*Can't use minus*

Declaring data types. FORTRAN has five data types. Three are numeric, the integer, real, and complex types; the other two are character and logical types. The variable name is related to the type of data stored by an appropriate *type declaration* statement.

***INTEGER* statement.** Identifies variables for storing integer data. The general form

```
INTEGER VAR1,VAR2, . . . ,VARN
```

where VAR1,VAR2, . . . ,VARN are any acceptable FORTRAN variable or function names,

causes all variables listed to be of the type integer.

EXAMPLE

```
INTEGER AGE,WEIGHT
```

Declares AGE and WEIGHT as integer variables.

***REAL* statement.** Identifies variables for storing real data. The general form

```
REAL VAR1,VAR2, . . . ,VARN
```

where VAR1,VAR2, . . . ,VARN are any acceptable FORTRAN variable or function names,

causes all variables listed to be of type real.

EXAMPLE

```
REAL NETPAY
```

Declares NETPAY a real variable and allows us to use it, for example, as the location for storing net salary, where fractions of dollars are significant.

***COMPLEX* statement.** Identifies variables for storing complex data. The general form is

```
COMPLEX VAR1,VAR2, . . . ,VARN
```

where VAR1,VAR2, . . . ,VARN are any acceptable FORTRAN variable or function names.

Recall that complex data, as defined in mathematics, consist of a *real* part and an *imaginary* part. A complex FORTRAN variable is written as two numbers enclosed in parentheses. The first number is the real part and the second is the imaginary part. The numbers are actually stored in two adjacent memory locations, both of which are accessed by the single complex variable name.

EXAMPLE

```
COMPLEX ROTATN,DIRECN
```

Declares ROTATN and DIRECN to be complex variables.

***CHARACTER* statement.** Identifies variables to be used for storing data of type character, including any acceptable characters available on the given computer system. Character data are not used in arithmetic computations even if they consist entirely of numbers, as does a Social Security number.

There are three general forms of the CHARACTER statement:

FORM A

```
CHARACTER V1,V2, . . . ,VN
```

where V1,V2, . . . ,VN are acceptable FORTRAN variable or function names.

Variable names are listed without a length specification; the system assumes a length of one character. Any variable in the list of a CHARACTER statement in form A thus stores exactly one character.

EXAMPLE A1

```
CHARACTER ID
```

where ID is the name of a variable capable of storing one character.

EXAMPLE A2

```
CHARACTER INIT1,INIT2,INIT3
```

Each of these 3 variables stores a single character.

FORM B

```
CHARACTER V1*N1,V2*N2, . . . ,VN*NN
```

where V1,V2, . . . ,VN are variable names as described above and N1,N2, . . . ,NN are unsigned integer constants that define the lengths of V1,V2, . . . ,VN, respectively.

The length of each character variable is specified by the integer following the asterisk.

EXAMPLE B

```
CHARACTER ID,ID2*10,FNAME*8
```

ID stores 1 character, since no length is specified, the default length of 1 applies;
ID2 stores up to 10 characters; and
FNAME stores up to 8 characters.

FORM C

```
CHARACTER*K V1,V2, . . . ,VN
```

where V1,V2, . . . ,VN are variable names as described above and K is any unsigned integer datum specifying the length of V1,V2, . . . ,VN. A comma following K is optional in FORTRAN 77 but is forbidden in some other versions of FORTRAN.

EXAMPLE C

```
CHARACTER*15 FNAME,LNAME,CITY
```

Each of the variables FNAME, LNAME, and CITY stores up to 15 characters.

LOGICAL statement. At times, it is essential to include variables whose only values are *true* or *false*. For example, if one operation is to be performed for odd numbers and another for even numbers, a variable called FLAG might be used to determine which process to execute. If a test of FLAG indicated a value of false, it could signal an odd number and the execution of one process, whereas a value of true could signal an even number and call for the other process. Whenever decisions are to be made in a FORTRAN program, variables like FLAG are very useful.

Such variables, whose only values can be true or false, are called *logical* variables. The name of a logical variable is formulated according to the same rules that apply to any FORTRAN variable. When a logical variable is assigned true or false, the values are written

.TRUE. *or* **.FALSE.**

The LOGICAL statement is used to declare a variable for storing these logical values. Its general form is

```
LOGICAL VAR1,VAR2, . . . ,VARN
```

where VAR1,VAR2, . . . ,VARN are any acceptable FORTRAN variable or function names.

IMPLICIT statement. There are situations where it is convenient to declare a whole group of variables as a single type without specifying each variable name. The IMPLICIT statement identifies a group of variable names as being of a certain type according to the letter of the alphabet with which those names begin. The general form is

```
IMPLICIT Type (L1-L2)
```

where Type refers to one of the types INTEGER, REAL, COMPLEX, CHARACTER, LOGICAL, or any other FORTRAN data type, and L1 and L2 define the range of letters, in alphabetical order, with which the names of the variables of that type begin.

If there is only one letter inside the parentheses, all variable names beginning with that single letter are implicitly assumed to specify variables of the indicated type. Consider these examples:

EXAMPLE 1

```
IMPLICIT INTEGER(A-D)
```

specifies that any variable or function names that begin with A,B,C, or D identify INTEGER variables.

EXAMPLE 2

```
IMPLICIT REAL (A-Z)
```

causes *all* variable or function names to be of type REAL.

EXAMPLE 3

```
IMPLICIT CHARACTER (C)
```

identifies all variable or function names that begin with C as being CHARACTER variables of length 1 (default).

Undeclared variables. If a variable is not declared, FORTRAN makes the variable type INTEGER if its name begins with I, J, K, L, M, or N. Otherwise it is of type REAL. Only types integer and real occur in the default mode.

- *Always declare program variables.*

Although the default makes it possible to avoid declaring variables, we urge you to always declare them. The only exception might be an occasional variable used to store temporary data or a variable used as an index. Declaring variables helps make your program more understandable, a goal well worth the effort.

Selecting names. A standard translating program for FORTRAN 77 assumes that you follow these rules for variable names, and thus assure that the program is correctly executed. The rules do not, however, help to make the program any more readable by engineers. You are therefore urged to make variable names as meaningful as possible. This will help you as you develop your program, and especially if you need to review or revise your program long after you first write it. To show how names can help make things clear, we present two solutions to the problem.

Problem 2.1
Analyzing a Subdivision Lot

SITUATION A common problem in private surveying practice is the analysis of undeveloped subdivision lots for a potential buyer, to determine what can and cannot legally be built on the lot.

Suppose that the lot is 80' × 150'. City land use laws require a setback of a minimum of 35' to the front of the building, and zoning regulations allow only single family houses with no construction within 10' of any property line. There is an alley at the back of the property with a right of way extending 25' into the property.

OBJECTIVE Write a procedure to calculate

1. the maximum square footage available for building,
2. the percentage of total land available for building,
3. the width and depth of the largest building for the property.

SOLUTION 1

```
Read X and Y
Compute A = X minus (10+10)
Compute B = Y minus (35+25)
Compute C = product of A and B
Compute D = product of X and Y
Compute E = ratio of C to D
Compute F = product of E and 100
Print C, F, A, and B
End
```

This procedure does everything that the problem requires. However, to recognize that F, for instance, is the percentage of land available for building, you must carefully trace all the steps.

SOLUTION 2 This procedure is exactly like the previous one except that more meaningful variable names are chosen.

```
Read TOTWTH and TOTDPH
Compute AVWTH = TOTWTH minus (10+10)
Compute AVDPTH = TOTDPH minus (35+25)
Compute AVAREA = product of AVWTH and AVDPTH
Compute TOTARA = product of TOTWTH and TOTDPH
Compute ARATIO = ratio of AVAREA to TOTARA
Compute AREAPC = product of ARATIO and 100
Print AVAREA, ARATIO, AVWTH, and AVDPTH
End
```

Here, even a quick reading makes it apparent what is happening at each step, because the variable names are meaningful in the context of the problem.

FORTRAN PROGRAM We have not yet discussed all the concepts necessary to understand a complete FORTRAN program, but we present this program now to demonstrate the close relationship between a good solution procedure, shown above, and the corresponding FORTRAN program.

```
PROGRAM SUBDIV
REAL TOTWTH,TOTDPH,AVWTH,AVDPTH,AVAREA
REAL TOTARA,ARATIO,AREAPC
READ*,TOTWTH,TOTDPH
AVWTH = TOTWTH-(10+10)
AVDPTH = TOTDPH-(35+25)
AVAREA = AVWTH*AVDPTH
TOTARA = TOTWTH*TOTDPH
ARATIO = AVAREA/TOTARA
AREAPC = ARATIO*100
PRINT*, AVAREA, ARATIO, AVWTH, AVDPTH
END
```

This program can be entered into a computer. If two numbers are provided, TOTWTH and TOTDPH, the program produces the answers requested.

FORTRAN Syntax

The remainder of this chapter defines the rules of word usage and punctuation marks for some of the statements essential to the writing of FORTRAN programs. This aspect of program statements is called *syntax*. It includes input/output conventions, statements for structuring and operating the code, and system library functions.

Input/Output in FORTRAN

Variable data input and the printing of computed output are the main ways you can use a FORTRAN program. Program lines are structured according to a simple set of positional rules. These make the program able to run on the computer and also make it easy to see from the printed program what is being done. READ statements allow you to feed data into computer memory, either from the program or from a keyboard, and PRINT and WRITE statements allow you to see the results on a computer screen or print them on paper.

The use of position. FORTRAN 77 requires that the 80 spaces available in a line of code be used in accordance with the following conventions.

Position 1. Begin a line with the letter C or an asterisk to indicate that the line is a *comment* line. Comment lines describe the code. Sometimes the task of a group of program lines is described by one or more comment lines preceding the functional code.

Any information that makes the code more understandable should be included in comment lines. Comment lines are not translated and do not cause any action by the computer. They are, however, printed whenever a program listing is requested and add significantly to the understandability of the program.

- *We recommend that position 1 be left blank if the line is not a comment line.*

Positions 2–5. Reserve these positions for a reference number, also called a *statement number*. Statement numbers are unsigned integers from 1 to 99999 used to identify statements so that, as is necessary, program control may be transferred to a statement out of sequence. If the program contains a large number of statements, and you find it necessary or convenient to use more than four digits for the statement number, use position 1 to allow five digits.

- *We recommend that position 1 not be used for statement numbers unless necessary, since it makes programs less readable.*

Position 6. Reserve this position for a character to indicate that a line is continued from the previous line. If a program statement is longer than one line, place a character other than 0 in position 6 of each continued line and continue the statement in positions 7-72. In this book, we use a plus sign (+) as the continuation symbol, but *any* character except 0 is acceptable. Continuation symbols are not used when continuing comment lines.

Positions 7–72. These positions are used for the actual code, the words and symbols we are studying in this book.

Positions 73–80. These positions are ignored by FORTRAN translators. Some programmers use them for short comments or annotations. They may be left blank. The code in this book is shown only through position 75; we include all comments in comment lines.

EXAMPLES

```
1234567                              These numbers mark the first 7 positions
 100  READ*,I,J                      Line identified by statement number 100
      PRINT*,I,J                     All functional code begins in position 7
      IF (I .EQ. J) GO TO 100        References statement number 100
     +                               Continued code line, marked in position 6
C   THIS IS A COMMENT LINE;          Only comment lines use position 1
C   THEY CONTINUE WITH ONLY THE POSITION 1 MARKER
```

Unformatted READ statement. For FORTRAN the statement easiest to use for entering data into computer memory for later processing is the *unformatted* READ statement, also called *list-directed input.* There are two forms of this statement, one for entering data only through the keyboard, and the other for entering data from some specified input unit including the keyboard.

FORM A

```
READ*,Var-list
```

where Var-list represents any list of acceptable FORTRAN variables separated by commas. Sometimes referred to as the *list* of the READ statement.

FORM B

```
READ(N,*) Var-list
```

where the integer N identifies the input unit from which data are read. The integer 5 is commonly used to designate a keyboard. The asterisk in both forms indicates unformatted input and is required in FORTRAN 77.
These statements must begin in position 7 of the line.

▪ *Whenever a READ statement appears in FORTRAN, corresponding data must be provided at the time that the program is run.*

EXAMPLE 1 For the program segment

```
REAL VAR1, VAR2, VAR3
CHARACTER NAME*10
READ*,VAR1,VAR2,VAR3,NAME
```

provide a data line like this with the four needed values:

```
5,10.6,15.92,'ROBERT'
```

Note that four items of input must be entered, corresponding to the four variables in the list of the READ statement. The first three data items must be numbers and the fourth item must be a string of no more than 10 characters enclosed in single quotation marks.

When the READ statement is executed in conjunction with the input data provided, the value stored in location VAR1 becomes the real number 5.0, in VAR2 the real number 10.6, in VAR3 the real number 15.92, and in NAME the character data ROBERT.

Notice that the order of variables in the READ statement corresponds to the order of the input data. Also note that the input data are separated by commas or blank spaces. This is characteristic of data read by unformatted READ statements. Alternatively, each of the four values could have been entered on a separate line if there were some reason to do so. There must be exactly as many data items provided as there are variables in the READ statement.

Normally the type of each datum entered on the data line must match the type of the variable corresponding to it in the associated READ statement. It is possible to enter integer data into a real variable, in which case the integer data are automatically stored as real data, but real data may not be entered into an integer variable. Thus, 5 is input as integer data but stored as the real number 5.0 because VAR1 is declared a real variable.

- *Character data must be enclosed in single quotation marks or apostrophes, as shown by the data 'ROBERT' in Example 1.*

EXAMPLE 2 For the program segment

```
INTEGER NUMBER, ZIP
REAL VALUE
READ*, NUMBER, VALUE, ZIP
```

these data value are entered:

```
296, 236.41
5656
```

This READ has 3 variables and the input data provide 3 numbers in two lines. All 3 numbers *may* be on one line; it doesn't matter how many lines are used as long as 3 numbers are provided.

Note that the first and third variable names are type integer and the first and third numbers in the data are entered without decimal points. The second variable VALUE is type real and the second data item has a decimal point. The correspondence between type of variable and type of data provided is very important.

- *Remember, all data must be provided when the program is executed.*

Unformatted* PRINT *and* WRITE *statements. Also called *list-directed output* statements, these statements are used to produce a visual copy of data electronically stored in computer memory. There are two general forms of this statement, one for displaying data only on a computer screen, the other for displaying the data either on the screen or on some other specified output unit.

FORM A

```
PRINT*,Out-list
```

where the asterisk is used to indicate the absence of a format specification and
Out-list refers to any collection of constants, variables, or arithmetic expressions whose values are to be displayed.
Causes output to be displayed on the computer screen.

FORM B

```
WRITE(N,*) Out-list
```

where the unsigned integer N designates the output unit on which the values are to be written. The integer 6 is commonly used to designate the video screen of the computer in which the program is being executed.

EXAMPLE 1 Suppose that a READ statement has already been executed, and the real variables VAR1, VAR2, and VAR3 contain the values 2.5, 10.0, and –3.1 respectively. Then the statement

```
PRINT*,VAR1,VAR2
```

when executed, causes the values stored in VAR1 and VAR2 to be displayed like this:

```
2.5                     10.0
```

EXAMPLE 2

```
WRITE(6,*) VAR3, VAR1+VAR2
```

This statement causes two numbers to be displayed. The first number is a copy of what is stored in VAR3 while the second number is the sum of the numbers stored at VAR1 and VAR2. The line of output looks like this:

```
-3.1                    12.5
```

EXAMPLE 3 The third example has five items separated by commas:

```
PRINT*,VAR1,'+',VAR2,'=',VAR1+VAR2
```

thus causing five pieces of information to be printed as follows:

```
2.5         +           10.0          =          12.5
```

Each of the five items appears in the output line spaced across the line. Item 1 is the value of VAR1; item 2 is the string constant +; item 3 is the value of VAR2; item 4 is the string constant =; and item 5 is a number equal to the sum of VAR1 and VAR2.

Each item in the output list of the original PRINT statement corresponds to one item on the output line.

EXAMPLE 4 For this example:

```
PRINT*,'THE SUM OF THE VARIABLES IS ', VAR1+VAR2+VAR3
```

the output produced is

```
     THE SUM OF THE VARIABLES IS 9.4
```

This PRINT statement has two items specified for output, the string enclosed in single quotation marks and the sum of numbers stored in locations VAR1, VAR2, and VAR3. The string constant is 27 characters long and, therefore, requires a field of at least that width. The sum 9.4 is displayed to the right of the string.

Notice that these PRINT and WRITE statements cause identical effects if their output lists are identical. The value of the WRITE statement over the PRINT statement will become apparent when we discuss output on devices other than video screens.

Structural Statements

These FORTRAN statements identify the beginning and the end of a program or specify the end of an action. Thus they indicate program structure. Three of the most common structural statements, PROGRAM, END, and STOP, are discussed here; others are presented in later chapters.

PROGRAM statement. This identifies the beginning of the program—only comment statements may precede it—and assigns a name. Its form is

```
PROGRAM NAME
```

where NAME represents any valid FORTRAN variable name.

This statement is not required by the rules of FORTRAN 77 but we recommend it as a convenient method for assigning your program an identifying name. If the PROGRAM statement appears, it must precede all statements with the exception of comment statements. Although the PROGRAM statement described here is a part of FORTRAN 77, some translating programs (compilers) do not accept it in this form.

END statement. Every FORTRAN program and subprogram must conclude with a statement that signals the compiler that the end of the program or subprogram has been reached. This statement is the END statement and has the form

```
END
```

- *This must be the last statement of the program or subprogram.*

STOP statement. The third structural statement is the STOP statement, whose form is simply

```
STOP
```

It may appear anywhere and as often in a program as makes logical sense. When this statement is executed it brings an immediate halt to any further program execution.

The major difference between END and STOP statement is that a STOP statement may be used anywhere in a program to stop execution. An END statement is used only at the physical end of a program, and thus can terminate a program only at its natural termination point. Also, STOP statements may include a reference number, while the END statement, which is nonexecutable, can never contain anything but the word END.

The use of a STOP statement in FORTRAN 77 is optional, but other versions of FORTRAN may require it.

Problem 2.2 Writing a Program Module

SITUATION You have been assigned to write a module, or subsection, for a larger program that is to input data, calculate values based on the data, and report the calculated values.

Among other advantages, writing programs in modules saves one from having to write and test an entire program all at once. Modules can be writen as separate, very simple programs, allowing each step to be tested before being incorporated into the larger program. This makes it easier to find any problems and identify their source.

When a module is being written, clear and simple input and output procedures are usually added to simplify testing and checking. The module we are writing has such simplified read and write elements. When the finished module is ready to be included in the final program, input and output procedures are substituted that receive actual data from and pass it back to the final program.

Note that the output statements are exceptionally clear, with all input and output elements included and carefully labelled. Errors are thus unlikely to slip through in the testing process.

OBJECTIVE This program reads three numbers, then prints each number with an identifying message on a separate line. Also, a part of the output is a line of digits to help determine the horizontal spacing of the rest of the output. Some sums are included in the output.

FORTRAN PROGRAM

```
10        PROGRAM SAMPLE
11        REAL NUM1,NUM2,NUM3
12        READ*,NUM1,NUM2,NUM3
13        PRINT*,'0123456789012345678901234567890123456789'
14        PRINT*,'THE VALUE OF THE FIRST VARIABLE IS ',NUM1
15        PRINT*,'THE VALUE OF THE SECOND VARIABLE IS ',NUM2
16        PRINT*,'THE VALUE OF THE THIRD VARIABLE IS ',NUM3
17        PRINT*,'NUM1 + NUM2 = ',NUM1 + NUM2
18        PRINT*,'NUM2 + NUM3 = ',NUM2 + NUM3
19        WRITE(6,*) 'NUM1 + NUM3 = ',NUM1 + NUM3
20        WRITE(6,*) 'THE SUM OF ALL 3 NUMBERS IS ',
21       +NUM1 + NUM2 + NUM3
22        END
```

The numbers at the left of each program line are not a part of the program but are used to refer to individual lines in the discussion.

OUTPUT When this program is executed with input data of 5, 50, and 500, the output is

```
0123456789012345678901234567890123456789
THE VALUE OF THE FIRST VARIABLE IS 5.0
THE VALUE OF THE SECOND VARIABLE IS 50.0
THE VALUE OF THE THIRD VARIABLE IS 500.0
NUM1 + NUM2 = 55.0
NUM2 + NUM3 = 550.0
NUM1 + NUM3 = 505.0
'THE SUM OF ALL 3 NUMBERS IS 555.0'
```

DISCUSSION Line 10 gives the name SAMPLE to this program and results in no other action.

Line 11 declares three variables, NUM1, NUM2, and NUM3, as real variables.

Line 12 provides for the input of three numbers to be stored in NUM1, NUM2, and NUM3. As a result of the data provided, 5 is stored at NUM1, 50 at NUM2, and 500 at NUM3.

Line 13 produces an output line of 40 digits intended to help count the characters in each remaining line of output.

Line 14 displays the string bounded by the pair of single quotation marks followed by the value stored in NUM1. Similarly, lines 15 and 16 display both string and numeric output.

Lines 17 and 18 also each display a line of output in which there is a string followed by a number that is the result of the addition called for by the last item in the PRINT statement.

Lines 19 and 20 (and 21) are unformatted WRITE statements that perform actions similar to those of the preceding PRINT statements.

Line 21 is a continuation of line 20 and, therefore, has a plus sign in position 6, immediately to the left of position 7, where all statements begin.

Exercises 2.1

1. Give a correct response for each of the following:

a. Why is machine language rarely used by the average programmer?

b. What are some advantages of assembly language over machine language?

c. Give two examples of machine-dependent languages.

d. Give three examples of machine-independent languages.

e. Define these words; *bit, byte, word.*

f. What category of languages is referred to as high-level? Low-level?

g. List some advantages for standardizing a programming language.

h. What is meant by a *constant* in FORTRAN?

i. What is meant by a *variable* in FORTRAN?

j. How do *integer* and *real* constants differ?

k. How do *constant* and *variable* differ?

2. Identify all incorrect *variable* names in the following list and state why each is incorrect.

VARIABLE	NUMBR	KOOL	XX1	X1	JOB 1
SQUARE	2X	KOLD	IXX2	NET	DEGREE
DON'T	X!1	A 15 B	JXY	WAGE	WARM
GAS-PUMP	NEW	'ABC'	NEWX	MAX	SUM
PRIME	OLD/NEW	KOUNT	OLDX	MIN	NOFTST
I/O	25	COUNT	INPUT	RATE	LENGTH
IN OUT	A25	FOOT*	OUTPUT	INDOOR	RATIO
ENTER	NO.	$100	GRADE	LEAST	NTEST
IN	PRIMNO	D100	TESTNO	OUTDOOR	SCCRE
INOUT	FACTOR	LAST			

3. When preparing FORTRAN statements for processing by a computer system, what special use is made of each of the following designated positions in any given line?

Position 1	Positions 2-5
Position 6	Positions 7-72

Computational Statements

We consider next the methods used in FORTRAN to perform arithmetic calculations. Six arithmetic operations are available in FORTRAN: Addition, subtraction, multiplication, division, exponentiation, and negation.

Addition. The symbol used for addition is +, just as in mathematics. Thus, to indicate the sum of two variables NUMBR1 and NUMBR2, we write

```
NUMBR1+NUMBR2
```

Subtraction. Again, the symbol is a familiar one from mathematics, the minus sign –. The difference of two variables NUMBR1 and NUMBR2 is written

```
NUMBR1-NUMBR2
```

Multiplication. In mathematics a common symbol used is the × or times sign. Unfortunately, most people think of the × and the letter X as interchangeable. As you know from the discussion earlier in this chapter on naming variables, X is a legitimate name for a FORTRAN variable. When communicating with a computer there must be no ambiguity, so to avoid that problem, the asterisk * is used to indicate multiplication. For instance, the product of the variables RATE and HOURS is written

```
RATE*HOURS
```

Division. In mathematics a common method of indicating division is to place the dividend over the divisor and draw a short horizontal line between them, as

$$\frac{15}{22}$$

An alternative method is to use a slash, as in 15/22. This is the method used in FORTRAN, because it lends itself more easily to the limitations of computer input devices. Thus, the general form for division in FORTRAN is

```
VAR1/VAR2
```

where VAR1 and VAR2 represent any valid FORTRAN constants or variables.

If at least one of the operands, VAR1 or VAR2, is of type real, then the quotient is real. If both operands are of type integer, then the quotient is of type integer.

Truncating the result. If the real number 12.6 is stored in variable SUM, then the quotient SUM/3 is the real number 4.3. If the integer value 195 is stored in variable N, then the quotient N/50 is 3, the largest integer less than or equal to the true quotient. Notice the loss of any fractional portion in the quotient when division of integers occurs. This chopping off of the fractional part is call *truncation.*

Type of an operation. This method of determining the *type* of a result applies to addition, subtraction, and multiplication as well as division:

- *Only if **both** operands are of type integer is the result of type integer.*

Exponentiation. In mathematics, a *superscript*, a small number a little above and to the right, is used to designate that a variable is raised to some power. For example, y^2 means the value obtained by raising y to the second power. In FORTRAN, a *double asterisk* is placed between the number to be raised to a power and the power. Thus Y**2 means Y raised to the second power. Expressed in general terms, a variable raised to a variable power is written

```
VAR1**VAR2
```

This expression has the value resulting from raising the value of variable VAR1 to the power specified by the value of variable VAR2. So, if 5 is stored at VAR1 and 3 at VAR2, then the expression has the value 125. Note that either or both VAR1 and VAR2 may be real. Thus a number may be raised to a fractional power.

Negation. The preceding arithmetic operations are all binary in the sense that *two* operands are required. There are certain mathematical operations, called *unary* operations, in which only one operand is required. One of these available in FORTRAN is negation. The symbol for negation is the minus sign, –. To indicate the negation of a variable, B, we write

`-B` *or* `(-B)`

Whatever value is stored in variable B will be negated, so that (–B) will have a value equal to the contents of B with the opposite sign.

Arithmetic expressions. A combination of variables and constants together with arithmetic operation symbols is an *arithmetic expression*. In common use, the term has been extended to include a numeric variable by itself, a numeric constant by itself, or any combination of these together with arithmetic symbols. Here are some examples of arithmetic expressions:

EXAMPLES

```
A
5
A*5
(A*5)+B/6
X**2-4*8
X+Y/3*T
```

Hierarchy of arithmetic operations. Since arithmetic expressions may often have more than one meaning, it is important to know which interpretation is used by the FORTRAN compiler. Recall from mathematics that if the five fundamental arithmetic operations occur in the same expression, they are to be computed in this order: first, exponentiation in order from right to left; second, multiplication and division from left to right; and third, addition and subtraction also from left to right.

Mathematics further provides parentheses to indicate which portion of an expression is computed first. With multiple sets of parentheses, the expression within the innermost parentheses is computed first, then the expression in the next-innermost parentheses, and so on. Fortunately, all of these hierarchical rules apply in FORTRAN.

To shed further light on the situation we consider four examples. Where applicable, assume that the value stored in A=5 and in B=3. Assume also that A and B have been declared integer variables.

EXAMPLE 1 `7+3*A-B**2`

First compute the square of B, which is 9, to get

```
7+3*A-9
```

The product 3*A is calculated next. Since A is 5, 3*A is 15, and now the expression is

```
7+15-9
```

Here, addition and subtraction operations have equal priority and are performed from left to right. Therefore, 7+15 is computed first to give 22, after which 9 is subtracted to yield the final value of 13.

EXAMPLE 2 This expression has the same variables, constants, and operation symbols as Example 1 but now parentheses have been inserted.

```
7+(3*(A-B))**2
```

Let's apply the hierarchical rules to evaluate this expression. Starting in the innermost parentheses means that A–B must be calculated first, yielding a result of 2. Now the original expression becomes

```
7+(3*2)**2
```

Next we find the product of 3 and 2 inside the parentheses, which is 6. The expression to be evaluated now is

```
7+6**2
```

The exponentiation operator has higher priority, so 6**2 is computed, giving 36. Finally we evaluate 7+36 to obtain the value of the original expression as 43.

So the use of parentheses changed the value of the expression.

■ *Always be alert in presenting and using arithmetic expressions that involve more than one operation.*

EXAMPLE 3 `2*A/B*7+B**2**3`

In this expression the exponentiation operator appears twice in succession. In mathematics this situation would appear like this:

$$B^{2^3}$$

The interpretation would be B to the power of 2^3 or B^8.

In order to comply with this interpretation from mathematics, FORTRAN provides that multiple appearances of the exponentiation operator are performed from right to left. Therefore, we evaluate the original expression using the following steps:

`2*A/B*7+B**2**3`	*2**3 is computed first*
`2*A/B*7+B**8`	*B**8 is computed next*
`2*A/B*7+6561`	*2*A is computed next*
`10/B*7+6561`	*10/B is computed next*
`3*7+6561`	*3*7 is computed next*
`21+6561`	*21+6561 is computed next*
`6582`	

With B and 10 both integer values, note that 10/B is the integer value 3.

EXAMPLE 4 `-A*B+100*(90/100)`

The use of parentheses in this expression requires the division operation to be done first. Here are the steps in the evaluation:

`-A*B+100*(90/100)`	*90/100 is computed first, resulting in zero because this is integer division*
`-A*B+100*0`	*A*B is computed next*
`-15+100*0`	*100*0 is computed next*
`-15+0`	*−15+0 is computed next*
`-15`	

Note that when the negation operation is not enclosed in parentheses, its precedence is the same as for subtraction.

Assignment statement. Now that we know how arithmetic expressions are evaluated, we are ready to discuss the process of storing or *assigning* the results to a variable. The FORTRAN statement to accomplish this is called the *assignment statement* and has the form

```
RESULT = VAR
```

where the equals symbol is interpreted to mean *is assigned* and VAR is any acceptable arithmetic expression or string constant.

EXAMPLE 1 `RESULT = 3*B`

means: the variable RESULT is assigned the product of 3 and B. The actions that occur in the computer are

1. Multiply 3 by the contents of B.
2. Erase whatever was stored in location RESULT.
3. Assign the product of 3 and B to location RESULT.

Here are more examples of assignment statements with brief explanations of what actions take place. Assume the following declarations:

```
REAL VAR,A,X
INTEGER J
CHARACTER NAME*5
```

EXAMPLE 2
```
VAR=126.5
```

Assigns the constant 126.5 to variable VAR.

EXAMPLE 3
```
VAR=VAR*2+1
```

The current value of variable VAR is multiplied by 2 and 1 is added to that product. This result replaces the previous contents of VAR.

EXAMPLE 4
```
NAME = 'ALI'
```

The string ALI replaces whatever was stored in variable NAME.

EXAMPLE 5
```
J=7.3*A-23
```

The expression on the right is evaluated (result is 13.5 if A is 5.) and truncated because the integer variable J is to contain the final result. Therefore, the integer 13 is stored in J.

EXAMPLE 6
```
X=(X+1)*(3-8/3)+2**3
```

Assume the current value of X is 2.5. The steps in evaluating the arithmetic expression are

```
(2.5+1)*(3-8/3)+8
(3.5)*(3-2)+8
3.5*1+8
3.5+8
11.5
```

Then X is assigned the new value 11.5. Note that the result is a real number because the operand X on the right is a real variable, in spite of the fact that all constants are integers.

Mixed mode arithmetic expressions. The representations of integer and real values in computer memory are fundamentally different, so we need to be well aware of what happens if an arithmetic expression contains *both* kinds. Expressions containing both real and integer values are called *mixed mode* expressions.

We've already seen that if one or more operands in an arithmetic expression are real then the value of the whole expression is real. Only if all variables and constants in an arithmetic expression are of integer type will the entire expression be of integer type. In addition, it is important to note that the FORTRAN compiler handles each parenthetical part separately in determining which are integer and which are real.

EXAMPLE 1 Suppose that the integer 5 has been stored in integer variable N, the integer 6 in integer variable M, and the real value 4.0 in real variable A. Now consider this expression:

```
(3+A)*(N/M+1)
```

The rightmost parenthetical group consists only of integer type value, causing integer arithmetic to be performed within that group. The result is 1 since N/M = 0 with N = 5 and M = 6.

The leftmost parenthesized group has the real value 7.0, so that when the result of the left group is multiplied by the result of the right group, the entire expression has the real value 7.0.

Therefore, *portions* of arithmetic expressions may result in integer values, though the entire expression will be of type real as long as at least one operand is real.

The following two examples are both a little more complex. In both, assume 2.5 is stored at A, 10.2 at B, 5 at N, 6 at M, and 10 at L.

EXAMPLE 2 Consider the expression

```
M/L*A+N/M*B
```

Here are the steps in evaluating it:

```
M/L=6/10=0
0*A=0*2.5=0.0
N/M=5/6=0
(0*2.5)+(0*10.2)=0.0+0.0=0.0
```

Does it surprise you that an arithmetic expression with no zero values initially and no subtraction operation should ultimately have the value zero? It does most people. The reason, of course, is that integer division results are sometimes unexpectedly zero. Note that the final value is of type real because of A and B in the original expression.

EXAMPLE 3 Consider the expression

```
A*M/L+B*N/M
```

The steps evaluating it are

```
A*M=2.5*6=15.0
(A*M)/L=15.0/10=1.5
B*N=10.2*5=51.0
(B*N)/M=51.0/6=8.5
```

Therefore,

```
A*M/L+B*N/M=1.5+8.5=10.0
```

You probably noticed that these two examples involve the same operations, though the order of the variables is different. The results are not the same at all. The reason, of course, is that the rearranged order in Example 3 eliminated all integer arithmetic, thus giving no unexpected zeros.

Thus far, references to mixed mode expressions may have given the impression that this is a concern only when real and integer operands are involved. This is not true. Mixed mode arithmetic operations can occur among any types of numeric data.

Type of mixed mode expressions. Consider this general form of an arithmetic expression:

```
OPRND1 OP OPRND2
```

where OPRND1 and OPRND2 are two operands in a FORTRAN expression and OP is any of the binary operations +, –, *, /, and **.

When OPRND1 and OPRND2 are of the same type there is no mixed mode. But if they are of different data types, the expression is of mixed mode and the following rules apply in determining the type of the result:

1. If one of the two operands is of type real and the other one is of type integer, the result is of type real.
2. If one of the two operands is of type complex or double precision, the result is of type complex or double precision.

Therefore, if an arithmetic expression with several operations in it has at least one complex operand, the final result of all operations is of type complex. If there is no operand of type complex but at least one of type real, then the result is of type real. With neither complex nor real operands, the result is of type integer.

SAMPLE PROGRAM

Consider this program as we give some examples of mixed mode expressions:

```
1        PROGRAM MIX
2        INTEGER A
3        REAL B
4        COMPLEX C
5        C = (2.1, 7.0)
6        B = 3.6
7        A = 2
8        C = A * B + C + (2,3)
9        PRINT*,C
10       C = C * B
11       PRINT*,C
12       A = C
13       B = C
14       PRINT*,A,B
15       END
```

If this program is executed, the output is

```
11.3000          10.0000
90.4000          80.0000
90               90.4
```

Line 5 assigns a complex value to C. Therefore, both C and the constant (2,3) are complex numbers. When both are involved in the expression, as in line 8, the result is complex. This result is stored at variable C.

Line 9 calls for displaying the contents of variable C as the first output line.

Line 10 causes a real number to multiply both parts of a complex number, producing another complex number. This result is stored at variable C.

Line 11 calls for displaying the new value of C as the second output line.

Line 12 causes the integer portion of the real part of the complex number stored at C to be stored in the integer variable A.

Line 13 causes the real part of the complex number at C to be stored in the real variable B.

Finally, line 14 calls for displaying the integer at A and the real number at B as the third output line.

Exercises 2.2

1. Write a single FORTRAN statement equivalent to each of these mathematical equations. Each letter represents a different variable. When two or more letters are written together, we mean their product.

a. $$x = \frac{a^2 + b^2 + ab}{1 + \frac{a}{a+b}}$$

b. $$v = (a - 2b)^3 (3a + b)^2$$

c. $$w = \frac{-b + \sqrt{b^2 - 4ac}}{2a}$$

d. $$t = (a^n)^m + a^n a^m$$

e. $$p = 37(\sqrt[3]{a^2} + \sqrt{a^3}\,) / (\sqrt{a\sqrt{b}} + a)$$

f. $$y = a + \frac{1}{1 + \frac{1}{1+a}}$$

g. $$z = (a^{b^2} + b^{a^2})\,(a + b + \frac{ab}{a+b})$$

h. $$u = abc + \frac{1}{ab} + \frac{bc}{ab + bc} + \frac{ab + bc + ac}{\frac{a+b+c}{abc}}$$

2. Determine the value that is stored in real variable X or integer variable IX as each of the following FORTRAN statements is executed with A=200, B=10, and C=5. Assume A, B, and C are declared integer variables.

a. `X=A*C + (B*C)**2`

b. `X=(A+B)*C/B*C`

c. `X=B**2**3/A**2`

d. `IX = (A+B)**(B+C)*(5/9)`

e. `IX = (9/5)*(A-32)`

f. `IX = (A+B+30*C) * 1/3`

g. `IX = A*(10/200) * C`

h. `X = A * C * (10/200)`

i. `IX = C/B + C**2*A`

j. `X = C**2*A + C/B`

k. `IX = (A+B+30*C)*(1/3)`

l. `X = (B/A)*(A/B)**C`

m. `X = (A/B*B/A)**C`

Rounding and Truncation

Variables can be composed of an infinite set of digits, but in making computations it is sometimes necessary and often useful to restrict the number of significant digits. Some numbers cannot be stored or printed on some computers. In other cases, manipulating long strings of numbers consumes a great deal of time without improving the usefulness of the result. So computers round or truncate numbers. The two processes are different, and when used will produce different results. An awareness of how these processes are used will help you avoid computational traps.

Rounding. Suppose we have a real number containing *n* digits (integer or fractional) that we wish to round to *m* digits (where *m* is less than *n*). In mathematics, we proceed as follows: If the digit in position $m+1$ from the left is less than 5, we drop all digits to the right of the *m*th digit that are also to the right of the decimal point; digits to the left of the decimal point are changed to zeros. If the digit in position $m+1$ is 5 or more, we add 1 to the *m*th digit and treat the digits to the right of the *m*th digit as in the previous case.

Here are some examples:

EXAMPLE 1 Round 32.68717 to four significant digits. Result: 32.69.

The digit in position five is 7, a number greater than 5, so 1 is added to the fourth digit.

EXAMPLE 2 Round 2.8998 to three significant digits. Result: 2.90.

The digit in position four is 9, a number greater than 5, so 1 is added to the third digit. But 1 added to 9 gives 0 plus a carry digit, which then makes the 8 in position two 9, yielding 2.90.

EXAMPLE 3 Round 21.398 to two significant digits. Result: 21.

The 3 in position three is less than 5, so the three digits to the right of the second position are dropped.

EXAMPLE 4 Round 238,691 to four significant digits. Result: 238,700.

The fifth digit is 9, so we increase the fourth digit to 7 and change the fifth and sixth digits to zeros.

Truncation. Another method of shortening the number of significant digits in a variable is *truncation*. In the earlier section on division of integers, we used truncation to drop any fractional digits, leaving an integer result. Truncation in FORTRAN usually means exactly that.

However, one can also speak of truncating to some number of digits, an alternative to rounding. When such truncation occurs, all digits to the right of the specified digit are dropped or changed to 0 regardless of their size. For example, if 20 is divided by 3 and the result is truncated to two digits, the result is 6.6. The true quotient is 6.66666 . . . , but all the sixes after the second are dropped. Note that if this number is *rounded* to two digits, the result is 6.7.

Uses of rounding. In FORTRAN, a displayed real number is rounded to the greatest number of digits allowed by the system. A number stored internally is also rounded to keep as many digits as the computer allows.

EXAMPLE In order to impress you with the importance of the computer's inability to store all fractions in their exact representation we present an example.

QUESTION A Suppose the variable X is assigned the value resulting from dividing 1.0 by 300.0. If the computer being used allows for storing the equivalent of eleven significant digits, then X is assigned the value .0033333333333.

Suppose, next, that Y is initially assigned the value 0.

Now suppose the value at X is added repeatedly 300 times to the value at Y. (This seems like it should have the same effect as multiplying X by 300.)

- *What value do you think is stored at Y after such repeated additions?*

QUESTION B Now assume a variable A is defined by

```
A=(1-Y)*10**14
```

where Y is the result of 300 additions of X.

- *What value do you think is stored at A?*

FORTRAN PROGRAM The common answers given to the two questions just posed are 1 and 0, respectively. However, those answers are incorrect, as you can discover for yourself by running this FORTRAN program

```
      PROGRAM TRUNC
      REAL X,Y,A
      X=1.0/300
      Y=0
      DO 10 I=1,300
           Y=Y+X
 10   CONTINUE
      A=(1-Y)*10**14
      PRINT*, 'A = ',A,'Y = ',Y,'X = ',X
      END
```

The output of this program is

```
A = 230.686     Y = 0.999999     X = 3.33333E-3
```

In the program, we include the lines

```
      DO 10 I=1,300
           Y=Y+X
 10   CONTINUE
```

to add X to the variable Y 300 times. This FORTRAN structure will be discussed later as a convenient means of accomplishing 300 additions.

ALTERNATE PROGRAM

Now suppose than instead of performing 300 additions of X to Y we simply assign to Y the result of multiplying X by 300. The program would then appear like this:

```
PROGRAM TRUNC
REAL X,Y,A
X=1.0/300
Y=300*X
A=(1-Y)*10**14
PRINT*, 'A = ',A,'Y = ',Y,'X = ',X
END
```

This revised program has the output we expect:

```
A = 0      Y = 1.00000      X = 3.33333E-3
```

In both of these programs the value of X is exactly the same. The results differ because of the method used to compute the value of Y. In the first program, repeated additions result in repeated roundings—with unexpected results. In the second program, no such repeat operations occur. One multiplication of 300 and X produces the final value of Y.

▪ *The student should be alert to the possibility of incorrect results because of faulty computation techniques.*

Problem 2.3
Computing Radar Vectors

SITUATION

You have been assigned to write a module for a collision avoidance program for a passenger ship. The program as a whole evaluates the position and projected course of radar objects (other ships, icebergs, etc.) ahead of the ship. It does this by comparing, at 30-second intervals, the positions of an object on a rectangular grid.

OBJECTIVE

Your assignment is to write a module to convert the two grid positions for an object into a vector defined by magnitude and direction. Other modules will work out from this vector the speed and course of the object, convert units of measure, and evaluate the object's risk of collision.

This module may be called from various points within the program, and reports will be passed to three other modules. Your module must thus accept a broad range of input variables and provide output in a simple, standard form.

Begin by stating the problem in a highly general form: Given two points, $P1$ with coordinates $(x1, y1)$ and $P2$ with coordinates $(x2, y2)$, find the slope and length of the line joining the two points.

ALGORITHM

1. Read the values for X1, Y1, X2 and Y2.
2. Compute slope using the formula SLOPE = (Y2–Y1) / (X2–X1).
3. Compute the length using the formula

   $$distance = \sqrt{(x1 - x2)^2 + (y1 - y2)^2}$$

4. Report the values for SLOPE and LENGTH.

PROGRAM

```
PROGRAM VECTOR
REAL X1, X2, Y1, Y2, SLOPE, LENGTH
PRINT *, 'ENTER THE COORDINATES OF THE FIRST POINT'
READ *, X1, Y1
PRINT *, 'ENTER THE COORDINATES OF THE SECOND POINT'
READ *, X2, Y2
SLOPE = (Y2 - Y1) / (X2 - X1)
LENGTH = SQRT((X1-X2) * (X1-X2) + (Y1-Y2) * (Y1-Y2))
PRINT *, 'THE SLOPE IS ', SLOPE
PRINT *, 'THE LENGTH IS ', LENGTH
END
```

Note that in the computation of LENGTH, a function SQRT was used. It computes the square root of the expression within the parentheses to its right.

Problem 2.4
Determining a Course

SITUATION You are now assigned to write the module that will convert the vector to a course. It will accept the slope from the previous module, adjust it for our ship's current heading, and find the direction in which the radar object is moving.

An artificial vector coordinate system always locates the ship on which we are traveling at (0,0) with the y axis positive in the direction the ship is moving. Once again, we wish to keep the module as generalized as possible.

Given the slope of the radar object's motion in the artificial coordinate system, determine its course as a compass bearing.

SOLUTION This requires two steps: First the radar object's slope must be converted to a course relative to our ship, in the artificial polar form. Then the ship's current heading must be added to it to find the radar object's compass course. The slope will be simply *arctan(slope)*. This module will receive the ship's heading from another module in the larger program.

ALGORITHM

1. Read values for SLOPE and HEADING.
2. Compute RELCRSE = ARCTAN(SLOPE).
3. Compute ABSCRSE = RELCRSE + HEADING.
4. Report results.

FORTRAN PROGRAM

```
PROGRAM OBJCRS
REAL SLOPE,HEAD,RELCRS,ABSCRS
PRINT*,'ENTER SLOPE OF RADAR OBJECT'
PRINT*,'AND CURRENT SHIP HEADING'
READ*,SLOPE,HEAD
RELCRS = ATAN(SLOPE)
ABSCRS = RELCRS+HEAD
PRINT*,'WHEN THE SHIP HEADING IS: ',HEAD
PRINT*,'A RADAR OBJECT WITH SLOPE: ',SLOPE
PRINT*,'HAS A COURSE OF: ',RELCRS,' RELATIVE TO THE SHIP'
PRINT*,'AND IS ON A COURSE OF: ',ABSCRS
PRINT*,'BY THE COMPASS.'
END
```

Note that in computing RELCRS the system function ATAN was used. This function computes the arctangent of SLOPE. (See Appendix B.)

PROGRAM DESIGN ISSUE

Writing a program in modules is not only easier, for very large programs it is the only reasonable way. But there is a danger. The module interfaces account for a very high proportion of software bugs, and especially for the intermittent problems that are hardest to detect and even harder to fix. So when you work on modular programs, as with Problems 2.3 and 2.4, it is important to carefully define the function and scope of each module and define the input and output criteria. These questions may help in your work:

Is the module responsible for detecting and stopping bad input data? If not, which module is responsible, and how can it be insured that revisions of the program do not separate the modules in such a way that errors can pass through?

Is the module responsible for detecting and stopping bad output data? If yes, which aspects of data quality does it check: Missing values? Zero denominators? Undefined codes?

Is the module performing more than one distinct function? If so, it might be better to replace the module with separate modules for each task. This can make future revisions of the program much easier.

Problem 2.5
Describing a Gas Cloud

SITUATION You're building a computer model of the interactions of atoms and ions in hydrogen at very high temperatures. This model might be used in the development of bootstrapping or cold-start procedures for nuclear fusion reactors or in fluid flow studies for the design of a nuclear space propulsion system. One key function of the model is working out the distribution of quantum states of the electrons in the gas. You know the apparent atomic radius, which for hydrogen is the distance from the single electron to the nucleus, and from that the model computes the probability of finding excited 4s ions.

OBJECTIVE Given the value of r, the distance of an electron from the nucleus of an hydrogen atom, the probability of finding that electron in the 4s excited state is proportional to $f(r)$, where

$$f(r) = \left(1 - \frac{3r}{4} + \frac{r^2}{8} - \frac{r^3}{192}\right)^2 e^{(-r/2)}$$

Compute that probability.

ALGORITHM

1. Read the value for R.
2. Compute X = 1 – ((3R)/4) + ((R**2)/8) – ((R**3)/192)
3. Compute Y = X*X.
4. Compute Z = E**(–R/2)
5. Compute Y*Z as the desired value for F(R).

FORTRAN PROGRAM

```
      PROGRAM GASCLD
      REAL X, Y, Z, RMAN, R, FR
      INTEGER REXP
C*
C*    RMAN IS THE MANTISSA OF R AND
C*    REXP IS THE EXPONENT OF R IN SCIENTIFIC NOTATION FORM.
C*
      PRINT *, 'ENTER THE RADIUS IN 2 PARTS, THE MANTISSA & THE EXPON'
      READ *, RMAN, REXP
      R = RMAN * 10**REXP
      X = 1 - 3*(R/4) + R*R/8 - R*R*R/192
      Y = X*X
      FR = Y*Z
      PRINT *, 'THE PROBABILITY IS PROPORTIONAL TO ', FR
      END
```

The COMMENT Statement

No matter how careful we are in developing the structure and organization of a program so that its logic is easily followed and understood, it is not possible to make it as understandable as prose in one's native language. The COMMENT statement is provided in FORTRAN to help us keep our programs clear and understandable.

The COMMENT statement begins with the letter C or the asterisk * in the first position in the line. The rest of the line contains the comment itself. This statement is not executed in running the program, and accomplishes nothing toward the solution of the problem for which the program was written. Its only purpose is to allow for information to be inserted within the program so that anyone reading a program listing will better understand the program's logic.

■ *We repeat: No effect on the problem solution results from COMMENT statements. Their usefulness is to increase the readability and understandability of a program listing.*

Dennis Van Tassel, in his book on program style,[2] considers COMMENT statements as either *prologue* or *explanatory* comments. These categories are useful in presenting guidelines to help you develop skill in using COMMENT statements effectively.

Prologue comments. These appear at the beginning of a program or subprogram or before any group of code statements. Prologue comments can do many things:

1. Describe briefly what the program, subprogram, or group of statements accomplishes.
2. List and explain important variables.
3. List all array variables (described later) and briefly describe their use.
4. Describe in detail input data required by the program.
5. Describe in detail all possible output generated by the program.
6. List any special instructions needed to correctly execute the program.
7. List the program author, date of completion, company or institution of affiliation, and related information.
8. List any subprograms and describe their functions.

2. Van Tassel, D., *Program Style, Design, Efficiency, Debugging, and Testing* (Englewood Cliffs, NJ: Prentice-Hall, 1974).

9. Summarize any special scientific method or procedure used in the program. A reference should be included for further study.
10. Estimate computer memory and cpu requirements for executing the program.
11. Explain any special operating instructions.
12. Describe any special cases that the program cannot process.
13. List all data and problem-formulation limitations of the program.

EXAMPLE

```
C***********************************************************************
C*    PROGRAM NAME:           EXAMPLE                                  *
C*    AUTHORS:                A. BEHFOROOZ, M. HOLOIEN                 *
C*    DATE:                   OCTOBER, 1990                            *
C*    PURPOSE:                TO PROVIDE AN EXAMPLE OF PLACEMENT OF    *
C*                            COMMENT LINES IN A PROGRAM OR SUBPROGRAM. *
C*    VARIABLE DEFINITIONS:   NUM=NUM OF CASES.                        *
C*                            OBSV=OBSERVED VALUE.                     *
C*                            ESTV=ESTIMATED VALUE.                    *
C*    ARRAY DEFINITIONS:      A=ONE-DIMENSIONAL ARRAY OF SIZE 100      *
C*                              FOR STORING OBSERVED VALUES.           *
C*                            B=TWO-DIMENSIONAL ARRAY OF SIZE 200 × 2  *
C*                              FOR STORING THE DIFFERENCES            *
C*                              AND THEIR SQUARES OF THE OBSERVED VALUES. *
C*    INPUT:                  NUM=NUMBER OF CASES.                     *
C*                            NUM IS FOLLOWED BY THAT SPECIFIED        *
C*                            NUMBER OF OBSERVED VALUES.               *
C*    OUTPUT:                 VALUE OF CHI-SQUARED AND THE             *
C*                            ASSOCIATED DEGREES OF FREEDOM.           *
C*    SCIENTIFIC METHOD:      THE CHI-SQUARED GOODNESS OF FIT IS USED. FOR *
C*                            DETAILS SEE ANY APPLIED STATISTICS TEXTBOOK. *
C*    USING THE PROGRAM:      BEFORE EXECUTION, USER MUST ENTER        *
C*                            LINE 39 OF THE PROGRAM AS THE DEFINING   *
C*                            EQUATION BY WHICH THE ESTIMATED VALUE OF X *
C*                            IS COMPUTED. LINE 39 IS ENTERED AS FOLLOWS: *
C*                              EST(X)=ANY FORTRAN EXPRESSION INVOLVING X *
C*    SUBPROGRAM USED:        NONE                                     *
C*    MEMORY/TIME REQUIRED:   AVERAGE                                  *
C*    SPECIAL OPERATING INSTRUCTIONS:     NONE                         *
C*    SPECIAL CASE:           THE PROGRAM WILL NOT WORK FOR NEGATIVE   *
C*                            INPUT VALUES.                            *
C*    LIMITATIONS:            NO MORE THAN 100 OBSERVED VALUES CAN BE  *
C*                            PROCESSED.                               *
C***********************************************************************
```

Explanatory comments. COMMENT statements can also clarify any program logic that is otherwise difficult to follow. When using explanatory comments, assume that the reader is familiar with the program language. Here are some unrelated sample comment lines:

EXAMPLES

```
C      GO TO STOP IF END OF DATA.
C      BRANCH TO ERROR ROUTINE IF NEGATIVE ACCOUNT NUMBER.
C      RE-ENTER DATA IF BLANK LINE IS READ.
C      REJECT OFF-LIMIT DATA.
C      INPUT DATA FROM FILE XTRA.
C      PRINT HEADINGS FOR OUTPUT.
```

Placement. Although there are no rules for the use of COMMENT statements, it is useful to follow a couple of guidelines:

1. Separate comments from program statements by one blank line. To do this, insert a COMMENT statement consisting only of the C in position 1 or a C* in positions 1 and 2, with the rest of the line blank.
2. Use asterisks to enclose comments in boxes. Separation can also be achieved by proper use of indentation.

EXAMPLE

```
C***********************************************************************
C*     THE NEXT FIVE PROGRAM STATEMENTS COMPUTE                        *
C*     CHI-SQUARE.                                                     *
C***********************************************************************
C

       (PROGRAM LINES)

C
C***********************************************************************
C*     THIS LOOP INITIALIZES ARRAY A.                                  *
C***********************************************************************
C

       (PROGRAM LINES)
```

We conclude this section with three problems, showing complete solutions including FORTRAN programs.

Problem 2.6 Studying Gas Mileage

SITUATION As an automotive engineer, you are trying to study the relation between the reported gas mileage of cars operated in various cities and their Carnot efficiencies. The Carnot efficiency, the maximum possible for any engine that converts heat to mechanical work, is defined by

```
1-(TL/TH)
```

where TL is the temperature into which heat is being released, here the outside environment, and
TH is the temperature from which heat is being drawn, here the

cylinder of the engine. Both are absolute temperatures, measured in degrees Kelvin or Rankine.

To do the study, you have data from recording thermocouples that give cylinder temperatues in several test cars driven in different cities over a period of several months. You also have the National Weather Service hourly temperatures for those cities during that period. The cylinder temperatures are in degrees Celsius, the weather temperatures in degrees Fahrenheit.

OBJECTIVE Write a program that will convert the environmental temperature to degrees Celsius, convert both temperatures to the Kelvin scale, and calculate the Carnot efficiency. Output all the temperatures calculated.

ALGORITHM

1. Input environmental temperature in degrees Fahrenheit and cylinder temperature in degrees Celsius.
2. Convert environmental temperature to degrees Celsius: (5/9)(F−32).
3. Convert both temperatures to degrees Kelvin: C+273.16.
4. Calculate the Carnot efficiency.
5. Output the input data, all temperature conversions, and the calculated Carnot efficiency.

FORTRAN PROGRAM

```
PROGRAM CONVN
REAL FENV,CCYL,CENV,KCYL,KENV,EFFCY
READ*,FENV,CCYL
CENV=(5.0/9.0)*(FENV-32)
KENV=CENV+273.16
KCYL=CCYL+273.16
EFFCY=1-(KENV/KCYL)
PRINT*,FENV,CCYL,CENV,KCYL,KENV,EFFCY
END
```

In order for this program to run successfully, input data must be provided at the time the program is executed.

PROGRAM WITH COMMENTS Although the preceding problem statement and solution are a satisfactory disposition of the problem, if a user of the program had available only the program listing of eight statements, it probably would not be completely clear what the program accomplishes. This would be especially true if the user knew nothing about Carnot efficiency or the relationship between the three temperature scales. Here is an example of not only a correct, but an understandable program:

```
      PROGRAM CONVN
C*************************************************************************
C*    PROGRAM DEFINITION                                                 *
C*         THIS PROGRAM READS ENVIRONMENTAL TEMPERATURE                  *
C*         IN DEGREES FARHENHEIT                                         *
C*         & CYLINDER TEMPERATURE IN DEGREES CELSIUS,                    *
C*         CONVERTS BOTH TO DEGREES KELVIN,                              *
C*         CALCULATES THE CARNOT EFFICIENCY AND                          *
C*         CONVERTS IT TO CELSIUS DEGREES                                *
C*         AND PRINTS THE RESULTS.                                       *
C*************************************************************************
C*    VARIABLE DEFINITIONS                                               *
C*         FENV IS ENVIRONMENTAL TEMPERATURE IN DEGREES FAHRENHEIT.      *
C*         CCYL IS CYLINDER TEMPERATURE IN DEGREES CELSIUS.              *
C*         KENV IS ENVIRONMENTAL TEMPERATURE IN DEGREES KELVIN.          *
C*         KCYL IS CYLINDER TEMPERATURE IN DEGREES KELVIN.               *
C*         EFFCY IS CARNOT EFFICIENCY.                                   *
C*************************************************************************
C*                                                                       *
      REAL FENV,CCYL,CENV,KCYL,KENV,EFFCY
      PRINT*,'ENTER ENVIRONMENTAL TEMPERATURE IN DEG F'
      READ*,FENV
      PRINT*,'ENTER CYLINDER TEMPERATURE IN DEG C'
      READ *,CCYL
      CENV=(5.0/9.0)*(FENV-32)
      KENV=CENV+273.16
      KCYL=CCYL+273.16
      EFFCY=1-(KENV/KCYL)
      PRINT*,'REPORTED ENVIRONMENTAL TEMPERATURE, DEG F ',FENV
      PRINT*,'REPORTED CYLINDER TEMPERATURE, DEG C ',CCYL
      PRINT*,'ENVIRONMENTAL TEMPERATURE, DEG K ',KENV
      PRINT*,'CYLINDER TEMPERATURE, DEG K ',KCYL
      PRINT*,'CARNOT EFFICIENCY ',EFFCY
      END
```

It is clear that the inclusion of comments does a great deal to elucidate the program and its functions. We know here what the numbers input and output mean. Without the comment lines, a user would be hard pressed to know what either input or output was. We urge beginning programmers to develop early the habit of including comments so that the user is made aware of what the program accomplishes.

Note also that we have added program lines that label the input and final results. The user receives not just a jumble of numbers at the end, but a clearly labeled printout of temperatures and efficiency. Users tend to feel much more comfortable with such a program than one that gives no clue as to what the input or output represent. Furthermore, identifying the input to be entered by the user helps assure that input data are correct.

Problem 2.7
Storing Explosive Chemicals

SITUATION Your company needs to put up warehouses to store ammonium nitrate, a serious explosion hazard. Federal safety regulations governing such storage facilities require that no part of any warehouse extend into the circle which circumscribes any other warehouse.

Since you will want to make maximum use of the expensive ground area available, you will want to know how much warehouse space a given radius (distance from the center of the building to a corner) will give you, how much area Federal regulations require, and the ratio between those. Assuming the warehouses are to be four-sided, a square warehouse will make the most effective use of space.

OBJECTIVE Input the radius of a circle and compute and output

1. The area of the circle.
2. The area of the largest square contained within the circle.
3. The ratio of the result of Objective 1 to the result of Objective 2.

Use the value 3.1416 for the constant *pi*.

ALGORITHM

1. Input radius and store in RADIUS.
2. Compute the area of the circle using the equation.

   ```
   CAREA=RADIUS*RADIUS*3.1416
   ```

3. Compute the area of the largest square contained within the circle according to the formula

   ```
   SAREA=RADIUS*RADIUS*2
   ```

4. Compute the ratio.

   ```
   RATIO=CAREA/SAREA
   ```

5. Output the results.

FORTRAN PROGRAM

```
      PROGRAM AREA
C***********************************************************************
C*    PROGRAM DEFINITION                                               *
C*         PROGRAM TO READ RADIUS OF A CIRCLE,                         *
C*         COMPUTE AREA OF THE CIRCLE,                                 *
C*         COMPUTE AREA OF THE LARGEST SQUARE CONTAINED IN THE CIRCLE, *
C*         AND COMPUTE THE RATIO OF CIRCLE AREA TO SQUARE AREA.        *
C*         IT ALSO PRINTS THE THREE COMPUTED VALUES.                   *
C***********************************************************************
```

```
C*    VARIABLE DEFINITION                                                  *
C*         RADIUS IS THE GIVEN RADIUS OF A CIRCLE.                         *
C*         CAREA IS AREA OF CIRCLE.                                        *
C*         SAREA IS AREA OF SQUARE.                                        *
C*         RATIO IS THE RATIO OF THE TWO AREAS.                            *
C*         PI IS 3.1416.                                                   *
C***********************************************************************
C*                                                                         *
      REAL RADIUS, CAREA, SAREA, RATIO, PI
      PI = 3.1416
      READ*, RADIUS
      CAREA = RADIUS * RADIUS * PI
      SAREA = RADIUS * RADIUS * 2
      RATIO = CAREA / SAREA
      PRINT*, 'THE RADIUS GIVEN IS ', RADIUS
      PRINT*, 'THE AREA OF THE CIRCLE IS ', CAREA
      PRINT*, 'THE AREA OF THE SQUARE IS ', SAREA
      PRINT*, 'THE RATIO OF THE TWO AREAS IS ', RATIO
      END
```

Problem 2.8
Timing Building Inspections

SITUATION Industrial insurance normally requires any area in which things of value are stored, or where there is any risk of loss of life in the event of a fire, to be proteted by a sprinkler system. The sprinkler system is inspected by an insurance company engineer at regular intervals, depending on how critical the area is.

OBJECTIVE Write a module for a larger program that will be used in scheduling inspections for facilities where one or more years will elapse between inspections. Given the date of the last inspection, your module is to report the number of full years since the last inspection; no greater precision will be needed.

SOLUTION If today's date, expressed as year, month, day, is TY,TM,TD and the inspection date is IY,IM,ID, then the years since the last inspection is computed by

```
(TY-IY)+((TM-IM)/12)+((TD-ID)/365.25)
```

This solution is based on dividing the year into 12 equal months, and is thus not quite accurate. But the variation from true value is actually less than 2%, or one week. Since inspection schedules routinely vary by as much as a month for reasons of convenience, and the result is going to be truncated to an integer in any case, there is little reason to introduce a more complicated and more accurate algorithm. If there is any risk that this code might be re-used in a program where accuracy is more critical, a more sophisticated algorithm might be needed.

FORTRAN PROGRAM

```
      PROGRAM INSPCTDT
C*************************************************************************
C*    PROGRAM DEFINITION                                                 *
C*         THIS PROGRAM PROVIDES AN APPROXIMATING FUNCTION TO            *
C*         CALCULATE YEARS SINCE LAST SPRINKLER INSPECTION.              *
C*************************************************************************
C*    VARIABLE DEFINITIONS                                               *
C*         TY,TM,TD ARE TODAY'S YEAR,MONTH,DAY RESPECTIVELY.             *
C*         IY,IM,ID ARE YEAR,MONTH,DAY OF LAST INSPECTION.               *
C*         YEARS IS YEARS SINCE LAST INSPECTION.                         *
C*         PLANT IS NAME OF INSPECTED FACILITY.                          *
C*************************************************************************
C*    INPUT SPECIFICATION                                                *
C*         TY,IY ARE 4-DIGIT INTEGERS.                                   *
C*         TM,TD,IM,ID,YEARS ARE 2-DIGIT INTEGERS.                       *
C*         PLANT IS 1 TO 15 CHARACTERS.                                  *
C*************************************************************************
C*                                                                       *
      INTEGER TY,TM,TD,IY,IM,ID,YEARS
      CHARACTER PLANT*15
C*
      READ*,TY,TM,TD
      READ*,PLANT,IY,IM,ID
C*
      YEARS=(TY-IY)+((TM-IM)/12)+((TD-ID)/365.25)
C*
      PRINT*,'THE LAST INSPECTION AT ',PLANT,' WAS ',YEARS,
     +      ' YEARS AGO.'
      END
```

String Data Operations

Besides processing numeric information, a computer is able to process information consisting of letters and other characters. We call such data *string data* or *character data*. Just as arithmetic operations process numeric data, certain operations are reserved for processing character data. We introduce two string data operations here: Concatenation and the substring operation.

Concatenation. Suppose A is a character variable of *m* characters and B is a character variable of *n* characters. *Concatenation* of A and B creates a string of the *m* characters of A followed immediately by the *n* characters of B. The symbol in FORTRAN for concatenation is double slash //. Thus we indicate the concatenation of character variables A and B as

```
A // B
```

EXAMPLE 1 Consider the following program segment:

```
CHARACTER A*8,B*12,C*20
A =' AS GOOD'
B =' AS THIS ONE'
C = A // B
```

After the last statement has been executed, variable C contains the characters

```
 AS GOOD AS THIS ONE
```

■ *Note that blank spaces are legitimate characters in a string.*

EXAMPLE 2 Here is another example of using spaces:

```
CHARACTER A*8,B*12,C*20
B='  THIS     '
A='OR THAT'
C=B // A
```

After the execution of these statements the contents of C is

```
  THIS     OR THAT
```

where the two spaces before THIS and the five spaces after it are preserved in the concatenation of B and A.

EXAMPLE 3 Here is another example, giving different spacing results.

```
CHARACTER A*4,B*3,C*5,D*7,E*12
A='THIS'
B=' OR'
C=' THAT'
D=A // B
E=D // C
```

After the execution of these statements the contents of E is

```
THIS OR THAT
```

You are urged to verify this result by examining the contents of variable A, B, and C at each line of the program segment.

If a character variable is too small to contain all the characters assigned to it, as many of the leftmost characters of the assigned string as possible will be stored while excess characters to the right are lost.

EXAMPLE 4 Consider this program:

```
PROGRAM CHAR
CHARACTER*10 A, B
CHARACTER C*15
READ*, A, B
C = A // B
PRINT*, A, B, C
END
```

Suppose it is run four times with these sets of input data:

```
4A    'ALI'   'BEHFOROOZ'
4B    'MARTIN O. HOLOIEN' 'ALI BEHFOROOZ'
4C    'A' 'B'
4D    '1234567890' '1234567890'
```

The four resulting sets of output are

```
4A     ALI          BEHFOROOZ    ALI        BEHFO
4B     MARTIN O.    ALI BEHFOR   MARTIN O. ALI B
4C     A            B            A          B
4D     1234567890   1234567890   123456789012345
```

ANALYSIS A careful analysis of the output gives us some insights into the way character data are handled.

4A Variables A and B are each specified as having length 10, and C as having length 15. The input provided for A is only three characters and that for B is nine characters.

For A the output consists of the letters A,L,I, and seven spaces.

B is output as the nine letters B,E,H,F,O,R,O,O,Z and one space.

The concatenation of A and B, stored in variable C, is output as the 15 characters A,L,I, seven spaces, B,E,H,F, and O.

Note that when the input provided for a character variable is not enough to fill the entire length of the variable, the unfilled rightmost characters become blank spaces.

4B For both variables A and B, more characters are provided as input than the ten-character length at which they are both declared.

A consists of the ten characters M,A,R,T,I,N,space,O,period, and space.

B consists of the ten characters A,L,I,space,B,E,H,F,O,and R.

C consists of the ten characters of variable A plus the first five characters of variable B to make up its specified 15 characters.

Therefore, we can conclude that if the length of the character string provided as input for a character variable is not as long as the length specified for the variable, then blank spaces are automatically filled into the rightmost part of the variable. If *more* characters are provided as input than the length specified for the variable, then characters are taken from the left part of the input string to fill the length of the variable. You are urged to analyze the output for 4C and 4D to verify these statements.

The substring operation. A second string operation available in FORTRAN is the *substring* operation. This operation accesses a specified collection of characters in a given string. We indicate a substring operation on variable STRING as

```
STRING(I:J)
```

> where I and J are integer constants or variables such that I is less than or equal to J and both I and J are not greater than the length of the character variable STRING.

The default value for I is one and for J it is the length of the string STRING. For example, STRING(:5) means the first five characters of string STRING and STRING(5:) means the last N–4 characters of STRING where N is the length of STRING.

EXAMPLE 1 Let's consider an example to illustrate this operation. Suppose ST has been declared as a character variable of length 15 and that variable B has been declared as a character variable of length 5. Then the statement

```
B = ST(3:5)
```

will cause the third through the fifth characters of ST to be stored in the first 3 positions of variable B. Note that the substring symbol (3:5) appears immediately to the right of the variable on which it is to operate.

EXAMPLE 2 Here is a complete program to illustrate further uses of the substring operation.

```
      PROGRAM STRING
      CHARACTER ST1*20,ST2*15,ST*15
      READ*, ST1, ST2
C***********************************************************************
C*    RECALL THAT IF THE 2ND INTEGER IN THE SUBSTRING SYMBOL           *
C*    IS OMITTED, THEN WE INTEND TO SPECIFY THE RIGHTMOST CHARACTER    *
C*    OF THE STRING IN THE SUBSTRING SYMBOL. THUS IN THIS PROGRAM      *
C*    ST2(6:15) AND ST2(6:) ARE EQUIVALENT.                            *
C***********************************************************************
      ST = ST1(1:5) // ST2(6:)
      PRINT*, ST1, ST2, ST
      END
```

CASE A Suppose we run the program with this input:

```
'ALI' 'BEHFOROOZ'
```

The three letters of the name ALI are stored in the leftmost three positions of variable ST1 and the next seventeen positions of ST1 are filled in with blank spaces.

The nine letters in BEHFOROOZ are stored in the leftmost nine positions of variable ST2 and the next six positions of ST2 are filled in with blank spaces.

In ST are stored the first five characters of ST1 (three letters and two blanks) followed by the last ten characters of ST2 (since only ten positions remain in ST and those ten positions will be filled from the rightmost characters of ST2, namely, the letters R,O,O, and Z, and six blank spaces).

The output of this program consists of the contents of the three variables ST1, ST2, and ST, and would appear as follows:

```
ALI                   BEHFOROOZ          ALI  ROOZ
```

CASE B Suppose we run the program again with this new input:

```
'ALI BEHFOROOZ OR' 'MARTIN O. HOLOIEN'
```

The output this time would be

```
ALI BEHFOROOZ OR     MARTIN O. HOLOI     ALI BN O. HOLOI
```

In this case ST2, with length 15, is capable of storing only the first 15 characters of the input.

```
'MARTIN O. HOLOIEN'
```

CASE C We present one more set of input to be used with STRING:

```
'FFIVE NEXT FIFTEEN'          'LAST NINE CHARACTERS'
```

The output produced this time is

```
FFIVE NEXT FIFTEEN     LAST NINE CHARA     FFIVENINE CHARA
```

ST1, with specified length of 20, is large enough to store all of the input data provided.

However, ST2, with specified length of 15, is *not* large enough to contain the 20 characters of input data provided. Therefore, ST2 contained only the first 15 characters.

The substring operations caused characters 1 through 5 of ST1 and characters 6 through 15 of ST2 to be used in the concatenation operation, resulting in the output at the right.

A repeated variable. With arithmetic operations, the same variable could appear on both sides of the equal sign in an assignment statement. For example,

$$b = a + b$$

is a valid and sometimes useful statement. However, a similar statement involving string operations

```
ST = ST1 (1:3) // ST (1:9)
```

with variable ST on both sides of the equals sign

does not produce the results in ST that you expect.

EXAMPLE

Let's examine a program to help us understand what causes the problem:

```
PROGRAM TEST
CHARACTER ST*12, ST1*3
ST = ' EXAMPLES'
ST1 = 'TWO'
ST = ST1(1:3) // ST(1:9)
PRINT*,ST
END
```

This program performs the following steps:

1. Determines ST1 (1:3)
2. Assigns the results of step 1 to ST.
3. Assigns characters in positions 1 through 9 *one at a time* to positions 4 through 12 of ST.

   That is, a copy of the first character of ST is stored in position 4,
   A copy of the second character of ST is stored in position 5.
   A copy of the third character is stored in position 6.
   A copy of the fourth character (originally copied from position 1) is stored in position 7.
   And so on until position 12 is filled from the character occupying position 9.

   The contents of ST are modified 9 times after the first 3 characters are filled with the 3 characters of ST1.

To make clear what actually happens when the line

```
ST = ST1 (1:3) // ST (1:9)
```

is executed, the following table shows the contents of ST at ten different times. Time 0 is after positions 1-3 are filled with the characters of ST1. Subsequent times show the position-by-position filling described in step 3 above.

Time	*Contents of* ST
0	TWO
1	TWOT
2	TWOTW
3	TWOTWO
4	TWOTWOT
5	TWOTWOTW
6	TWOTWOTWO
7	TWOTWOTWOT
8	TWOTWOTWOTW
9	TWOTWOTWOTWO

Once more, remember that this illustrates the *potential problem* that arises when the same variable appears on both sides of the equals sign in an assignment statement.

REVISION To obtain the *intended results*, PROGRAM TEST should be written as follows:

```
PROGRAM TEST
CHARACTER ST*12, ST1*3, TEMP*9
ST = ' EXAMPLES'
ST1 = 'TWO'
TEMP = ST(1:9)
ST = ST1(1:3) // TEMP
PRINT*,ST
END
```

The output of this program is

```
TWO EXAMPLES
```

Note that it is perfectly valid to use the substring operation within an assignment statement. It is simply a matter of understanding exactly what happens. For example, the statement

```
ST (1:5) = ST(7:11)
```

calls for position 1 through 5 of ST to be filled with a copy of the characters in positions 7 through 11 of the same variable. Thus, if the contents of ST are originally

```
ABCDEFGHIJKL
```

executing the above statement results in

```
GHIJKFGHIJKL
```

Exercises 2.3

1. Examine each of the following FORTRAN statements individually and independently of each other. Those that are incorrect are to be so identified and a reason given for calling them incorrect. Where it is important, assume that variables are properly defined.

.1	`READ NUM1,NUM2,NUM3`	.28	`REAL I,J,X`
.2	`NUM1=NUM2/!NUM3`	.29	`END = START`
.3	`X*X=X**2`	.30	`CHARACTER 2*A,B,C*3`
.4	`READ*,A, A+B`	.31	`A+2 = A+4!2`
.5	`PRINT*,A A+B`	.32	`FIVE = 0`
.6	`A(1:5)=B(1:3) // A(1:6)`	.33	`TEN = 2*FIVE`
.7	`CHARACTER THIS, OR, THAT`	.34	`IMPLICIT LOGICAL(A)`
.8	`COMPLEX END, READ, WRITE`	.35	`LOGICAL A NAME`
.9	`COMPLEX END, READ, WRITE`	.36	`A= B // C(1:10)`

```
.10   CHARACTER 2*A*3B
.11   LAST = END OR 0
.12   IMPLICIT REAL(A,B)
.13   IMPLICIT CHARACTER(A-Z)
.14   IMPLICIT REAL(X)
.15   PRINT*, 'A+B = ' , A + B
.16   LOGICAL REAL,INTEGER
.17   PRINT*,SUM, ' = TOTAL'
.18   B = B * (B+1)/A TIME B
.19   CHARACTER 10*NUM1,NUM2,NUM3
.20   X = (X+Y) / ZERO
.21   IMPLICIT (A TO Z)
.22   READ*, 10, 20
.23   X OR Y = Y OR X
.24   A(1:5)=B(2:7)
.25   X=X // Y
.26   INTEGER A OR B
.27   STOP = END
```

```
.37   AB=A(1:10) // B(1:10)
.38   A = A(1:10)
.39   PRINT*
.40   A=B**!B
.41   X2 = X*2
.42   A(1:4)=A(5:8)
.43   IFA = THEN = ELSE
.44   STOP = END
.45   TWO = 2.5
.46   READ*
.47   CHARACTER A*2,B*3
.48   200A = 100A * 2
.49   IMPLICIT INTEGER(I-N)
.50   X = A(1:10)
.51   LOGICAL A,B
.52   PRINT*, 'A+B', = , A + B
.53   LOGICAL REAL,VAR
.54   A = B * AX(AX+1)
```

2. The following programs should run and produce output on any computer system that has a FORTRAN translating program. Give the output generated by each one if it were executed with indicated input data.

a.

```
INTEGER NUM
PRINT*, 'WHAT IS YOUR STUDENT NUMBER?'
READ*, NUM
PRINT*, 'YOUR STUDENT NUMBER IS', NUM
END
```

Assume 810001 is input datum for NUM.

b.

```
REAL AVE,SUM
INTEGER NUM1,NUM2
READ*,NUM1,NUM2
SUM=NUM1+NUM2
AVE=SUM/2
PRINT*, 'THE TWO NUMBERS ARE: ',NUM1,NUM2
PRINT*,NUM1, '+' ,NUM2, '=' ,SUM
PRINT*, 'THE AVERAGE OF THE 2 NUMBERS IS', AVE
END
```

Assume 8 and 12 are input data for NUM1 and NUM2, respectively.

c.

```
READ*,CENTIG
FAHR = CENTIG * 9.0/5.0 + 32.
PRINT*, 'CENTIGRADE','FAHRENHEIT'
PRINT*,CENTIG,FAHR
END
```

Assume 40. is input datum for CENTIG.

d.

```
READ*,X,Y
AREA=X*Y
PER=(X+Y)*2
PRINT*,'SIDE ONE OF A RECTANGLE',X
PRINT*,'SIDE TWO OF A RECTANGLE',Y
PRINT*,'AREA OF THAT RECTANGLE IS',AREA
PRINT*,'PERIMETER IS',PER
END
```

Assume 5 and 8 are input data for X and Y, respectively.

3. The following FORTRAN programs each have at least one fatal error, an error that makes it impossible for the program to be executed. Identify the errors and provide corrected statements.

a.

```
READ*,A,B
X=A+B
PRINT*,X,A*B
READ*,N+M
PRINT*,N+M
END
```

b.

```
PRINT*'HEADING LINE'
PRINT*,'************'
READ*,ONE,TWO
THREE=ONE+TWO
PRINT*,ONE+TWO,EQUALS,THREE
END
```

c.

```
READ*,F
C=5/9*(F-32)
PRINT*,'F DEGREES', 'C DEGREES'
PRINT*,F,C
PRINT*,A,A*2
END
```

System Library Functions

Many common but relatively complex computational processes are used again and again by different people—for example, finding the square root of a positive real number. This process is difficult to describe step by step, no matter which of the several available methods one chooses. However, if you construct one program module to derive a square root, anyone can insert it in a program when they need to find a square root.

FORTRAN makes a number of such stored programs available as *system library functions* or *FORTRAN library functions*. The appendix provides a complete list of system library functions available in FORTRAN 77. We discuss here how to use selected library functions you are likely to want early in your programming studies.

Using a library function. To use a library function we need only provide the correct *name* of the function followed by a pair of parentheses in which is identified the object on which the function is to operate. We call the object the *argument* or *parameter* of the function.

EXAMPLE 1 For example, suppose we have a positive number stored at real variable X and we want to compute the square root of X, storing the result at real variable Y. The following statement accomplishes this:

```
Y = SQRT(X)
```

where SQRT is the FORTRAN name for the square root function, and the parentheses enclose the object of SQRT; this is the function argument or parameter.

Using a FORTRAN library function is no more difficult than providing its correct name and an argument. As with simple FORTRAN variables, library functions may be used in assignment statements, in arithmetic or appropriate string expressions, in PRINT statements, and as arguments of other library functions. Thus, all of the following are valid examples of using the library function SQRT:

EXAMPLES

```
A = B *(R+SQRT(S))
PRINT *, A, B, SQRT(T)
Z = SQRT (X+SQRT(B))
```

System library functions are used in FORTRAN statements in much the same manner as simple FORTRAN variables.

Common functions. Here are the more important FORTRAN system library functions, each listed with its correct name, an argument name reminding you of the type of the argument, and a brief description of what it does.

FUNCTION 1

```
SQRT(R)
```

computes the square root of a real value stored at R. The result is also real.

FUNCTION 2

```
INT(R)
```

produces an integer value that is the greatest integer less than or equal to the real value at R.

FUNCTION 3

```
ABS(R)
```

produces a real value that is the same as the real value at R if R is zero or positive but is the negative of R if R is negative. This result is called the *absolute value* of R.

FUNCTION 4

```
MAX0(I1,I2, . . . ,IK)
```

determines the greatest of the K integers I1, I2, . . . ,IK and makes that integer value available in the program statement where it appears.

FUNCTION 5 `MIN0(I1,I2, . . . ,IK)`

is like the MAX function except that the *smallest* of the K integers is returned to the program.

FUNCTION 6 `FLOAT(I)`

produces a real value that represents the integer value at `I`.

FUNCTION 7 `MOD(I1,I2)`

computes the integer remainder when the integer value at `I1` is divided by the integer value at `I2`. This is called the *modular quotient* of `I1` and `I2`.

FUNCTION 8 `EXP(R)`

computes the real result when E = 2.178 . . . is raised to the real power R.

FUNCTION 9 `LEN(STRING)`

computes the length, or number of characters, of the string STRING. The result is an integer value.

FUNCTION 10 `ICHAR(C)`

produces the integer value code for the single character represented by argument C.

FUNCTION 11 `CHAR(I)`

produces the single character value that has the code equal to the integer value `I`.

FUNCTION 12 `INDEX (ST1,ST2)`

searches the character string ST1 to see if substring ST2 is contained in it. If substring ST2 is contained in ST1, then this function returns the integer value equal to the leftmost position in ST1 where the substring ST2 first occurs.

A complete list of FORTRAN library functions is found in the appendix.

These examples use some of the system library functions we have just described, with CST a character variable of length 4, `I` an integer variable, and all other variables of type real.

EXAMPLE 2 `Y = INT(X/4)`

The real value at X is divided by 4. The greatest integer less than or equal to that quotient is stored at Y.

EXAMPLE 3 `X = ABS (3 - SQRT(x))`

First the square root of the value at X is computed. The result is subtracted from 3. Then the absolute value of the difference is computed and stored at X.

EXAMPLE 6 `Z = FLOAT(MOD(I,20)) / 15`

The modular quotient of `I` and 20 is computed. The resulting integer value is changed to an equal real value which is then divided by 15. The real result is then stored at Z.

EXAMPLE 9

```
CHARACTER CST*4
Y = LEN(CST) + LEN('QRSTUV')
```

Here the length of CST (4) is added to the length of the string QRSTUV (6). The result (10) is stored as a real number at Y.

EXAMPLE 10

```
I = ICHAR('A')
```

The integer code for the letter A used by the computer system on which this statement is executed is assigned to I.

EXAMPLE 11

```
CST = CHAR(22) // 'BC'
```

The character whose code (on the computer system on which this statement is executed) is the integer 22 is concatenated with the string BC. The resulting character string is stored in CST.

The random number generator. There is one last function that we want to discuss even though it is not one of the system library functions available in FORTRAN 77. It is, however, available in most function libraries, and is used in almost the same manner as other system library functions.

This function is called the *random number generator*. It generates pseudo random numbers from 0 to 1, with the second endpoint excluded. Although the function RANDOM requires an argument, it makes no difference what that argument is—we call this a *dummy* argument. Here are some examples:

EXAMPLE 1

```
X = RANDOM(1)
```

A random number between 0 and 1 is produced and stored in real variable X.

EXAMPLE 2

```
Y = RANDOM(1)*99 + 1
```

A random number between 0 and 1 is multiplied by 99 and 1 is added to the product. The resulting number stored in real variable Y is a real number between 1 and 100, endpoints excluded.

EXAMPLE 3

```
D=INT(RANDOM(1)*9 + 1)
```

A random number between 0 and 1 is multiplied by 9 and 1 is added to the product. Then the INT function computes the greatest integer less than or equal to the computed result. The resulting integer finally stored in variable D is a single digit from 1 to 9.

Summary

In this chapter we learn about the three levels of programming language: Machine languages, assembly languages, and high-level languages. A resume of the historical development of FORTRAN is followed by an introduction to basic concepts needed to write programs in FORTRAN, including the use of constants and variables.

Data declaration statements define variables as real, integer, complex, logical, or character. The general forms of these statements are

```
INTEGER Var-list
```

declares all variables in Var-list as integer variables.

```
REAL Var-list
```

where Var-list represents a list of one or more variable names separated by commas,

declares all variables in Var-list as real variables.

```
LOGICAL Var-list
```

declares all variables in Var-list as logical variables.

```
COMPLEX Var-list
```

declares all variables in Var-list to be complex variables. Each complex variable stores two real values corresponding to the real and imaginary parts of the complex number stored.

```
CHARACTER V1*N1,V2*N2, . . . ,VN*NN
```

where Nl,N2, . . . ,NN represent integers specifying the maximum number of characters in each of the associated character variables.

```
CHARACTER*K Var-list
```

where K is an unsigned integer specifying the maximum number of characters in each of the variables.

The IMPLICIT statement enables the programmer to specify a set of variables as being of a certain type according to the first letter of their names.

EXAMPLE 1

```
IMPLICIT INTEGER (A-D)
```

causes all variables whose names begin with A, B, C, or D to be considered of type INTEGER.

EXAMPLE 2

```
IMPLICIT REAL (X-Z)
```

causes all variables whose names begin with X, Y, or Z to be considered of type REAL.

EXAMPLE 3

```
IMPLICIT CHARACTER (M)
```

causes all variables whose names begin with M to be of type CHARACTER, each capable of sorting one character.

Input and output statements include:

```
READ*,Var-list
READ(N,*) Var-list
PRINT*,Out-list
WRITE(N,*) Out-list
```

where Var-list refers to zero or more variables separated by commas,
Out-list refers to zero or more variables, constants, or arithmetic expressions, and
N refers to an input or output device.

Comment lines insert non-funcional, clarifying information for those reading the printed program. The ***STOP statement*** halts further program execution. The ***END statement*** must be the last line in any program, and the ***PROGRAM statement***, if it is used, must be the first line except for comment lines. The PROGRAM statement names the program.

The hierarchy of arithmetic operations. When two or more operations of the same priority appear in the same arithmetic expression, they are executed in order from left to right, except for multiple exponentation (double asterisks), which is executed in order from right to left.

**	*has highest priority*
/ *and* *	*have second priority*
+ *and* -	*have lowest priority*

As in mathematics, parentheses may be used to specify order of operations. Expressions inside the innermost parentheses are evaluated first, then those within the next-innermost pair, and so on until all operations have been performed.

Concatenation and substring operations both operate on character strings. The symbol for concatenation is // (double slash). Substring operations are specified using the form

```
A//B
```

where A and B are variables.

EXAMPLE 1 If ST1, ST2, and ST3 are all character variables, then the statement

```
ST3=ST1 // ST2
```

causes the character string made up of the string at ST1 followed by the string at ST2 to be stored at ST3. Of course, the length of ST3 must be large enough to accommodate the combined string made up of ST1 and ST2.

EXAMPLE 2 The statement

```
ST2=ST1(3:9)
```

causes the substring consisting of characters 3 through 9 of ST1 to be stored in ST2. We assume both ST1 and ST2 have been properly specified to accomodate strings of the lengths given.

For a complete list of ***system library functions*** see the appendix.

End of Chapter Exercises

1. For each of the following situations write FORTRAN statements to produce the required results.

a. Input number of miles, output equivalent number of kilometers.

b. Input pounds, output equivalent kilograms.

c. Input degrees Fahrenheit, output equivalent degrees centigrade.

d. Input yards, output equivalent meters.

e. Input acres, output equivalent square kilometers.

f. Input cubic feet, output equivalent cubic meters.

g. Input gallons, output equivalent liters.

2. Write a FORTRAN program to input two numbers, compute what percent the first number is of the second, and output both numbers input as well as the computed percent.

3. Write a FORTRAN program to input three numbers $x1$, $x2$, and $x3$, and find their average $\bar{x}$, where

$$\bar{x} = \frac{x1 + x2 + x3}{3}$$

Also find the standard deviation *sd* where

$$sd = (1/3)\sqrt{(\bar{x} - x1)^2 + (\bar{x} - x2)^2 + (\bar{x} - x3)^2}$$

and the relative percentage *rp* for each number where

$$rp1 = \frac{x1}{x1 + x2 + x3} * 100$$

and similarly for $rp2$ and $rp3$. Output the standard deviation and the three relative percentages.

4. Write a FORTRAN program that inputs the necessary dimensions for each of the following geometric figures and outputs the perimeter.

a. Square (one dimension)

b. Rectangle (two dimensions)

c. Diamond (one dimension)

d. Circle (one dimension)

e. Right triangle (lengths of two legs from which the hypotenuse can be computed)

5. Write a FORTRAN program to solve the following problem where the only input is the thickness of the paper and the output is the number of times the paper must be folded:

Suppose you are given a piece of paper as large as needed and are always able to fold the paper no matter how many thicknesses there are. Every time the paper is folded, the resulting layers form a thickness twice the thickness before it was folded. If the paper is originally 1/64 inch thick, how many times must the paper be folded so that the thickness of the folded piece is at least one yard?

PROGRAM DESIGN ISSUE

This problem is in many ways typical of those you will encounter in business. Instead of being presented in simple math, the problem statement is in general prose. It may seem that the few sentences stating the problem are adequate, but a closer look raises several questions:

Are there unstated tolerances? *At least 1 yard* means *greater than or equal to 1 yard*, but what if it is 0.998 yards thick? Do you fold again?

Will we want to use this program again? If so, it would be desirable to make the 1 yard input a variable instead of writing it into the program. It might also be handy to set up a variable that stores the final thickness—you may need it next time around.

Is there any need to store the thickness at each individual fold? The easiest way to approach this problem may be the use of logarithms, but if you will need the individual results later, an iteration solution may need to be considered.

6. Write a FORTRAN program that accepts three names each having a maximum length of twenty characters and produces the following output:

a. The first letter of each of the three names all on the same line.

b. A single character string of length 3 made up of the first letters of the three names.

c. A line of output on which appear three character strings, each of them made up of the ninth, tenth, eleventh, and twelfth letters of one of the three names.

d. A single string of length 21 such that it contains the first seven characters of the first name, characters 8 through 14 of the second name, and characters 14 through 20 of the third name.

7. The combined resistance of three resistances $r1$, $r2$ and $r3$ connected in parallel is given by the equation

$$cr = \frac{1}{\frac{1}{r1} + \frac{1}{r2} + \frac{1}{r3}}$$

Develop an algorithm and a FORTRAN program to read three resistance values and compute their combined resistance.

8. Develop an algorithm and a FORTRAN program to read the radius of a sphere and compute the sphere's volume and surface area.

9. The element thorium decomposes according to the following formula, in which t is the elapsed time:

$$\textit{amount decomposed} = (\textit{initial amount}) * e^{(-0.693 * t * 10^{(-10)})/1.5}$$

Develop an algorithm and a FORTRAN program to read values for the initial amount of thorium and the elapsed time, then compute the amount of thorium decomposed.

Chapter 3

Selection Structures in FORTRAN

So far, we have primarily been using one type of FORTRAN structure, the one-task-after-another *sequential* structure. Now we proceed to *selection* structures, those that use preliminary decisions to determine the task order. There are two major categories of selection structure, the *two-way* structure, set up to choose between two cases using an IF . . . ELSE structure, and the *multi-way* structure, where more than two cases are considered.

Two-way Selection Structures

The general form of the two-way selection structure is represented in pseudocode as follows:

```
1       IF (Condition) THEN
2            Statement 1        True block statements;
3            Statement 2        also called a THEN block.
             .
             .
             .
7            Statement M
8       ELSE
9            Statement M+1      False block statements;
10           Statement M+2      also called an ELSE block.
             .
             .
14           .
15           Statement N
        ENDIF
```

where Statements 1, 2, . . . , N are any executable program statements.

At the entry to a two-way selection structure (line 1), a condition is given and tested for being true or false.

If this condition is true, the program executes statements 1 through M, the *true block* statements. The program then finds ENDIF and executes whatever statement comes immediately next.

If this condition is false, statements 1 through M are ignored and the program executes statements M+1 through N, the *false block* statements, followed by the statement immediately after ENDIF.

Note that in both cases the normal exit from a two-way selection structure is at the ENDIF statement.

To illustrate the two-way selection structure let us study some examples using ordinary English statements.

EXAMPLE 1

```
IF the value of Variable B is positive, THEN
      Add A to B;
      Report the Result;
ELSE
      Add X to B;
      Report both X and the Sum;
ENDIF.
```

EXAMPLE 2

```
IF it is raining, THEN
      Call friends Jane, Pete, and Mary;
      Prepare lunch for the four of us;
      Watch the football game on television;
ELSE
      Call friends Mike and Lee;
      Prepare for a camping trip;
      Go camping;
ENDIF.
```

EXAMPLE 3

```
IF a test is scheduled for tomorrow, THEN
      Get extra materials at library;
      Spend the evening in my room studying;
      Get a decent night's rest;
ELSE
      Plan a party;
      Arrange for finances to pay for refreshments;
      Invite friends;
      Purchase refreshments;
      Ask two friends to help serve refreshments;
      Enjoy the party;
      Eventually get to bed;
ENDIF.
```

In each example, the first line contains a condition between the words IF and THEN that may be judged true or false. This line is followed by statements of action for the true case. The ELSE line introduces statements of action for the false case. This general structure is called the *IF-THEN-ELSE structure*. It has two useful variations, the IF-THEN structure and the logical IF.

IF-THEN structures. When the ELSE or false block contains *no* statements, it simply disappears, leaving the form

```
IF (Condition) THEN
      Statement 1
      Statement 2
      .
      .
      Statement M
ENDIF
```

If the condition is true, statements 1 through M are executed, followed by the statement after ENDIF.

If the condition is false, execution skips to the statement directly following ENDIF.

We discuss *IF-THEN* selection structures later in this chapter.

Logical IF structures. If the IF or true block has only one statement, and there is no statement in the ELSE or false block, the single true-block statement replaces the THEN at the end of the IF line:

```
IF (Condition) Statement
```

The entire structure thus consists of one line. There is no need for the THEN word to clue the program to execute the statement, nor do you need the ENDIF statement to exit the structure. If the condition is true, the statement is executed and program execution passes to the next line. If the condition is false, the statement is ignored and the program proceeds to the next line. Here is an example of a *logical IF* structure:

EXAMPLE

```
IF (it is raining) take your umbrella.
```

The Syntax of Conditions

Three types of expressions are especially useful in building selection structures: *relational*, *logical*, and *compound relational* expressions. All combine arithmetic or string expressions with FORTRAN operators.

Relational expressions. A *relational expression* is a combination of arithmetic or string expressions and relational operators. There are six relational operators in FORTRAN, shown in Table 3.1. These are all *binary* operators because they require two arithmetic expressions or character strings as operands. Their operation is similar to six comparison symbols in mathematics.

TABLE 3.1 *Relational operators in FORTRAN*

Relational operator	*Its application in FORTRAN*	*Meaning*
.EQ.	A.EQ.B	A is equal to B
.NE.	A.NE.B	A is not equal to B
.LT.	A.LT.B	A is less than B
.GT.	A.GT.B	A is greater than B
.LE.	A.LE.B	A is less than or equal to B
.GE.	A.GE.B	A is greater than or equal to B

The general form of a relational expression is

```
Operand RELOPR Operand
```

where Operand is any acceptable FORTRAN expression, and RELOPR is one of the relational operators.

The result of a relational expression is always one of the logical values, true or false.

Let's examine four relational expressions and determine their values. Assume that the real variables A=10.0 and B=2.0, and the integer variable N=5.

EXAMPLE 1 `A+1 .GT. N*B`

Observe that A+1=11 and N*B=5*2=10. Therefore, the value of this relational expression is true.

EXAMPLE 2 `A/B .EQ. N`

Observe that A/B=10.0/2.0=5.0; N is the integer 5. Therefore, the value of this relational expression is true. Recall that the FORTRAN compiler takes care of the mixed data types in the expression.

EXAMPLE 3 `3*(A+B)/4 .LE. 2*A+5*B-21.01`

First we evaluate the left operand: A+B=12.0. Then we compute 3*(A+B)/4=3*12.0/4=36.0/4=9.0.

Now we evaluate the right operand: 2*A=20.0 and 5*B=10.0. Then we compute 2*A+5*B–21.01=20.0+10.0–21.01=30.0–21.01=8.99.

Since 9 is not less than or equal to 8.99, the relational expression has the value false.

As you can tell from these examples, the rules for evaluating arithmetic expressions are applied to each of the operands in the relational expression.

EXAMPLE 4 `ST(1:5) .LE. ST1(1:2) // 'END'`

First, this statement concatenates the first two characters stored at ST1 with the word END.

This result is automatically stored in a temporary location whose contents are then compared to the first five characters stored at ST.

If the value of the numeric code for the first five characters of ST is less than or equal to the numeric code for the characters in the temporary storage location, the relational expression has value true; otherwise it is false.

Comparing character strings. Note that when a relational expression involves the comparison of two character strings, as in Example 4, the comparison occurs character by character from left to right in both strings. The question of one string being less than or equal to the other is answered on the basis of the numeric code for each single character.

EXAMPLE For example, suppose that the numeric codes for letters is such that A < B < C < . . . < Z and that ST1='ABC' and ST2='ABD'. Then the relational expression

```
ST1 .LE. ST2
```

has value true because the code for C is less than the code for D.

Two character strings are considered equal if and only if they have an equal number of characters with identical characters in corresponding positions in both strings. If the strings have unequal length, the shorter string is expanded with blank space(s).

Although it is not incorrect, avoid comparing character string expressions with arithmetic expressions. The processes used in comparing such expressions are complex and the principles of comparison are difficult to understand. Such comparisons are occasionally useful, but only if you are absolutely clear what will happen when the instructions are executed.

Logical expressions. A *logical expression* is a combination of two or more relational expressions together with the logical operators .AND., .OR., and .NOT. The functions of these operators correspond closely to the functions performed by English words *and*, *or*, and *not*.

Binary operators. Let's begin by reviewing how these logical conjunctions are used in simple English statements. Suppose we have statements A and B.

STATEMENT A `It is warm.`

STATEMENT B `It is raining.`

When statements A and B are connected with *and* we get the statement

`It is warm` ***and*** `it is raining.`

This is called a *compound* statement and it is possible to determine whether it is true or false. If statements A and B are both true, then the compound statement is also true. However, if it is false to say, *It is warm*, then to say, *It is warm* ***and*** *it is raining*, is also false. Similarly, if statement B, *It is raining*, is false, the compound statement is false.

- *The compound statement* A .AND. B *is true only if statements* A *and* B *are both true.*

Now let's use the same statements A and B, but connect them with *or* to get the compound statement

`It is warm` ***or*** `it is raining.`

Although the grammar seems a bit awkward, we can discuss whether this compound statement is true or false. If it is false to say, *It is warm*, but true to say, *It is raining*, then it is true to say, *It is warm* ***or*** *it is raining.* Similarly, if statement A is true, the compound statement using *or* is true regardless of the condition of statement B. Only if both statements A and B are false is the *or* statement relating A and B false. To summarize:

- *Given two statements* A *and* B, *the compound statement* A .OR. B *is false only if* A *and* B *are both false.*

The conjunctions *and* and *or* are used to connect two simple statements to form a compound statement. This is a *binary* operation. Thus *and* and *or* can be called *binary logical operators* because they operate on two statements and result in the logical considerations of truth or falsity.

***The unary operator* NOT.** The word *not* in English also has important implications for truth or falsity. *Not* reverses the truth or falsity of a statement in which it is inserted. Again consider statement A:

```
It is warm.
```

By inserting *not*

STATEMENT C
```
It is not warm.
```

we obtain a new statement, C, that is the negative of statement A. Therefore, if statement A is true, the *not* of A, or the *negation* of A, is false. If A is false, the negation of A is true. Sometimes the negation of a statement is called its *complement*.

Since the use of *not* involves a single statement, it can be thought of as a *unary logical operator.*

Compound relational expressions. Recall our discussion earlier in this chapter of relational expressions like A .GT. B and A*B .LE. C. When we connect two or more such relational expressions with the .AND. or .OR. operator, or precede one such expression by the .NOT. operator, we get a *compound relational expression.* Here are some examples written in FORTRAN. Assume that the values 2, 3, and 6 are stored at locations A, B, and C, respectively.

EXAMPLE 1
```
(A .GT. B) .AND. (A*B .LE. C)
```

A .GT. B has the value false.

A*B .LE. C has the value true.

The .AND. of a false expression and a true expression is false. (Recall our discussion of logical operators in simple English statements.) Therefore, this compound relational expression has the value false.

EXAMPLE 2
```
(A .GT. B) .OR. (A*B .LE. C)
```

In this example we have the .OR. of a false expression and a true expression. Thus the value of the compound expression of this example is true.

EXAMPLE 3
```
.NOT. (A .GT. B)
```

The expression A .GT. B has the value false. Therefore, .NOT. (A .GT. B) has the value true.

EXAMPLE 4
```
.NOT. (A .GT. B) .OR. (A*B .LE. C)
```

In this example .NOT. (A .GT. B) has the value true and A*B .LE. C has the value true. Therefore, the compound relational expression, which is the .AND. of two true statements, also has the value true.

EXAMPLE 5 Consider one more example of a compound relational expression in which we assume the same values previously stored in variables A, B, and C.

```
(A .GT. B) .AND. ((A .LE. C) .OR. (B .NE. C)) .OR. .NOT. (A .EQ. B)
```

We begin evaluation inside the innermost parentheses. A .LE. C has value true because A = 2 and C = 6. B .NE. C has value true because B = 3 and C = 6. (A .LE. C .OR. B .NE. C) thus has the value true.

A .GT. B has the value false. Thus, the .AND. operates on a false value and a true value, making the compound expression false. (A .EQ. B) has the value false. .NOT. (A .EQ. B) has the value true. Therefore, the final .OR. relates a false expression with a true expression and has the value true.

Priority of operations. Recall from Chapter 2 that there is a priority of execution among arithmetic operations, with exponentiation executed first, followed by multiplication and division, the lowest priority being given to addition and subtraction. With operations of equal priority, execution occurs from left to right, except for exponentiation, which is done from right to left. Parentheses interrupt this priority, and the innermost parentheses are processed first.

Among relational operations, .EQ., .NE., .GT., .LT., .GE., and .LE. all have equal priority and are executed, left to right, before the binary logical operations .AND. and .OR. The following list shows the operations discussed so far and the priority assigned when no parentheses are used.

`**`	*Highest priority*
`* , /`	*2nd priority*
`+ , -`	*3rd priority*
`All relational operations`	*4th priority*
`.NOT.`	*5th priority*
`.AND.`	*6th priority*
`.OR.`	*Lowest priority*

The GO TO statement. There is one more statement that will be useful as we proceed to work with selection structures, the GO TO statement. In the simplest selection structures, THEN block and ELSE block instructions directly follow the IF statement. If, however, you are repeatedly using a particular computational module, it is useful to be able to present it once in the code sequence and simply refer the program to it instead of reinserting all the code in each relevant block. Such a reference is accomplished by using the GO TO statement in the form

```
GO TO N
```

where N represents the reference number of the next statement to be executed.

Using Simple Selection Structures

With this new FORTRAN syntax in mind, we can explore some examples of simple selection structures. The first examples use relational expressions within a logical IF statement:

EXAMPLES

```
IF(A .GT. B+X) X=25.2
```

The value of B+X is computed and compared with the value of A. If A is greater than B+X, then X is set to 25.2; otherwise, X remains the value it was. In both cases the next statement executed is the one on the following line.

```
IF(FIRST .EQ. 'SECOND') LAST=FIRST

IF(A*B-1 .NE. A*(B-1)) B=0

IF((A*A-1) .GE. 6.0) STOP

IF((A .LE. 3) A=A*5/B-1

IF((X+Y)*(X-Y) .GT. X*Y+25) GO TO 25

IF(R-S .LT. 0.6) GO TO 100
```

These next examples use compound relational expressions in the logical IF statement:

EXAMPLE 1

```
IF((B .EQ. 5) .AND. (A*A .LT. 100))STOP
```

First, the value stored at variable B is compared with 5. If they are equal, the value of B. EQ. 5 is true. Otherwise it is false.

Then the value at A is multiplied by itself and the product is compared with 100. If the product is less than 100, the value of A*A .LT. 100 is true; otherwise, it is false.

Finally, the .AND. of the values of the two relational expressions is determined. Recall that if both relational expressions have the value true, then the .AND. of them has the value true; otherwise, the .AND. has the value false. If the .AND. value is true, the STOP at the right of the IF statement is executed, thus causing a halt to any further program execution. If the .AND. value is false, the program statement immediately following the IF statement is executed next and further program execution depends on each subsequent statement.

EXAMPLE 2

```
IF((A+B .GT. C) .OR. (A-B .LT. C)) GO TO 200
```

The sum of the values at A and B is compared to the value at C. If the sum of A and B is greater than C, then the value of this first relational expression is true; otherwise, it is false.

Next, the difference of the values at A and B is compared to the value at C. If the difference between A and B is less than C, then the value of this second relational expression is true; otherwise, the value is false.

Finally, the .OR. of the values of the two relational expressions is determined. Recall that the .OR. has value true if either of the operands has value true; otherwise, the .OR. has value false. If the .OR. has the value true, then the statement GO TO 200 is executed, and program control is transferred to the statement at reference number 200. If the .OR. has the value false, GO TO 200 is *not* executed; instead, the program proceeds to the next statement.

EXAMPLE 3

```
IF((A .GT. B) .AND. ((B .LE. C) .OR. (A .GE. B-C)))STOP
```

Start inside the innermost parentheses and compare the value at B with the value at C. If the B value is less than or equal to the C value, the value of B .LE. C is true; otherwise, its value is false.

Then the value at A is compared with the difference of the values at B and C. If the A value is greater than or equal to the difference, the value of the relational expression A .GE. B–C is true; otherwise, its value is false.

Next, the .OR. of the values of these two relational expressions is determined. The .OR. has value true if either of the two relational expressions has value true; otherwise, the .OR. value is false.

Now the value at A is compared to the value at B. If the A value is greater than the B value, then the value of the relational expression A .GT. B is true; otherwise, its value is false.

Finally, the .AND. of this .OR. value and the value A .GT. B is determined. If the .AND. value is true, the STOP statement is executed; otherwise, the program moves to the next statement.

EXAMPLE 4

```
IF(.NOT.(A .EQ. B) .OR. (B+A .GT. -C)) X=50
```

The first operation performed is the relational operation .EQ., within the parentheses. If the contents of A and B are the same, then A .EQ. B has the value true; otherwise, its value is false.

Next, the negative of the value at C is compared to the sum of the values at B and A. If the sum is greater than the negative of the value at C, then the relational expression has the value true; otherwise, its value is false.

The next operation executed is the .NOT. of the value A .EQ. B, which reverses its value from true to false or false to true.

Finally, the .OR. of the negation of A .EQ. B and the value of B+A .GT. −C is executed. If the result of the .OR. operation is true, then X is set to 50. If the .OR. value is false, then the value of X is left as it is—it is *not* set to 50. In either case, the program continues with the next line.

Now, let's look at logical IF statements in the context of segments of FORTRAN code. In these examples we use both relational expressions and compound relational expressions.

EXAMPLE 5

```
PRINT*, 'ENTER A NUMERIC VALUE FOR A'
READ*, A
IF (A .GT. 0) THEN
    PRINT*, A
ELSE
    PRINT*, -A
ENDIF
```

A numeric value is read in for variable A and then compared with zero. If the value is greater than zero, the value is output. However, if the value is less than or equal to zero, then the *negative* of the A value is output. In other words, this program segment reads a value and displays its absolute value.

EXAMPLE 6

```
PRINT*, 'PLEASE ENTER 3 NUMERIC VALUES'
READ*, A, B, C
IF ((A .GE. B) .AND. (B .GE. C)) THEN
    PRINT*, 'THE VALUES ', A, B, C,' ARE IN ORDER'
ELSE
    PRINT*, 'THE VALUES ', A, B, C,' ARE NOT IN ORDER'
ENDIF
```

This time 3 numeric values are read, one for each of variables A, B, and C. Then a compound relational expression compares the value of A with that of B and the value of B with that of C. If A < B < C, then a message is displayed that reports the 3 numbers are in order. If the result is something other than A < B < C, an alternative message is displayed that reports the 3 numbers are not in order.

EXAMPLE 7

```
PRINT*, 'PLEASE ENTER 4 NUMERIC VALUES'
READ*, A, B, C, D
IF (A/B .EQ. B/C) THEN
    PRINT*, 'THE FOLLOWING NUMBERS FORM A GEOMETRIC PROGRESSION'
    PRINT*, A, B, C, D
    PRINT*, A/B,  ' IS THE PROGRESSION RATE'
ENDIF
```

This time 4 values are required as input data. The quotient of the first 2 numbers is compared with the quotient of the second 2 numbers. If these quotients are equal, a message is displayed that the 4 input numbers form a geometric progression. If the quotients are not equal, this segment does nothing.

Problem 3.1A
Calculating Storm Drainage

SITUATION A shopping center parking lot is drained by a storm sewer 2.5 feet in diameter. This sewer allows a flow of 3 feet per second. The lot is 2 acres in size.

OBJECTIVE Write a program that will calculate, for a given rainfall in inches per hour, how much water, in cubic feet per second, flows through the sewer and how much backs up and floods the parking lot. There are no alternate drains or gutters, and the parking lot is lower than its surroundings.

ANALYSIS Begin by getting the variables into common dimensions. First, convert from rainfall in inches per hour per acre to rainfall in cubic feet per second. One acre is 43,600 square feet, and to convert from acre-inches to cubic feet we need also to divide by 12. To move from hours to seconds, we divide by the number of seconds in an hour, 3,600. This gives us the formula

$$1 \; \textit{acre-inch/hour} = 43600/(12*3600) \; \textit{cubic feet/second}$$

Next, compute the maximum flow the sewer can carry—again in cubic feet per second. This is equal to the cross-sectional area of the sewer, π times the sewer radius squared or $\pi*(2.5\text{ft}/2)^2$, times the rate of flow in the pipe, which is 3ft/sec.

There are two cases to consider: Either the influx of rain is less than or equal to the maximum flow rate, in which case the sewer caries all the water and there is no flooding. Or the influx is greater than the maximum flow rate, in which case the sewer operates at capacity and the remaining water floods the parking lot.

ALGORITHM

1. Input rainfall, sewer diameter, maximum flow rate, and the parking lot area.
2. Calculate the influx of water:

   $\textit{influx} = 43600(\textit{rainfall})(\textit{parking lot area})/(12*3600)$
3. Calculate sewer cross section area:

   $\textit{cross section} = \pi(\textit{sewer diameter}/2)^2$
4. Calculate maximum sewer drainage:

   $\textit{maximum drainage} = (\textit{sewer speed})(\textit{sewer cross section})$
5. If influx is less than or equal to drainage, there is no flooding.

6. If influx is greater than drainage, the flooding is equal to the difference between the two.
7. Report initial conditions and outcome.

FORTRAN PROGRAM

```
      PROGRAM SEWER
C*************************************************************************
C* THIS PROGRAM CALCULATES SEWER FLOW AND FLOODING                       *
C* FOR A SPECIFIED RAINFALL, SEWER, AND PARKING LOT.                     *
C*************************************************************************
C* VARIABLE DEFINITIONS                                                  *
C*    RAIN IS INCHES OF WATER FALLING PER HOUR.                          *
C*    INFLUX IS RAIN CONVERTED TO CU FT/SEC.                             *
C*    DIAMTR IS SEWER DIAMETER IN FT.                                    *
C*    PLAREA IS PARKING LOT AREA IN ACRES.                               *
C*    XSAREA IS SEWER CROSS SECTIONAL AREA IN SQ FT.                     *
C*    SEWSPD IS SPEED OF WATER IN SEWER IN FT/SEC.                       *
C*    SEWMAX IS MAXIMUM WATER SEWER CAN CARRY IN CU FT/SEC.              *
C*    SEWFLW IS WATER ACTUALLY FLOWING IN SEWER IN CU FT/SEC.            *
C*    FLOOD IS WATER BACKING UP ONTO PARKING LOT IN CU FT/SEC.           *
C*************************************************************************
C*
      REAL RAIN,INFLUX,DIAMTR,PLAREA
      REAL XSAREA,SEWSPD,SEWMAX,SEWFLW,FLOOD
C*
      READ*,RAIN,SEWSPD,DIAMTR,PLAREA
      INFLUX=43600*RAIN*PLAREA/(12*3600)
      XSAREA=3.1416*(DIAMTR/2)**2
      SEWMAX=SEWSPD*XSAREA
C*
      IF (INFLUX .LE. SEWMAX) THEN
         FLOOD=0
         SEWFLW=INFLUX
      ELSE
         FLOOD=INFLUX-SEWMAX
         SEWFLW=SEWMAX
      ENDIF
C*
      PRINT*,'A RAINFALL OF ',RAIN,' INCHES/HOUR ON A'
      PRINT*,'PARKING LOT OF ',PLAREA,' ACRES WITH A SEWER'
      PRINT*,'OF DIAMETER ',DIAMTR,' FEET AND SPEED OF FLOW OF'
      PRINT*,SEWSPD,' FT/SEC WILL RESULT IN ',SEWFLW,' CUBIC FEET'
      PRINT*,'OF WATER PER SECOND FLOWING THROUGH THE SEWER'
      PRINT*,'AND ',FLOOD,' CUBIC FEET PER SECOND OF WATER'
      PRINT*,'BACKING UP ONTO THE PARKING LOT.'
      END
```

Problem 3.1B
Assessing the Chance of Flood

SITUATION A citizens' group has hired your construction firm to give expert testimony about flooding from a shopping mall parking lot into a residential neighborhood that caused significant damage to several homes. The flooding happened between 3A.M. and 5A.M. on a Sunday morning, so there were no witnesses as to whether it actually was the parking lot that overflowed, causing the flooding. A surveyor has determined that the parking lot, which covers 6 acres, could hold 4 acre-feet of flood waters before the excess overflowed into the neighborhood.

The citizens feel the mall owners were responsible for the flooding by not installing a drain with sufficient capacity to handle runoff from the lot.

OBJECTIVE Modify the program from Problem 3.1A to determine whether the mall owners are legally responsible for the flood. The following additional information is available: It rained 1.4 inches per hour for 1:47 hours. The mall storm sewer is 2 ft in diameter and has a flow speed of 2.7ft/sec.

ANALYSIS The most important thing to notice is that the values in the previous program are included as variables, not hard-coded (the values themselves are not written into the FORTRAN code). This enables you to reuse most of that code. The issue now is simply whether, by the end of the storm, the accumulated floodwater in the lot was more than 4 acre-feet. This can be computed simply by multiplying the duration of the storm in seconds by the previously established variable FLOOD, which shows the rate of accumulation of water, then converting the resulting cubic feet of water to acre-feet and comparing.

ALGORITHM The algorithm is the same as for Problem 3.1A, except that there is additional information for step 1, and step 7 is replaced by the following steps.

1. Also input the total hours and minutes of the storm, and the flood capacity of the parking lot in acre-feet.

7. If flooding is calculated to be 0, report that the overflow probably did not occur.
8. If flooding is greater than 0, prepare a report by converting to the appropriate dimensions:

8.1 Convert storm hours and minutes to total length of storm in seconds.

8.2 Multiply total length of storm in seconds by FLOOD to obtain total accumulated water in cubic feet.

8.3 Divide cubic feet by 43600 to obtain acre-feet.

8.4 Compare accumulated water in acre-feet with lot capacity.

8.4.1 If accumulated water is greater than capacity, report that overflow probably occurred.

8.4.2 If accumulated water is less than capacity, report that overflow probably did not occur.

FORTRAN PROGRAM

To modify the code, we first need to introduce the new variables, so after the REAL statements already listed on line 1 of PROGRAM SEWER we add this line:

```
REAL STMHRS,STMMIN,STMSEC,CUFT,ACFT,PLCAP
```

where STMHRS, STMMIN, and STMSEC are the duration of the storm, CUFT and ACFT are equivalent measurements of total accumulated water, and PLCAP is the flood-holding capacity of the parking lot.

Then, we add three of these variables to the READ statement in line 3:

```
3       READ*,RAIN,SEWSPD,DIAMTR,PLAREA,STMHRS,STRMIN,PLCAP
```

Now, we simply replace the PRINT statements in lines 14-20 with this:

```
14      IF (FLOOD .EQ. 0) THEN
15          PRINT*,'THERE WAS PROBABLY NO OVERFLOW.'
16      ELSE
17          STMSEC=3600*STMHRS+60*STRMIN
18          CUFT=STMSEC*FLOOD
19          ACFT=CUFT/43600
20          IF (ACFT .LE. PLCAP) THEN
21              PRINT*,'THE PARKING LOT OVERFLOWED.'
22          ELSE
23              PRINT*,'THERE WAS PROBABLY NO OVERFLOW.'
24          ENDIF
25      ENDIF
26      END
```

Problem 3.1C Reconciling Observations

SITUATION

Just when you thought you were through with storm sewers forever, the mall owners find three witnesses who testify that they saw the mall lot flooded out to a stated point, but no further, on the morning of the flood. The time has been determined to have been exactly 5:42A.M. and the water height indicates that the lot was holding 2.9 acre-feet. The rain stopped at 4:52A.M. You are again called as an expert witness.

OBJECTIVE Answer these questions:

1. Assuming the parking lot was full at the end of the rainstorm, what was the actual rate of flow in the storm sewer?
2. Is this result consistent with the amount of flooding you computed before? Or is it more or less?
3. Is it possible that there was no flooding at all? Or that the flooding was much more severe than you had previously computed?
4. If the flooding now seems more or less severe than originally computed, by what percentage does your estimate change?

ANALYSIS Once again, you can modify the previous code. Unfortunately, when you modified the code last time, you did not add the new variables to the comments—so you may need to spend some time figuring out what they mean. This time, in addition to adding the code lines shown below, modify the comments to include the variables introduced both here and in Problem 3.1B.

The problem now is simply to compare the rates of flow calculated from eyewitness reports with those calculated before. If the two match, there is no difference in flooding estimates. If new rates are higher, flooding is likely to have been less than thought—it may not have flooded at all. If rates are lower, flooding will have been greater.

FORTRAN PROGRAM We present here only the new block of code, which you may simply add to the end of the previous program. In addition, you will need to add a REAL statement after line 1, as in Problem 3.1B, defining the new variable types. You should also add descriptions of the new variables in the comment lines: OBSCAP is the observed capacity of the parking lot; TRUFLW is the sewer flow rate calculated from the observed water level; TRUFLD is the flooding calculated from TRUFLW; PCTCHG is the percentage by which the original estimate was wrong; TRUAFT is the recalculated amount of accumulated water in acre-feet.

```
26        TRUFLW=(PLCAP-OBSCAP)*43600/(50*60)
27        IF (INFLUX .LE. TRUFLW) THEN
28            PRINT*,'NEW RESULT IS CONSISTENT WITH NO FLOODING.'
29            PRINT*,'SOME INFORMATION IN THIS CASE IS FAULTY.'
30        ELSE
31            IF (TRUFLW .EQ. SEWMAX) THEN
32                PRINT*,'ORIGINAL CALCULATIONS WERE ACCURATE.'
```

```
          ELSE
              TRUFLD=INFLUX-TRUFLW
              IF(TRUFLW .LT. SEWMAX) THEN
                  PCTCHG=100*((TRUFLD/FLOOD)-1)
                  PRINT*,'NEW RESULT INDICATES ',PCTCHG,' MORE.'
              ELSE
                  PCTCHG=100*(1-TRUFLD/FLOOD)
                  PRINT*,'NEW RESULT INDICATES ',PCTCHG,' LESS.'
                  TRUAFT=TRUFLD*STRMSEC/43600
                  IF (TRUAFT .LE. PLCAP) THEN
                      PRINT*,'NOT ENOUGH TO OVERFLOW.'
                  ELSE
                      PRINT*,'BUT STILL ENOUGH TO OVERFLOW.'
                  ENDIF
              ENDIF
          ENDIF
      ENDIF
      END
```

As you can see, selection structures allow a FORTRAN program to solve increasingly complicated problems and to resolve abstract information into more easily used forms. We will return later to these nested IF-THEN-ELSE structures. For now, we hope you understand the power and flexibility possible with selection structures.

Multi-way Selection Structures

We have been considering structures that process input information in such a way as to reduce operational choices to *yes* or *not-yes*—the IF-THEN structures. We now proceed to explore program tools that allow for many different paths of operation. We begin with a problem to illustrate the usefulness of these structures.

Problem 3.2 Calculating Photon Energy

SITUATION Often a program module will not only calculate a value needed for the larger program, but will also filter out bad or meaningless data to avoid getting spurious results. In this situation, you are working in an observatory. Photons can be recorded and measured for frequency. From that frequency, Planck's equation can be used to compute the energy of the photon:

$$e = h\nu$$

where ν is frequency in hertz (1 hertz = 1 cycle/sec),
h is the constant $6.63\text{x}10^{-34}$ joules/sec, and
e is energy in joules.

OBJECTIVE You have been asked to write a program module to calculate the energy of a photon, given its frequency. Note that the range of frequencies is from as low as a few hertz up through 10^{23} hertz, but there are these restrictions:

1. A frequency, by definition, cannot be negative.
2. Zero frequency would correspond to a physically impossible photon of zero energy.
3. The detector used in this experiment is unreliable when energies are large enough to cause positron-electron pair production—that is, above about 1 million electron volts or $1.602\text{x}10^{-13}$ joules.

ANALYSIS The simple computation of energy is at the heart of the program, but we also need to add checks for impossible negative and zero frequencies and for large frequencies where the figures may be unreliable. Since the two impossible frequencies are mutually exclusive, we may check for them independently.

ALGORITHM

1. Input the frequency.
2. If the frequency is negative, warn the user that frequencies cannot be negative, and stop.
3. If the frequency is zero, warn the user that this corresponds to a zero energy photon, which is impossible, and stop.
4. If neither of the above is true, compute ENERGY = FREQCY*6.63E–34.
5. If ENERGY>1.602*10E–13, report the energy and warn the user that the result may be unreliable.
6. Otherwise, simply report the energy.

FORTRAN PROGRAM

```
      PROGRAM PHOTON
C***********************************************************************
C* THIS PROGRAM CALCULATES THE ENERGY OF A PHOTON                       *
C* FOR A GIVEN FREQUENCY.                                               *
C***********************************************************************
C* VARIABLE DEFINITIONS                                                 *
C*     FREQCY IS FREQUENCY IN HERTZ.                                    *
C*     ENERGY IS ENERGY IN JOULES.                                      *
C***********************************************************************
C*
      REAL FREQCY,ENERGY
C*
      PRINT*,'ENTER FREQUENCY IN HERTZ.'
      READ*,FREQCY
C*
      IF (FREQCY .LT. 0) THEN
          PRINT*,'FREQUENCIES CANNOT BE NEGATIVE.'
          STOP
      ENDIF
C*
      IF (FREQCY .EQ. 0) THEN
          PRINT*,'FREQUENCY CORRESPONDS TO A PHOTON OF ZERO ENERGY,'
          PRINT*,'WHICH IS PHYSICALLY IMPOSSIBLE.'
          STOP
      ENDIF
C*
      ENERGY=FREQCY*6.63E-34
      IF (ENERGY .GT. 1.602E-13) THEN
          PRINT*,'PHOTON ENERGY IS ',ENERGY,' JOULES.'
          PRINT*,'WARNING: RESULT MAY BE IN ERROR BECAUSE OF'
          PRINT*,'POSSIBLE DETECTOR ERROR DUE TO ELECTRON'
          PRINT*,'POSITRON PAIR PRODUCTION.'
          STOP
      ENDIF
C*
      ENERGY=FREQCY*6.63E-34
      PRINT*,'PHOTON ENERGY IS ',ENERGY,' JOULES.'
      END
```

ELSEIF-THEN Structures

If you study Problem 3.2 and its solution—both the algrorithm and the FORTRAN program—you will recognize that four different paths of action can result depending on the input value: rejection of negative values, rejection of null values, report of the energy level with a warning of its possible inaccuracy, and simple report of the energy level.

Problem 3.2 presents a four-way selection structure, an example of a *multi-way* selection structure. In the problem, each segment of the structure begins with an IF-THEN statement and ends with an ENDIF.

Between appear sets of action statements. The program proceeds until the data satisfy one of the IF-THEN statements, then executes the associated actions and stops.

There is another way to handle multi-way selection: the ELSEIF-THEN structure. This is a simpler way to have FORTRAN move through multiple choices. Here is the general form of ELSEIF-THEN multi-way selection:

```
IF (Condition 1) THEN
      { Action set 1 }
ELSEIF (Condition 2) THEN
      { Action Set 2 }
ELSEIF (Condition 3) THEN
      { Action set 3 }
      .
      .
      .
ELSEIF (Condition K-1) THEN
      { Action set K-1 }
ELSE
      { Action set K }
ENDIF
```

The entire multi-way structure begins with an IF-THEN statement and ends with an ENDIIF. In between are several ELSEIF-THEN conditional statements. Each condition in a multi-way selection structure is a relational statement, for example:

EXAMPLES

```
A .GT. 0
(X+Y)*2 .LE. (R+S)/T
```

Following each condition appear sets of statements designated Action set 1, Action set 2, and so on. These action sets consist of one or more FORTRAN statements.

Only one of these action sets will actually be performed because of the selection done by the conditional statements. If the result of testing condition 1 gives a result of false, the program moves to the next ELSEIF and tests condition 2. The first condition that results in true causes the corresponding action set to be performed, after which control transfers to the statement immediately following the ENDIF statement. Thus, condition `I` is tested only if the preceding `I`–1 conditions have all tested false.

Note that the final ELSE statement and its action set are optional. If the ELSE clause is omitted and all conditions test false, no action set is performed and control transfers to the statement immediately following the ENDIF.

PROBLEM 3.2 REVISED To illustrate how an ELSEIF-THEN structure makes a program solution both more readable and more understandable than the repeating IF-THEN-ENDIF structure, let us look at a revised FORTRAN solution to Problem 3.2. Here we replace the series of IF-THEN-ENDIF statements with the ELSEIF-THEN structure.

FORTRAN PROGRAM

```
      PROGRAM PHOTNB
C***********************************************************************
C* REPEAT COMMENTS FROM PROGRAM PHOTON WITHOUT CHANGE.                 *
C***********************************************************************
C*
      REAL FREQCY,ENERGY
C*
      PRINT*,'ENTER FREQUENCY IN HERTZ.'
      READ*,FREQCY
      ENERGY=FREQCY*6.63E-34
C*
      IF (FREQCY .LT. 0) THEN
          PRINT*,'FREQUENCIES CANNOT BE NEGATIVE.'
      ELSEIF (FREQCY .EQ. 0) THEN
          PRINT*,'FREQUENCY CORRESPONDSON OF ZERO ENERGY,'
          PRINT*,'WHICH IS PHYSICALLY IMPOSSIBLE.'
      ELSEIF (ENERGY .GT. 1.602E-13) THEN
          PRINT*,'PHOTON ENERGY IS ',ENERGY,' JOULES.'
          PRINT*,'WARNING: RESULT MAY BE IN ERROR BECAUSE OF'
          PRINT*,'POSSIBLE DETECTOR ERROR DUE TO ELECTRON'
          PRINT*,'POSITRON PAIR PRODUCTION.'
      ELSE
          PRINT*,'PHOTON ENERGY IS ',ENERGY,' JOULES.'
      ENDIF
      END
```

Problem 3.3 Classifying Utility Needs

SITUATION A utility holding company has recently acquired a gas and electric company. The holding company has energy use forecasting software that classifies residences by whether they should be counted as part of peak energy demand for gas or electricity and for winter or summer. Codes for this software are given in the first table. The newly acquired utility company has records classifying homes by the type of heating and whether or not they have central air conditioning. The codes used for homes in the records of the gas and electric company are listed in the second table.

Forecasting software codes

Code	*Gas* *Peak in winter*	*Electric* *Peak in summer*	*Electric* *Peak in winter*
1	Y	Y	Y
2	Y	Y	N
3	Y	N	Y
4	Y	N	N
5	N	Y	Y
6	N	Y	N
7	N	N	Y
8	N	N	N

Old utility record codes

Code	*Meaning*
1	Electric heat, central air conditioning
2	Gas heat, no central air conditioning
3	Electric heat, no central air conditioning
4	Gas heat, central air conditioning
5	Other heat, no central air conditioning

OBJECTIVE Write a program to translate the classifications of the gas and electric company into the codes of the new holding company, so that the data may be used to forecast gas and electric needs.

ANALYSIS Clearly all that need be done is to assign each of the old utility codes to a new holding company code. The simple conversion would be

1 to 5
2 to 4
3 to 7
4 to 2
5 to 1

Codes 1, 3, and 6 have no equivalents in the old system, so none of the units will be matched to them.

This type of problem is common in programs where data have come from heterogenous sources. Since all the conversions are mutually exclusive, each line of the conversion table simply becomes an IF-THEN or an ELSEIF-THEN statement, followed by an action line replacing the old code with the new. Theoretically the conversions could execute in any order with the same result.

In this case, if none of the conditions are satisfied, there was clearly some input mistake, and an error message should appear.

FORTRAN PROGRAM

```
1        PROGRAM TRCODE
   C************************************************************************
   C* THIS PROGRAM CONVERTS NORWEST G&E RESIDENCE CODES TO                 *
   C* OCTOPUS CORP. DEMAND FORECAST CODES.                                 *
   C************************************************************************
   C* VARIABLE DEFINITIONS                                                 *
   C*     OLDCOD IS NORWEST G&E RESIDENCE CODE.                            *
   C*     NEWCOD IS OCTOPUS CORP. DEMAND FORECAST CODE.                    *
   C************************************************************************
   C*
2        INTEGER OLDCOD,NEWCOD
3        LOGICAL BADCOD
4        BADCOD = .FALSE.
   C*
5        PRINT*,'ENTER NORWEST G&E CODE'
6        READ*,OLDCOD
   C*
7        IF (OLDCOD .EQ. 1) THEN
8            NEWCOD=5
9        ELSEIF (OLDCOD .EQ. 2) THEN
10           NEWCOD=4
11       ELSEIF (OLDCOD .EQ. 3) THEN
12           NEWCOD=7
13       ELSEIF (OLDCOD .EQ. 4) THEN
14           NEWCOD=2
15       ELSEIF (OLDCOD .EQ. 5) THEN
16           NEWCOD=1
17       ELSE
18           PRINT*,'WARNING: BAD CODE DETECTED!'
19           BADCOD = .TRUE.
20       ENDIF
21       IF (.NOT. BADCOD) PRINT*,'OCTOPUS CORP. CODE IS ',NEWCOD
22       END
```

Suppose the code processed by this program is a 3.

Line 6 of the program results in a 3 being stored in OLDCOD.

Lines 7 and 9 are both false, and no change is made to NEWCOD through line 10.

Line 11 is value true, so line 12 changes NEWCOD to 7.

None of the remaining conditions are true; there are no more changes.

Finally, line 21 results in the printout

```
OCTOPUS CORP. CODE IS 7
```

After that, control passes to line 22, and the program terminates.

If the code is something other than 1, 2, 3, 4, or 5, line 18 is executed, indicating invalid data, and line 19 sets a signal BADCOD indicating this.

Line 21 causes a check of BADCOD. If BADCOD is true, then no new code is printed. If BADCOD is false, the new code is printed.

Nested IF-THEN-ELSE Structures

With two-way selection structures, there are two sets of instructions, an IF-THEN block and an ELSE block. No restrictions are placed on the kinds of statements that are included within these two blocks of statements. It is even possible to include another IF-THEN or IF-THEN-ELSE statement, creating a *nested* IF-THEN-ELSE structure.

In nesting, it is essential that each IF-THEN-ELSE be paired with its own ENDIF. In order to keep track of the pairs of statements and keep elements in correct order, it is useful to indent each level of statement the same number of spaces on the line. This also increases the readability of the program. Consider the following example.

Problem 3.4 Checking Ballistic Trajectories

SITUATION Your firm is supplying the software for a ballistic missile warning system. The path of each object on the radar screen is analyzed to determine whether or not it is a parabola—indicating a ballistic trajectory.

If the path is parabolic, a regression program estimates the parabola. The result is converted to the form

$$ax^2 + bx + c = 0$$

Two roots of the equation are needed because, when converted into the proper coordinate system, they will correspond to the launch point and the impact point of the missile.

Let us explore the possible cases. If we let $d = b^2 - 4ac$, we can use different values of d to determine certain characteristics of the roots of the equation.

CASE 1 $d > 0$

CASE 1A $a \neq 0$ and $b \neq 0$

There are two unequal real roots given by the equations

$$x1 = \frac{-b + \sqrt{b^2 - 4ac}}{2a}$$

$$x2 = \frac{-b - \sqrt{b^2 - 4ac}}{2a}$$

CASE 1B $a = 0$ and $b \neq 0$

There are two equal real roots such that $x1 = x2 = -c/b$

CASE 1C $a = 0$ and $b = 0$

Either $c = 0$ and there is no equation, or there is a contradiction.

CASE 2 $d = 0$

There are two equal real roots such that $x1 = x2 = -b/2a$

CASE 3 $d < 0$

There are no real roots. Note that if a root is not real, the estimation that the curve is a parabola is probably in error.

OBJECTIVE You have been asked to write a module that will compute the roots of the equation for any estimated coefficients *a*, *b*, and *c*.

ANALYSIS This solution recognizes all possible cases discussed in the problem statement.

1 $a \neq 0$

CASE 2 **1.1** $b^2 - 4ac = 0$

$x1 = x2 = -b/2a$

CASE 1A **1.2** $b^2 - 4ac > 0$

$$x1 = (-b + \sqrt{b^2 - 4ac})/2a$$

$$x2 = (-b - \sqrt{b^2 - 4ac})/2a$$

CASE 3 **1.3** $b^2 - 4ac < 0$

No real roots.

CASE 1B **2** $a = 0$

2.1 *b* not equal to 0

$x = -c/b$

CASE 1C **2.2** $b = 0$

2.2.1 *c* not equal to 0

Contradiction.

2.2.2 $c = 0$

$0 = 0$

ALGORITHM From this analysis we can develop a pseudocode solution:

```
1.  Read A, B, C
2.  If A is not equal to 0 then
3.     If B*B -4AC = 0 then
4.        X1 = X2 = -B/2A
5.        Report X1 and X2
6.     Else
7.        If B*B -4AC > 0 then
8.           X1 = ( - B + SQRT(B*B - 4AC))/2A
9.           X2 = ( - B - SQRT(B*B - 4AC))/2A
10.          Report X1 and X2.
11.       Else
12.          Report that there are no real roots.
13.       Endif
14.    Endif
15. Else
16.    If B is not equal to 0 then
17.       X = -C/B
18.       Report X
19.    Else
20.       If C = 0 then
21.          Report 0 = 0
22.       Else
23.          Report that there is a contradiction
24.       Endif
25.    Endif
26. Endif
```

Note the IF-THEN-ELSE structures:

Lines 2 through 26,
Lines 3 through 14,
Lines 7 through 13,
Lines 16 through 25, and
Lines 20 through 24.

FORTRAN PROGRAM The numbers at the left of the program lines are only for reference in the discussion that follows.

```
1       PROGRAM QUAD
2       REAL A, B, C, X1, X2, D
3       READ *, A, B, C,
4       D = B*B - 4*A*C
5       IF (A .NE. 0) THEN
6           IF (D .EQ. 0) THEN
7               X1 = -B/(2*A)
8               X2 = X1
9               PRINT*,'X1 = ', X1, ' X2 = ', X2
10          ELSE
11              IF (D .GT. 0) THEN
12                  X1 = (-B + SQRT(D)) / (2*A)
13                  X2 = (-B - SQRT(D)) / (2*A)
14                  PRINT*,'X1 = ', X1, ' X2 = ', X2
15              ELSE
16                  PRINT*,'THERE ARE NO REAL ROOTS'
17              ENDIF
18          ENDIF
19      ELSE
20          IF (B .NE. 0) THEN
21              X1 = -C/B
22              PRINT*,'X = ', X1
23          ELSE
24              IF (C .EQ. 0) THEN
25                  PRINT*,'0 = 0'
26              ELSE
27                  PRINT*,'CONTRADICTION IN COEFFICIENTS'
28              ENDIF
29          ENDIF
30      ENDIF
31      END
```

Now this program contains IF-THEN-ELSE structures corresponding to those mentioned in the pseudocode:

Lines 5 through 30,
Lines 6 through 18,
Lines 11 through 17,
Lines 17 through 29, and
Lines 24 through 28.

This solution demonstrates a multilevel nested IF-THEN-ELSE structure.

Problem 3.5
Estimating Air Moisture

SITUATION Weather simulation and forecast programs are used to study natural phenomena such as global warming or the effects of El Niño. One of the problems is an extreme sensitivity to initial conditions. Very small differences in beginning values of the variables tend to alter the final result dramatically. Many of the equations used are of a *lagged variable* type, where a single value is important at successive intervals in the computation, each time having a fraction of its previous effect.

One useful weather forecast equation stipulates that a snowpack of size p will melt at n% per day, so that each day the remaining snowpack is (100–n)% of the previous day's pack. A second equation computes air moisture downwind as a function of exposure to snowpack over the previous n days. This gives us an equation for the total snowpack exposure s of the wind that is of the lagged variable type:

$$s = f\,[p_{\text{initial}}(1 + (1-n) + (1-n)^2 + (1-n)^3 + \ldots + (1-n)^{d-1} + (1-n)^d)]$$

Because the larger forecasting model is sensitive to very small errors, it is important to make sure that the means of computing this equation does not introduce any errors. As we previously discussed, computers commonly truncate decimal numbers in order to store them in memory. If such numbers are used repeatedly, the inconsequential difference introduced by truncation will be repeatedly magnified until significant errors are obtained.

This is called a *truncation error*. In order to minimize such errors, it is often necessary, before solving for a function, to run a numerical experiment to determine the best way to calculate its value.

OBJECTIVE We can state the snowpack equation in the general form

$$s = 1 + a + a^2 + a^3 + \ldots + a^d$$

where $a = 1 - n$

Given values for a and d, compute the value of this geometric series and compare the result with the value obtained using the formula

$$s = \frac{1 - a^{(n+1)}}{1 - a}$$

to determine whether there is any truncation error. Both formulas are exact expressions for the sum of n terms of a geometric series.

ALGORITHM

1. Read values for A and D.

2. Compute S using repeated summing. Call it SUM1.

3. Compute S using the non-summing formula. Call it SUM2.

4. If SUM1 = SUM2, report "NO TRUNCATION ERROR."

4.1 Else report the amount of truncation error.

FORTRAN PROGRAM

```
      PROGRAM  TRUNC
      REAL A,SUM1,SUM2
      INTEGER D,I
      PRINT*,'ENTER THE VALUE FOR A'
      READ*,A
      PRINT*,'ENTER THE VALUE FOR D'
      READ*,D
      SUM1=1
      I=1
10    IF (I < D) GOTO 20
          SUM1=SUM1+A**I
          I=I+1
      GOTO 10
20    SUM2=(1-A**(D+1)) / (1-A)
      IF (SUM1 .NE. SUM2) THEN
          PRINT*,'TRUNCATION ERROR = ', ABS(SUM1-SUM2)
      ENDIF
      END
```

Problem 3.6 Testing Barometers

SITUATION A manufacturer of precision barometers finds that the torsional balance that the barometers use to measure pressure is only approximately linear in response, and that some balances indeed distort the barometric readings beyond acceptable limits. The error caused by the torsional balance must be reduced to below the level of precision of the instrument.

A precisely calibrated pressurizing system is used to test precision. Three specific, known situations are reproduced, and the barometer is used to measure each. The relation between the known values and the registered pressure is checked to see whether it is linear. As the barometer continues to show linear response across smaller and smaller pressure intervals, its measurements are shown to be more and more exact. At very small intervals, the measured high, medium, and low values are checked against the known values.

This known-pressure system is controlled by placing precisely measured masses onto a piston that then pressurizes the chamber containing the barometer. To control the influence of daily fluctuations in ambient air pressure, the three measurements are taken in a rapid sequence—all within a few seconds.

The known pressure is specified on the piston head in milligrams. The barometer measures pressure to .01 millibar.

OBJECTIVE You have been asked to write the key module, to determine whether the key points are linear and in the correct order. No conversion of units of measure is required.

ANALYSIS The problem can be broken down into two simple stages:

1. Given the coordinates of the three points *p*1, *p*2, and *p*3 in the rectangular coordinate plane, determine whether or not they lie on the same straight line.
2. If they do, determine whether *p*2 and *p*3 are on the same side of *p*1 or on opposite sides.

ALGORITHM

1. Read coordinates for points *p*1, *p*2, and *p*3.
2. Compute the slope, SLOPE1, of the line through *p*1 and *p*2.
3. Compute the slope, SLOPE2, of the line through *p*1 and *p*3.
4. If SLOPE1 = SLOPE2, then report that the points are on the same line and *p*2 and *p*3 are on the same side of *p*1.
5. If SLOPE1 = –SLOPE2, then report that the points are on the same line with *p*2 and *p*3 on opposite sides of *p*1.
6. Else report that the points are not on the same line.

FORTRAN PROGRAM

```
PROGRAM LINEAR
REAL X1, X2, X3, Y1, Y2, Y3, SLOPE1, SLOPE2
PRINT*,'ENTER THE COORDINATES OF P1'
READ*, X1, Y1
PRINT*,'ENTER THE COORDINATES OF P2'
READ*, X2, Y2
PRINT*,'ENTER THE COORDINATES OF P3'
READ*, X3, Y3
SLOPE1 = (Y2-Y1) / (X2-X1)
SLOPE2 = (Y3-Y1) / (X3-X1)
IF (SLOPE1 .EQ. SLOPE2) THEN
    PRINT*,'P1, P2, AND P3 ARE ON THE SAME LINE AND'
    PRINT*,'P2 AND P3 ARE ON THE SAME SIDE OF P1.'
ELSEIF (SLOPE1 .EQ. -SLOPE2) THEN
    PRINT*,'P1, P2, AND P3 ARE ON THE SAME LINE AND'
    PRINT*,'P2 AND P3 ARE ON OPPOSITE SIDES OF P1.'
ELSE
    PRINT*,'P1, P2, AND P3 ARE NOT ON THE SAME STRAIGHT LINE.'
ENDIF
END
```

PROGRAM DESIGN ISSUES When working with data near the limits of accurate measurement, it is very important to remember that programs themselves have no common sense. A program does not know that unreal roots to an equation indicate a probable data error as in Problem 3.4. Nor that truncation errors may be a problem in cases of sensitive dependence on initial conditions, as in Problem 3.5. Nor that 3 colinear points do not prove accuracy in very small intervals if the points are not in the right order, as in Problem 3.6.

To give your program some common sense, think about how you know that an answer or result is "obviously" wrong, and find a way to describe *obviously wrong* in FORTRAN. Notice that these three problems use three strategies for protecting against nonsense.

Problem 3.4 identifies cases where the mathematical expression corresponds to something that cannot exist in the real world situation described.

Problem 3.5 inserts prior to the main program a series of short programs to conduct numeric experiments on the functions and equations that will be used and determine their behavior in the presence of errors. The results of these experiments may suggest ways to filter out bad input and bad output.

Problem 3.6 finds a test that is mathematically independent of the main calculation to use to distinguish suspect cases. Here, the basic determination of colinearity is checked by looking for *betweenness.*

Exercises 3.1

1. Answer the following questions:

a. What is meant by a mixed-mode expression? Give three examples.

b. What are the FORTRAN symbols for the various arithmetic operations?

c. What is the priority of arithmetic operations?

d. What is the effect of parentheses on this priority?

e. What are the relational operators in FORTRAN?

f. What are the logical operators in FORTRAN?

g. What action occurs when a GO TO statement is executed?

h. Identify the type of IF statement in each of the following:

```
IF(A.GT.B)STOP
IF(A.LT.A+B)GO TO 20
IF(A.LT.B.OR.A.GT.C)A=B+C
IF(A*B.GT.-A)A=-B
```

i. Give a definition of a loop.

j. What is meant by an infinite loop?

k. What two methods are used to control the number of times a loop is executed?

2. For each of the following IF statements, indicate whether or not the statement is syntactically correct. If it is not correct, identify the error and propose a correction.

a. `IF(A+B)GO TO 10`

b. `IF(A.GT.B)10`

c. `IF(B)2.3`

3. For each of the following simple logical IF statements, indicate whether or not the statement is syntactically correct. If not correct, identify the error and propose a correction.

a. `IF(A+B .GT. A)A+B=C`

b. `IF(STOP .EQ. END)END=0`

c. `30 IF(A .GT. B)GO TO 30`

d. `IF(A+B .EQ. A)GO TO 10`

e. `IF(A .GT. 5)GO TO 5`

f. `IF('A' .LT. AB)AB+'AB'`

g. `IF(A .NE. 'AB')GO TO 20`

h. `IF(A .E. AB)GO TO 20`

i. `IF(A+B .GE. A-B)A+B=X-B`

j. `IF(A+B .LE. A-B)PRINT*,A+B.A-B`

4. For each of the following compound logical IF statements, indicate whether or not the statement is syntactically correct. If it is not correct, identify the error and propose a correction.

a. `IF(A.GT.B.AND..LT.C)GO TO 10`

b. `IF(A+B.OR.2.LT.5)GO TO 20`

c. `IF(A*B.AND.A-B.GT.A+B)A=B`

d. `IF(A.GT.B.AND.(A.LT.B.OR.B.LT.C).AND.A.LT.C)A=B+C`

e. `IF(.NOT.A.EQ.B)A=-B`

f. `IF(A.OR.B.NOT.C.OR.D)GO TO 10`

g. `IF(A.GT.(B*A)**2.OR.(A*B/2).AND.B.LT.5.6)GO TO 40`

h. `IF(((A.GT.B).AND.(B.LE.C)).OR.((A.NE.2*C).AND.(A.EQ.C)STOP`

i. `IF((A.GT.B).OR.(B.GT.C).OR..NOT.(A.LT.B))GO TO 50`

j. `IF(A+B+C.LE.A-B+C .AND. THIS.EQ.THAT)SET X TO 5`

k. `IF(A+B.GT.A-B)LET B=-A`

l. `IF(A+B.EQ.2.5)THEN A=5.5`

m. `IF(A*B**2.NE.B*A**2)ELSE B=A**2`

n. `IF(2*3..GT.A.AND.2.EQ.B)GO TO 20`

o. `IF(A.EQ.B)GO TO=20`

5. Determine whether or not there are errors in any of these uses of IF statements, define the error(s), and correct them.

a.

```
10   IF (A.LT.B)THEN
        X=A+B
        GO TO 10
     ELSE
        Y=A+B
     ENDIF
```

b.

```
10   IF(A-B.EQ.A+B)THEN
        IF(B.EQ.A+B)THEN
           B=B+1
           GO TO 10
        ELSE
           B=0
           GO TO 10
        ENDIF
     ENDIF
```

c.

```
IF(A+B.GT.A.AND.A-B.LT.B)THEN
    A=A+B
    IF(A.GT.100.)A=100
ELSE
    A=200
ENDIF
```

d.

```
IF(A+B.LT.2.5 .AND. A-B.GT.3)THEN
      IF(A*B.EQ.6 .OR. A*B.GT.8)THEN
        IF(X.EQ.2.1)THEN
            A=X*B
        ELSE IF(X.LT.2.0)
            A=X/B
        ELSE
            A=X*A
        ENDIF
ENDIF
```

e.

```
IF(A.AND.B.EQ.A.AND.C.)THEN
    A=A*C
ELSE
    IF(A+B.GT.X)THEN
        IF(X.GT.5)THEN
            A=X+1
            PRINT*,A
        ELSEIF(X.LT.5.0)
            A=X-1
            PRINT*.A
        ENDIF
    ELSE
        PRINT,'INCORRECT INPUT'
        STOP
    ENDIF
ENDIF
```

f.

```
IF(IFLAG.EQ.1)THEN
    PRINT*,'JANUARY'
ELSEIF(IFLAG.EQ.2.AND.ICOLD.LE.-10)
    PRINT*,'FEBRUARY NORTHEAST'
ELSEIF(IFLAG.EQ.3)PRINT*,'SPRING IS COMING.'
ELSEIF(IFLAG.GT.3.AND.IFLAG.LT.7)
    PRINT*,'SPRING IS HERE.'
    IF(IFLAG.GE.7.AND.IFLAG.LT.10)PRINT*, 'HOT SUMMER.'
ELSEIF(IFLAG.GT.9)PRINT*,'BACK TO FALL.'
ENDIF
```

g.

```
      IF(FLAG.NE.PASS)THEN
 20     KPASS=KMIN
        KMIN=TEMP
        TEMP=KPASS
      ELSEIF(FLAG.EQ.PASS)
        PRINT*,'ALL SORTED'
        PASS=MIN=TEMP=0
        GO TO 20
      ENDIF
```

h.

```
10    IF(SPACE.GE.100)THEN
        PRINT*,'SPACE IS AVAILABLE.'
        IF(CAR.GE.5)THEN
          PRINT*,'SHIPMENT SHOULD START.'
        ELSEIF(CAR.LT.5)
          PRINT*,'WAIT FOR CARS TO ARRIVE.'
        ENDIF
        SPACE=200
        GO TO 10
      ENDIF
```

i.

```
      IF(A.LT.145)THEN
          PRINT*,A, 'IS NOT ENOUGH.'
      ELSE
          IF(A.GT.350)THEN
              PRINT*,A, 'TOO MANY.'
          ELSE
              LOW=1
              HIGH=12
              IF(LOW.LT.HIGH)THEN
                  MID=(LOW+HIGH)/2
                  IF(A.LT.AREA)THEN
                      HIGH=MID-1
                  ELSE
                      IF(A.GT.AREA)THEN
                          HIGH=MID+1
                      ELSE
                          NUM=NUM+1
                          LOW=HIGH+1
                      ENDIF
                  ENDIF
              GO TO 10
              ENDIF
          ENDIF
      ENDIF
```

Simple IF-GO TO Program Loops

One of the most significant capabilities of any programming language is the ability to repeat a given set of program statements many times while having that set of statements appear only once in the program. This property is what is called a *program loop* or *repetition structure* of the programming language. Repetition structures are fully discussed in Chapter 5, but here we introduce the simplest manually controlled loop structures. These loops use the logical IF and GO TO statements. We will find them extremely useful.

EXAMPLE Let's start with a simple example. Suppose there are some number of data lines to be processed, where each data line contains two numbers, the first an integer that is a student identification number and the second a test score for that student. For each line of input data, the program is to produce a line of output containing the two input numbers. Obviously, this is a trivial problem. Input is followed by output until all input data have been processed. If there were only one line of input data the program would be relatively simple.

SOLUTION 1

```
PROGRAM READ1
C***********************************************************************
C*     PROGRAM DESCRIPTION                                             *
C*         THIS PROGRAM READS 1 LINE OF INPUT DATA AND PRINTS          *
C*         1 LINE OF OUTPUT CONSISTING OF THE NUMBERS ENTERED AS INPUT. *
C***********************************************************************
C*     VARIABLE DEFINITION                                             *
C*         NUMBER IS THE STUDENT ID NUMBER.                            *
C*         TEST IS THE STUDENT'S TEST SCORE.                           *
C***********************************************************************
C*
      INTEGER NUMBER, TEST
      PRINT*, 'ENTER ID NUMBER AND TEST SCORE'
      READ*, NUMBER, TEST
      PRINT*, NUMBER, TEST
      END
```

This solution handles the processing of a single line of input data but cannot handle more than one line. What we want is a program that handles many lines of input data.

One way to accomplish this is to include as many of the triple PRINT/READ/PRINT statements as there are lines of input data. Each triple would process one line of input data. However, it seems particularly inefficient to use many copies of the same three instructions. Furthermore, such a program would process exactly the same number of input lines as there are triples of PRINT/READ/PRINT statements—and only that number.

We would like a program that would not repeat statements and that could handle a flexible number of input lines. The solution is to use a logical IF statement to introduce a loop or repetition structure into the program. Thus, we can process as many lines of input data as required.

Control with dummy data. The first step is to add a dummy line of data at the end of the valid data being input. These data are also called *sentinel* or *trailer data.* Dummy data are carefully selected to signal the end of the program—they are not to be processed as are the valid data preceding them.

In the problem currently being solved, student ID numbers are typically unsigned integers and test scores are typically nonnegative numbers. We can then add to the end of the input data a dummy line containing –1 for both the ID number and the test score. We then insert a test line in the code to exit the loop and terminate processing when a student ID number of –1 is read.

SOLUTION 2

```
      PROGRAM RDMANY
C***********************************************************************
C*    PROGRAM DESCRIPTION                                              *
C*        THIS PROGRAM READS AND PRINTS INPUT VALUES UNTIL             *
C*        AN INPUT VALUE OF -1 IS READ AS THE VALUE FOR ID             *
C*        NUMBER, AT WHICH TIME THE PROGRAM TERMINATES.                *
C***********************************************************************
C*    VARIABLE DEFINITIONS                                             *
C*        NUMBER IS STUDENT ID NUMBER.                                 *
C*        TEST IS TEST SCORE.                                          *
C***********************************************************************
C*
      INTEGER NUMBER, TEST
      PRINT *, 'ENTER ID NUMBER AND TEST SCORE'
      READ *, NUMBER, TEST
 10   IF (NUMBER .LT. 0) GO TO 20
          PRINT *, NUMBER, TEST
          PRINT *, 'ENTER ID NUMBER AND TEST SCORE. END WITH -1, -1.'
          READ *, NUMBER, TEST
      GO TO 10
 20   STOP
      END
```

The logical IF statement is identified as statement number 10. This reference number is used by the GO TO statement near the end of the program to transfer control back to the IF statement.

The sequence of five executable statements starting with the IF statement is repeatedly performed until the READ statement results in a negative value in both NUMBER and TEST—that is, until the dummy data arrives.

Then the IF statement finds NUMBER less than zero, and the GO TO 20 portion of the statement sends the program to line 20, STOP, causing program action to terminate.

Note again that dummy data like −1 entered as values for ID number and test score are not processed like the valid data. They are simply signals to exit the loop structure.

Condition-controlled loops. If you review Solution 2, you will see that it contains only two more statements than Solution 1, the logical IF and the GO TO. Yet Solution 2 processes correctly all the lines of data input—as many lines as are entered—while Solution 1 processes only one line of input data.

This is the strength of program loops: They make it possible to repeat certain actions again and again without significantly lengthening the program. In this example, it is not known how many times the statements in the loop are performed because it depends on the number of input values entered. Repetition continues until the condition of negative ID number is detected, then action terminates. Such a loop is referred to as a *condition-controlled* loop: The condition of a negative number controls the repetition of the loop statements.

WHILE-DO loops. Although standard FORTRAN 77 does not, many versions of FORTRAN do include the WHILE-DO statement to make it even easier to write condition-controlled loops. This is its general form:

```
WHILE (Condition) DO
      Statement 1
      Statement 2
      Statement 3
      .
      .
      .
      Statement K
ENDWHILE
```

In standard FORTRAN 77, one substitutes a GO TO structure, with the loop defined using a reference number.

```
10  IF (.NOT. (Condition)) GO TO 100
        Statement 1
        Statement 2
        Statement 3
        .
        .
        .
        Statement K
    GO TO 10
100 Any acceptable FORTRAN statement
```

Statement numbers 10 and 100 are arbitrary numbers and may be any unsigned integer from 1 to 99999.

If the condition is true, statements 1 through K are performed and the condition is tested again.

If the condition is still true, statements 1 through K are executed again.

The condition is tested again, and as long as the condition remains true statements 1 through K are executed again.

As soon as the condition has the value false, control transfers to the statement immediately following the WHILE-DO structure, statement 100.

As you read this explanation of the simple WHILE-DO loop, you will certainly realize that if such a loop is to terminate, at least one of the statements 1 through K must at some point make a change in the condition so that its value changes from true to false. Otherwise, the loop will repeat indefinitely, and we have the undesirable situation called an *infinite loop*.

Referring back to the previous example, you will see that the statement with the potential of affecting Condition is the READ statement. As soon as the program reads negative input data, for instance, Condition becomes false and the loop terminates.

Counter-controlled loops. A second commonly used method for controlling the number of times a loop is executed involves the use of a *counter* whose value is changed by 1 each time the loop actions are performed. When the counter attains a predetermined value, the loop is terminated.

The COUNT statement. To use counter-controlled loops, we need the COUNT statement:

FORM 1

```
COUNT = COUNT + 1
```

This is a standard assignment statement. When it is executed, the current value stored in location COUNT is added to 1 and the sum is stored back in location COUNT.

Thus if 0 is stored in location COUNT before its first execution, after the first execution the value stored in COUNT is 1.

If the statement is executed a second time, the value stored in COUNT is 2.

If it is executed a third time, the value 3 is stored in location COUNT.

Each time the statement is executed, the value of COUNT is increased by 1. Thus, the program maintains in location COUNT a continuous record of the number of times the statement has been executed.

It is also possible to set variable COUNT to a predetermined value and then decrease it by 1 at each execution. There are situations where such a decreasing counter is more appropriate to monitor loop repetitions. The statement then has the form

FORM 2

```
COUNT = COUNT - 1
```

If COUNT initially has the value 10 stored in it, the first execution stores the value 9 in location COUNT.

If the statement is executed a second time, the value stored in COUNT is 8.

If this process continues, the statement is executed ten times before the value stored in COUNT is 0.

Now let's return to our example. This time the program contains a loop controlled by a counter instead of by a test for sentinel data. Suppose there are 50 lines of input data.

SOLUTION 3

```
      PROGRAM RDMANY
C***********************************************************************
C*    PROGRAM DEFINITION                                               *
C*        THIS PROGRAM READS A TOTAL OF 50                             *
C*        DATA LINES AND PRINTS THE DATA.                              *
C***********************************************************************
C*    VARIABLE DEFINITION                                              *
C*        NUMBER IS STUDENT ID NUMBER.                                 *
C*        TEST IS TEST SCORE.                                          *
C*        COUNT IS TO COUNT NUMBER OF LINES                            *
C*        READ.                                                        *
C***********************************************************************
C*
      INTEGER NUMBER, COUNT, TEST
      COUNT=0
 10   IF(COUNT.GE.50)GO TO 20
          READ*, NUMBER, TEST
          PRINT*, NUMBER, TEST
          COUNT=COUNT+1
      GOTO 10
 20   STOP
      END
```

This third solution is no better than Solution 2. It simply demonstrates another, and sometimes useful, method of controlling loops. As an exercise, modify this program so that it will process any number of input lines instead of exactly 50. Obviously, this will make the program more general and, therefore, useful to more people. A more direct implementation of the loop structure uses DO loops, discussed in Chapter 5.

Problem 3.7
Screening for Null Values

SITUATION Mechanical engineering problems associated with fluid flow and vibratory motion, important, for example, in designing subway trains or jet engines, often have quite important results derived from the ratio of two functions. If the denominator function is zero, or close to zero, the ratio becomes undefined or inappropriately large, and is thus useless. It is important to know what values of an input variable may bring the denominator of an important ratio close to zero, so that a test can be set up to screen out those values.

OBJECTIVE One of the best ways to assess input values is to set up a simple numeric experiment as a prolog to the program. Assume that the function $f(x)$ will appear in the denominator of some expression in the main program. You want to write a prolog to screen out null values.

ANALYSIS A straightforward way of doing that is to find a value $x0$ such that $f(x0) = 0$. This value is called a *zero* of $f(x)$. There exist many functions for which it is impossible to find an exact value for $x0$, for example:

$$f(x) = 3^3 - 2x^2 + 3$$

One method of determining whether or not a function has a zero in the interval $[a, b]$ is to compute $f(a)$ and $f(b)$. If $f(a) < 0 < f(b)$, then there is at least one value $x0$ where $a < x0 < b$ and $f(x0) = 0$.

We may not be able to find an exact value for $x0$—quadratic functions are an exception; we can be exact by using the quadratic formula. But even an approximate value is useful, call it y, where $|f(y)| < e$, and e is a specified arbitrarily small positive value.

INFORMAL ALGORITHM Several algorithms find approximate zeros of functions, among them the *bisection* algorithm.

1. The first estimate uses $y = (a + b)/2$. Let us call the first estimate y_1.

2.1 If $f(y) > 0$ then we know that $x0$ is in the interval $[a,y]$, and we compute the second estimate, y_2, using the equation $y_2 = (a+y_1)/2$.

2.2 If $f(y_1) < 0$, we know that $x0$ is in the interval $[y_1,b]$ and we compute the second estimate from the equation $y_2 = (y_1+b)/2$.

3. Starting with any *i*th *y* estimate y_i, the next *y* estimate y_{i+1} is the midpoint of an interval determined by the value of $f(y_i)$. This process is continued until $|f(y_i)| < e$.

3.1 If $f(y_i) > 0$, then y_i is the right endpoint of the interval whose midpoint is the value of y_{i+1}.

3.2 If $f(y_i) < 0$, then y_i is the left endpoint of the interval.

EXAMPLE Before we write a more formal version of the bisection algorithm, let us apply it to the function

$$f(x) = 3x^3 - 2x^2 + 3.$$

A quick computation tells us that $f(0) = 3$ and $f(-1) = -2$, so our choice for the interval $[a,b]$ is the interval $[-1,0]$. So the first estimate for y is $(-1+0)/2 = -0.5$.

Then compute $f(-0.5) = (-0.375) - (0.5) + 3 > 0$. The next estimate for y is the midpoint of the interval $[-1, -0.5]$ with a value $(-1 + (-0.5))/2 = -0.75$.

Evaluating the function at -0.75 gives approximately 0.7, so $f(-0.75) > 0$. Consequently, the next estimate for y is the midpoint of the interval $[-1, -0.75]$ with a value $(-1 + (-0.75))/2 = -0.875$.

Evaluating $f(x)$ using this latest y value gives approximately -0.460621, so $f(-0.875) < 0$. The next y estimate is thus the midpoint of the interval $[-0.875, -0.75]$. Computing the midpoint gives $(-0.875 + (-0.75))/2 = -0.8125$.

Evaluating $f(-.08125)$ gives approximately 0.71, greater than zero. Therefore, the next estimate for y is the midpoint of the interval $[-0.8125, -0.75]$, or -0.78125.

The zero we are looking for is now known to be in the interval $[-0.78125, -0.75]$. As we expected, the interval becomes smaller and smaller. The process continues until the midpoint y of the interval is such that $|f(y)| < e$, where e is an arbitrarily small number. The value of e must be specified at the beginning of the program.

ALGORITHM Here is a formal presentation of the bisection algorithm:

1. Obtain the function, F (X).
2. Obtain values for A and B such that F (A) < 0 < F (B).
3. Obtain a value for E, the acceptable error when finding a zero of F(X).

4. Compute X = (A+B)/2.
5. Compute F (X).
6 If F(X) > 0, assign B to have the value X.
7 If F(X) < 0, assign A to have the value X.
8. Compute a new X value such that

   NEW X = (current A-value + current B-value) / 2
9. If the absolute value of F(NEW X) > E, repeat the process from step 4.
10. Report the current value of NEW X.
11. End.

FORTRAN PROGRAM

Next we develop a FORTRAN program. Since we have not yet discussed a method whereby a definition for F(X) can be easily read into a program, we shall accomplish step 1 of the algorithm by defining F(X) in a function statement within the program. To solve for a different function, change the function statement line of the program before execution. For the moment, let us assume that we want to find an approximate zero for the function $F(X) = XE^X - 2X - 1$

```
      PROGRAM FUNCT
C***********************************************************************
C*    THIS PROGRAM COMPUTES AN APPROXIMATE ZERO FOR THE FUNCTION       *
C*        F(X) = XE**X - 2X - 1                                        *
C*    WITHIN THE INTERVAL [1, 2]                                       *
C***********************************************************************
C*
      REAL A, B, AORIG, BORIG, XOLD, XNEW, E, F
C*
C*    E IS THE ERROR TOLERANCE BETWEEN AN EXACT ZERO AND AN            *
C*    APPROXIMATE TO BE COMPUTED BY THIS PROGRAM. THE VALUE            *
C*    E DETERMINES HOW MANY SUCCESSIVE APPROXIMATIONS FOR A ZERO       *
C*    ARE COMPUTED BEFORE A RESULT IS REPORTED.                        *
C*    THE FOLLOWING STATEMENT IS CALLED A FUNCTION STATEMENT           *
C*
      F(X) = X * EXP(X) -2*X -1
      PRINT *, 'ENTER VALUES FOR A, B, AND E'
      READ *, A, B, E,
      AORIG = A
      BORIG = B
      XOLD = A
      XNEW = (A+B)/2
```

```
10   IF (ABS(XOLD-XNEW) .LE. E) GOTO 20
        IF (F(XNEW) .LT. 0) THEN
            A = XNEW
        ELSE
            B = XNEW
        ENDIF
        XNEW = (A+B)/2
     GO TO 10
20   PRINT*, XNEW, 'IS AN APPROXIMATE ZERO IN THE INTERVAL ',
    +    'FROM ', AORIG, ' TO ', BORIG
     END
```

If another function were defined in the function statement, the program would compute an approximate zero for that new function. It is relatively easy to adapt to a new function by replacing the function statement line before running the program. More advanced FORTRAN programs allow one to enter the function at the time of execution, but such refinements are beyond the scope of this book.

Exercises 3.2

1. Study each of the following programs and determine the output.

a. Assume an input value of 62.

```
PROGRAM SCORE
INTEGER ISCORE
PRINT*,'INPUT YOUR TEST SCORE'
READ*,ISCORE
IF(ISCORE.GE.90)PRINT*,'YOUR GRADE IS A.'
IF(ISCORE.LT.90.AND.ISCORE.GE.80)PRINT*,'YOUR GRADE IS B.'
IF(ISCORE.LT.80.AND.ISCORE.GE.70)PRINT*,'YOUR GRADE IS C.'
IF(ISCORE.LT.70.AND.ISCORE.GE.60)PRINT*,'YOUR GRADE IS D.'
IF(ISCORE.LT.60)PRINT*,'YOUR GRADE IS F.'
END
```

b. Modify the program in Exercise 1a to output

```
YOUR SCORE IS ______ YOUR GRADE IS _______
```

c. Specific input is not given; simply *describe* the output.

```
PROGRAM GRADE
REAL TOTAL
INTEGER N,SCORE,NSTUDT
CHARACTER GR
READ*,N,TOTAL
```

```
      PRINT*,'STUDENT NO.','SCORE','GRADE'
100   READ*,NSTUDT,SCORE
      SCORE=(SCORE/TOTAL)*100
      GR='A'
      IF (SCORE .LT. 90) GR='B'
      IF (SCORE .LT. 80) GR='C'
      IF (SCORE .LT. 70) GR='D'
      IF (SCORE .LT. 60) GR='F'
      PRINT*,NSTUDT,SCORE,GR
      N=N-1
      IF(N .GT. 0) GO TO 100
      END
```

d. After you have determined the output of the program in Exercise 1c, rewrite it to insert appropriate comment lines. The program should be as easily understandable as possible.

e. Relate the output of this program to whatever the input might be.

```
      PROGRAM ROUND
      READ*,X
      N=X+0.5
      PRINT*,N
      END
```

f. Describe what this program does with input, regardless of the specific number provided.

```
      PROGRAM EVEN
      READ*,N
      I=(N/2)*2-N
      IF(I.EQ.0)PRINT*,N,' IS AN EVEN NUMBER'
      IF(I.NE.0)PRINT*,N,' IS AN ODD NUMBER'
      END
```

g. Describe output with respect to the number provided for N.

```
      PROGRAM SEVEN
      INTEGER N.KOUNT
      READ*,N
      IF(N.LT.7)GO TO 20
      KOUNT=0
      I=0
15    I=I+7
      N=N-1
      KOUNT=KOUNT+1
      IF(N.GE.7)GO TO 15
      PRINT*,'THERE ARE',KOUNT,'SEVENS IN',N
      STOP
20    PRINT*,'THERE ARE NO SEVENS IN',N
      END
```

h. Describe output in relation to input.

```
      PROGRAM MULTP
      INTEGER N,M,MULT,FACT,RESULT
      IF(M.GT.N) FACT=M
      IF(M.GT.N) MULT=N
      RESULT=0
 10   MULT=MULT-1
      RESULT=RESULT+FACT
      IF(MULT.GT.0)GO TO 10
      PRINT*,N,'X',M,'=',RESULT
      END
```

Elementary Error Correction

It will be handy now to introduce techniques to locate and remove errors in a program submitted for execution and said to be error-free. There are two principal types of basic errors.

1. ***Misspelling special words or use of incorrect punctuation.*** These errors are called *syntax* errors. Most syntax errors are discovered and identified by the compiler and result in error messages called *diagnostic messages*, or simply *diagnostics.* To correct them one reenters the program lines in which errors were detected. The program is then executed again.
2. ***Improper conception of the problem or incorrect procedures.*** In either case some incorrect logical thinking has occurred; hence this kind of error is called a *logic* error. A program with logic errors may be syntactically correct and may correctly accept input data. It may even execute in what seems to be a correct run, yet the output is incorrect. Or execution may come to an unexpected halt without processing all input data.

The following problem will demonstrate the process of removing errors from simple programs.

Problem 3.8 Correcting a Rounding Program

OBJECTIVE Input a positive number and round it to the nearest integer. If the number is exactly halfway between two integers, round it to the next higher one. The program should check that the input datum is positive; if it isn't, the program should print an appropriate error message. If input datum is positive, output should give the rounded value.

ALGORITHM

1. Read number A.
2. If A is negative, report an appropriate message and stop processing.
3. Add 0.5 to the value of A. The integer part of this sum is the rounded value of A.
4. Report the result and stop processing.

FLAWED FORTRAN PROGRAM 1

This program approximately expresses the pseudocode procedure, except that we have deliberately included some errors. Examine the program to see how many errors seem obvious to you. Then compare your responses with the analysis that follows.

```
 070   PROGRAM ROUND
 080   REAL A
 090   INTEGER I
 120   A = A + 0.5
 130   IF)A .GT. 0)THEN
 140       READ*, A
 150       I = A
 160       PRINT*, 'THE ROUNDED VALUE OF ', A, ' IS ', I
 170   ELSE
 180       PRINT*, 'BAD INPUT'
 190   ENDIF
 200   END
*** ERROR LIST FOR THIS PROGRAM ***
 120          A = A + 0.5
    (120) - CAUTION A IS NOT SET ABOVE
 130          IF)A .GT. 0)THEN
    (130) - FATAL—MISSING ( OR EXTRA )
    (130) - FATAL—MISSING ( OR EXTRA )
                     END
THE FOLLOWING ERROR HAS OCCURRED AT LINE 120 OF THE SOURCE PROGRAM
MODE 4 ERROR—ATTEMPT TO USE UNSET DATA AREA, OR ZERO DIVIDED BY ZERO.
ENSURE CODE IS INITIALIZED—USE MNF (Z)—AND CHECK DIVISIONS.
```

ERROR ANALYSIS

An error message calls attention to actual errors or to situations that are likely to be errors. In the error list, a copy of line 120 is printed, followed by this message:

```
CAUTION A IS NOT SET ABOVE
```

In other words, up to this point in the program, previous to line 120, no value has been assigned to location A by a READ or an assignment statement. This may not be an error: If the program does not place a value in a memory location, the compiler uses the last value stored there, and A may have a stored value.

Usually, such an omission is an oversight and should be corrected. To eliminate the error we move the READ statement for A from line 140 to line

115 and eliminate line 140 completely. The value of A does not change between line 115 and line 140, and there is no need to repeat the READ.

The next error messages refer to line 130:

```
FATAL—MISSING ( OR EXTRA )
FATAL—MISSING ( OR EXTRA )
```

The compiler cannot exactly determine what the error is but it points out that there is something wrong with the parentheses—there are not the same number of left- and right-facing parentheses. A look at line 130 reveals quickly that the parenthesis to the right of IF should have been right-facing instead of left-facing.

The correction is made by reentering line 130 with the right-facing parenthesis following IF.

Finally, after printing a copy of the END statement, this diagnostic message is given:

```
THE FOLLOWING ERROR HAS OCCURRED AT LINE 120 OF THE SOURCE PROGRAM
MODE 4 ERROR—ATTEMPT TO USE UNSET DATA AREA, OR ZERO DIVIDED BY ZERO.
ENSURE CODE IS INITIALIZED—USE MNF (Z)—AND CHECK DIVISIONS.
```

This final error message, about the use of "unset data area," will be eliminated when the position of the READ statement is moved to line 115. If we make these corrections, we have an improved program:

FLAWED FORTRAN PROGRAM 2

```
070  PROGRAM ROUND
080  REAL A
090  INTEGER I
115  READ*, A
120  A = A + 0.5
130  IF (A .GT. 0) THEN
150      I = A
160      PRINT*, 'THE ROUNDED VALUE OF ',A,' IS ',I
180  ELSE
190      PRINT*, 'BAD INPUT'
200  ENDIF
210  END
```

Assuming that the input datum was 23.79, the output produced is

```
THE ROUNDED VALUE OF 24.2900 IS 24
```

Although the program is now free of syntax errors, there must be at least one logic error. The datum input is 23.79, but it is reported in the output statement as 24.2900.

Somehow, Program 2 does not keep the originally entered number to print at line 160. A look at the program reveals that we use A in two different ways in line 120—to denote both the number originally entered for rounding and the number used in the rounding process.

If we change the A on the left of the equals sign to X, and in line 150 change the corresponding A to X, then the correct input value is output and the number is correctly rounded.

This revised program is now correct, as shown by two sets of confirming results:

CORRECT FORTRAN PROGRAM 3

```
070   PROGRAM ROUND
080   REAL A, X
090   INTEGER I
115   READ *, A
120   X = A + 0.5
130   IF (A .GT. 0) THEN
150       I = X
160       PRINT*, 'THE ROUNDED VALUE OF ',A,' IS ',I
170   ELSE
180       PRINT *, 'BAD INPUT'
190   ENDIF
200   END
```

With input datum 23.79, the output is

```
THE ROUNDED VALUE OF 23.7900 IS 24
```

With input datum 123.47, the output is

```
THE ROUNDED VALUE OF 123.470 IS 123
```

Indentation and Structure

The observant reader will have noticed that many of the program examples given in this chapter have some lines indented beyond others. In some cases indents are followed by further indents. Although indentation is not required by FORTRAN 77, it makes programs more understandable.

Indentation visually groups related program lines. This allows one to scan the program and easily see which lines belong to each program block. It also enables one to visually associate paired statements, such as IF-THEN and ENDIF statements, even though they are separated in the code—and perhaps even interrupted by other, nested IF-THEN-ENDIF structures.

For example, in rounding program 3, the two lines

```
I = X
PRINT*, 'THE ROUNDED VALUE OF ',A,' IS ',I
```

are indented to make it clear that these two statements are the action block for the conditional statement

```
IF (A .GT. 0) THEN
```

to be executed if the relational expression is true. When the two action statements are complete, control passes to the END statement. These indented lines thus provide visual evidence of how the logic of a program flows. The program thus becomes more readable and understandable.

For further examples of the use of indentation see the programs in Exercise 3 at the end of this chapter.

Summary

In this chapter we have considered FORTRAN statements used in building programs that can make choices and follow through with appropriate actions. Previous syntax was entirely based on executing each line of code in sequential order. Selection structures, and the iteration or loop structures that are discussed in Chapter 5, allow one to specify non-linear orders for program execution.

Conditional statements based on relational expressions form the basis of FORTRAN selection structures. Programs still read through the code one line at a time, from the top down, but we may now instruct the program to make decisions to skip lines, to repeat lines, or to move to a line in the program either further along or further back than the current line.

Here are the general forms of the statements discussed:

Logical IF statement.

```
IF (Condition) Statement
```

where Condition represents a simple or compound relational (logical) expression and Statement represents any executable FORTRAN statement except another IF statement.

GO TO statement.

```
IF (Condition) GO TO N
```

where N represents the reference number of the statement to be executed next. GO TO may refer to lines either above or below the line in which it appears.

IF-THEN-ELSE structure.

```
IF (Condition) THEN
    { IF block }
ELSE
    { ELSE block }
ENDIF
```

where IF block and ELSE block represent one or more executable FORTRAN statements.

When the condition is true, statement(s) in the IF block are executed and ELSE block statement(s) are completely ignored, control moving from the IF block to the statement following the ENDIF.

When the condition is false, the IF block is ignored and ELSE block statement(s) are executed.

It is legitimate to omit the ELSE statement and the ELSE block. In this case, if the condition is true, IF block statement(s) are executed, then the statement following ENDIF. If the condition is false, control transfers directly to the statement following ENDIF.

ELSEIF statement, a useful option in IF-THEN-ELSE structures.

```
IF (Condition 1) THEN
    { Block 1 }
ELSEIF (Condition 2) THEN
    { Block 2 }
    .
    .
    .
ELSEIF (Condition N) THEN
    { Block N }
ELSE
    { ELSE block }
ENDIF
```

If condition 1 is true, the statement(s) in block 1 are executed, followed by the statement immediately after the ENDIF.

If condition 1 is false, condition 2 is tested. If it is true, block 2 statements are executed, followed by the statement immediately after ENDIF.

In general, when condition `I` is true, the statement(s) in block `I` are executed followed by the statement after ENDIF. If condition `I` is false, the next condition is tested and similar actions occur.

If no condition is true, and an ELSE statement is present, the ELSE block statement(s) are executed. If there is no ELSE statement or ELSE block, program control goes to the statement following ENDIF.

WHILE-DO structure.

```
WHILE (Condition) DO
    { DO block }
ENDWHILE
```

In versions of FORTRAN that do not include direct implementation of the WHILE-DO use IF (.NOT. Condition) GO TO N.

We also discussed simple loops, covered in full in Chapter 5, elementary error correction techniques, and the usefulness of indentation in writing understandable programs.

End of Chapter Exercises

1. The following program is written to compute the sum of even integers from 2 to 1000. However, the program contains some logic errors, so it does not perform the desired task. Find and correct these errors.

```
       ISUM=2
       I=2
 30    ISUM=ISUM+I
       I=I+2
       IF(I.LT.1000)GO TO 30
       PRINT*,ISUM
       END
```

2. This program is supposed to take as input an integer greater than 10 and output the digits of the integer vertically with the units digit first. For example, if the integer input is 9368, the output should be

```
8
6
3
9
```

Check to see if there are any logic errors in this program.

```
       PROGRAM 2
       INTEGER NUMB,NEWNUM,DIGIT
       READ*,NUMB
 15    IF(NUMB.LT.10) GO TO 35
          NEWNUM=NUMB/10
          DIGIT=NUMB-NEWNUM*10
          NUMB=NEWNUM
          PRINT*,DIGIT
          GO TO 15
 35    PRINT*,NUMB
       END
```

3. Review the following programs for correctness. For those that are incorrect, identify the error(s) and suggest corrections for both syntax and logic errors. If the program is free of errors, specify its output with respect to the input data.

a.

```
 20    READ*,N
       IF(N.LT.0)THEN
          M=-N
          PRINT*,M,' IS THE ABSOLUTE VALUE OF ',N
       ELSEIF(N.EQ.0)
          PRINT*,'TRY AGAIN.'
          GO TO 20
```

```
      ELSEIF(N.GT.0)
          PRINT*,'THE ABSOLUTE VALUE OF A POSITIVE'
          PRINT*,'NUMBER IS THE NUMBER ITSELF.'
          PRINT*,'TRY AGAIN'
          GO TO 20
      ENDIF
      END
```

b.

```
      READ*,N,M
      L=N+M
      LL=N-M
      LLL=M-N
      IF(L.EQ.LL)THEN
          PRINT*,'M MUST BE ZERO.'
      ELSEIF(L.EQ.LLL)
          PRINT*,'N MUST BE ZERO'
      ENDIF
      PRINT*,'NEITHER M NOR N IS ZERO.'
      END
```

c.

```
 10   READ*,N,M
      IF(N.LE.0)THEN
          PRINT*,'INCORRECT INPUT FOR N.'
          PRINT*,'N MUST BE A POSITIVE INTEGER.'
          PRINT*,'ENTER N AND M AGAIN.'
          GO TO 10
      ELSE
          IF(M.LE.0)THEN
              PRINT*,'INCORRECT INPUT FOR M.'
              PRINT*,'M MUST BE A POSITIVE INTEGER.'
              PRINT*,'ENTER N AND M AGAIN.'
              GO TO 10
          ENDIF
      ENDIF
      END
```

d.

```
      READ*,A,B,C
      IF(A.EQ.0)THEN
          X=-C/B
          PRINT*,B,'*X+',C,'=0'
          PRINT*,'IMPLIES X=',X
      ELSE
          D=B*B-4*A*C
          IF(D.EQ.0)THEN
              X=-B/2.
              PRINT*,A,'*X*X+',B,'*X+',C,'=0'
              PRINT*,'IMPLIES X=',X
```

```
      ELSEIF(D.GT.0)
          X1=(-B+D).(2.*A)
          X2=(-B-D)/(2.*A)
          PRINT*,A, '*X*X+',B, '*X+',C, '=0'
          PRINT*,'IMPLIES X=', X1, 'AND X=',X2
      ENDIF
  ENDIF
  END
```

e.

```
  READ*,X,Y,Z
  IF(X.GE.Y)THEN
      IF(X.GT.Z)THEN
          IF(Y.GT.Z)THEN
              PRINT*,X,Y,Z
          ELSE
              PRINT*,X,Z,Y
      ELSE
          PRINT*,Z,X,Y
  ELSE
      IF(X.GE.Z)THEN
          IF(Y.LE.Z)THEN
              PRINT*,Z,Y,X
          ELSE
              PRINT*,Y,Z,X
          ENDIF
      ELSE
          PRINT*,Y,X,Z
      ENDIF
  ENDIF
  END
```

4. In Exercise 3b there is a logic error. Every time the program is run it prints

```
NEITHER M NOR N IS ZERO.
```

Correct the error so that the output corresponds to the input data.

5. In Exercise 3c there are two logic errors. As given, the program checks separately for the validity of data input for N and M. If either one of them is invalid, the program requests both values to be reentered. Also, only M or N is rechecked for validity, although both must be reentered and an error could be present in the one not checked. Rewrite the program to correct these errors in logic.

6. You may recognize that Exercise 3d deals with solutions to the quadratic equation $ax^2 + bx + c = 0$. The program handles situations where $d = b^2 - 4ac \geq 0$, but does nothing with the case in which $d < 0$. Modify the program to include this case as well. Also, change the program so that the PRINT statement for the equation A*X*X + B*X + C = 0 occurs only once in the program.

7. In Exercise 3e, the program was intended to accept three numbers and output them in descending order. As given, it works correctly for certain sets of three numbers but not for any three numbers. Modify the program so that it is correct for any three numbers given as input.

8. This program is intended to find the first half of string ST and output it. Review the program to see whether it does the job correctly.

```
PROGRAM HALF
INTEGER M
CHARACTER ST*10
READ*,ST
M=LEN(ST)
ST=ST(1:M/2)
PRINT*,ST
END
```

9. This program is supposed to reverse the order of the characters in string ST. Find the errors in it.

```
PROGRAM REVERSE
CHARACTER ST*10, STR*10
INTEGER M
READ*,ST
STR=''
M=10
STR=STR//ST(M:M)
M=M-1
PRINT*,STR
END
```

▪ *The rest of these exercises define a situation for which you are to write a* FORTRAN *program. The exercises are arranged approximately in order of increasing difficulty.*

10.a. Input two integers, M and N, and compute the sum of the integers from M to N inclusive. Output M, N, and the sum, including some identifying information.

b. Compute and report only the odd integers.

c. Compute and report only the even integers.

11. Enter the coordinates for each of 4 points in a plane where it is assumed that point A is designated by coordinates (XA, YA), point B by (XB, YB), point C by (XC, YC), and point D by (XD, YD). Write a program to determine if ABCD is

a. A square.

b. A rectangle.

c. A parallelogram.

d. A trapezoid.

e. None of the above.

12. Input any number, determine its integer part and its fractional part, then produce the output

```
INTEGER PART XXXX FRACTIONAL PART .XXXX
```

where the X's represent appropriate digits.

For example, if the number input is 396.8210, the output should be

```
INTEGER PART 396 FRACTIONAL PART .8210
```

13. In mathematics, given any positive integer n, the number called n factorial (denoted $n!$) is defined as $n! = n*(n-1)*(n-2)* \ldots *(2)*(1)$. Write a FORTRAN program that inputs any positive integer N, where N is less than or equal to 15, computes N!, and produces the output XX FACTORIAL = XXXXX where the X's represent appropriate digits. Thus, if the number input for N is 6, the output should be 6 FACTORIAL = 720

14. Input a single-digit code and a number. Assume that if the code is positive, the number input is in English units and needs to be converted to metric units. If the code is negative, the reverse is true. The output should be of the form

```
__________ POUNDS = ________ KILOGRAMS
```

Use these codes and units:

Code	*English unit*	*Metric unit*
1	Pound	Kilogram
2	Gallon	Liter
3	Degree Fahrenheit	Degree Celsius
4	Yard	Meter
5	Square yard	Square meter
6	Cubic yard	Cubic meter
7	Mile	Kilometer
8	*Stop any further program action*	

Thus, if the two numbers input were 1 and 3.3, the output would be

```
3.3 POUNDS = 1.5 KILOGRAMS
```

15. This program is to input data from a checking account and print a monthly report of activity. The first line of input data provides the beginning balance. Each other line of input data contains a transaction code (1 for deposit, 2 for withdrawal, 0 for no more transactions), a 6-digit date in the form DDMMYY, and the amount of the transaction. Assume that transactions are input in chronological order. Output is to be a report, including headings, that looks like this:

```
TRANSACTION          DATE          AMOUNT          BALANCE
                                                   1357.62
DEP                  051282         17.50          1375.12
WDR                  051482        100.00          1275.12
 .                     .              .                  .
 .                     .              .                  .
 .                     .              .                  .
```

The beginning balance is alone on the first line. Numeric codes 1 and 2 are translated to DEP and WDR.

16. This program is to provide a simple analysis of gasoline usage. The input consists of beginning mileage, ending mileage, gasoline used in gallons, and cost per gallon. The output should include headings as follows:

```
TOTAL MILES  GALLONS USED  MILES/GAL  TRIP COST
XXXX.X       XXX.X         XX.X       XXX.XX
```

17. This program is to compute the current value A of an amount invested at compound interest. The input is principal PRIN, annual interest rate RATE, compounding period P, a fraction of a year entered as 1, 0.5, 0.25, 0.08333, etc., and the number of years N for which the money is invested. The formula is A = PRIN (1.0 + RATE*P)**(N/P). Output should be

```
___ DOLLARS INVESTED AT ____ PERCENT FOR ___ YEARS WILL HAVE THE VALUE ____
```

18. This program is to compute the Nth power of a number X, where N is a positive integer, by doing repeated multiplications.

a. Input N and X, and compute X**N by performing an appropriate number of multiplications. Output should be

```
______ RAISED TO THE _______ POWER = __________
```

b. This time, use the minimum number of multiplications. For example, to compute x^5 first compute Y = X*X, then X**5 = Y*Y*X. This requires only three multiplications rather than the four in X*X*X*X*X.

19. This program is to compute a schedule of monthly payments for a mortgage of P dollars borrowed at an annual rate of RATE for N years. The input values are the principal borrowed P, the annual interest rate RATE, and the number of years N. Use this formula for monthly payment:

```
Monthly payment = (P*R*(R + 1)**M)/((R = 1)**(M - 1))
```

where R = RATE/12 and M = N*12.

Output should be a payment schedule in this form:

```
MONTH        INTEREST PD     PRINCIPAL PD          BALANCE
  .               .                .                  .
  .               .                .                  .
  .               .                .                  .
```

20. Write a program that outputs a multiple choice test item and accepts as input a response to the item. If the answer selected is correct, the program outputs the word CORRECT and stops. If the answer is wrong, the program outputs INCORRECT and the message TRY AGAIN., and then outputs the test item again, repeating until the correct choice is input. An example of the type of test item is

```
THE CURRENT U.S. PRESIDENT IS
1) RONALD REAGAN
2) JAMES CARTER
3) GEORGE BUSH
4) NONE OF THE ABOVE
```

21. COMPS, Inc. uses 5 different salary schedules for its employees:

Schedule	*Average salary in $*	*No. of employees*
1	12,000	10
2	15,000	17
3	18,000	20
4	21,000	18
5	26,000	8

The corporation plans to give raises such that the overall increase is 8%. Write a program to compute and output the following:

a. Total money needed for the raise.

b. Overall average pay for all employees before the raise.

c. Overall average pay for all employees after the raise.

d. New average salary for each schedule and the dollar amount of the raise for each group of employees.

22. The real estate tax on residential homes is computed as follows:

Assessed valuation V	*Computed tax*
$30,000 or less	$800
$\$30,000 < v \le \$50,000$	$800 + 1% of valuation over $30,000
$\$50,000 < v \le \$80,000$	$800 + 1.2% of valuation over $30,000
$\$80,000 < v \le \$120,000$	$800 + 1.4% of valuation over $30,000
$v > \$120,000$	$800 + 1.5% of valuation over $30,000

Write a program with the assessed valuation of a home as input that computes the real estate tax. Output the assessed valuation and the amount of the tax.

23. Write a program to accept input of any positive real number of at most twelve digits and output, one at a time on separate lines, each of the digits in the number beginning with the leftmost one.

24. A container has ten red balls numbered 00, 01, . . . , 09 and ten black balls numbered 10, 11, . . . , 19. Assume that outside of the container are as many additional similarly numbered red and black balls as needed for the following process. Write a program using the RAND function described in Chapter 2 to simulate the drawing of balls from the container. You might use the occurrence of 0 to represent red and 1 to represent black. The procedure for drawing and adding balls to the container is

a. Determine the color of the ball to be drawn.

b. Determine the number on the ball to be drawn.

c. Add to the container a ball of opposite color but identical number to that on the ball drawn.

The output should be as follows:

```
DRAW            BEFORE DRAW                       AFTER DRAW
         NO. RED          NO. BLACK        NO. RED          NO. BLACK
1        10               10               ...              ...
2        ...              ...              ...              ...
```

Continue this process until 100 balls have been drawn.

25. You are given this list of the first 41 U.S. presidents and their ages at inauguration. Write a program that reads these data from the keyboard and produces the following output:

a. The name and age of the youngest president.

b. The name and age of the oldest president.

c. The number of presidents older than 50.

d. The number of presidents older than 65.

e. The number of presidents younger than 50.

f. The average age of the presidents at inauguration.

	President	*Age*		*President*	*Age*
1	G. Washington	57	22	G. Cleveland	47
2	J. Adams	61	23	B. Harrison	55
3	T. Jefferson	57	24	G. Cleveland	55
4	J. Madison	57	25	W. McKinley	54
5	J. Monroe	58	26	T. Roosevelt	42
6	J.Q. Adams	57	27	W.H. Taft	51
7	A. Jackson	61	28	W. Wilson	56
8	M. VanBuren	54	29	W.G. Harding	55
9	W.H. Harrison	68	30	C. Coolidge	51
10	J. Tyler	51	31	H. Hoover	54
11	J.K. Polk	49	32	F.D. Roosevelt	51
12	Z. Taylor	64	33	H.S. Truman	60
13	M. Fillmore	50	34	D. Eisenhower	62
14	F. Pierce	48	35	J.F. Kennedy	43
15	J. Buchanan	65	36	L.B. Johnson	55
16	A. Lincoln	52	37	R. Nixon	56
17	A. Johnson	56	38	G. Ford	61
18	U.S. Grant	46	39	J. Carter	52
19	R.B. Hayes	54	40	R. Reagan	69
20	J.A. Garfield	49	41	G. Bush	64
21	C.A. Arthur	50			

26. You are given a set of numbers ending with the sentinel number 999.999. Write an algorithm and program to read the numbers, determine the sum of the absolute values of the numbers, and find their range (the difference between the largest number and the smallest).

27. You have a set of numbers ending with sentinel number –999.99. Write an algorithm and program to read the set only once and, excluding the sentinel data, find

a. The number n of numbers in the set.

b. The number of negative numbers in the set.

c. The sum of the negative numbers.

d. The number of positive numbers in the set.

e. The sum of the positive numbers.

f. The arithmetic mean $\overline{X}$ (the average) of all the numbers.

g. The variance of the numbers where

$$Variance = \left(\sum_{i=1}^{n} X_i^2 - n * \overline{X}^2 \right) / n$$

28. Write an algorithm and program to read a single positive integer N and do the following tasks:

a. For N < 15, compute N factorial = N! = N*(N–1)*(N–2) * . . . *2*1.

b. For 20 ≤ N <100, compute the sum of the squares of the integers 1,2,3, . . . , N.

c. For 100 ≤ N < 1000, compute the sum of the odd integers 1, 3, 5, . . . , N.

d. For N ≥ 1000, compute the square root of N, then stop.

29. For positive integers X and Y, write an algorithm and program to find the maximum value of the function 2X**2 + 3XY where the sum of X and Y is at least 2 but does not exceed 10. Output the maximum value for the function and the integer values of X and Y that produce that maximum.

PROGRAM DESIGN ISSUES

This represents a common problem in modern design engineering: *Optimization under constraint*. The general form is "Given the restrictions for independent variables, what is the maximum or minimum value to which the dependent variable can be brought?" In Exercise29, the values of X and Y, the independent variables, are constrained by their relationships to each other.

Asking the following questions may help you plan for optimization: ***How much of the range of possible answers can be excluded automatically?*** These answers need not be calculated. Here, if you simply calculate sums and results for all the permutations of two numbers between 1 and 9, simply throwing away combinations whose sum did not fall within bounds, it would be very inefficient. Can you think of a way to have the system calculate only the numbers it needs to? HINT: think of each X as defining a set of acceptable Y's.

Does the function you are trying to maximize have a single global maximum for the range? If so, watch out for *corner solutions*, the cases where the optimum is found at a point corresponding to extreme maxima or minima of all independent variables. It may indicate that better results can be obtained if the constraints are relaxed.

Before running an optimization program, always figure out the maximum number of iterations it may have to make. Where the number is very large, reduce it by setting up strategies that do not involve sampling the whole space. This necessarily runs the risk of missing an isolated local maximum which is in fact the true global maximum.

30. Given two integers, the greatest common divisor GCD of the two integers is the largest integer that divides both of them. For example, the GCD of 12 and 16 is 4 since it divides both numbers and it is the largest such divisor. Write an algorithm and program that reads any two integers, finds their GCD, and reports the two numbers and their GCD with appropriate identifying information.

31. An integer is called a *perfect number* if its value is equal to the sum of all its divisors including 1. For example, 6 is a perfect number because the sum of its divisors (1 + 2 + 3) equals 6. Write an algorithm and a program to find and display the five smallest perfect numbers.

32. In a right triangle, if c is the length of the hypotenuse and a and b are the lengths of the two legs, then $c^2=a^2 + b^2$. Write a program to find the 10 sets of smallest integer values for a, b, and c that satisfy this equation. Display the 10 sets of three numbers together with appropriate identifying information.

33. In mathematics, Euler's number e is the limiting value of an expression. This number is represented by the equation

$$e = 1 + \frac{1}{1!} + \frac{1}{2!} + \frac{1}{3!} + \ldots + \frac{1}{n!} + \ldots$$

where $n!$ is defined as in Exercise 28.

Write an algorithm and a program to compute E correct to twelve decimal places; then report that value. *Hint:* You will need to compute N! so that 1/N! is less than .0000000000001.

34. An integer is divisible by 9 if the sum of its digits is divisible by 9. For example, the number 729 is divisible by 9 (9*81 = 729). The sum of its digits is 7 + 2 + 9 = 18, which we know is divisible by 9. We can also show that 18 is divisible by 9 by applying the same sum-of-digits rule, where 1 + 8 = 9.

Write an algorithm and a program that accepts any positive integer as input and then applies the sum-of-digits rule to the original integer and to successive sums of digits until the last sum is exactly 9 or less than 9. If the last sum is exactly 9, the original integer is divisible by 9 and a message should be output saying

```
XXXXX is DIVISIBLE BY 9.
```

If the last sum is less than 9, output the message

```
XXXXX IS NOT DIVISIBLE BY 9.
```

In both of these output messages, XXXXX represents the original integer input to the program.

35. Write an algorithm and program to play the following game:

a. Request the player to input age, month of birth, and year of birth, each as a two-digit number. For example, 16,05,75 means a player is sixteen years old and was born in May of 1975.

b. Use the RAND function to determine randomly a unique position form 1 to 6 for each of 6 input digits in a 6-digit number. The result from the input digits 1, 6, 0, 5, 7, 5 might be the number 710655.

c. Tell the player the computer has produced a 6-digit number from their birthdate and they will have at most 15 chances to guess the number by keying the guess on the terminal.

d. After each guess, determine which digits, if any, are correct and output appropriate messages. For example, if the player guesses 517650 as the number generated in section b, the output might be as follows:

```
CORRECT DIGITS ARE:
THE 1 IN POSITION 2
THE 6 IN POSITION 4
THE 5 IN POSITION 5
```

e. Write the program so that play continues until the correct 6-digit number is guessed or until the player has had 15 attempts.

f. At the end of each game, ask the player to enter 0 if no more playing is desired and 1 if another game is to be played.

36. The citizens of Moorhead have completed surveys from which the following data were obtained:

a. Respondent's sex, with 0 = male and 1 = female.

b. Marital status, with 0 = single, 1 = married, and 2 = other.

c. Age, in years.

d. Education, with 0 = less than high school, 1 = high school, 2 = college but no degree, 3 = 4 yr. degree, and 4 = graduate degree.

Write a program to input these data until an age of 0 is encountered and compute the following statistics:

e. Percent of all respondents over 65.

f. Percent of all respondents over 21.

g. Percent of single females.

h. Percent of single males.

i. Percent of single females with a 4-year degree.

j. Percent of single males with a 4-year degree.

k. Average age of single males.

l. Average age of single females.

m. Assuming that education code 0 means an average of 6 years of education, 1 means 12 years, 2 means 14 years, 3 means 16 years, and 4 means 19 years, determine the average years of education for males.

n. Determine the average years of education for females.

The program should generate appropriate output for all statistics.

37. A sequence of integers defined as

$$f(n) = \begin{cases} 1 \ if\ 0 < n \leq 2 \\ f(n-1) + f(n-2) \ if\ n > 2 \end{cases}$$

is called a Fibonacci sequence. Write an algorithm and program to compute and report the first 40 Fibonacci numbers.

38. The function $f_k(m, n) = (1/2)(m+n-1)(m+n-2) + n = k$ is called an *inverting* function. Write an algorithm and program that computes and reports the values for M and N for each value of K from 1 through 20.

39. Factorial N is usually defined as N! = N*(N−1)*(N−2)* . . . *3*2*1. Stirling's formula for computing $n!$ is

$$n! = \sqrt{2\pi\, n}\ (n/e)^n$$

where $e = 2.718282$.

Develop an algorithm and a program to check the accuracy of Stirling's formula for N = 10, 11, . . . , 20.

40. Given a set of N numbers (X1, X2, X3, . . . , XN) we define the arithmetic mean of this set by the equation

$$XBAR = (X1 + X2 + X3 + \ldots + XN) / N$$

The geometric mean of the same set of numbers is given by:

$$Y = \sqrt[N]{X1 * X2 * X3 * \ldots * XN}$$

The harmonic mean of the same set of N numbers is given by:

$$Z = N / (1/X1 + 1/X2 + 1/X3 + \ldots + 1/XN)$$

Develop an algorithm and a program to read a set of N numbers and compute and report the 3 mean values defined above.

41. The correlation coefficient for 2 sets of numbers with N numbers per set ($x1, x2, x3, \ldots, xn$ and $y1, y2, y3, \ldots, yn$) is defined as follows:

$$cc = \frac{n\,(\Sigma xi * yi) - (\Sigma xi) * (\Sigma yi)}{\sqrt{(n\,\Sigma xi^2 - (\Sigma xi)^2)\,(n\,\Sigma yi^2 - (\Sigma yi)^2)}}$$

Develop an algorithm and a program to read two equally-sized sets of numbers and compute the correlation coefficient for the 2 sets. Remember that we have not yet learned how to store all members of a set of numbers. To avoid reading the input data more than once, compute all values that are needed for summing immediately as X-values and Y-values are read in X/Y pairs.

Chapter 4
Arrays

Previous chapters focused on problem solving and led you to organize solutions to problems and write some short but meaningful FORTRAN programs. As tools, we have selection structures and one form of loop control using the GO TO statement. Now we turn our attention to specifying input values, focusing on the structured data type called an *array* or *subscripted variable.*

Using Collections of Values

Each value stored in computer memory must be named in some way in order to be used in a FORTRAN program. We have so far been giving each value a unique name, but in processing a collection of functionally related values—sometimes a large collection—we cannot always do so. For example, a surveyor may be dealing with slope data from 200 gradient test sites, or a traffic engineer may be analyzing the flow patterns of 10,000 automobiles. In such situations we must be able to refer to values without having to create a unique name for each value in the collection. From mathematics, we borrow two very useful concepts, the *vector* and the *matrix.*

The mathematical vector. Mathematicians long ago developed a method for keeping track of a collection of data by using *subscript* notation to create what is called a *vector.* For example, if the surveyor wishes to refer to those 200 slopes by using the subscript notation, she can write

EXAMPLE 1 $S_1, S_2, S_3, \ldots, S_{200}$

where the group name S refers to all slopes, and subscripts 1 to 200 denote data for the specific sites.

Similarly, the automobile locations can be referred to as

EXAMPLE 2 $L_1, L_2, L_3, \ldots, L_{10,000}$

where L is the group name for auto location data and the subscript identifies the datum for a specific vehicle.

The number of elements—200 in the surveyor's case—in the vector is called the *size* of the vector.

The mathematical matrix. Another way to structure a large collection of related data is to arrange the data in a *matrix* of rows and columns. In this case, the relationships among the data are expressed by their row and column positions in the matrix.

EXAMPLE

For example, consider some data associated with the ten employees of a firm. In particular, suppose we have arranged these data in some order, here beginning in row 1 with the data for the employee with the most seniority and moving to row 10 with the data for the employee with the least. Then we arrange the hours worked by each person in columns for the days of the week. Here's the resulting matrix:

8	10	8	7	8	4	0
8	9	8	8	8	2	0
8	8	8	8	8	2	1
8	7	8	8	8	1	1
8	8	8	8	8	0	0
8	8	8	8	7	0	1
6	8	8	6	7	0	0
8	5	8	8	6	0	0
7	8	8	8	7	0	0
8	6	6	8	6	0	0

There are ten rows and seven columns. Each row corresponds to an employee and each column corresponds to a day of the week—let's begin with Monday. Thus, the number of hours worked on Tuesday by the employee with the most seniority is 10.

It is convenient to think of this set of data as one collection and assign it the name HOURS.

Each member of the set HOURS is uniquely identified by the row and column in which it appears. Therefore, the number of hours worked on Tuesday by the first employee can be denoted as $\text{HOURS}_{1,2}$ where the first subscript indicates the row (employee) and the second subscript the column (day). Here, $\text{HOURS}_{1,2} = 10$.

The matrix itself is the collection of objects, usually numbers, in rows and columns and sometimes in layers. Each datum is specified by the name of the set (HOURS) with subscripts specifying row and column. If layers of rows and columns are needed, as when including data for several companies in the matrix HOURS, a third subscript denotes the layer, in this case the company. The specification for our sample worker in company 3 is then $\text{HOURS}_{1,2,3}$. Although it is possible to imagine situations where it might be useful to have more than three subscripts, we will not use more than three in this book. When there are three they are commonly called the *row*, *column*, and *layer* subscripts.

The matrix of ten rows and seven columns in our example is called a 10-by-7 matrix, also denoted 10x7. So a matrix of *m* rows and *n* columns is called an $m \times n$ matrix. If there are P layers, the matrix is called an $m \times n \times p$ matrix. An element in matrix M, say the element in row i and column j of layer k, is denoted by $M_{i,j,k}$.

The FORTRAN array. In FORTRAN we refer to vectors and matrices (the plural of matrix) as *arrays*, and classify them as one-, two-, or three-*dimensional* arrays. Sometimes they are referred to as single-, double-, or triple-*subscripted* arrays. A one-dimensional array is simply a row of data, a two-dimensional array includes both rows and columns, and a three-dimensional array includes layers as well. Any array of more than one dimension is termed a *multidimensional* array.

Subscripts in FORTRAN. Arrays are constructed and used just as in mathematics. But standard computer programs, microcomputers and computer terminals have no provision for entering a number or letter dropped halfway below the text line, so we cannot use subscripts as is done in mathematics. So in FORTRAN, subscripts are kept in the normal line, enclosed in parentheses. Items are still separated by commas.

The subscripted mathematical variable T_5 is thus denoted T(5) in FORTRAN, and $HOURS_{1,2,3}$ is denoted HOURS(1,2,3). Notice that the vector or matrix names (T and HOURS) are kept, with the subscripts enclosed in parentheses rather than appearing below the name.

Declaring an Array

In order to be able to use a subscripted variable in FORTRAN—as is the case with any variable—one must name it and declare its type. Recall that FORTRAN allows a name to have a maximum length of six characters and to use only letters and digits—and the first character must be a letter. We have learned about using the INTEGER, REAL, LOGICAL, COMPLEX and CHARACTER type declaration statements, in which any named variable identifies a single storage location. Now arrays, with their collections of functionally related values, may also be declared using one of the type declaration statements, or a special declaration statement, the DIMENSION statement.

The DIMENSION statement. The DIMENSION statement allows the programmer to set aside a series of memory locations for related data using just one name. Subscripts are used to denote each unique location. It has the general form

```
DIMENSION VAR1(N), VAR2(M,N), VAR3(M,N,P)
```

where VAR1, VAR2, and VAR3 are any acceptable FORTRAN variable names and
M, N, and P represent any unsigned integer ***constants*** within the limitations of the given computer memory.

With a DIMENSION statement used to declare an array, a data type statement must also be included to declare the data type; otherwise, the default data type declaration prevails, based on the first letter of the variable name.

In order to understand how the DIMENSION statement is used, let's look at a situation in which arrays become increasingly useful.

Problem 4.1A
Storing State Populations

OBJECTIVE As part of a population survey, you want to store the census counts for each of the 50 United States.

SOLUTION Use a subscripted variable with the array name STATE. The DIMENSION statement would then be

```
INTEGER STATE
DIMENSION STATE(50)
```

This statement sets aside 50 adjacent computer words all having the name STATE, each uniquely identified by an appropriate subscript.

When a DIMENSION statement is used to declare an array, a data type statement like INTEGER must also be included; otherwise the default data type is declared based on the first letter of the variable name.

Thus, if array STATE contains the populations of the states in alphabetic order, then

`STATE(1)`	*Stores the populaion of Alabama*
`STATE(2)`	*Stores the population of Alaska*
.	
.	
.	
`STATE(50)`	*Stores the population of Wyoming*

The DIMENSION statement does not actually cause anything to be stored, it only sets aside the adjacent memory locations. Other statements are required to actually store numbers in these locations.

Using type declaration statements. In the problem above, the INTEGER statement is included along with the DIMENSION statement. An alternative would be to simply use the INTEGER statement alone instead of combining it with the DIMENSION statement to declare the array STATE. In this problem, you want STATE to be an integer variable and an array of 50 locations. The single statement to accomplish this is

```
INTEGER STATE(50)
```

There is no need to use a DIMENSION statement to declare the array. The INTEGER statement—or the CHARACTER, REAL, or other type declaration statements—can perform both functions.

Problem 4.1B
Dividing the Populations by Sex

OBJECTIVE Now you want to store the population for each state divided by sex.

SOLUTION The most obvious way is to set up two arrays, in which the first stores the female populations and the second the male populations, with the statement

```
INTEGER FSTATE(50), MSTATE(50)
```

This statement sets aside 50 adjacent memory locations under the array name FSTATE and 50 more under the array name MSTATE.

Note again that the INTEGER statement does not place information into the arrays, nor does it specify the order in which the information is stored; it simply sets aside and names the locations. An associated READ statement will place the data in the order desired.

ALTERNATE SOLUTION Another method for storing this data is to use a two-dimensional array and call it BISTAT. The following statement reserves and names the appropriate memory locations:

```
INTEGER BISTAT(50,2)
```

This statement sets aside 100 adjacent memory locations under the array name BISTAT as one array of 50 rows and 2 columns. BISTAT(1,1) now stores the female population of Alabama, BISTAT(1,2) stores the male population of Alabama, and so on.

Problem 4.1C
Keeping Records by Age and Sex

OBJECTIVE You would now find it useful to divide the population figures again, this time into four age ranges, preschool, school age (to 24), adult (to 55), and mature.

SOLUTION A The most obvious solution is to set up four arrays for each sex, using the statements

```
INTEGER FSTATP(50), FSTATS(50), FSTATA(50), FSTATM(50)
INTEGER MSTATP(50), MSTATS(50), MSTATA(50), MSTATM(50)
```

The 4 arrays beginning with F store the populations for the 4 age ranges of women, and the 4 arrays beginning with M store the populations for the 4 age ranges of men.

This solution takes 400 computer words, organized in 8 different arrays, to include the appropriate categories and subcategories of population.

SOLUTION B Another solution, building on the two-dimensional array presented in 4.1B, is to set up four 2-dimensional arrays, one for each of the ages:

```
INTEGER PSTATE(50,2), SSTATE(50,2), ASTATE(50,2), MSTATE(50,2)
```

The variable names refer here to the ages, the first subscript to the state, and the second subscript to the sexes.

This solution also takes 400 computer words. The advantage of using four 2-dimensional arrays instead of eight 1-dimensional arrays lies mostly in the greater ease of program access: There's one fewer set of array names to access in manipulating the information. You'll see how this works as we move on.

SOLUTION C The most compact way to assemble this data is in one 3-dimensional array, with one dimension for each aspect of the population we want to track. The statement is

```
INTEGER STPOP(50,4,2)
```

The variable name STPOP refers to the population data as a whole, while the subscripts refer to the subdivisions, the first by the 50 states, the second by the 4 age ranges, and the third by the 2 sexes.

The population of school age women in Alabama is to be stored in STPOP(1,2,1), while that of male adults in Alabama is STPOP(1,3,2) and female adults STPOP(1,3,1).

Evaluating alternatives. All three of these solutions take 400 computer words. All three organize the data in ways acceptable to FORTRAN. But there are differences; each of the organizations is useful in circumstances that depend on the structure of the program as a whole and the uses to which the data in the arrays are put. Which array works best in which circumstance is an understanding that comes with experience.

We'll now look at a more complex progression of arrays using various data types. These advanced problems help us increase an understanding of the practical uses of arrays in various engineering situations; however, it is not necessary to understand the physics of the problems in order to see how FORTRAN provides flexible array options to meet varying circumstances.

Problem 4.2A
Identifying Atomic Nuclei

SITUATION Your firm is developing a very large supercomputer program to be used in simulating the operation of a nuclear reactor. Several processes within the reactor—fission, neutron capture, and the emission of alpha and beta particles and positrons—cause the transmutation of a nucleus of one element into one or more nuclei of another element.

OBJECTIVE You have been assigned to write the module that identifies a new nucleus from the atomic number for that nucleus calculated by another part of the program. Your module takes as input the atomic number and is to output the correct abbreviation from the periodic table of elements.

ANALYSIS One way to accomplish the result would be to write a series of ELSEIF statements—but it would take more than 100 to cover all the possibilities! If we look at the periodic table as a one-dimensional array, with each atomic number defining a row, we can define a subscripted variable to store all the abbreviations and access them using the atomic number.

SOLUTION If we name the array ELEMNT, the CHARACTER statement declares the data type of each element and the size and vector or matrix structure of the array.

```
CHARACTER ELEMNT(110)*2
```

This statement sets aside 110 adjacent computer words to identify the 110 chemical elements in the periodic table. Each location will store a two-character datum. All of these locations have the same name, ELEMNT, but each is uniquely identified by the appropriate subscript, an atomic number from 1 to 110. Thus,

```
ELEMNT(1)      stores H for hydrogen, atomic number 1
ELEMNT(2)      stores He for helium, atomic number 2
.
.
.
ELEMNT(110)    stores Fm for fermium, atomic number 110
```

The statement only sets aside adjacent memory locations—it does not cause any data to be stored. Other statements are required in order to actually store the abbreviations in these memory locations.

Problem 4.2B
Forecasting Probable Changes

SITUATION In the first round of developing the reactor model, we ignored the possibility of newly formed nuclei absorbing neutrons and transmuting again. Most of the new nuclei have short halflives, so it is not very probable that a nucleus is hit twice by stray neutrons before it transmutes into another element through normal alpha or beta decay.

But now we are refining the model, and this less likely occurence needs to be taken into account. The probability of any nucleus absorbing a second neutron is related to a computed number called the *cross section of nuclear absorption* for each element, as well as its halflife.

OBJECTIVE Write a module so that the program can look up the transmuted element's cross section for nuclear absorption at the same time that it identifies its halflife. Other modules will account for the influences of neutron flux and distribution in the reactor space.

SOLUTION We now construct two one-dimensional arrays, each with a row for each element. Two statements establish these arrays:

```
REAL HLFLIF(110)
REAL XSECTN(110)
```

This time 110 adjacent memory locations are set aside to store halflife figures under the array named HLFLIF and 110 more to store cross section values under the array name XSECTN. Both are in rows according to atomic number.

Here again the REAL statements do nothing with the contents of the memory locations they establish. They simply set aside the number of computer words specified inside the parentheses of each array name and allow for the program to use those words by calling them with the array name and its subscripts.

Neither the contents nor the order of storing information in these arrays is determined here. Storing order is determined by the order in which data are entered in conjunction with the READ statement that causes input to the arrays.

ALTERNATE SOLUTION Since all data here are of type real and in the same 110 rows, we can combine the information in one 2-dimensional array ELDATA. The data type and array declaration are simple:

```
REAL ELDATA(110,2)
```

Sets aside 220 adjacent memory locations under the name ELDATA, providing space for 110 rows and 2 columns of items, each location having the name ELDATA and being uniquely specified by a combination of two subscripts.

Here, ELDATA(1,1) is available to store the halflife for hydrogen, the same as HLFLIF(1) above, while ELDATA(1,2) can be used to store hydrogen's cross section for nuclear absorption.

Problem 4.2C Considering Isotopes

SITUATION Further refinement of the reactor model requires identifying isotopes of elements, since their different halflives and cross sections lead to different probabilities of changes due to chemical interactions and atomic decay.

OBJECTIVE You have been asked to expand your module to return for a given atomic mass, calculated by another part of the program, these sets of data:

1. The abbreviation of the name of the element from the periodic table. There are, of course, 110 elements.
2. Identification of the isotope along with the appropriate neutron absorption cross section and the halflife in seconds. There are fewer than 700 isotopes, between 2 and 6 for each element in the periodic table.
3. Certification of which valence numbers, from one to three per isotope, are possible. Valence numbers range from –7 to +7.

SOLUTIONS We show here two alternate methods for storing this data. Each method has times when it would be preferred over the others, but none is clearly correct or incorrect. As you gain programming experience, be alert to choosing the method that makes writing your particular program as easy as possible.

FORM A One way to accomplish the task is by using a set of one- and two-dimensional arrays:

```
CHARACTER ELEMNT(110)*2
INTEGER VALNCE (110,15)
REAL ISODAT(700,3)
```

The first line sets aside locations to store the abbreviation of the periodic element name in rows corresponding to the atomic numbers of the elements.

The second line creates a matrix in which each row contains 15 columns corresponding to the 15 possible valences (–7 to +7 including 0). The integer 1 in a given column indicates that that particular valence is possible for an element, whereas 0 indicates that it is not. The rows correspond to the atomic numbers of the elements, columns to the valence numbers, –7, –6, . . . , 0, 1, . . . , 7.

The third line reserves space to store atomic numbers for all the isotopes, along with neutron absorption cross section and halflife. Rows correspond to the atomic mass. This matrix not only accesses information on the isotopes, but acts as an index to the atomic numbers for the first two matrices.

In this set of arrays, data are stored with like data for quick access. A given atomic mass will produce immediately the cross section and halflife figures from ISODAT. The atomic number can then be used to retrieve the abbreviation from ELEMNT and the valence information from VALNCE. No computations are necessary; this method uses 3970 data locations.

FORM B Here, we combine the isotope data with the periodic data in a three-dimensional array and valence data with ELEMNT in a two-dimensional array.

```
REAL ATMINF(110,3,7)
CHARACTER ELEVAL(110,4)*2
```

The first statement creates a matrix with rows corresponding to atomic numbers; columns for storing mass, cross section, and halflife; layers for isotope numbers from –3, the lightest, to +3, the heaviest. Mass 0 indicates an isotope number doesn't exist; there are in that case 0 entries in the other columns as well.

The second statement creates a two-dimensional array combining valence states from –7 to +7 with the element abbreviation. Where fewer than 3 valence states exist, the third or second and third repeat the last valid number. Note that valence numbers are stored as characters not as numeric values.

This method uses 3190 data locations, but requires a complex computation to derive atomic number from atomic mass, to assign an isotope number, and to interpret the valence data. The advantage here is that the columns and layers of one row of ATMINF and the corresponding row of ELEVAL contain all relevant information about one periodic element. Solutions like this are useful when storage space is at a premium and the module is not often used, so that computation time is not an important factor.

PROGRAM DESIGN ISSUES

Frequently it is useful to develop a common relationship table, or *relation,* for use by many different programs, including some that are not yet anticipated. Such a relation allows one unique identifier to be used to look up other relevant data, as here with nuclear data, or for the wheel base of all cars of a given make and model, or types of fire extinguishers and nonconducting ingredients. The relation develops over time and may be accessed as needed. For such a program, you might consider these design issues:

Can data be stored in a standard order? If the data are in ascending or descending order, search routines in other programs will be able to use that fact.

How often does the data need to change? This determines what facilities you need for updates. Also, are any security precautions needed for changes, updates, or deletes?

What happens if someone tries to put invalid data into the array? What should happen?

Choosing an array declaration. As we see from these problems, there are several steps to consider in using an array. One must name the array, define the subscripts, set aside the memory locations, define the data type, and eventually assign data to the memory locations. We do not deal here with assigning data, but show two main methods to accomplish the other tasks: First, a DIMENSION statement declares the array, including naming and subscripting, and a type declaration statement defines the data type. Second, a type declaration statement simply declares the array with its name, subscripts, and data type.

- *We recommend that you include the subscripts that specify the array in its data type declaration statement.*

Using a separate DIMENSION statement to declare the array is not incorrect, but it adds a line of code without contributing to the clarity or functionality of the program.

However you declare the array, be sure that the array specification—the subscripts in parentheses—go in *either* the data type statement *or* the DIMENSION statement, but not in both.

Here are some further examples of array declarations using type declaration statements.

EXAMPLE 1
```
LOGICAL FLAG(80)
```

Defines FLAG as a logical array of size 80.

EXAMPLE 2
```
REAL INDEX(20,3),WAGE(20)
```

Defines INDEX as a two-dimensional array of size 20x3 and WAGE as a one-dimensional array of size 20.

EXAMPLE 3
```
CHARACTER NAME(12),CAPTAL(50)*12
```

Defines NAME as a character array of size 12 where each member of the array can store only one character and CAPTAL as a character array of size 50 where each member of the array can store up to twelve characters.

Full set FORTRAN 77 arrays. What we have so far presented about using arrays is valid for many versions of FORTRAN, including the standard subset of FORTRAN 77. In addition, relative to the issues we have raised, the full set of FORTRAN 77 has some special capabilities that may prove useful.

There are two alternative general statements in full set FORTRAN 77 to declare a one-dimensional array. They are similar to the forms we have used already:

FORM A
```
DIMENSION VAR1(N1:N2), . . . ,VARN(P1:P2)
```

FORM B
```
Type VAR1(N1:N2), . . . ,VARN(P1:P2)
```

where Type is one of the declaration types INTEGER, REAL, CHARACTER, LOGICAL, and so on;
VAR1, . . . ,VARN are any acceptable FORTRAN variable names; and
N1, N2, P1, and P2 are negative, zero, or positive integers such that N1 < N2 and P1 < P2 and each pair of integers defines the range of integer values for the subscript.

Notice that this form allows us to specify not only the number of subscripts in each array, but also the integer range of those subscripts by using the colon notation. Here are some examples declaring one-dimensional arrays:

EXAMPLE 1

```
DIMENSION ACCT(5:10), PRICE(1989:1992)
```

Declares ACCT as a one-dimensional array of the six elements ACCT(5), ACCT(6), ACCT(7), ACCT(8), ACCT(9), and ACCT(10).

It also declares the one-dimensional array PRICE of which there are 4 members: PRICE(1989), PRICE(1990), PRICE(1991), and PRICE(1992).

EXAMPLE 2

```
INTEGER DEMAND(1:10), AGE(-5:0)
```

Declares both DEMAND and AGE as one-dimensional integer arrays where DEMAND has ten members with subscripts 1, 2, 3, . . . , 10 and AGE has six members with subscripts –5, –4, –3, –2, –1, and 0.

EXAMPLE 3

```
REAL NUM(-5:5)
```

Defines the real array NUM with eleven members with subscripts –5, –4, . . . , 0, 1, 2, . . . , 5.

EXAMPLE 4

```
LOGICAL SWITCH(0:5),FLAG(-1:1)
```

Declares SWITCH and FLAG as one-dimensional arrays of type LOGICAL. SWITCH has six members with subscripts from 0 to 5, and FLAG has three members with subscripts –1, 0 and 1.

Multidimensional arrays. In the full set of FORTRAN 77 one may specify up to seven subscripts for a given application, giving the capability of specifying up to seven-dimensional arrays. The general forms for declaring such multidimensional arrays are

FORM A

```
DIMENSION VAR1(ML:NL, . . . ,MK:NK), . . . ,VARN(IL:JL, . . . ,IP:JP)
```

FORM B

```
Type VAR1(ML:NL, . . . ,MK:NK), . . . ,VARN(IL:JL, . . . ,IP:JP)
```

with K ≤ 7 and P ≤ 7,
where VAR1, . . . ,VARN are any valid FORTRAN variable names;
ML, NL, . . . , MK, NK are negative, zero, or positive integers such that MK ≤ NK;
and similarly IL ≤ JL, . . . , IP ≤ JP.
In the case of the integers ML, NL, . . . , MK, NK, IL, JL, . . . , IP, JP, each pair defines the range of integer values allowed for the subscripts of the given array.

Here are some specific examples:

EXAMPLE 1

```
DIMENSION YEARP(1989:1993, 1:6), MONTH(1:12)
```

Declares YEARP a two-dimensional array whose row-subscript may range from 1989 to 1993 and whose column-subscript may range from 1 to 6. This array could be used, for example, to store the prices of six different items for the years 1989, 1990, 1991, 1992, and 1993.

Also declared is the one-dimensional array MONTH with twelve members whose subscripts may range from 1 to 12.

EXAMPLE 2

```
INTEGER POPUL(1:50, 1:4, 0:1, 1980:1989)
```

Declares POPUL to be a four-dimensional integer array whose first subscript ranges from 1 to 50, its second subscript from 1 to 4, the third from 0 to 1, and the fourth subscript ranges from 1980 to 1989.

Array POPUL could be used to store population data for the fifty United States, for each of four age ranges, for male and female, and for each of the ten years 1980 through 1989.

EXAMPLE 3

```
CHARACTER NAME(1:100, 0:1)*20
```

Declares NAME to be a character array having two subscripts, the first ranging from 1 to 100 and the second from 0 to 1, thus giving the array 200 members, each of them able to store up to 20 characters.

This array could be used to store the names, in 20 or fewer letters, of 100 airline pilots and 100 navigators, where the second subscript designates position.

EXAMPLE 4

```
REAL SUPPLY(1980:1984, 10:19, -1:1), PRICE(1980:1984, 10:19)
```

Declares two real arrays, SUPPLY and PRICE.

SUPPLY is a three-dimensional array that could, for example, store the quantities of inventory items numbered 10–19 for the years 1980–1984 that fell in each of three categories: Overstock with a third subscript -1, items shipped when stocked with third subscript 0, or backordered items with third subscript 1.

PRICE is a two-dimensional array that could store the prices of the 20 items for each of the same years.

Rules for Using Arrays

We can now state eight basic rules for using arrays and present examples of how they work.

1. A variable may be defined as an array by either a DIMENSION statement or a type declaration statement.
2. A single DIMENSION or type declaration statement may declare more than one variable.
3. More than one DIMENSION or type declaration statements may appear in any one program.
4. A single variable can be defined as an array only once in any one program.
5. A subscripted variable must be defined in a DIMENSION or type declaration statement before it is used in any other program statement.

6. DIMENSION and type declaration statements must appear at the beginning of the program before any executable statements but after the PROGRAM statement.

7. Once a variable has been defined as an array, it should be used with the defined number of subscripts (later we discuss exceptions in which it appears without subscripts).

8. In the full set of FORTRAN 77, the DIMENSION or type declaration statement may specify not only the number of subscripts but also the allowable integer ranges.

Let's now consider some applications of the preceding rules as related to a sample DIMENSION statement. This statement holds throughout all of the examples that follow:

STATEMENT

```
DIMENSION A(20), B(3,6), C(-5:0,0:3,20:22)
```

EXAMPLES

`A(15)`	*Valid.*
`A(NAME)`	*Valid provided NAME is an integer variable less than or equal to 20 and greater than 0.*
`A(I=J*K)`	*Invalid; assignment is not permitted in subscripts.*
`A(J*K)`	*Valid provided* $J*K \geq 1$ *and* $J*K \leq 20$.
`A(30)`	*Invalid;* $30 > 20$.
`A(K+I*J)`	*Valid provided* $K+I*J \geq 1$ *and* $K+I*J \leq 20$.
`B(0,1)`	*Invalid; 0 subscripts are not allowed.*
`B(6,2)`	*Invalid; the first subscript exceeds 3.*
`B(3*I)`	*Invalid; only 1 subscript is used, but 2 were specified.*
`B(I,J)`	*Valid provided* $I \geq 1$ *and* $I \leq 3$ *and* $J \geq 1$ *and* $J \leq 6$.
`B(2,I*J)`	*Valid if I*J is between 1 and 6, inclusive.*
`B(2+K*J,K-I*J)`	*Valid provided 2+K*J is between 1 and 3 inclusive, and K–I*J between 1 and 6 inclusive.*
`B(I-2,3*I)`	*Invalid. If* $I = 2$, *first subscript is 0, not in the range. If* $I < 2$, *first subscript is negative, and invalid. If* $I > 2$, *second subscript* > 6, *not in the range.*
`C(1,1,20)`	*Invalid; the first subscript is not in the range −5 to 0.*
`C(I,J,I+J)`	*Invalid; there are no integers for I and J such that I is in the range −5 to 0, J in the range 0 to 3, and I+J in the range 20 to 22.*
`C(-2,0,20)`	*Valid.*
`C(I,J,K)`	*Valid provided I, J, and K all fall within range.*
`C(-2,20)`	*Invalid; only 2 subscripts appear, 3 were specified.*

Array Input and Output

So far in our discussion of input and output variables used with READ, PRINT, and WRITE statements we have included only simple variables. Now that we have created multidimensional variables, we need to include them in both input and output statements. It's surprisingly easy: Whenever a single element of an array is to be input or output, it is handled in the same way as a simple variable except that subscripts identify the element. Consider these examples:

EXAMPLE 1

```
READ*,A(11)
```

Reads one value and stores it in A(11).

EXAMPLE 2

```
READ*,B(2,3)
```

Reads one value and stores it in B(2,3).

EXAMPLE 3

```
READ*,VALUE(K,J)
```

Reads one value and stores it in memory location VALUE(K,J), where K and J are previously defined within the boundary values specified in the statement that defines VALUE as an array.

EXAMPLE 4

```
PRINT*,A(3)
```

Causes the printing of the contents of A(3).

EXAMPLE 5

```
WRITE(6,*)A(11),B(2,J)
```

Causes the printing of the contents of A(11) and B(2,J), where J is previously defined as an integer within the boundary values specified in the statement that defines B as an array.

These examples all store or print one value into or from an array. Sometimes it is desirable to input or output an entire array. In such a case the array name without subscripts appears in the input or output statement. Consider the following program:

EXAMPLE 6

```
      PROGRAM TABLES
      INTEGER TABLE(10),I
      READ*,TABLE
      I=1
 10   IF (I .GT. 10) GO TO 20
          IF (TABLE(I) .LT. 0) TABLE(I)=0
          I=I+1
          GO TO 10
 20   PRINT*,TABLE
      END
```

The READ statement causes the input of 10 numbers and stores them in TABLE(1), TABLE(2), . . . , TABLE(10).

The next five lines result in any negative members of array TABLE being set to 0.

The PRINT statement causes all 10 members of the integer array TABLE to be printed, including those set to 0.

- *In what order does the computer store data when only the array name is given?*

Where array TABLE is single-subscripted, the answer is easy. The numbers are stored sequentially in TABLE(1), TABLE(2), . . . , TABLE(10).

- *What happens when an array has two subscripts?*

Two likely methods come to mind—let's first consider an example:

EXAMPLE 7

Suppose array A is defined with two subscripts:

```
INTEGER A(3,4)      or      INTEGER A(1:3,1:4)
```

Suppose also that the statement

```
READ*,A
```

appears and that the numbers 1, 3, 5, 7, 9, 11, 13, 15, 17, 19, 21, and 23 are provided in that order.

ROW-MAJOR ORDER

From the fact that the INTEGER statement specifies 3 rows and 4 columns, one possible order for storing the numbers assumes that they are entered by row with 4 elements per row. The numbers are stored like this:

```
Row 1        A(1,1)=1
             A(1,2)=3
             A(1,3)=5
             A(1,4)=7
Row 2        A(2,1)=9
             A(2,2)=11
             A(2,3)=13
             A(2,4)=15
Row 3        A(3,1)=17
             A(3,2)=19
             A(3,3)=21
             A(3,4)=23
```

COLUMN-MAJOR ORDER

Another possible order for storing the numbers assumes that they are entered by column, with three elements per column. Now, the numbers look like this:

```
Column 1     A(1,1)=1
             A(2,1)=3
             A(3,1)=5
Column 2     A(1,2)=7
             A(2,2)=9
             A(3,2)=11
Column 3     A(1,3)=13
             A(2,3)=15
             A(3,3)=17
```

```
Column 4     A(1,4)=19
             A(2,4)=21
             A(3,4)=23
```

Mathematicians refer to these two orderings of the elements of an array as *row-major* and *column-major*. Computer scientists use the same terminology.

- *FORTRAN uses column-major ordering.*

FORTRAN INPUT

Given the program segment

```
INTEGER A(3,4)
READ*,A
```

and the input values 1, 3, 5, 7, 9, 11, 13, 15, 17, 19, 21, and 23, the values in array A are

```
A(1,1)=1
A(2,1)=3
A(3,1)=5
A(1,2)=7
A(2,2)=9
A(3,2)=11
A(1,3)=13
A(2,3)=15
A(3,3)=17
A(1,4)=19
A(2,4)=21
A(3,4)=23
```

FORTRAN OUTPUT

FORTRAN also uses column-major ordering in output. Thus, if we assume that A is the same 3x4 array, the statement

```
PRINT*,A
```

results in the elements of array A being printed in the following order:

```
A(1,1),A(2,1),A(3,1),A(1,2),A(2,2),A(3,2),A(1,3),A(2,3),A(3,3),A(1,4),A(2,4),A(3,4)
```

When three-dimensional arrays are used there is again the question of how FORTRAN orders the elements. We illustrate the FORTRAN method with the following example:

EXAMPLE

```
INTEGER A(2,3,2)      or      INTEGER A(1:2,1:3,1:2)
READ*,A
```

Segment array A is of size 12 and, therefore, the READ statement requires 12 numbers to fill it. Suppose that the input data provided are 1, 2, 3, 4, 5, 6, 7, 8, 9, 10, 11, and 12. The program segment would result in storage as follows:

```
A(1,1,1) = 1
A(2,1,1) = 2
A(1,2,1) = 3
A(2,2,1) = 4
```

```
A(1,3,1) = 5
A(2,3,1) = 6
A(1,1,2) = 7
A(2,1,2) = 8
A(1,2,2) = 9
A(2,2,2) = 10
A(1,3,2) = 11
A(2,3,2) = 12
```

It is also possible to specify the order in which we want data to be stored in an array by explicitly giving the subscripts, as here:

EXAMPLE

```
      PROGRAM ARRAY
      INTEGER A(10), B(2,5), I, J
      I = 1
10    IF (I .GT. 10) GO TO 20
         READ *, A(I)
         I = I+2
      GO TO 10
20    J = 1
30    IF (J .GT. 5) GO TO 40
         READ *, B(1, J)
         J = J+1
      GO TO 30
40    J = 1
60    IF (J .GT. 5) GO TO 50
         READ *, B(2, J)
         J = J+2
      GO TO 60
50    STOP
      END
```

This program reads 5 integers into array A at locations A(1), A(3), A(5), A(7), and A(9).

Then it reads 5 integers into array B storing them at locations B(1, 1), B(1, 2), B(1, 3), B(1, 4), and B(1, 5).

Following that, 3 more integers are read and stored at locations B(2, 1), B(2, 3), and B(2, 5).

Locations B(2, 2) and B(2, 4) have no values stored by this program, nor do locations A(2), A(4), A(6) and A(8).

More will be said about array processing in the next chapter.

Initializing an Array

For simple variables, we use one assignment statement for each variable. With arrays, each of which may contain numerous elements with one name, this method is too cumbersome. Here's an example of the statement to initialize the simple variables A and C:

SIMPLE EXAMPLE

```
INTEGER A
CHARACTER C*3
A = 0
C = 'CAT'
```

In the case of an array, one method to initialize two or more elements with the same array name is first to decide how we want to set the variables, then write a program that initializes them for us to those values. For example:

EXAMPLE

Consider these declarations:

```
INTEGER A(100), I
CHARACTER C(100)*3
```

Now suppose we want to initialize all members of array A to zeros and all members of array C to blank spaces. This may be done with the following program segment:

```
      I = 1
 2    IF (I .GT. 100) GO TO 5
          A(I) = 0
          C(I) = '   '
      GO TO 2
 5    (Rest of program)
```

The DATA statement. An even easier method to initialize arrays uses the DATA statement. Its general form is as follows:

```
DATA VAR1,VAR2, . . . ,VARN/Data-list/
```

where VAR1,VAR2, . . . ,VARN represent any set of acceptable FORTRAN variable names—including arrays, and
/Data-list/ represents one value for each variable to be stored in the specified variables.

The data in the list are separated by commas and the entire data list is enclosed within a pair of slashes. If a given datum is to be used more than once, enter first the number of times the datum is to be used, insert an asterisk, and then put the datum.

The variable list and data list must match each other item for item in both number and data type. Mismatches in either of these situations causes some FORTRAN compilers to produce a warning. If there are more data items than variables, the message is something like

```
DATA CONSTANT LIST TOO LONG
```

This type of mismatch may not cause a problem, but since it should not normally occur, the programmer is reminded of the possibility that incorrect data constants have been provided.

If there are more variables than data items, the warning is something like

```
DATA VARIABLE LIST TOO LONG
```

Although this type of mismatch does not cause a fatal error in compiling the program, it does result in the excess variables being uninitialized. Note that in this case some FORTRAN compilers automatically initialize every numeric variable to 0 and every character variable to blanks.

In the following DATA statements, assume variables and data values have matching data types.

EXAMPLE 1

```
DATA A,B/20,10/
```

A is assigned the value 20 and B the value 10.

EXAMPLE 2

```
DATA A,B,C/15,2*1.0/
```

A is assigned the value 15 and both B and C are assigned the value 1.0. Note the use of the asterisk to indicate repetition of a value, where the number of repetitions is indicated by the integer left of the asterisk.

EXAMPLE 3

```
DATA X,Y,Z/'XY','XYZ','XY/YZ'/
```

X is assigned the character 'XY', Y is assigned the character string 'XYZ', and Z is assigned the character string 'XY/YZ'.

EXAMPLE 4

```
DATA A/20/,B,C/'AB',25.6/
```

A is assigned the value 20, B is assigned the string AB, and C is assigned the value 25.6.

EXAMPLE 5

```
DATA A,B,C,D/4*0,3/
```

All four of the variables A, B, C, and D are assigned the value 0 and the remaining data item, 3, is left unassigned. This situation would produce a warning message telling about the discrepancy between the variable list and the data list but would not result in a fatal error.

EXAMPLE 6

```
REAL A(1:100),B(0:9,-10:9)
DATA A,B/100*1,200*0/
```

A is a one-dimensional array of size 100 and B is a two-dimensional array of size 200 (10 rows x 20 columns). When the variable names appear in the DATA statement without subscripts, as here, all locations of the arrays are to be assigned the given values. Therefore, all 100 locations of array A are assigned the value 1.0 and all 200 locations of array B are assigned the value 0.

EXAMPLE 7

```
INTEGER A(20,10),B(5)
DATA B,A(10,10)/1,2,3,4,0,1/
```

Here A and B appear in an INTEGER statement with subscripts. A is defined as an integer array of 20 rows and 10 columns for a total of 200 memory locations.

Similarly, B is an integer array of 5 locations.

In the DATA statement, since B appears without subscripts, all 5 of its memory locations are individually assigned values: B(1)=1, B(2)=2, B(3)=3, B(4)=4, and B(5)=0. Then one of the elements of array A, A(10,10), is assigned the value 1.

The DATA statement is a nonexecutable statement in FORTRAN, although it does result in the assignment of values to specified variables. As is the case with all nonexecutable statements except FORMAT statements:

- *DATA statements must precede all executable statements in the program or subprogram.*

Using Arrays to Solve Problems

Let's now look at some problems that combine what we've learned of arrays to address complex problems by processing collections of related data.

Problem 4.3 Handling a Relation with an Array

SITUATION Utility companies and other very large users purchase new electric cable by the foot and sell used and scrap cable to salvage companies by the pound. The weight-length ratio depends on the type of cable. Types of cable are named by gauge numbers, alphanumeric names, or letter codes. In order to correctly calculate depreciation, your company needs to calculate the salvage value of every cable purchase.

OBJECTIVE Write a program to relate the cable type names to the corresponding weight-length ratios and store them in an array, making the constructed array available for depreciation calculations.

The general problem is one of handling a *relation*, the set of weights and lengths in the weight-length ratios, by means of an array. So we will solve the problem by developing an algorithm and a program to read information about any relation and store that information in an array.

ANALYSIS Given two finite sets A and B, the cross product A x B of the two sets is the set of all possible pairs such that one member of each pair comes from each of the two sets.

If A is the set [*a*, *b*, *c*]

And B is the set [1, 2, 3, 4]

Then A x B = { $(a, 1), (a, 2), (a, 3), (a, 4), (b, 1), (b, 2), (b, 3), (b, 4), (c, 1), (c, 2), (c, 3), (c, 4)$ }.

A relation R between elements of the two sets consists of the following:

a is related to 1,
b is related to 2, and
c is related to 3.

So, symbolically,

R = { $(a, 1), (b, 2), (c, 3)$ }.

and it is easy to see that R is a subset of A x B.

Now suppose set A has *m* elements and set B has *n* elements. We use an *m* x *n* array to represent the relation R.

Let's call the array itself R. Each of the *m* rows in array R corresponds to one of the members of set A and each of the *n* columns in array R corresponds to one of the members of set B.

For each member *i* of set A that is related to a member *j* of set B, store the integer 1 in row *i* column *j* of array R. The array representation of R is thus

```
1    0    0    0
0    1    0    0
0    0    1    0
```

ALGORITHM

1. Declare an array, R, of appropriate size to be able to accommodate all possible relations between sets A and B.
2. Initialize array R to zeros.
3. Read the size M of set A and the size N of set B.
4. Read one relation between the members of A and B as the pair of integers I and J.
5. Set the element in rowI and column J to 1.
6. Repeat process from step 4 until all relations have been read.

FORTRAN PROGRAM

```
      PROGRAM RELATN
C**** IN THIS PROGRAM WE ASSUME THAT THE LARGEST VALUE FOR M AND N
C**** IS 100
      INTEGER R(100,100), I, J
      DATA R/10000 * 0/
      PRINT *, 'ENTER NUMBER OF ELEMENTS IN SET A'
      READ *, M
      PRINT *, 'ENTER NUMBER OF ELEMENTS IN SET B'
      READ *, N
      PRINT *, 'ELEMENTS OF SET A ARE REPRESENTED BY INTEGERS'
     +    PRINT *, ' 1 THROUGH ', M
```

```
      PRINT *, 'ELEMENTS OF SET B ARE REPRESENTED BY INTEGERS'
     +    PRINT *, ' 1 THROUGH ', N
      PRINT *, 'ENTER AN ELEMENT OF SET A FOLLOWED BY A BLANK'
      PRINT *, 'SPACE FOLLOWED BY AN ELEMENT OF SET B TO WHICH'
      PRINT *, 'IT IS RELATED. IF DONE, ENTER 0,0.'
      READ *, I, J
10    IF (I*J .EQ. 0) GO TO 100
          IF (I .LT. 0 .OR. J .LT. 0 .OR. I .GT. M .OR. J .GT. N) THEN
              PRINT *, 'FIRST NUMBER MUST BE BETWEEN 1 AND ', M
              PRINT *, 'SECOND NUMBER MUST BE BETWEEN 1 AND ', N
              PRINT *, 'PLEASE ENTER THE PAIR OF NUMBERS AGAIN.'
          ELSE
              R(I, J) = 1
          ENDIF
          PRINT *, 'ENTER ANOTHER PAIR OF NUMBERS.'
          READ *, I, J
      GO TO 10
100   (Here enter program statements that make use of relation R.)
      END
```

Sets, relations, and matrices. Many types of information may be seen as *relations*, multidimensional sets of information that may be stored in an array. Suppose that the members of set A are cities in Africa and the members of set B are cities in Spain. A city in set A is said to be related to a city in set B if there is a direct airline flight between them. Thus, the array R for this relation would have a 1 in those positions representing African cities in set A for which there is a direct flight to the Spanish city in set B, and zeros everywhere else. Such an array may be used to report the frequency of direct flights between cities as well as similar kinds of information.

The FORTRAN program from Problem 4.2 can be easily adapted to handle this matrix of relations between cities. In order to investigate flight frequency or other specifics, program statements producing appropriate results are inserted in the program beginning at statement 100.

Problem 4.4
Computing Potential Energy

SITUATION A Wimshurst motor is a type of rotary electrostatic motor that can be treated, in its simplest case, as an electric dipole between the plates of a capacitor. The Wimshurst motor is extremely efficient, converting almost all the electrical potential to mechanical work. It is also fully reversible, acting with equal efficiency simply by turning it in reverse, and potentially very light in proportion to power output. It is thus proposed for use in a space probe.

OBJECTIVE Your firm is developing a prototype Wimshurst motor. As a first step, you are asked to write a program to compute the potential energy of the rotor. The equation is

$$U = -p \cdot E$$

where U is the potential energy,
p is the moment of the dipole, a vector with its direction from negative to positive poles and its magnitude equal to the charge on the rotor times its diameter, and
E is a vector expressing the force and direction of the electric field, in this case that between the plates of a capacitor.

This equation introduces us to the computation of the dot product of two vectors.

ANALYSIS Suppose that we have n sets of dipole charge and electric field strength data, each represented by a pair of numbers (x_i, y_i).

Suppose also that p, let us call it vector A, has elements consisting of all of the x-coordinates of the n data sets and E, let us call it vector B, consists of all the y-coordinates of the sets.

Recall that the dot product of two vectors is the sum of the products of the data pairs that define the vectors, as expressed

$$A \cdot B = x_1{}^*y_1 + x_2{}^*y_2 + x_3{}^*y_3 + \ldots + x_n{}^*y_n$$

Develop an algorithm that reads all the members of vectors A and B, then computes their dot product.

ALGORITHM

1. Declare 2 one-dimensional arrays of appropriate maximum size.
2. Read an integer N specifying the number of members in each of vectors A and B.
3. Read the N members of vector A, then of vector B.
4. Compute the dot product and report it.

FORTRAN PROGRAM

```
      PROGRAM DOTPRD
      REAL A(100), B(100), PROD
      INTEGER N, I
      PRINT *, 'ENTER THE DIMENSION OF BOTH VECTORS.'
      READ *, N
      PRINT *, 'ENTER THE ELEMENTS OF VECTOR A ONE PER LINE.'
      I = 1
10    IF (I .GT. N) GOTO 20
         READ *, A(I)
         I = I+1
      GOTO 10
```

```
20    PRINT *, 'ENTER THE ELEMENTS OF VECTOR B ONE PER LINE.'
      I = 1
30    IF (I .GT. N) GOTO 40
          READ *, B(I)
          I = I + 1
      GOTO 30
40    PROD = 0
      I = 1
50    IF (I .GT. N) GOTO 100
          PROD = PROD + A(I) * B(I)
          I = I + 1
      GOTO 50
100   PRINT *, 'THE DOT PRODUCT OF VECTORS A AND B IS ', PROD
      END
```

Solving linear equations. Linear equations are often used to describe situations in all the engineering disciplines. The following general solution for a linear equation, called the *Gauss-Seidel method*, will both demonstrate the use of arrays and prove very useful later.

A system of n linear equations in n unknowns may be represented as follows. Our objective is to solve for the n unknowns.

$$a_{11} x_1 + a_{12} x_2 + \ldots + a_{1n} x_n = b_1$$
$$a_{21} x_1 + a_{22} x_2 + \ldots + a_{2n} x_n = b_2$$
$$\vdots$$
$$a_{n1} x_1 + a_{n2} x_2 + \ldots + a_{nn} x_n = b_n$$

PROCEDURE

The Gauss-Seidel method of finding roots for such a system of equations requires that the equations be rewritten as follows:

$$a_{11} x_1 = b_1 - a_{12} x_2 - a_{13} x_3 - \ldots - a_{1n} x_n$$
$$a_{22} x_2 = b_2 - a_{21} x_1 - a_{23} x_3 - \ldots - a_{2n} x_n$$
$$a_{33} x_3 = b_3 - a_{31} x_1 - a_{32} x_2 - \ldots - a_{3n} x_n$$
$$\vdots$$
$$a_{nn} x_n = b_n - a_{n1} x_1 - a_{n2} x_2 - a_{n3} x_3 \ldots - a_{nn-1} x_{n-1}$$

so that each equation isolates a different unknown on the left side of the equation.

Then estimate values for unknowns $x_2, x_3, x_4, \ldots, x_n$.

Substitute these estimates into the system to compute a value for x_1.

Next substitute the computed value for x_1 and the original estimates for $x_3, x_4, \ldots, x_n$ into the system of equations and compute a new value for

x_2. At this point we have computed values for x_1 and x_2 and estimates for all the other unknowns.

Now substitute the computed values for x_1 and x_2 together with the estimates for $x_4, x_5, \ldots, x_n$ and compute a new value for x_3.

Continue computing a new value for each next unknown not yet computed until computed values have been obtained for all of $x_1, x_2, x_3, \ldots, x_n$. Note that at each step of this process the latest values obtained for all unknowns are used in the computation of the next unknown.

When values have been computed for all n unknowns, start the process all over again. This time use the latest computed values for the unknowns rather than the original estimates to compute a second set of values for all n unknowns.

After computing a second set of values for the unknowns, the process is repeated a third time, using the second set of computed values. This repetition continues until the differences between the last computed value and the next-to-last computed value for each of the n unknowns is less than some predefined acceptable error value E.

Two concerns should be brought to your attention:

1. Because of the manner in which we compute x_i it is necessary to ensure that a_{ii} not be zero for $i = 1, 2, 3, \ldots, n$.
2. It is possible that this process will not yield sets of values for the unknowns such that the latest computed value for a given unknown becomes ever closer to the preceding computed value for that unknown. That is, the process may not converge, in which case it will not be possible to satisfy the condition that $|x_{i,\text{new}} - x_{i,\text{old}}| < \text{E}$ for $i = 1, 2, \ldots, n$.

Therefore, to ensure that our solution program does not go into an infinite loop, we introduce an iteration counter and stop the repetitive process when this counter exceeds some specified value.

EXAMPLE Here is a simple example to illustrate the Gauss-Seidel method. Suppose the system of equations to be solved is as follows:

$$x_1 - 2x_2 = 1$$
$$x_1 - 4x_2 = 4$$

First we rewrite the equations in the Gauss-Seidel required form:

$$x_1 = 1 + 2x_2 \qquad \textit{or} \qquad x_1 = 1 + 2x_2$$
$$4x_2 = 4 - x_1 \qquad\qquad x_2 = 1 - 0.25x_1$$

Suppose we guess a value of zero for x_2. Since the original estimates can be almost any value, small numbers are usually selected.

Now compute x_1 using the first equation. This yields a value of 1 for x_1.

Next substitute 1 for x_1 in the second equation to obtain a value of 0.75 for x_2.

Now go back to the first equation, substitute this latest value for x_2, and compute a value of 2.5 for x_1.

Suppose that the predetermined small value that stops the repetition is 0.05. Here is the list of values we would compute if the original estimates for the two unknowns are 0 and 0:

x_1	x_2
0	0
1	0.75
2.5	0.375
1.75	0.5625
2.125	0.46875
1.9375	0.515625
2.03125	0.4921875
1.984375	0.5139063
2.027812	0.4930468

At this point the differences between the last two computed values for both unknowns are less than 0.05, so the process stops. These last values are accepted as the solution to this system of equations.

If you solve the system of equations by an exact method, the solution is

$$x_1 = 2$$
$$x_2 = 0.5$$

Note that the computed set of values in the table above are converging to these exact values.

If other original estimates are made for the two unknowns, for example, 1 and 1, the resulting computations would converge to the same solution. In other words, whether the computed values converge or do not converge is independent of the choice of original estimates for the n unknowns.

Therefore, we may now proceed to solve the original problem, using 1 as the original estimate for all unknowns.

SOLUTION As you may deduce, the system of linear equations given at the beginning of this section may be written in the form of a matrix equation:

$AX = B$

where A = $a(1,1)\ a(1,2)\ a(1,3) \ldots a(1,n)$, $X = x(1)$, and $B = b(1)$

$a(2,1)\ a(2,2)\ a(2,3) \ldots a(2,n)$ $\quad x(x)$ $\quad b(2)$

$a(3,1)\ a(3,2)\ a(3,3) \ldots a(3,n)$ $\quad x(3)$ $\quad b(3)$

. . .

. . .

. . .

$a(n,1)\ a(n,2)\ a(n,3) \ldots a(n,n)$ $\quad x(n)$ $\quad b(n)$

Note again that before any part of the repetitive process begins, we must make sure that a_{ii} is not equal to zero for all $i = 1, 2, \ldots, n$. The solution below assumes that this requirement has been met.

ALGORITHM

1. Read the allowable error ERR for stopping the process.
2. Read a value for the maximum number K of iterations to be performed.
3. Initialize the unknowns all to 1.
4. Divide all elements in row 1 of matrix A by A(1,1), divide all elements in row 2 of matrix A by A(2,2), and so on until all elements in row N of matrix A have been divided by A(N,N). Call the new matrix obtained as a result of these divisions matrix C.
5. While the iteration counter is less than K and acceptable solution has not been found

   Compute X(1) based on X(2), X(3), X(4), . . . , X(N)
   Compute X(2) based on X(1), X(3), X(4), . . . , X(N)
   Compute X(3) based on X(1), X(2), X(4), . . . , X(N)
   .
   .
   .

   Compute X(N), based on X(1), X(2), X(4), . . . , X(N−1)
   End of While structure.
6. If the iteration counter is greater than or equal to K, then Report that a solution has not been found.

   Else Report X(1), X(2), . . . , X(N) as the solution to the system of equations.

FORTRAN PROGRAM

```
      PROGRAM GAUSID
C***
C***  THIS PROGRAM REQUIRES THAT ARRAY A CONTAIN THE
C***  COEFFICIENTS OF THE UNKNOWNS IN THE SYSTEM TO BE SOLVED.
C***  IT ALSO REQUIRES THAT ARRAY B CONTAIN THE CONSTANT TERMS OF
C***  THE SYSTEM TO BE SOLVED. WE ASSUME A MAX OF 50 EQUATIONS
C***  AND 50 UNKNOWNS.
      REAL A(50, 50), B(50), C(50, 51), X(50), DIFF, ERR, P
      LOGICAL ERROR
      INTEGER N, K, COUNT, I
      PRINT *, 'ENTER THE MAXIMUM ERROR TO BE TOLERATED.'
      READ *, ERR
      PRINT *, 'ENTER THE MAXIMUM NUMBER OF ITERATIONS ALLOWED.'
      READ *, K
      { Insert here statements necessary to read values for arrays }
      { A and B and their size N. }
      I = 1
 10   IF (I .GT. N) GOTO 40
          X(I) = 1
          C(I,N+1) = B(I) / A(I,I)
          J = 1
 20       IF (J .GT. N) GOTO 30
              C(I,J) = A(I,J) / A(I,I)
              J = J+1
          GOTO 20
 30       I = I+1
      GOTO 10
 40   ERROR = .FALSE.
      COUNT = 1
 50   IF (COUNT .GE. K .OR. DIFF .LT. O) GOTO 100
          I = 1
 55       IF (I .GT. N) GOTO 80
              P = C(I, N+1)
              J = 1
 60           IF (J .GT. N) GOTO 70
                  P = P - C(I,J)*X(J)
                  J = J+1
              GOTO 60
 70           X(I) = X(I) + P
              DIFF = DIFF + ABS(P)
              I = I+1
          GOTO 55
 80       DIFF = DIFF - ERR
          COUNT = COUNT + 1
      GOTO 50
 100  IF (COUNT .GE. K) THEN
          PRINT *, 'NO SOLUTION HAS BEEN FOUND IN ',COUNT,
     +            'ITERATIONS.'
          ERROR = .TRUE.
      ENDIF
      RETURN
      END
```

If this subroutine returns a value of TRUE for parameter ERROR, then no solution has been found in the specified number of iterations. Otherwise, array X will be returned with the *n* values that solve the system of equations passed to this module as parameters A and B.

Summary

In this chapter we have presented concepts related to arrays. An array is a collection of computer memory locations all having the same name and distinguished from one another by the use of single, double, or triple subscripts. A variable is defined as an array by the DIMENSION statement or any of the type declaration statements. Here are some general forms of array-definition statements:

EXAMPLES

```
DIMENSION VAR1(N1), VAR2(N2), . . . , VARN(NN)
INTEGER VAR1(N1), VAR2(N2), . . . ,VARK(NK)
REAL VAR1(N1), VAR2(N2), . . ., VARJ(NJ)
CHARACTER VAR1(N1)*K1, VAR2(N2)*K2, . . . ,VARN(NN)*KN
DIMENSION VAR1(M1:N1),VAR2(M1:N1,M2:N2),
+VAR3(M1:N1,M2:N2,M3:N3)
REAL VAR1(M1:N1,M2:N2)
INTEGER VAR2(M1:N1,M2:N2,M3:N3,M4:N4)
```

where VAR1, VAR2, . . . , VARN represent variable names,
M1, . . . , M4 and N1, . . . , NN represent integer constants that define the sizes of the arrays, and
K1, K2, . . . , KN in the CHARACTER statement, are integer constants specifying the maximum number of characters each member of the array is to hold; if this is not specified the number of characters is assumed to be 1.

Two and three-dimensional arrays are specified similar to any of the first four examples.

We then listed the rules for using arrays, which you should review.

Next, we discussed, with examples, the input of data to and output of reports from arrays. Here, it is useful to know the DATA statement. Its general form is

```
DATA VAR1, VAR2, . . . , VARN/Data1, Data2, . . . , DataN/
```

where VAR1, . . . , VARN are variable names and
Data1, Data2, . . . , DataN are the actual data to be stored.

If a given datum is to be used more than once, enter first in the data statement the number of times it is to be used, insert an asterisk, and then put the datum, as in

EXAMPLE

```
DATA V1, V2, V3, V4/4*0/
```

indicates that the datum 0 is to be used 4 times; that is, zero is the datum stored in all the variables.

If an array name appears without subscripts, all elements of the array are assigned values by the DATA statement; the full number of values must appear between the slashes following the array name.

End of Chapter Exercises

1. Indicate which of the following statements are true and which are false. Change those that are false to become true.

a. A DATA statement is an executable statement.

b. The statement

```
DATA A(10)/10 * 0/
```

will initialize A(1) through A(10) to the value zero.

c.
```
DATA A/5.2/, B/6.7/
```
is a correct FORTRAN statement if A and B have previously been declared of type REAL.

d. An INTEGER statement in FORTRAN must follow all the DATA statements in that program.

e. FORTRAN 77 allows for the declaration of arrays only up to dimension 3.

f. An array may not have a negative subscript in FORTRAN 77.

g. FORTRAN 77 allows for the use of a real variable as subscript of an array.

h. The following declaration is valid in FORTRAN 77:

```
INTEGER A(1.1, . . . , 1.9)
```

i. DATA statements are generally used to simplify initialization of variables in FORTRAN.

j. Only one DATA statement may validly be included in any FORTRAN program.

2. Determine which of the following are correct FORTRAN 77 statements and which contain errors. For those that are incorrect, make the changes needed to correct them.

```
DIMENSION A(10) B(20)
DIMENSION A, B(10)
INTEGER OUT(-10:10), IN(-5:0, 5:10)
DIMENSION A(10, 20), B(5, 6, 10)
DIMENSION IF(10), GOTO (20)
DIMENSION X(1000, 1000), Y(100, 200, 20)
DIMENSION X(2, 3, 5, 5)
INTEGER VAR1, VAR2(5)
INTEGER X(1), X(2), X(3)
CHARACTER A(20), *10
DIMENSION A(7:10), B(10)
REAL IN(10, 20), A(50)
CHARACTER*10, A(5), B, C(10)
REAL A, B, C(20)
REAL NUM(1), NUM(5)
```

3. Identify all syntax errors in each of the following program segments. Assume default data type based on the first letter of a variable name unless otherwise declared.

a.
```
      INTEGER A(2,10)
      DATA A/1,2,3,4,5,6,7,8,9,10*0.10/
      REAL B(20)
      DATA B/20*1/
```

b.
```
      INTEGER X, Y
      DIMENSION X(10), Y(10)
      DATA X/10*1/,Y/10*0/
 10   IF(Y .GT. 0) GO TO 20
      X(Y) = X * Y
      Y = Y + 1
      GO TO 10
```

c.
```
      INTEGER ARY(10), F(10), X, I
      DATA ARY/10*0/
      F(X) = ARY(1)*X
      ARY(I) = I*10
```

4. Write a FORTRAN program to read 2 sets of integers $x_1, x_2, \ldots, x_n$ and $y_1, y_2, \ldots, y_m$, where n and m are not necessarily equal. Each of the sets of numbers is terminated with sentinel data of –9999. Your program must read the values of n and m; you may assume that they do not exceed 100.

a. $\sum_{i=1}^{n} x_i$

b. $\sum_{i=1}^{n} x_i^2$

c. $\bar{x} = (1/n)\sum_{i=1}^{n} x_i, \quad \bar{y} = (1/m)\sum_{i=1}^{m} y_i$

d. $(1/n)\sum_{i=1}^{n} (x_i - \bar{x})^2, \quad (1/m)\sum_{i=1}^{m} (y_i - \bar{y})^2$

e. $(1/n)\sum_{i=1}^{n} x_i^2 - \bar{x}^2$

5. Write a program, using the following specifications, to score a multiple-choice test and output certain associated reports.

LIMITS

1. At most there should be 150 items in the test.
2. At most 200 students will take the test.
3. The correct response to each test item is a single letter or digit.
4. Each item has an integer point value from 1 to 9.

INPUT

Instructor-related data.

1. The number N of students taking the test.
2. The correct responses in order from item 1. If there are 80 or fewer items, 1 line is needed for correct responses; otherwise use 2 lines.
3. The point value of all test items in the same order as the correct responses. As with correct responses, use 1 or 2 lines depending on the number of items.

Student-related data; one set for each student.

1. Student identification number in 6 positions.
2. Student responses in the same order as correct responses. The student response to item 1 is in position 7, immediately following the student ID number; the rest follow in order. As with correct responses, 1 or 2 lines will be needed.

OUTPUT

1. Mean score for all students, and the standard deviation.
2. A summary of test results including these columns:

```
ITEM          CORRECT     INCORRECT     % CORRECT
NUMBER        RESPONSES   RESPONSES     RESPONSES
```

3. Student identification numbers and scores sorted in descending score order.
4. Student identification numbers and scores sorted in ascending ID number order.
5. For each student, a report showing

```
STUDENT NUMBER XXXXXX          SCORE XXXX
STUDENT RANK ON TEST XXX       GRADE X
```

For the grade, assign A if score is in the top 10% of the class, B in the next 20%, C in the middle 40%, D in the next 20%, and F in the bottom 10%.

6. A table presenting this information:

```
ITEM          STUDENT     CORRECT       POINTS PER
NUMBER        RESPONSES   RESPONSES     ITEM
```

PROGRAM DESIGN ISSUES

Programs like this one, whose main function is to take data stored in an array or set of arrays and convert it into something that can be quickly read and understood, are called *report writers.* They are a vital part of the job in almost any area of engineering or scientific community, for information calculated or retrieved from the computer does little good if it cannot be assimilated enough for human beings to act on it.

When you write a report writer, questions you might need to think about include:

Who is going to be reading this? How sophisticated are they about the numbers printed? Is there any risk that they will pass it on to someone less technically sophisticated? Could generic notes to help the untutored reader be included automatically with each report?

Is the report potentially of interest to many more people than the ones to whom it will be first sent? If so, copies are likely to be requested. Later, there are likely to be many requests for changes and modifications in the structure of the report. It might be wise to plan to make the report very easy to modify by using lots of comments and numerous small single-function modules.

Is it possible to make sure that no record is read more than once? This will greatly improve efficiency.

Chapter 5

Iteration Structures in FORTRAN

We have already noticed how the solution to certain types of problems requires us to be able to repeat a set of actions in a FORTRAN program. We've built some simple *iteration structures*, or *loops*, around the GO TO statement. This is a very direct way of handling iteration, but by no means the only way available in FORTRAN. In fact, there is a wide range of powerful structures and techniques for iteration.

Since iteration structures are so effective in utilizing the power of a computer system it is important that you become adept at constructing them. This chapter explains the use of special FORTRAN statements and other techniques to implement iteration structures. We first consider iteration structures as algorithms and discuss basic structure. Then the discussion and problems present the techniques for implementation.

Constructing Iteration Structures

Every iteration structure should consist of one *entry point*, an *iteration body*, and one *exit point*. In addition, the structure needs to establish an initial value for, or *initialize*, the iteration number or variable(s), or both, and then use these in testing for the *exit condition*. These elements are usually arranged in one of two ways:

FORM A

```
Entry point and Initialization
execute Iteration body
Exit condition
If false
      repeat from execute Iteration body
If true
Exit point
```

FORM B

```
Entry point and Initialization
Exit condition
If false
      execute Iteration body
      return to Exit condition
If true
Exit point
```

The main difference between these forms is the different position of the exit condition test. It either follows the iteration body, as in form A, or precedes it, as in form B. When the test follows the iteration body, the instructions in the loop are performed at least once before exiting, no matter what the exit values are. When the test precedes the iteration body, the computer will skip the iteration body altogether, given exit values that immediately register true.

Entry and exit. An iteration structure must always be entered at the entry point. This ensures that appropriate initialization takes place. The entry point is usually at the top of the program or program segment.

For the exit point, the *normal* or *default* placement is as the first statement immediately following the iteration body. This is both the most common and the best structured exit point. Before using any other point for exit, you should have good reason, and remember that any nonstandard exit point position must be specified in the iteration body.

Iteration body. The iteration body consists of a statement or a series of statements that are executed a variable number of times, depending on the initialization values and on the statements in the body itself.

Here are some examples of iteration structures. These all use form B, with the exit condition before the loop.

EXAMPLE 1

```
      PROGRAM VARANC
      REAL NUMBER, MEAN, SUM, SUMSQ, VAR
      INTEGER COUNT
C*
      COUNT=0
      SUM=0
      SUMSQ=0
      READ*,NUMBER
C***********************************************************************
C*                      COMPUTE MEAN AND VARIANCE                     *
C***********************************************************************
 3    IF (NUMBER .EQ. 99999) GOTO 5
          SUM = SUM + NUMBER
          SUMSQ = SUMSQ + NUMBER * NUMBER
          COUNT = COUNT + 1
          READ*,NUMBER
      GOTO 3
C*
 5    MEAN = SUM / COUNT
      VAR = (SUMSQ - COUNT * MEAN * MEAN)/COUNT
      WRITE*,'THE VARIANCE IS ',VAR
      END
```

In this example the entry point is where COUNT, SUM, SUMSQ and NUMBER are all initialized. The exit point is at statement 5.

Statements between the first READ statement and statement 5 constitute the iteration structure.

EXAMPLE 2 This example is a program *segment*, so the usual statements appearing at the beginning of a program are purposely omitted.

```
.
.
.
      READ*,N
100   IF (N .LE. 0) GO TO 110
          READ*,NUM
          SUM = SUM+NUM
          SUMSQ = SUMSQ+NUM*NUM
          N = N-1
      GO TO 100
110   PRINT*,SUM,SUMSQ
.
.
.
```

The entry point is at the first READ statement and the exit point is the PRINT statement.

EXAMPLE 3 Here's the same program segment modified to test for data errors as an exit condition.

```
.
.
.
      READ*,N
100   IF (N .LE. 0) GO TO 110
          READ*,NUM
          IF (NUM .LT. 0) GO TO 150
          SUM = SUM+NUM
          SUMSQ = SUMSQ+NUM*NUM
          N = N-1
      GO TO 100
110   PRINT*,SUM,SUMSQ
.
.
.
150   PRINT*,'ERROR IN INPUT DATA.'
.
.
.
```

The entry point is at the first READ statement where N is initialized.

There are two exit points. The normal exit is the first PRINT statement where the value of SUM and SUMSQ are printed. The second exit point is at statement 150, which is executed only if input data are negative—which in this case would mean they are invalid. This second exit is a provision for an abnormal situation, so such an exit point is often called an *abnormal exit*.

▪ *Good programming style dictates that if possible there be only one exit.*

Exit control. Let's consider how each of these examples controls the number of repetitions of the iteration body.

Example 1 exits the loop on the condition that the value read for NUM is 99999. The number of repetitions is unknown in advance of entering the loop. It is dependent on the insertion of a dummy datum, namely 99999, being added at the end of the input data. This allows the number of values, and thus the number of repetitions, to vary directly with the number of items to be processed. Since the number of repetitions is controlled by the occurrence of a given condition, we refer to this type of iteration structure as a *condition controlled* iteration structure.

In Examples 2 and 3, the number of repetitions N is known in advance. This value is read at the entry point, and each iteration of the loop reduces N by 1. Exit from the loop occurs after N repetitions, when the reduced number N reaches a value of 0. In order to change the number of repetitions, the number read in as N must be changed. This is the second principal type of loop, the *counter controlled* iteration structure.

Example 3 presents an exception to the normal process of counter controlled structures. The abnormal exit condition reduces the number of repetitions by arbitrarily terminating the loop immediately in cases where an error is found, no matter what the current value of N.

Forms of Iteration

The two main methods used in FORTRAN to control the number of repetitions of the iteration body are the ones in the above examples, counter control and condition control. Counter control depends on a set number of iterations and a counter that registers each repetition until the pre-set number is achieved. Condition control depends on the inclusion of dummy data at the end of the input string to trigger the exit from the loop. Each of these has its special forms in FORTRAN.

Counter Controlled Structures

Counter controlled iterations in FORTRAN have four common features:

Index. The *counter* of the number of repetitions or iterations.

Initial value. The initialization value of the index.

Final value. The exit value of the index.

Step value. The amount of increase or reduction in the index during each iteration.

Looking at Examples 2 and 3 above, the *initial value* of the *index* is N, its *final value* is 0, and the *step value* is –1.

These and the other examples we've seen so far use the simplest of counter controlled structures, with appropriate initialization statements and an IF . . . GO TO statement. Another convenient FORTRAN method for counter controlled iterations uses a single statement called the DO statement.

Writing a DO statement. This statement combines all four of the basic features of a counter controlled structure. Two forms of the DO statement are specified in the full set FORTRAN 77 Standard. These are designated by the type of the index as the *integer* DO statement and the *real* DO statement.

The integer DO. The integer DO statement has been available since the very beginning of FORTRAN. It has the general form

```
DO N INDEX = INIT,FINAL,STEP
```

> where N is the reference number of the last program statement in the loop, INDEX is an integer variable, INIT is the initial value of the index, FINAL is the final value of the index, and STEP is the value of the increment or decrement.

In FORTRAN 77, one has the official option of putting a comma to the right of N, but many FORTRAN compilers do not permit a comma there and will return an error message. Therefore, we do not use a comma to the right of the reference number in any DO statement.

Note that all variables are integers. INIT, FINAL, and STEP may be integer constants, variables, or arithmetic expressions.

EXAMPLE If the value of STEP is the constant 1, it may be omitted together with the preceding comma, giving the statement

```
DO 50 INDEX = 1,10
```

Because no step value is specified, this statement implies that the step value is 1.

The real DO. The real DO statement is a more recent introduction, included only in the full set FORTRAN 77. Other versions of FORTRAN are likely to allow only the integer DO. The general form of the real DO statement is the same as for the integer DO except that INDEX, INIT, FINAL, and STEP are all real constants, variables, or arithmetic expressions.

- *Using the real form of the DO loop may result in round-off errors. The integer form is thus preferred unless there is a clear and overriding need to use the real form.*

The CONTINUE statement. There is one other requirement in writing a DO loop: The last statement, with reference number N, must be executable. It may not be another DO statement or a selection structure statement such as GO TO or IF-THEN. So FORTRAN introduces an executable CONTINUE statement. The CONTINUE statement does not cause any action in the program. It simply causes the program to proceed, continuing the loop until the iteration counter reaches zero.

Always use a CONTINUE statement at the end of a DO loop to avoid using any invalid statement in that position. The form is

```
      DO N INDEX = INIT,FINAL,STEP
         Iteration body
 N    CONTINUE
```

The statement number is always the integer N directly following DO in the DO statement.

Executing a DO statement.

Each DO statement requires three specified values, INIT, FINAL, and STEP, and a value for the reference number N. When a DO statement is executed, it causes the following steps to be performed:

1. The FORTRAN 77 compiler calculates the number of times that the iteration occurs. If the initial value of the iteration is the integer I, the calculation uses the three specified values as follows:

   ```
   I=((FINAL-INIT)/STEP)+1
   ```

   If I is less than or equal to 0, the loop is not executed even once. However, if I is greater than zero, the loop begins.

2. I is called the *iteration counter*. Each time the loop is executed, I is decreased by 1 until one of the following occurs:

   a. A statement is executed that results in a transfer out of the loop, *an abnormal exit*.

   b. A STOP statement is encountered in the loop, *also an abnormal exit*.

   c. I becomes zero and the exit condition is satisfied, *a normal exit*.

3. The value stored in variable INDEX is set to the value stored in the location INIT.

4. All statements on the lines following the DO statement are executed, up to and including the CONTINUE statement whose reference number is N. This N is the number following the word DO in the DO statement.

5. After the execution of statement N, the value stored in INDEX is replaced by the sum of STEP and the previous value of INDEX. This loop continues until one of the incidents in step 1 occurs. If the loop is not ended by an abnormal exit the iteration occurs I times, and execution passes to the statement next after the CONTINUE statement.

Now we'll look at some complete DO loops. As you study these examples, determine the number of times the READ statement is executed. Assume in every case that I has data type integer and X has data type real.

EXAMPLE 1

```
      DO 20 I=1,5
         READ *, X
         Y=X*I
         PRINT *, Y
 20   CONTINUE
```

The iteration counter is ((5 – 1) / 1) + 1 = 5, so the READ statement, and the two statements following it, are executed 5 times. Five values are read for X, 5 values are used for I in the assignment statement, and 5 values for Y are printed by line 20.

EXAMPLE 2

```
      DO 20 I=10,1
         READ *, X
         PRINT *, X
 20   CONTINUE
```

The steps in this loop are not executed at all because the iteration counter is ((1 – 10) / 1) + 1, which is –8. A negative iteration counter prevents any processing of the loop.

EXAMPLE 3

```
      DO 20 IND=10, 1, -1
         PRINT *, IND
 20   CONTINUE
```

The iteration counter is computed as ((1 – 10) / (–1)) + 1, which is 10, so the PRINT statement is executed 10 times. The index IND goes from an initial value of 10 to a final value of 1 in steps of –1.

EXAMPLE 4

```
      N=2
      DO 50 I=1, N
         N=N+1
         PRINT *, N
 50   CONTINUE
```

At the entry of the iteration structure, N has the value 2. The iteration counter is thus computed as ((2 – 1) / 1) + 1, which is 2. The iteration body consisting of the statements N = N + 1 and PRINT*, N is executed twice. The values output for N are 3 and 4.

If this program segment were processed by a compiler other than a FORTRAN 77 compiler, the results would be radically different. In fact, the execution of the loop would go on endlessly because the final value N of the counter is being continuously increased and is, therefore, never equaled by the current value of the index I. Other compilers will not stop the iteration until I and N are equal. Only FORTRAN 77 will compute the iteration counter and stop after two repetitions.

EXAMPLE 5

```
      DO 60 X=0.1, 1.0, 0.01
         PRINT *, X
 60   CONTINUE
```

This example illustrates the possibility of minor errors in numbers owing to the finite representation in a binary computer of a decimal number. The iteration counter is ((1 – .1) / .01) + 1, which is 91, so the loop is executed 91 times. The expected output is

```
0.10000000
0.11000000
0.12000000
0.13000000
 .
 .
 .
0.98000000
0.99000000
1.00000000
```

If you run the following complete program version of Example 5

```
      PROGRAM XAMPL5
      REAL X
      DO 60 X=.1,1,.01
         PRINT *, X
 60   CONTINUE
      END
```

and compare the results with the expected output, not only may some lines of your output differ from the expected output but you may also find that the loop counter is not 91. Such unexpected results are due to a truncated or rounded representation of .01 in the computer system.

EXAMPLE 6

```
      DO 30 I=1, 10, 2
         READ *, X
         IF (X .LT. 0) STOP
         SUM = SUM + X
 30   CONTINUE
```

This iteration counter is 5, the largest integer less than or equal to ((10 – 1) / 2) + 1. In this loop the value input for X is tested for being less than 0; if it is, the program stops processing. If no negative number is input, the body of the iteration structure is executed 5 times.

EXAMPLE 7

```
      DO 30 I=1, 10, 2
         READ *, X
         IF (X .LT. 0) GOTO 50
         SUM = SUM + X
 30   CONTINUE
      .
      .
      .
 50    . . .
```

If a negative value is input for X, control transfers out of the loop to the statement with reference number 50. If all numbers input are positive, the iteration body is executed 5 times—as in Example 6.

- *Such a transfer out of the iteration body should normally not be used.*

Using another compiler. Other than FORTRAN 77, most FORTRAN compilers process DO loops in a significantly different manner. Where the DO statement is

```
DO N INDEX = INIT,FINAL,STEP
```

1. The value stored at INIT is assigned to INDEX as the initial value and the loop is performed the first time.
2. At the end of the body of the loop the value stored at STEP is added to the current value of INDEX and the sum is stored back in INDEX.
3. The new value of INDEX is compared with the value at FINAL.

a. If STEP is greater than 0 the loop terminates when INDEX becomes greater than the value at FINAL.

b. If STEP is less than 0 the loop terminates when INDEX becomes less than the value at FINAL.

You are urged to find out exactly how the compiler available to you processes DO loops, because results from certain processes may differ quite a bit from those obtained using a FORTRAN 77 compiler.

Now let's consider two complete examples in which we apply these latest programming concepts.

Problem 5.1 Checking Pressure Records

SITUATION Your firm has been conducting some biological work that requires conditions of very high sterility in a positive pressure chamber. A positive pressure chamber is kept at an air pressure slightly higher than the ambient pressure; in the event of a small rupture or leak, any potential contaminants will be blown out of the chamber. To ensure the integrity of the work, the difference between inside and outside pressure is recorded in pounds per square inch every 15 minutes. As long as the difference is positive, the chamber is functioning properly.

It has become necessary to check for a possible breach of sterility within the past six months. The magnitude of the breach is unimportant, but elapsed time since the breach is critical. The longer the time, the more data must be regarded as suspect.

Contamination may have occurred if the pressure difference was 0; it almost certainly did occur if the pressure difference was negative. Data were recorded with the most recent records first, but since any breach will compromise all subsequent records, it is desirable to check the earliest records first.

ANALYSIS A quick first pass through the data will allow us to find out whether there were any negative pressure incidents, count the number of such incidents, and create a code for suspected breaches so they can be sorted to check the most serious incidents first. We can accomplish this by generalizing the problem as follows.

OBJECTIVE A set of no more than 100 numbers is provided, including a sentinel datum of –999.999. Using these data, perform the following:

1. Determine the number of numbers N in the set.
2. Print the N numbers in the reverse of the order in which they are provided.
3. Change every negative number in the set to 0 and determine the number of such negative numbers.
4. Print the new set of numbers and the count of negative numbers.

ALGORITHM

1. Set aside an array, ANUM, for storing up to 100 numbers and initialize a counter N for counting the number of numbers to read until sentinel datum is detected. Also initialize a counter NEG for counting negative numbers that are input.
2. Read a number X. If it is sentinel datum or the maximum of 100 numbers have been read, proceed to step 4.
3. Increase N by 1 and assign to the Nth position in the array the number X. Then repeat the process from step 2.
4. Print the N numbers stored in array ANUM beginning with the number at ANUM (N) then ANUM (N–1), and so on to ANUM(1).

5. Check each number in array ANUM for being negative. If it is, set the number to 0 and increase NEG by 1.
6. Print each number in array ANUM, now modified to contain zeroes in place of negative numbers.
7. Print the number of negative numbers.
8. End.

Program

```
      PROGRAM NEGCHK
C***********************************************************************
C*    PROGRAM DEFINITION                                               *
C*        SEE THE TEXT FOR COMPLETE DESCRIPTION OF THE PROBLEM.        *
C***********************************************************************
C*    VARIABLE DEFINITION                                              *
C*        ANUM IS THE ARRAY OF NUMBERS READ.                           *
C*        N IS THE COUNT OF TOTAL NUMBERS.                             *
C*        NEG IS THE COUNT OF NEGATIVE NUMBER.                         *
C*        X IS THE NUMBER JUST READ.                                   *
C*        I IS THE LOOP INDEX.                                         *
C***********************************************************************
C*
      REAL ANUM(100), X
      INTEGER N, NEG, I
C*
      N = 0
      NEG = 0
C*
C***********************************************************************
C*    HERE A TOTAL OF N NUMBERS ARE READ ONE AT A TIME.                *
C*    IF THE NUMBER READ IS NOT -999.999. IT IS STORED IN ARRAY ANUM.  *
C***********************************************************************
C*
      READ*,X
 10       IF ((X .EQ. -999.999) .OR. (N .GE. 100)) GOTO 20
          N = N + 1
          ANUM(N) = X
          READ*,X
      GOTO 10
C*
 20   PRINT*,' A TOTAL OF ',N,' NUMBERS WERE READ.'
      PRINT*,' THE LIST IN REVERSE ORDER IS:'
      DO 30 I = N,1, -1
          PRINT*,ANUM(I)
 30   CONTINUE
C*
C***********************************************************************
C*    SET ANY NEGATIVE NUMBER IN ARRAY ANUM TO ZERO                    *
C*    AND COUNT NUMBER OF NEGATIVE NUMBERS.                            *
C***********************************************************************
C*
```

```
      PRINT*,'THE LIST WITH NO NEGATIVE IS:'
C*
      DO 40 I = 1,N
          IF (ANUM(I) .LT. 0) THEN
              NEG = NEG + 1
              ANUM(I) = 0
          ENDIF
          PRINT*,ANUM(I)
 40   CONTINUE
C*
      PRINT*,'THERE ARE ', NEG, ' NEGATIVE NUMBERS.'
      END
```

Problem 5.2 Computing Sums

OBJECTIVE Read a positive integer N, less than or equal to 10,000 and compute the following sums. Include a test to select a positive N not greater than 10,000. The output is the value obtained for each sum, appropriately identified.

PART A $1 + 2 + \ldots + N$

PART B $1^2 + 2^2 + \ldots + N^2$

PART C $1^3 + 2^3 + \ldots + N^3$

PART D $1 + 3 + \ldots + M$

where M is the largest odd integer less than or equal to N.

PART E $2 + 4 + \ldots + K$

where K is the largest even integer less than or equal to N.

ALGORITHM

1. Initialize five variables SUMA, SUMB, SUMC, SUMD, and SUME for accumulating sums.
2. Read an integer N and test that it is positive and no greater than 10,000. If either condition is not satisfied, output an error message and stop processing.
3. Set up a loop to compute the first 3 sums SUMA, SUMB, and SUMC.
4. Set up a loop to compute the fourth sum SUMD.
5. Subtract SUMD from SUMA to compute the final sum SUME.
6. Print each of the 5 sums with appropriate identification.
7. End.

FORTRAN PROGRAM

```
      PROGRAM SUMS
C***********************************************************************
C*                         PROGRAM DEFINITION                          *
C*    SEE THE TEXT FOR A COMPLETE DEFINITION OF THE PROBLEM.           *
C***********************************************************************
C*                         VARIABLE DEFINITIONS                        *
C*    SUMA IS THE SUM OF ALL INTEGERS FROM 1 TO N.                     *
C*    SUMB IS THE SUM OF SQUARES OF INTEGERS FROM 1 TO N.              *
C*    SUMC IS THE SUM OF CUBES OF INTEGERS FROM 1 TO N.                *
C*    SUMD IS THE SUM OF ODD INTEGERS FROM 1 TO N.                     *
C*    SUME IS THE SUM OF EVEN INTEGERS FROM 1 TO N.                    *
C*    I IS THE LOOP INDEX.                                             *
C*    ERROR IS A LOGICAL VARIABLE RELATED TO INPUT DATA.               *
C***********************************************************************
C*
      INTEGER SUMA, SUMB, SUMC, SUMD, SUME, N, I
      LOGICAL ERROR
C*
C*    INITIALIZE
C*
      SUMA = 0
      SUMB = 0
      SUMC = 0
      SUMD = 0
      SUME = 0
      ERROR = .FALSE.
C*
C*    INPUT N AND VERIFY IT
C*
      READ*, N
      IF (N.LT.0 .OR. N.GT.10000) THEN
          PRINT*, 'ERROR IN INPUT ', N
          ERROR = .TRUE.
      ENDIF
      IF (ERROR) STOP
C*
C*    COMPUTE THE 5 SUMS
C*
      DO 10 I = 1, N
          SUMA = SUMA + I
          SUMB = SUMB + I*I
          SUMC = SUMC + I*I*I
 10   CONTINUE
C*
      DO 20 I = 1, N, 2
          SUMD = SUMD + I
 20   CONTINUE
```

```
C*
      SUME = SUMA - SUMD
C*
      PRINT*, 'THE NUMBER N IS ', N
      PRINT*, 'SUM OF INTEGERS FROM 1 TO N IS ', SUMA
      PRINT*, 'SUM OF SQUARES OF INTEGERS FROM 1 TO N IS ', SUMB
      PRINT*, 'SUM OF CUBES OF INTEGERS FROM 1 TO N IS ', SUMC
      PRINT*, 'SUM OF ODD INTEGERS FROM 1 TO N IS ', SUMD
      PRINT*, 'SUM OF EVEN INTEGERS FROM 1 TO N IS ', SUME
      END
```

EXERCISE Notice that four of the required computations are done in two separate loops. As an exercise, combine the two loops. Be sure to retain the program's clarity and ease of comprehension.

Exercises 5.1

1. Indicate which of the following statements are true or false. Remember that a statement must be considered false if any part of it is false. Figure out how to change those that are false so that they are true.

a. FORTRAN 77 allows at most two subscripts for any given variable.

b. A FORTRAN compiler stores a two-dimensional array in row-major order.

c. If a DIMENSION statement is to appear in a program, it must be the first statement in the program.

d. If an INTEGER statement is to appear in a program, it must immediately follow any DIMENSION statements, or if there are none, the INTEGER statement must come first.

e. The REAL statement may be anywhere in the program as long as any variables declared in it are not used until after its appearance.

f. FORTRAN stores matrices in column-major order.

g. When using DO loops, it is permissible to transfer into and out of the body of a loop.

h. Transferring into a DO loop is permitted if the programmer sets the index with an assignment statement before so doing.

i. Real-indexed DO loops are available in almost every version of FORTRAN.

j. The following is an incorrect statement:

```
DO I=1,1,1
```

k. One may use no more than ten DO loops in any given program.

l. It is not permissible to use the index of a DO loop in any statement that appears in the body of a DO loop.

m. Every DO loop *must* terminate in a CONTINUE statement or else it is incorrect.

n. There must be at least one statement between a DO statement and a CONTINUE statement in order to have a DO loop.

o. The terminating statement in a DO loop may be any executable statement.

p. In FORTRAN 77, it is permissible to use a variable as the subscript in a DIMENSION statement.

q. DIMENSION statements not only specify the *size* of subscripted variables but also cause values to be stored in the variables.

r. The CONTINUE statement is an executable statement.

2. Determine which of the following FORTRAN statements are syntactically correct and which contain errors. For those that are incorrect, make the changes necessary to correct them. Do not look for mismatched data types.

a. `READ*, A(1,2), A(I ,J,K)`

b. `PRINT*, A, B(10)`

c. `PRINT*, A(10, 20), A(5)`

d. `PRINT*, B(1, B(2, 6)`

e. `PRINT*, B(1) + B(2)`

f. `DATA A, B(5)/6*2/C/3.0/`

g. `DATA A, B, C/20*1, 3, 7/`

h. `DATA A/10./B/20./`

i. `10 CONTINUE`

j. `DO 20 I=1, 10, -1`

k. `DO 50 I=10, 1`

l. `DO 9 J=1, 5`

m. `DO 10 I=1, 5`

n. `DO 20 J=1, 1, 2`

3. In the following segments of FORTRAN programs, identify any syntax errors. Correct those statements that contain errors.

a.
```
      INTEGER A(10)
      READ*, A(2)
```

b.
```
      DIMENSION A(-8, 8)
      INTEGER A
      A(X) = X*X + 1
      READ*, X
      PRINT*, A(X)
```

c.
```
      DIMENSION A(10, 2)
      READ*, A
      DO 10 I=1, 10
         A(I,1) = A(I-1, 2)
 10   CONTINUE
```

d.
```
      DO 20 I=1, 10
      K=K+I
 20   DO 30 J=K, 100
 30   PRINT*, J
```

e.
```
      DIMENSION A(20)
      DO 20 I = 1,20
      READ*, A(I)
          T = A(I)+A(I+1)
          Q = A(I-1)+A(I)
          PRINT*, T, Q
 20   CONTINUE
      END
```

f.
```
      DIMENSION A(0:1,0:5),B(1:12)
      INTEGER A,B
C*
C*    THIS PROGRAM SHOULD COPY A(0,0) THROUGH A(0,5) INTO B(1) THROUGH B(6)
C*    AND A(1,0) THROUGH A(1,5) INTO B(7) THROUGH B(12)
C*
      READ*,A
      DO 2 I=0,5
          B(I)=A(0,I)
          B(I+6)=A(1,I)
 2    CONTINUE
```

g.
```
      DIMENSION A(100),B(10,10)
      READ*,A
      DO 10 I=1, 100
 10   B(I,I)=A(I)
```

h.
```
      INTEGER B(10,10)
      DO 10 I = 1,10
      DO 10 J = 1,10
          B(I,J)='*'
 10   CONTINUE
      PRINT*, (B(I,J),J=1,10)
 10   CONTINUE
```

i.
```
      INTEGER B(10,10)
      READ*, B
      DO 10 I=1,10
          PRINT*, B(I,I),B(I,I-1),B(I-1,I)
 10   CONTINUE
```

j.
```
      INTEGER A(50),B(5,10)
      READ*,A
      DO 20,J=1,5
      DO 20,I=1,10
 20   B(I,J)=A(I*J)
```

4. In the following programs, look for errors in program logic. As you identify errors, make the changes necessary to make the program solve the stated problem.

a. This program is intended to compute and print the sum of all odd integers from J to K, including one or both of J and K if they are odd.

```
      PROGRAM ODD
      INTEGER I, J, K, ISUM, JSUM, KSUM
      DATA JSUM, KSUM/2*0/
      READ*, J, K
      IF (K-J .LE. 0) THEN
          PRINT*, 'NO INTEGERS BETWEEN ', J, ' AND ', K
          STOP
      ENDIF
      DO 10 I=1, J, 2
          JSUM = JSUM + I
 10   CONTINUE
      DO 20 I=1, K, 2
          KSUM = KSUM + K
 20   CONTINUE
      ISUM = KSUM - JSUM
      PRINT*, 'SUM OF INTEGERS FROM ', J, 'TO ', K , ' = ',ISUM
      END
```

b. A *perfect number* is a positive integer such that the sum of all its factors equals the number itself. The smallest perfect number is 6, whose factors are 1, 2, and 3. The sum 1, 2, and 3 equals 6. This program is intended to find and print the second smallest perfect number.

```
      PROGRAM PERFEC
      INTEGER N,SUM,K
      DO 30 N=7, 10000
          SUM=0
          DO 20 J=1,N-1
              IF (N/J .EQ. N/FLOAT(J)) SUM = SUM+1
 20       CONTINUE
          IF (SUM .EQ. N) THEN
              PRINT*, 'THE SECOND PERFECT NUMBER IS ',SUM
              STOP
          ENDIF
 30   CONTINUE
      END
```

c. This program is intended to read an integer, then print each digit of the integer on a separate line beginning with the most significant digit.

```
      PROGRAM DIGIT
      READ *,N
      DO 10 I = 1,10
          X = N/10.0
          K = (X-N/10)*10
          PRINT *,K
10    CONTINUE
      END
```

The nested DO loop. Often situations will occur in solving problems where it is necessary to have a loop within a loop, a structure called a *nested* loop. Here is a structure with two nested DO loops:

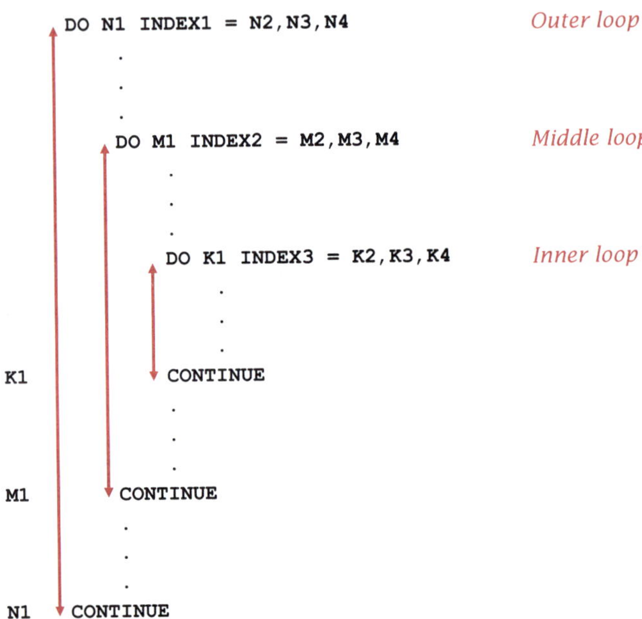

The index of the outer loop is initialized as specified in the first DO statement. The statements following the outer DO statement are executed until the next DO statement is encountered.

The index for the middle loop is initialized as specified in the second DO statement. The following statements are executed until the next DO statement is encountered.

The index of the inner loop is initialized and the statements in the body of the inner loop are executed once. The inner loop index is incremented or decremented according to its step size. If the index value is not greater than, or in specified circumstances less than, the specified final value for the index, the loop body statements are executed again. This inner loop process continues until the final value of the inner loop index is exceeded. At that point the inner loop is *completed* and program control passes to the following middle loop statements.

When the end of the middle loop is reached, its index is incremented or decremented as specified in the middle DO statement. Each time that the statements in the body of the middle loop are repeated, the index of the inner loop is again initialized and the inner loop statements executed until the inner loop is completed as before.

When the middle loop is completed in a similar fashion, the following statements are executed until the end of the outer loop is reached and its index modified according to the first DO statement. Repetition of the body of the outer loop, including new initializations and completions of both middle and inner loops, continues until the outer loop itself is completed.

Note that each time the body of an outer loop is executed, the nested loops are re-initialized and again completed. The re-initialization and completion continue until the outer loop itself is completed. Three other important characteristics of the diagram should be noted:

1. Each nested loop is ***completely contained*** within another loop.
2. Each loop index has a separate and ***unique variable name***.
3. Each loop ends with ***its own*** CONTINUE statement.

Now let's look at some examples of nested DO loops.

EXAMPLE 1

```
      DO 20 I=1,5
          K=I*I
          DO 10 J=1,5
              PRINT*,K*J
10        CONTINUE
20    CONTINUE
```

This program contains two loops. The loop with index J is the inner loop, so the entire loop, including the PRINT statement within it, is executed 5 times *for each value* of index I in the outer loop. Since I assumes 5 values, for each of which J assumes 5 values, a total of 25 lines of output are produced with one number on each line.

EXAMPLE 2

```
      DATA ISUM, JSUM, KSUM/3*0/
      DO 30 I=1,10
          ISUM = ISUM+1
          DO 20 J=1, 10, 2
              JSUM = JSUM+J
              DO 10 K=2,10,2
                  KSUM = KSUM+K
10            CONTINUE
              PRINT*,KSUM
20        CONTINUE
          PRINT*,JSUM
30    CONTINUE
      PRINT*,ISUM
```

In this three-loop example, ISUM is printed once, JSUM is printed 10 times, and KSUM is printed 50 times—5 times for each of the 10 JSUM calculations.

EXAMPLE 3

```
      DO 20 I=1,15,2
         DO 10 J=I,20
            PRINT*,I*J
10       CONTINUE
20    CONTINUE
```

The inner loop index J has a different initial value each time the outer loop is executed. J is initialized by the value of I, which changes with each iteration of the outer loop from 1 to 3 to 5 to 7 to 9 to 11 to 13 to 15.

The number of times the PRINT statement in the inner loop is executed thus reduces inversely to the value of I. When I = 1 the PRINT statement in the inner loop is executed 20 times. When I = 3 it is executed 18 times. The PRINT statement is thus executed a total of 20 + 18 + 16 + 14 + 12 + 10 + 8 + 6 = 104 times.

Rules for DO loops. From these examples, we can derive a set of useful rules for writing DO loops:

1. ***A DO loop must always be entered through its DO statement.*** This includes transfers to a DO loop. The DO statement properly initializes the index and computes the iteration counter.
2. ***Transfer out*** of a DO loop is permissible from a point other than the terminating statement, but this should be avoided in order to maintain program clarity.
3. ***Initial value***, ***final value***, and ***increment value*** may be constants, variables, or arithmetic expressions.
4. ***No overlapping of statements*** is allowed in nested loops. A single statement may terminate more than one loop, but this is not good programming style and should be avoided.
5. ***The DO loop must terminate with an executable statement***. Because the terminating statement cannot be a transfer type statement like GO TO or IF nor another DO statement, the CONTINUE statement is commonly used.

The implied DO loop. For READ, WRITE, DATA, and PRINT statements with data lists including subscripted variables, FORTRAN provides an *implied* DO loop. Processing proceeds very much like that in a DO loop but the loop is not explicitly specified.

EXAMPLE 1 Consider this program segment:

```
       REAL A(20)
       DO 15 I=1,N
           READ*,A(I)
 15    CONTINUE
```

Execution of this standard DO loop requires N lines of input where each line consists of a single number.

EXAMPLE 2 Now study this line of FORTRAN code:

```
READ*, (A(I),I=1,N)
```

This READ statement, like the loop above, requires N values to be input into A(1), A(2), . . . , A(N). However, this statement allows for all N values to be input from the same line, provided there is enough space.

The structure in Example 2 is an implied DO loop that has an effect similar to that of the DO loop in Example 1. The three general forms for implied DO loops are as follows:

FORM A

```
(A(I),I=N1,N2,N3)
```

for a single-subscripted value.

FORM B

```
((B(I,J),I=N1,N2,N3),J=M1,M2,M3)
```

for a double-subscripted variable where the order of I and J depends on the desired order of the input or output.

FORM C

```
(((C(I,J,K),I=N1,N2,N3),J=M1,M2,M3),K=L1,L2,L3)
```

for a triple-subscripted variable where the order of I, J, and K depends on the desired order of the input or output.

In each of these forms, the indices may be any acceptable integer variables and the parameters may be any integer constants, variables, or expressions—the same as for explicit DO loops. Furthermore, for two or three indices, the inner implied DO statement is executed first, then each succeeding outer one.

With multiple items. It is also possible to have more than one item in an implied loop.

EXAMPLE The statement

```
READ*,((A(I),B(I)),I=N1,N2,N3)
```

calls for pairs of input values starting with values for A(N1) and B(N1), followed by values for A(N1+N3) and B(N1+N3) and so on such that the subscript increases by N3 until the last pair of values whose subscripts are less than or equal to N2 are read.

When to use. Implied DO loops are used only to input, output, or initialize values for subscripted variables of one or more subscripts. In the following examples, assume that this variable declaration holds:

```
INTEGER A(-1:3),B(2,10),C(3,4,10)
```

If the increment is 1 it need not be specified as a parameter, just as in explicit DO loops.

EXAMPLE 1
```
READ*, (A(I),I=0,2)
```

expects three input numbers and stores them in A(0), A(1), and A(2).

EXAMPLE 2
```
READ*, (((B(I,J),J=1,10),A(I)),I=1,2)
```

expects 22 input numbers and, in the order entered, stores them in

```
B(1,1),B(1,2),B(1,3), . . . , B(1,10),A(1)
B(2,1),B(2,2),B(2,3), . . . , B(2,10),A(2)
```

EXAMPLE 3
```
READ*, (((C(I,J,K),J=1,2),I=2,3),K=1,10,2)
```

expects 20 input numbers and, in the order received, stores them as follows, in order from left to right and top to bottom:

```
C(2,1,1) C(2,2,1) C(3,1,1) C(3,2,1)
C(2,1,3) C(2,2,3) C(3,1,3) C(3,2,3)
C(2,1,5) C(2,2,5) C(3,1,5) C(3,2,5)
C(2,1,7) C(2,2,7) C(3,1,7) C(3,2,7)
C(2,1,9) C(2,2,9) C(3,1,9) C(3,2,9)
```

The numbers may be entered on a single line if there is space for them, or on more than one line.

In DATA statements. The use of an implied DO loop with DATA statements produces identical results with those just described for READ statements. Consider these examples:

EXAMPLE 1
```
INTEGER A(-1:3),B(2,10),C(3,4,10)
DATA A, (B(1,J),J=1,10)/5*0,10*1/
```

initializes to 0 all five elements of array A and initializes to 1 the first row of array B.

EXAMPLE 2
```
DATA(((C(I,J,K),J=1,2),I=2,3),K=1,10,2)/5*1,5*2,5*3,5*4/
```

initializes 20 of the 120 elements of array C as follows (read down the first column before proceeding to the second):

```
C(2,1,1)=1          C(3,1,5)=3
C(2,2,1)=1          C(3,2,5)=3
C(3,1,1)=1          C(2,1,7)=3
C(3,2,1)=1          C(2,2,7)=3
C(2,1,3)=1          C(3,1,7)=3
C(2,2,3)=2          C(3,2,7)=4
C(3,1,3)=2          C(2,1,9)=4
C(3,2,3)=2          C(2,2,9)=4
C(2,1,5)=2          C(3,1,9)=4
C(2,2,5)=2          C(3,2,9)=4
```

In PRINT and WRITE statements. The same implied DO loops given earlier can be used with PRINT or WRITE statements as well as READ. In such cases, as many numbers are printed per line as the system dictates.

EXAMPLE Another example of an implied DO loop will illustrate further. Consider the array declaration

```
INTEGER C(0:2,4:7,-5:4)
```

Suppose this INTEGER statement appears in the same program as the following three READ statements:

```
10    READ*,((C(0,I,J),J=-5,4),I=4,7)
20    READ*,((C(I,J,K),I=0,2),J=4,7)
30    READ*,(((C(I,J,K),K=-5,0)I=0,2),J=4,7)
```

When the READ on line 10 is executed, 40 values are read and stored in the following order:

```
C(0,4,-5),C(0,4,-4),C(0,4,-3), . . . ,C(0,4,3),C(0,4,4)
C(0,5,-5),C(0,5,-4),C(0,5,-3), . . . ,C(0,5,3),C(0,5,4)
C(0,6,-5),C(0,6,-4),C(0,6,-3), . . . ,C(0,6,3),C(0,6,4)
C(0,7,-5),C(0,7,-4),C(0,7,-3), . . . ,C(0,7,3),C(0,7,4)
```

The READ statement on line 20 results in 12 values being read and stored as follows, reading left to right and top to bottom:

```
C(0,4,K),C(1,4,K),C(2,4,K)
C(0,5,K),C(1,5,K),C(2,5,K)
C(0,6,K),C(1,6,K),C(2,6,K)
C(0,7,K),C(1,7,K),C(2,7,K)
```

In this case the value of K would have to be defined before the execution of the READ and must be in the range from –5 to 4, as specified in the accompanying INTEGER statement.

Finally the READ statement in line 30 causes the reading of 72 values that are stored as follows, from left to right:

```
C(0,4,-5),C(0,4,-4),C(0,4,-3),C(0,4,-2),C(0,4,-1),C(0,4,0)
C(1,4,-5),C(1,4,-4),C(1,4,-3),C(1,4,-2),C(1,4,-1),C(1,4,0)
C(2,4,-5),C(2,4,-4),C(2,4,-3),C(2,4,-2),C(2,4,-1),C(2,4,0)
C(0,5,-5),C(0,5,-4),C(0,5,-3),C(0,5,-2),C(0,5,-1),C(0,5,0)
C(1,5,-5),C(1,5,-4),C(1,5,-3),C(1,5,-2),C(1,5,-1),C(1,5,0)
C(2,5,-5),C(2,5,-4),C(2,5,-3),C(2,5,-2),C(2,5,-1),C(2,5,0)
C(0,6,-5),C(0,6,-4),C(0,6,-3),C(0,6,-2),C(0,6,-1),C(0,6,0)
C(1,6,-5),C(1,6,-4),C(1,6,-3),C(1,6,-2),C(1,6,-1),C(1,6,0)
C(2,6,-5),C(2,6,-4),C(2,6,-3),C(2,6,-2),C(2,6,-1),C(2,6,0)
C(0,7,-5),C(0,7,-4),C(0,7,-3),C(0,7,-2),C(0,7,-1),C(0,7,0)
C(1,7,-5),C(1,7,-4),C(1,7,-3),C(1,7,-2),C(1,7,-1),C(1,7,0)
C(2,7,-5),C(2,7,-4),C(2,7,-3),C(2,7,-2),C(2,7,-1),C(2,7,0)
```

Remember that the use of an array name without subscript designations in a data, input, or output statement assigns or retrieves values to or from the ***entire array***.

Condition Controlled Structures

Sometimes we cannot determine in advance the number of times the body of an iteration structure is to be executed. To control repetition, a condition is built into the loop that, when satisfied, terminates the loop. This condition may be placed either at the beginning or end of the loop body or within the loop body itself:

FORM A

```
Entry point
Exit condition                          At the beginning of the loop
If true
      execute Loop body
      return to Exit condition
If false
Exit point
```

FORM B

```
Entry point
execute first part of Loop body
Exit condition                          Within the loop body
If true
      execute rest of Loop body
      return to Entry point
If false
Exit point
```

FORM C

```
Entry point
Loop body
Exit condition                          At the end of the loop
If true
      return to Entry point
If false
Exit point
```

IF–GO TO statements. All three of these cases can be implemented using IF and GO TO statements. We demonstrate the three forms with three segments using essentially the same statements. The examples are meant simply to show the forms; only Example A is an appropriate program segment.

EXAMPLE A

```
      DATA COUNT, SUM, SUMSQ/3*0/
      READ*,X
 5    IF (X .LT. 0) GO TO 10           Condition
          COUNT=COUNT+1                Loop body
          SUM=SUM+X                    "
          SUMSQ=SUMSQ+X*X              "
          READ*,X                      "
      GO TO 5
 10   AVG=SUM/COUNT
      VAR=(SUMSQ-COUNT*AVG*AVG)/COUNT
      PRINT*,AVG,VAR
```

This loop is bounded by the IF statement with reference number 5 and the GO TO 5 statement. The condition is tested *before* the loop body so it is possible to completely skip executing the loop.

EXAMPLE B

```
      DATA COUNT, SUM, SUMSQ/3*0/
 5    READ*,X                              Part of loop body
         IF (X .LT. 0) GO TO 10            Condition
         COUNT=COUNT+1                     Rest of loop body
         SUM=SUM+X                         "
         SUMSQ=SUMSQ+X*X                   "
      GO TO 5
 10   AVG=SUM/COUNT
      VAR=(SUMSQ-COUNT*AVG*AVG)/COUNT
      PRINT*,AVG,VAR
```

This segment accomplishes the same results as Example A but this time the condition is tested within the loop body. ***Avoid this structure*** as it is difficult to understand.

EXAMPLE C

```
      DATA COUNT, SUM, SUMSQ/3*0/
 5    READ*,X                              Loop body
         COUNT=COUNT+1                     "
         SUM=SUM+X                         "
         SUMSQ=SUMSQ+X*X                   "
      IF (X .GE. 0) GO TO 5                Condition
      AVG=SUM/COUNT
      VAR=(SUMSQ-COUNT*AVG*AVG)/COUNT
      PRINT*,AVG,VAR
```

This time the condition is checked *after* the loop body, so the loop is executed at least once.

Although this program segment seems to solve the same problem as Examples A and B it has a ***logic error***. When the sentinel datum intended to stop the iteration is input at statement 5, it is processed by the loop body as if it were valid data. This placement of the test for the exit condition yields a program segment that does not solve the given problem.

WHILE-DO-ENDWHILE statements. A number of the commonly used FORTRAN compilers provide WHILE-DO and ENDWHILE statements designed specifically for condition controlled iteration structures. Although standard FORTRAN 77 does not have these features, they are very useful and help make a better-structured program, so we include them here. Until FORTRAN 77 adds these features, the same results can be accomplished using IF–GO TO structures.

The general format of WHILE–DO and ENDWHILE statements is as follows:

```
WHILE (Condition) DO
    Loop body
ENDWHILE
```

The word DO is usually optional.

The entry to the loop is the WHILE–DO statement, where the condition is tested.

If the condition is true all statements between the WHILE–DO and the ENDWHILE are executed, after which the condition is tested again. As long as the condition is true, this process continues.

The iteration is terminated when one of the following occurs:

1. The condition tested in the WHILE–DO becomes false.
2. A STOP statement within the loop body is executed.
3. A RETURN statement within the loop is executed.
4. A transfer out of the loop body occurs during the execution of the loop body.

The normal exit from a WHILE–DO loop is the statement immediately following the ENDWHILE. Abnormal exits may be the result of a RETURN, a STOP or a GO TO statement.

Because FORTRAN 77 does not support the WHILE–DO statement we shall not place much emphasis on the program structure made possible through its use. Nevertheless, if it is available in the FORTRAN compiler to which you have access we urge you to use it.

EXAMPLE

```
PROGRAM AVERAG
INTEGER COUNT, SUM, NUM, AVG
DATA COUNT, SUM, AVG/3*0/
READ*, NUM
WHILE (NUM .GT. 0) DO
    SUM = SUM + NUM
    COUNT = COUNT + 1
    READ*, NUM
ENDWHILE
AVG = SUM/COUNT
PRINT*, AVG, COUNT
END
```

This program reads and processes a set of one or more numbers until a 0 or negative number is encountered. The program reads the positive numbers, computes the average, and prints the count of positive numbers and their average.

The READ statement preceding the loop handles the unlikely situation where there are no positive numbers, only the sentinel null or negative datum. As written, ***the program does not correctly process this unlikely case*** to its conclusion; if the WHILE condition is false, the program still executes the statement immediately following the ENDWHILE, which could result in an attempt to divide 0 by 0. To avoid that attempted division as well as avoid reporting an undeclared value, the statements

```
AVG = SUM/COUNT
PRINT*, AVG, COUNT
```

could be replaced by the statements

```
IF (COUNT .GT. 0) THEN
    AVG = SUM/COUNT
    PRINT*, AVG, COUNT
ELSE
    PRINT*, 'NO AVERAGE COMPUTED.'
ENDIF
```

These changes allow division to occur only if COUNT is positive.

Using Iteration Structures

Being able to readily access information is one of the most important applications of computers. Randomly ordered information is no more valuable to us than raw data. Consequently, it is useful to learn methods for sorting data so that one can select portions of the data and make the selected data quickly available. Computer science research has produced many useful sorting methods, among them the two techniques used here. Both of them are appropriate examples of the use and usefulness of iteration structures. Problem 5.3A illustrates the sorting method known as either the *exchange sort* or the *straight selection sort*, and Problem 5.3B illustrates the *bubble sort*.

Problem 5.3A Checking Welds—a Straight Selection Sort

SITUATION Your company is operating a nuclear power plant. Nuclear Regulatory Commission regulations require that all of the weld xrays be available on very short notice, so that in an emergency the plant operators can quickly retrieve the ones they need to make informed decisions. Your solution to this requirement is to set up an electronic retrieval system for weld xrays. The system locates the xrays by joint number.

If the joint numbers in the data file are in ascending order, retrieval is much quicker than if the program must skip back and forth through the data. So you are asked to develop a quick and efficient way of sorting the list of joint numbers into ascending order—an example of a straight selection sort.

OBJECTIVE Read a set of N numbers, not more than 100, and store them in the array ANUM. Then sort this set of numbers in ascending order and store the sorted numbers back in array ANUM. The output of the program is the sorted numbers.

ALGORITHM

1. Read the numbers into array ANUM. Count them as they are read. Stop when sentinel datum –999,999 is encountered.

2. Sort the numbers, storing them back in array ANUM in sorted order.

3. Print array ANUM.

DETAIL

1.0 Define an array ANUM of size 100.

1.1 Initialize a number counter N to 0.

1.2 Input numbers into array ANUM until the sentinel datum –999,999 is reached.

2.0 Set loop index I to 1.

2.1 Find the smallest of the numbers at ANUM(I), ANUM(I+1), . . . , ANUM(N). Assume this smallest number is at ANUM(K).

2.2 Interchange ANUM(I) and ANUM(K).

2.3 Increase the index I by 1. If I is still less than N, repeat the process from step 2.1.

3.0 Output the N numbers in array ANUM.

MORE DETAIL The only complex step here is 2.1, so we explain one method for finding the smallest set of N numbers ANUM(1), ANUM(2), . . . , ANUM(N):

2.1.1 Beginning with I=1, assume that ANUM(I) is the smallest number in array ANUM, and store a copy of ANUM(I) in location SMALL.

2.1.2 Compare the entire array from ANUM(I) to ANUM(N), one at a time, with the value at SMALL.

2.1.3 If a number is found smaller than the current value of SMALL, the value at SMALL is replaced by that value and the location of that smaller number in array ANUM is stored at K. When all members of array ANUM from ANUM(I) to ANUM(N) have been compared with the number at SMALL, K will contain the position number of the smallest number.

2.1.4 Exchange ANUM(I) and ANUM(K). Increase I by 1, and repeat the process with the new value of I. By this process, when I reaches the value N−1, the whole array will be sorted in ascending order.

FORTRAN PROGRAM

```
      PROGRAM SORT
C***********************************************************************
C*                         PROGRAM DEFINITION                          *
C*    THIS PROGRAM INPUTS UP TO 100 NUMBERS,                           *
C*    SORTS THEM IN ASCENDING ORDER, AND OUTPUTS THE SORTED NUMBERS.   *
C***********************************************************************
C*                         VARIABLE DEFINITION                         *
C*    ANUM IS AN ARRAY OF SIZE 100 TO STORE THE SET OF NUMBERS.        *
C*    SMALL IS TO STORE THE SMALLEST NUMBER EACH TIME THROUGH THE LIST. *
C*    COUNT IS TO HOLD THE NUMBER OF NUMBERS READ INTO ARRAY ANUM.     *
C*    K IS THE POSITION OF SMALL IN ARRAY ANUM.                        *
C*    I, J ARE LOOP INDICES.                                           *
C***********************************************************************
C*
      REAL ANUM(100), SMALL, TEMP
      INTEGER COUNT, I, J, K
      COUNT = 0
      I = 1
      READ *, ANUM(I)
 10   IF ((ANUM(I) .EQ. -999999) .OR. (COUNT .GE. 100)) GOTO 12
          COUNT = COUNT+1
          I = I+1
          READ *, ANUM(I)
      GOTO 10
C*
C*******     THE NEXT STATEMENT ADJUSTS COUNT SO THAT SENTINEL DATUM
C*******     IS NOT INCLUDED.
C*
 12   IF (ANUM(I) .EQ. -999999) COUNT = COUNT-1
C*
      DO 15 I=1, COUNT-1
          SMALL = ANUM(I)
          K = I
          DO 14 J=I, COUNT
              IF (ANUM(J) .LT. SMALL) THEN
                  SMALL = ANUM(J)
                  K = J
              ENDIF
 14       CONTINUE
          TEMP = ANUM(I)
          ANUM(I) = ANUM(K)
          ANUM(K) = TEMP
 15       CONTINUE
C*
          PRINT *, (ANUM(I),I=1,COUNT)
      END
```

PROGRAM DESIGN ISSUES

Often, as here, the efficiency of searches and other procedures that involve iteration or physical operation of data storage systems is greatly increased by sorting search codes into an ascending or descending sequence. A front end sort subroutine as in this program can greatly improve the performance of a search program, if the sort subroutine is fast and efficient in its own right.

Some of the applicable design issues are:

How few steps can the subroutine use to test whether the array is already in ascending order? Or is there a procedure that will assure that it is in ascending order in fewer steps than it can be checked?

Is the subroutine efficient for almost right cases? For fully random cases? For mostly descending cases?

Can moving and copying be minimized by a brute force method that uses a lot of space? Or can we develop a faster algorithm?

Problem 5.3B
Using a Bubble Sort

OBJECTIVE

For the same problem, write an algorithm and a FORTRAN program using the bubble sort method. Assume that the number of elements in the array does not exceed 100.

ANALYSIS

The bubble sort technique compares each pair of adjacent members in the list to be sorted, starting with the first two numbers. If the number further into the list is smaller, the numbers are exchanged. If not, no change is needed. Continue comparing adjacent numbers until an entire pass can be made through the list without having to exchange a single pair of numbers.

EXAMPLE

To help clarify this procedure, we shall work through an example step by step. Suppose the original array is as follows:

```
121     217     67     81     200
```

When the first and second numbers are compared, no exchange is necessary because the smaller one is already in the first position.

When the second and third numbers are compared, an exchange is necessary. The following list results:

```
121     67     217     81     200
```

Now the third and fourth numbers are compared, resulting in an exchange. The list is

```
121     67     81     217     200
```

Finally, the fourth and fifth numbers of the latest version of the list are compared. Again an exchange is necessary, and the list becomes

```
121    67    81    200    217
```

Now we start at the beginning of the list again to see whether a complete pass through the list can be made without any exchanges. This time when elements 1 and 2 are compared, an exchange is required. After the exchange, the list looks like this:

```
67    121    81    200    217
```

Next, numbers 2 and 3 are compared, requiring an exchange. The resulting list is

```
67    81    121    200    217
```

A comparison of numbers 3 and 4 results in no exchange. It is not necessary to compare numbers 4 and 5 on this pass. Once one complete pass is made, at least the final number is in the correct position. Thus we complete the second pass through the list.

Again, start at the beginning of the list. A quick check assures you that a comparison of adjacent pairs all the way through the list requires no exchanges. The list is sorted as desired.

ALGORITHM

1.0 Initialize the logical variable CHANGE to the value true. We will make at least one pass through the list to determine whether any exchanges are necessary.

2.0 As long as CHANGE has the value true, perform steps 2.1 and 2.2.

2.1 Set CHANGE to false, assuming that no exchanges are necessary this time through.

2.2 Compare LIST(I) to LIST(I + 1), for I = 1, 2, . . . , N–1. For any I such that LIST(I) is greater than LIST(I + 1), exchange the contents of these two locations and set CHANGE to true.

3.0 Terminate processing. This will occur only if CHANGE still has the value false.

FORTRAN PROGRAM

```
      PROGRAM BUBSRT
C**************************************************************************
C*    PROGRAM DEFINITION SAME AS FOR PROBLEM 1                            *
C**************************************************************************
C*                         VARIABLE DEFINITIONS                           *
C*    NUM IS AN ARRAY OF SIZE 100 TO STORE THE NUMBERS TO BE SORTED.      *
C*    TEMP IS A VARIABLE FOR TEMPORARILY STORING A PARTICULAR             *
C*        ELEMENT OF ARRAY NUM.                                           *
C*    COUNT STORES THE NUMBER OF NUMBERS READ INTO ARRAY NUM.             *
C*    I IS A LOOP INDEX.                                                  *
C*    K IDENTIFIES THE POINT IN THE ARRAY TO WHICH SORTING IS COMPLETED.  *
C*    CHANGE IS A LOGICAL VARIABLE FOR SPECIFYING WHETHER OR              *
C*        NOT AN EXCHANGE OF VALUES HAS OCCURRED.                         *
C**************************************************************************
C*
      REAL NUM(100), TEMP
      INTEGER COUNT, I, K
      LOGICAL CHANGE
      COUNT = 0
      I = 1
      READ*, NUM(I)
 10   IF ((NUM(I) .EQ. -999999) .OR. (COUNT .GE. 100)) GOTO 12
          COUNT = COUNT+1
          I = I+1
          READ*, NUM(I)
      GOTO 10
 12   IF (NUM(I) .EQ. -999999) COUNT = COUNT-1
C*
      CHANGE = .TRUE.
      K = 1
 20   IF (.NOT. CHANGE) GOTO 30
          CHANGE = .FALSE.
          DO 100 I=1, COUNT-K
              IF (NUM(I) .LT. NUM(I+1)) THEN
                  CHANGE = .TRUE.
                  TEMP = NUM(I)
                  NUM(I) = NUM(I+1)
                  NUM(I+1) = TEMP
              ENDIF
 100      CONTINUE
          K = K+1
      GOTO 20
C*
 30   DO 200 I=1, COUNT
          PRINT*, NUM(I)
 200  CONTINUE
      END
```

Iterations in testing. The bubble sort technique sorts an array of the same type as that in Problem 5.3A, but it is generally a bit faster than the straight selection sort. The relative speed of the two techniques was actually tested using iteration structures. With an efficient code for each of the sort procedures, simply set up a FORTRAN program that will accomplish the following:

1. Produce a random list of numbers.
2. Submit it to the straight selection sort and keep track of how long it takes to sort the list.
3. Submit the same random list to the bubble sort and keep track of how long it takes to sort it.
4. Compare the speed of the two procedures.

If you set up this process within a loop, to run with several thousand pseudorandom number sets, you can process the results to find out which method is faster and determine the average difference in speed.

This technique of testing relative speeds by running many thousands of trials on sets of pseudorandom data is called the *Monte Carlo method* of testing. It is an extremely effective way to determine the relative advantages of two comparable procedures when there is no formal mathematical way to compare them.

Problem 5.4
Sorting Potatoes

SITUATION You work for a food processing company. It is vitally important that the ingredients used in processing be of consistent quality. The potatoes used in a variety of products have been sorted for many years by the same four employees, all of whom are now within 2 years of retirement. None of the sorters has trained any new worker, nor do they have any written system of how the potatoes are sorted—each of the workers simply *knows what is right*, and the four of them agree in their decisions 99% of the time.

When the workers retire, the company plans to replace them with an automated system that measures each potato for color, size, number of eyes, mass, and other items, classifies it, and drops it in the proper bin. But since the graders cannot describe their process, a special program called an *inference engine* must be written to deduce the rules from the various potato measurements and their classification by the graders.

The heart of an inference engine is a module that identifies *equivalence relations*. If an equivalence relation can be found, for example, between statistics such as

Mass < 250g
Eyes < 2
Firmness > 6psi
Water content > 94
Starch : sugar proportion < 12

and a consistent classification

Type B2 for canned whole small potatoes

then the automated machine will work adequately.

The inference engine itself works by clustering the data into arbitrary types. A matrix of measured type versus worker classification is then prepared and examined for equivalence relations.

OBJECTIVE You have been asked to write the module that will do the following:

1. Accept data in the form of a matrix of machine type by sorter type, in which 0 means that no potatoes belong to this combination of machine and sorter types and 1 means that at least one potato belongs to the combination. This notation is discussed further in the Technique section below.
2. Evaluate whether an equivalence relation is present.
3. Report back to the main program.

DEFINITION A relation R defined on a finite set A = {X1, X2, X3, . . . , XN} is said to be

1. *Reflexive* if for all XI in A, XI is related to XI. That is, each member of set A is related to itself.
2. *Symmetric* if for all XI and XJ such that if XI is related to XJ, XJ is related to XI. That is, XI is related to XJ if and only if XJ is related to XI.
3. *Transitive* if for all XI, XJ, and XK for which XI is related to XJ and XJ is related to XK, XI is also related to XK. That is, if XI is related to XJ and XJ is related to XK then XI is related to XK.

A relation that has all three of these properties is said to be an *equivalence relation.*

TECHNIQUE To represent a relation defined on a finite set of N elements, we use an N by N array R such that each of its rows and columns corresponds to an element of the set on which the relation is defined. (See Problem 4.3.) Thus, if XI is related to XJ for any I, J such that 1 <= I <= N and 1 <= J <= N, the member of array R in row I and column J is 1. If XI is not related to XJ, the element of R in row I and column J is 0.

EXAMPLE For example, suppose that A = {1, 2, 3, 4, 5} and that R is the relation on members of set A such that XI is related to XJ if and only if XI + XJ is an odd integer. The relation R is represented in array R as follows:

```
0    1    0    1    0
1    0    1    0    1
0    1    0    1    0
1    0    1    0    1
0    1    0    1    0
```

PROCESS Read the row and column positions in array R for which XI is related to XJ, then determine which, if any, of the properties reflexive, symmetric, or transitive, are true. Also determine if the relation is an equivalence relation.

ALGORITHM

1. Read pairs of integers specifying the row/column pairs I and J such that XI is related to XJ.
2. For all I = 1, 2, . . . , N if R(I, I) = 1 then R is reflexive. Otherwise R is not reflexive.
3. For all I = 1, 2, . . . , N and J = 1 , 2, . . . , N if R(I, J) = R(J,I) then R is symmetric. Otherwise, R is not symmetric.
4. For all I = 1, 2, . . . , N ; J = 1 , 2, . . . , N and K = 1, 2, . . . , N if R(I, J) * R(J, K) = 1 *and* R(I, K) = 1, then R is transitive. Otherwise, R is not transitive.
5. If R is reflexive and symmetric and transitive, then R is an equivalence relation. Otherwise, it is not an equivalence relation.

FORTRAN PROGRAM

```
      PROGRAM RELATN
C**** THE FOLLOWING LOGICAL VARIABLES WILL BE USED TO INDICATE
C**** THAT RELATION R HAS THE PROPERTIES WITH SIMILAR NAMES.
C**** WE ALSO ASSUME THAT THE SET ON WHICH RELATION R IS DEFINED
C**** WILL HAVE AT MOST 100 ELEMENTS.
C*
      LOGICAL REFL, TRANS, SYMET
      INTEGER R(100,100), N, I, J, K
      DATA R/10000 * 0/
      PRINT*, 'ENTER THE NUMBER OF ELEMENTS IN THE SET'
      READ*, N
      PRINT*, 'ENTER A PAIR OF INTEGERS SUCH THAT THE RELATION IS '
      PRINT*, 'TRUE FOR ELEMENTS SPECIFIED BY THESE INTEGERS.'
      PRINT*, 'ENTER ONE PAIR PER LINE. WHEN DONE ENTER 0 0'
      READ*, I, J
```

```
 10   IF (I*J .EQ. 0) GOTO 100
          IF (I.LT.0 .OR. I.GT.N .OR. J.LT.0 .OR. J.GT.N) THEN
              PRINT*, 'BOTH INTEGERS MUST BE GREATER THAN 0 '
              PRINT*, 'AND LESS THAN OR EQUAL TO ',N
              PRINT*, 'PLEASE ENTER AGAIN.'
          ELSE
              R(I, J) = 1
          ENDIF
          PRINT*, 'ENTER NEXT PAIR.'
          READ*, I, J
      GOTO 10
C***  AT THIS POINT THE RELATION IS STORED IN ARRAY R.
C***  NOW WE PROCEED TO CHECK FOR THE 3 PROPERTIES.
C*
 100  REFL = .TRUE.
      DO 120 I = 1, N
          IF (R(I,I) .NE. 1) REFL = .FALSE.
 120  CONTINUE
      IF (REFL) THEN
          PRINT*, 'THE RELATION IS REFLEXIVE.'
      ELSE
          PRINT*, 'THE RELATION IS NOT REFLEXIVE.'
      ENDIF
      SYMET = .TRUE.
      DO 150 I = 1, N
          DO 140 J = 1, N
              IF(R(I, J) .NE. R(J, I)) SYMET = .FALSE.
 140      CONTINUE
 150  CONTINUE
      IF (SYMET) THEN
          PRINT*, 'THE RELATION IS SYMMETRIC.'
      ELSE
          PRINT*, 'THE RELATION IS NOT SYMMETRIC.'
      ENDIF
      TRANS = .TRUE.
      DO 180 I = 1, N
          DO 170 J = 1, N
              DO 160 K = 1, N
                  IF ((R(I,J)*R(J,K) .EQ. 1) .AND. (R(I,J) .NE. 1)
     +                TRANS = .FALSE.
 160          CONTINUE
 170      CONTINUE
 180  CONTINUE
      IF (TRANS) THEN
          PRINT*, 'THE RELATION IS TRANSITIVE.'
      ELSE
          PRINT*, 'THE RELATION IS NOT TRANSITIVE.'
      ENDIF
```

```
IF (TRANS .AND. SYMET .AND. REFL) THEN
    PRINT*, 'THE RELATION IS AN EQUIVALENCE RELATION.'
ELSE
    PRINT*, 'THIS IS NOT AN EQUIVALENCE RELATION.'
ENDIF
END
```

Summary

DO loop. A DO loop is a collection of program statements repeated some finite number of times under the control of a DO statement and another statement identified in the DO statement. The general form of the DO statement follows:

```
DO R INDEX = exp1, exp2, exp3
```

where R is an integer constant specifying the reference number of the last statement in the loop;
INDEX is any integer variable (or real variable in the case of a real DO loop); and
exp1, exp2, and exp3 represent any constants, variables, or expressions resulting in integer (or real, in the case of a real DO loop) values.

The first of these three, exp1, is the initial value for INDEX, exp2 is the final value for INDEX, and exp3 is the increment to be used in going from the value of exp1 to the value of exp2.

Review the rules related to DO loops.

Implied DO loop. An implied DO loop is similar in action to a DO loop. It may be used only in input or output statements or in DATA statements, and has this form if the array is three-dimensional:

```
READ*, (((A(I,J,K), K=K1, K2, K3), J = J1, J2, J3), I = I1, I2, I3)
```

The index specified farthest to the left is assigned all its values first, then the index specified next in order to the right is assigned its values and for *each* different value of this index the leftmost specified index is again assigned all its values.

After all values for the second-specified index have been assigned, the next-specified index to the right is assigned its values. For *each* different value of this third index, the indices to its left are reassigned values as previously described.

Thus, this implied DO loop performs like a nested DO loop with three indices.

Nested DO loop. This structure has two or more complete DO loops, an inner loop entirely contained within a next innermost loop, which is entirely contained within another loop, and so on out to the outer loop. For *each* different value of the index of an outer DO loop, the index of the next inner loop is assigned *all* its specified values. This process continues inward, so that the index of the inner loop is assigned its specified values most often.

End of Chapter Exercises

1. Specify the output produced by each of the following programs:

a.
```
      PROGRAM A
      INTEGER INT(10),I,J
      DO 10 I=1,10
          DO 20 J=1,10
              INT (J)=I*J
 20       CONTINUE
          PRINT *,INT
 10   CONTINUE
      END
```

b.
```
      PROGRAM B
      CHARACTER A(-30:30)
      INTEGER I,J,K
      DO 10 I=-30,30
          A(I)='$'
 10   CONTINUE
      DO 20 I=-30,30,10
          PRINT *,A(I),
          DO 30 J=1,6
              PRINT *, (A(K),K=-30,30)
 30       CONTINUE
 20   CONTINUE
      END
```

c.
```
      PROGRAM C
      CHARACTER A(10,10)
      INTEGER I,J
      DO 10 I=1,10
          A(I,I)='$'
          A(I,11-I)='*'
 10   CONTINUE
      DO 20 I=1,10
          DO 20 J=1,10
              IF (A(I,J) .NE. '$' .OR. A(I,J) .NE. '*')A(I,J)=' '
 20   CONTINUE
      PRINT *,A
      END
```

d.

```
      PROGRAM D
      INTEGER I,K,N
      READ *,N
      IF (N .LT. 1 .OR. N .GT. 15) GO TO 30
      K=1
      DO 10 I=1,N
          K=K*I
          PRINT *,I,'FACTORIAL=',K
 10   CONTINUE
 30   PRINT *, 'N MUST BE BETWEEN 1 AND 15.'
      END
```

2. Given two positive integers M and N, write a program to compute the sum of all integers from M to N, inclusive; the sum of the even integers from M to N; and the sum of the odd integers from M to N. For the last two sums, include the integers M and N as appropriate.

3. Write a program that, for all positive integers I, J, and K from 1 to 1000, inclusive, finds all combinations of I, J, and K such that

$$I^2 + J^2 = K^2$$

4. Write a program that for all positive integers I, J, K, and L from 1 to 1000, inclusive, finds all combinations of I, J, K, and L such that

$$I^3 + J^3 = K^3 = L^3$$

5. A square matrix is called a *symmetric matrix* if it is equal to its transpose. Write a program that will read the elements of an N x N matrix A and determine if A is symmetric and report an appropriate message.

6. A square matrix is called a *diagonal matrix* if its only nonzero elements are on the diagonal from upper left to lower right. It is called *upper triangular* if all elements below this diagonal are zeros and *lower triangular* if all elements above this diagonal are zeros. Write a program that reads a square matrix no larger than N x N and determines if it is one of these three special matrices.

7. Let A be an M x N matrix and B an N x P matrix. Then the product matrix C of A and B is the matrix whose elements c_{ij} are computed as

$$c_{ij} = \sum_{k=1}^{n} a_{ik}\, b_{kj}$$

Write a program to compute the product of two matrices.

8. Write a program to find all integer solutions to the equation

$$x+y = 2(x-y)$$

where x is greater than or equal to y and both x and y are less than 1000.

9. Write programs to compute the values of each of the following series:

a. $$1 + \left(\frac{1}{8}\right) + \left(\frac{1}{27}\right) + \ldots + \left(\frac{1}{100}\right)$$

b. $$1 - \left(\frac{1}{2}\right) + \left(\frac{1}{3}\right) - \left(\frac{1}{4}\right) + \ldots - \left(\frac{1}{100}\right)$$

c. $$1 + \left(\frac{x}{1}\right) + \left(\frac{x}{2!}\right) + \left(\frac{x}{3!}\right) + \ldots + \left(\frac{x}{10!}\right)$$

where

$2! = 2 \cdot 1 = 2$

$3! = 3 \cdot 2 \cdot 1 = 6$

$4! = 4 \cdot 3 \cdot 2 \cdot 1 = 24$

$k! = k \cdot (k-1) \cdot (k-2) \ldots 1$

Compute values of this series for $x = 1,2,3, \ldots ,10$.

10. Write a program that reads any Roman numeral from I to XX and prints the equivalent decimal number. The twenty Roman numerals are I, II, III, IV, V, VI, VII, VIII, IX, X, XI, XII, XIII, XIV, XV, XVI, XVII, XVIII, IX, XX.

11. Consider five adjacent squares arranged as follows:

	1	
8	3	7
	5	

1OBJECTIVE Write a program to find all possible ways of placing a digit 1 through 8 in each of the squares so that no two squares having a common side contain consecutive digits. One such arrangement is shown on the figure.

12. ***The Random Walk problem.*** A rectangular room has a floor consisting of 1–inch square tiles. The dimensions of the room are M x N inches.

SITUATION Suppose a cockroach is placed on any given tile located at row I and column J, where I ≤ M and J ≤ N. Assume that the cockroach crawls from tile to tile at the rate of one tile per second, and that, from any single tile, it crawls randomly with equal probability to any of the eight tiles surrounding it, unless it is against the wall.

OBJECTIVE Write a program to compute the time needed for the cockroach to touch every tile on the floor at least once. Assume that 2 < M < 40 and 2 < N < 40 and that the cockroach cannot enter any given tile more than 50,000 times. If this maximum is reached before all tiles are touched, restart the cockroach at a different tile.

The output for each trial should be

1. The total number of seconds required.
2. The number of entries onto each tile.

3. A list of the tiles by position from the ones entered most often to the ones entered just once.

HINTS

Here are some hints for solving this problem:

1. Establish an array COUNT(M,N) to keep track of the number of entries to the tile whose position in the room is row M and column N.
2. If the cockroach is on tile (I,J), then the position of the next tile to which it moves is given by

```
(I+IMOVE(K), J+JMOVE(K))
```

where K is a random number from 1 through 8 and

```
IMOVE(1) = IMOVE(7) = IMOVE(8) = -1
IMOVE(2) = IMOVE(6) = 0
IMOVE(3) = IMOVE(4) = IMOVE(5) = 1
```

If we assume the arrangement of tiles with respect to the cockroach as follows:

3	4	5
2	0	6
1	8	7

A little thought will tell you the values to use for JMOVE(1) . . . JMOVE(8)

13. *The Magic Square Problem.* A magic square is an n x n matrix of integers from 1 to n^2 such that the sums of every row, column, and diagonal are equal. In fact, that sum will always be $(n/2) * (n^2 + 1)$

Mathematicians have shown that for all even values of n no magic square exists. For $n = 3$, here is a magic square:

6	1	8
7	5	3
2	9	4

Here is a magic square for $n = 5$:

15	8	1	24	17
16	14	7	5	23
22	20	13	6	4
3	21	19	12	10
9	2	25	18	11

ALGORITHM

Here is one algorithm for creating a magic square for a given N:

1. Place 1 in the center of the top row. Remember, N is odd.
2. Subsequent placement of successive numbers is done by moving diagonally upward to the left unless the number just placed is in the top in its column.
3. If the number just placed is the top one in its column, the next number is placed in the bottom square of the adjacent column to the left.

4. If there is no column to the left when applying step 2 or step 3, place the next number in succession in the appropriate row (as defined in steps 2 and 3) of the rightmost column of the matrix.
5. Every time the number just placed is a multiple of N, the next number is placed just below it in the same column, after which step 2 or 3 is applied.
6. Continue until the last number N has been placed.

OBJECTIVE Write a program to read an odd integer and produce a magic square.

PROGRAM DESIGN ISSUES Questions like these have been known for centuries, chiefly as amusements and puzzles. More recently, they have been found to have numerous applications in the mathematical description of communication networks, ranging from predicting flows of paper within large office buildings to creating software to control timesharing of long distance lines.

Frequently, when a problem involves optimizing one or more aspects of the flow of messages from point to point, the problem becomes identical at the abstract level with finding an arrangement like the Magic Square in Exercise 13 or the separation problem in Exercise 11. The drift of transmitting data away from perfect fidelity, a phenomenon familiar from the party game "Telephone," for a finite set of possible messages such as naval codebooks, phone numbers, or part orders is mathematically similar to the cockroach problem in Exercise 12.

Even though the mathematics of such problems has been explored for a very long time, they are still among the most challenging problems for the modern programmer. Here are some ways to plan an approach to your solutions:

Are there any identities or variables with a fixed relationship that can be exploited? For example, in the separation problem, if interger A must not adjoin integer B, the reverse is also true.

Is there a frame of reference in which the mathematics is unusually straightforward? For example, in Exercise 12, the distribution of probability of the cockroach's next move is always very clear if the square he's on is defined as (0,0).

Does the program have to find a particular solution? All the possible solutions? An indefinite number of solutions? Or the general solution? This is a hidden requirement that is far too often left out of specifications for problems of this type. For example, a program that has a single rule for generating a single magic square (one particular solution) may be less than useful if what is needed is a collection of choices; but often where a general solution is difficult or impossible to reach, and a complete solution set too large, all that may be needed is one solution that works.

Chapter 6

Subprograms

Thus far, it has been convenient to assume that each program presented was constructed as one unit. There have, of course, been subtasks within many of the programs, such as input, computation, and output; but we have made no concerted effort to group together within a program those statements that handle specific functions.

As your problem solving and programming skills develop to the point where you can deal with larger and more complex problems, you will find it very helpful to consider complex problems in segments. It is generally more efficient to develop and test solutions for smaller, more tightly defined problem segments than for massive, complex problems as a whole. The solutions to the smaller problems need only be connected together to build a satisfactory program to handle the overall problem.

Segmenting a Program

When computer programming is done in smaller sections such that each section is designed, written and tested separately, such sections are usually called *subprograms*. To qualify as a FORTRAN 77 subprogram, a collection of statements must conform to one of several specific formats, each of which has its own set of rules. The main formats are *function* and *subroutine* subprograms, each discussed in this chapter along with examples to clarify useful subprogram structures.

Reasons to subdivide a program. Many advantages of writing subprograms have become obvious as we have worked through the problems in this book. They are more efficient with resources, because with subprograms a larger number of teams can work on a problem at one time. And they are a good investment, because a solution in one context can easily be adapted to solve the same specific problem in other contexts. But the process of dealing with subprograms itself offers a number of advantages:

1. The limited series of steps is ***easier to comprehend*** than a larger collection of tasks.
2. Small segments are ***easier to structure***.
3. It's ***easier to spot logic errors*** than in a longer, more complex program.

4. The overall solution has ***clearer structure and tighter logic*** because each step has a more focused objective.
5. This can ***significantly reduce time*** for coding and debugging.
6. Appropriate subprogram structure reduces repetition, so ***less code is needed*** to accomplish a given task.
7. Modular, well-structured programs are ***simpler to maintain*** than monolithic non-modular programs.
8. Subprograms ***may eliminate the need for layering*** when a large program is developed for a computer with small memory.

The function statement. The role of a function statement in FORTRAN is similar to that of a formula in mathematics. It is a single line of FORTRAN code that has the appearance of an assignment statement, but a function is defined once and is used with different parameters as many times as needed.

The general form of a function statement has 3 parts:

```
Name(Arguments) = Definition
```

The ***function name*** precedes the first open parenthesis. A function name must conform to the same rules as those for naming variables. It is best to declare the data type using an appropriate declaration statement. Other wise, a default data type is assigned according to the first character of the function name, just as with ordinary variables.

The ***formal argument(s)*** appear inside the parentheses immediately following the function name. These formal arguments are the key variables in the expression to the right of the equals sign. Every function statement must have at least one formal argument. All arguments must be defined and given values before using the function.

The ***function definition*** is the expression following the equals sign.

A function statement is called into action by including its name and argument(s) in an expression, in an assignment statement, or as the actual argument of another function statement or subprogram.

Here are some sample function statements:

EXAMPLE 1

```
F1(X) = X**K
```

F1(X) is defined as the Kth power of X. Before F1(X) can be executed in the program, the variable X and the variable K must be defined. Consider the following program, in which a similar function statement appears:

```
PROGRAM SAMPL1
REAL A, F1
INTEGER K
F1(X) = X**K
READ *, A, K
PRINT *, A, K, F1(A)
END
```

Suppose the values read for A and K are 1.5 and 3, respectively. Since F1(X) is defined in the function statement as the Kth power of X, then F1(A) is the 3rd power of 1.5, or 1.5 * 1.5 * 1.5 = 3.375. Therefore, the output of the preceding sample program is

```
        1.5            3               3.375
```

In this example, A is the actual argument replacing formal argument X.

EXAMPLE 2

```
F2(X, Y, Z) = X*X + 2*X*Y + 3*Z*Z
```

Here, F2 has three formal arguments. The three actual arguments that replace these formal arguments must be defined in the program before any appearance of F2 in an executable statement. For example, the program

```
PROGRAM SAMPL2
INTEGER X, Y, Z
REAL R, F2
F2(X, Y, Z) = X*X + 2*Y*Y + 3*Z*Z
R = 0.5 * F2(3,2,1)
PRINT *,R, F2(1,1,1)
STOP
END
```

results in a value of 20 for F2(3,2,1), since the first argument is multiplied by itself, the second argument is multiplied by itself and that result multiplied by 2, and, finally, the third argument is multiplied by itself and that result multiplied by 3. Thus, R has a value of 10, and the output is

```
        10.0            6.0
```

As you can tell from these first two examples, formal arguments in function statements are placeholders for the actual variables or constants that appear when the function is used in the program. The operations specified for the formal arguments in the function expression are applied to the actual variables or constants provided when the function is used.

EXAMPLE 3

```
F3(X, Y) = SIN(X) + COS(Y)
```

We have seen already that a function definition may include other functions. Note that system library functions SIN and COS are used here.

EXAMPLE 4
```
F4(X, Y) = ALOG(X) + EXP(Y)
```

EXAMPLE 5
```
G1(X, Y) = ALOG10(X) * Y
```

In Examples 4 and 5, system library functions ALOG, EXP, and ALOG10 appear in the defining expression. Functions that are defined earlier in the program itself may also be used in the defining expression.

EXAMPLE 6
```
G2(A, B) = (A+B) * FF(A)
```

Here's a case in point. FF is such a function. Consider the program

```
PROGRAM SAMPL6
REAL FF, G2
INTEGER A, B, X
FF(X) = 3*X*X - 2*X
G2(A,B) = (A+B) * FF(A)
PRINT*, G2(2,1)
END
```

What is the output of this program? To determine what G2(2,1) is, we look to the defining expression for G2. We learn that the two arguments 2 and 1 are added, and the sum multiplied by FF(2).

The value for FF(2) is obtained by multiplying 3 times 2 times 2, which gives 12, then subtracting the product of 2 and 2, which is 4. Thus FF(2) is 12 – 4, or 8.

Back now to evaluating G2(2,1), we note that G(2,1) = (2+1) * 8 = 24. The output is the single number 24.

EXAMPLE 7
```
INTEGER I1
I1(A, B) = A+B
```

In this function statement the function name is of type integer; the value of `I1`(1.3,2.4) is the integer 3. Note that the defining expression for `I1` specifies that the sum of the two arguments must be computed, so from 1.3 + 2.4 we get 3.7. Then since the function name is `I1`, we truncate the value of 3.7 and have a final value of 3.

Rules for function statements. From these examples, we can distill a few simple but important rules:

1. A function statement is ***nonexecutable*** and should be defined with other nonexecutable statements at the beginning of the program or subprogram.
2. The data type of the function name should be declared by a ***data declaration statement***, or else FORTRAN default rules for variable types will apply.
3. A function statement must have ***at least one*** formal argument.
4. The formal arguments of a function statement must be ***simple variables***. An array variable or function name is not a valid argument for a function statement.

5. The value substituted for an argument may be a ***constant***, a ***variable***, an ***expression***, or another ***function name***.

Function Subprograms

A function subprogram consists of three or more—usually more—program statements of which the first must be a FUNCTION statement and the last an END statement. The form of the FUNCTION statement is

```
Type FUNCTION NAME(ARG1,ARG2, . . . ,ARGN)
```

where Type is optional and is any of the FORTRAN type declarations, NAME is any FORTRAN variable name, and
ARG1,ARG2, . . . , ARGN represent the formal arguments of the function subprogram; there must be at least one and no more than 63.

Between the FUNCTION statement and the END statement appear as many program statements as needed. In particular, one of these program statements must assign a value to NAME. When a function subprogram has finished running it returns the value assigned to NAME back to the calling program.

A function subprogram is called into action when its name and actual arguments, the items whose values replace the formal arguments, are included in an expression, in an assignment statement, or as an actual argument of another subprogram or function statement.

The function name type. Because a computed value is associated with the function name, the data type of the function name is important. Recall that if the data type of a variable is not explicitly declared, the type of that variable depends on the first letter of its name. This same rule applies to the data type of a function name.

EXAMPLE 1 In this example, the data types for the functions are declared using standard type declaration statements:

```
FUNCTION F1(A)
INTEGER F1
.
.
.
```

```
FUNCTION F2(A)
CHARACTER F2
.
.
.
FUNCTION NAME(F1,F2)
REAL NAME
```

F1 is declared type integer, F2 is declared type character, and NAME is declared type real.

As an alternative, the general form of the FUNCTION statement itself allows you to specify the data type at the beginning of the program line. For example, the previous three functions can be assigned the same data types using only FUNCTION statements:

EXAMPLE 2

```
INTEGER FUNCTION F1(A)
CHARACTER FUNCTION F2(A)
REAL FUNCTION NAME(F1,F2)
```

The treatment of a function name must be consistent with its type. A function declared type integer must be treated as type integer in the main program and in any subprogram in which it appears. This complex example shows the declaration and use of the FUNCTION named DIV:

EXAMPLE 3

```
      PROGRAM EXAMP3
      INTEGER DIV,RES
      REAL X,Y
      READ*,X,Y
      RES=DIV(X,Y)
      IF (RES .EQ. 0) THEN
          PRINT*,'NEITHER ',X,' NOR ',Y,' IS DIVISIBLE BY THE OTHER.'
      ELSEIF (RES .EQ. 1) THEN
          PRINT*,Y,' IS DIVISIBLE BY ',X
      ELSEIF (RES .EQ. 2) THEN
          PRINT*,X,' IS DIVISIBLE BY ',Y
      ENDIF
      END
      INTEGER FUNCTION DIV(A,B)
          INTEGER QUOT
          REAL A,B
          IF (A .GT. B) THEN
              QUOT=A/B
              IF (B*QUOT .EQ. A) THEN
                  DIV=1
              ELSE
                  DIV=0
              ENDIF
```

```
24          ELSE
25              QUOT=B/A
26              IF (A*QUOT .EQ. B) THEN
27                  DIV=2
28              ELSE
29                  DIV=0
30              ENDIF
31          ENDIF
32      END
```

The function subprogram extends from line 14 to line 32. The name of the function is DIV.

DIV determines whether or not two numbers are divisible one by the other. If the first number is divisible by the second (lines 18–19), DIV has the value 1.
If the second is divisible by the first (lines 25–26), DIV has the value 2.
If neither number is divisible by the other, as determined in the ELSE of either case (lines 21 and 28), DIV has the value 0.

In the main program (lines 1–13) we read two numbers X and Y (line 4), then apply function subprogram DIV to the two numbers (line 5) and test for a function value of 0 (line 6), 1 (line 8), or 2 (line 10).
If the value is 0, line 7 displays an appropriate message about the non-divisibility of the two numbers.
If the value is 1, line 9 displays a statement that the first number is divisible by the second.
If the value is 2, line 11 displays a statement that the second number is divisible by the first.

Thus, we have considered all cases of two numbers being divisible by each other.

Invoking a function subprogram. As shown in the example, a function subprogram may be called into action by including in an expression the function name along with its list of actual arguments (also called parameters). Another way of invoking a function is to have its name appear as the parameter of another subprogram.

When a function subprogram is invoked, program control goes to the first executable statement of the function. Statements in the function are executed sequentially until the END of the function is reached or a RETURN statement is encountered. In either case, control goes back to the point in the calling program where the function was invoked.

EXAMPLE Looking at the previous program, we see that the function DIV is invoked in line 5. At this point, program control goes to line 17, the first executable statement of the function DIV. Execution of statements continues to the END of function DIV at line 32.

Control then returns to the calling program at line 5, which assigns the value of DIV to RES. Execution continues through the selection structure from line 6 until the END of the main program at line 13, where the program terminates.

The RETURN statement. The END statement indicates the end of a function subprogram, at which time control returns to the calling program with the value of the function stored in the function name. You may, however, want more than one point at which return to the calling program can occur—if, for example, the value of the function is determined by two or more different computations, return to the calling program should occur as soon as one of them is completed. For these situations FORTRAN provides the RETURN statement, in form simply the reserved word

```
RETURN
```

appearing alone on a line as a statement in the function.

When a RETURN statement is encountered, it causes program control to return to the point in the calling program where the function was invoked, exactly the same results as the END statement. The difference between them is that only one END statement is permitted in a subprogram, but more than one RETURN statement may be used.

You will be tempted to use the RETURN when there are multiple points in the subprogram where return to the calling program should take place. But because it is more difficult to follow the logic of a program that provides for more than one exit point from a subprogram, we recommend that you not use this feature of FORTRAN even if it is available.

To help you develop the habit of using only one exit from a subprogram, we use the RETURN statement only in place of an END statement as the last statement of a subprogram. This is a legitimate use of the RETURN statement. Because RETURN is more expressive of the final function in a subprogram than is END, it makes the program more understandable.

Subroutine Subprograms

This form of subprogram begins with a SUBROUTINE statement and concludes with an END statement. Between these two statements may appear any other FORTRAN statements discussed in this book. The SUBROUTINE statement has the general form

```
SUBROUTINE NAME(PAR1,PAR2, . . . ,PARN)
```

where NAME is any acceptable FORTRAN variable name, and PAR1,PAR2, . . . ,PARN refer to formal arguments.

Formal arguments in a subroutine or function subprogram serve a somewhat different purpose than formal arguments in a function statement. In a function *statement*, formal arguments provide the means for passing information to the function. The result is available from the function to the main program usually only through the function name. On the other hand, in a subroutine or function *subprogram*, formal arguments are used as placeholders both for information passed *to* the subprogram and for results *from* the subprogram.

A subroutine subprogram may have as many as 63 different formal arguments or as few as none. With no arguments, the SUBROUTINE statement has this appearance:

```
SUBROUTINE NAME
```

The name assigned to a subroutine subprogram must comply with the rules for variable names in FORTRAN, but the data type of the name is nonexistent. The subroutine subprogram name is not a vehicle for bringing a result back to the calling program, as was the case with a function subprogram.

If there is more than one result from a subroutine subprogram, they are associated with one or more of its arguments. This will be illustrated when we present an example of a complete subroutine subprogram. The end of action in a subprogram is signalled by reaching the END statement or by executing a RETURN statement.

Calling a subroutine subprogram. As was previously stated, a subroutine subprogram does not return a value to the calling program through the subroutine name. Therefore, the simple appearance of the name will not call it into action. FORTRAN provides a special CALL statement with the form

```
CALL NAME(ARG1,ARG2, . . . ,ARGN)
```

where NAME represents the subroutine subprogram name, and ARG1,ARG2, . . . ,ARGN represent the actual arguments of subprogram NAME in one-to-one correspondence with PAR1,PAR2, . . . ,PARN.

If there are any arguments, the number of arguments specified in the CALL statement should be exactly the same in number and type as the formal arguments specified in the SUBROUTINE statement of the subprogram. The values used for arguments are determined at the time of executing the CALL statement and depend on the actual arguments in the CALL statement.

If there are no arguments in the subroutine subprogram, the form of the CALL statement is simply

```
CALL NAME
```

When a CALL statement is executed, program control transfers to the subroutine subprogram whose name as defined in the SUBROUTINE statement is the same as in the CALL statement. Program control remains in that subroutine subprogram until either a RETURN or an END statement is encountered. Then control returns to the calling program, either a main program or another subprogram.

Arguments. Arguments are the means by which information is carried back and forth between the calling program and the subroutine subprogram. Typically one or more arguments carry information *from* the calling program to the subprogram, and at least one argument carries the results of the subprogram action back *to* the calling program.

As you may recall from our discussion of arguments in connection with function statements, it is the position of an actual argument in the list of arguments of the calling statement and the position of the corresponding formal argument in the first statement in the subprogram that determine the information carried. In fact, a variable appearing in the same position in the calling statement and the FUNCTION or SUBROUTINE statement actually occupy the same memory location—even though the names used for the variables may be different in the two argument lists.

EXAMPLE 1

```
PROGRAM EXAMP1
REAL X,Y,X
READ*,X,Y,Z
CALL SUB1(X+Y,Z)
PRINT*,'THE ABSOLUTE VALUE OF ',X,' + ',Y,' IS ',Z
END
SUBROUTINE SUB1(A,B)
B = A
IF (A .LT. 0) B=-A
END
```

In the calling program values are input to variables X and Y.

Then subprogram SUB1 is called, and the sum of X and Y is passed to the subprogram as the first argument, called A.

In the subprogram, the second argument is assigned the value of the first argument if the first argument has a positive value. If the value of the first argument is not positive, the second argument is assigned a value that is the negative of the first argument.

Upon return of program control to the calling program, the value of Z is the absolute value of the sum of X and Y. This value is output with appropriate identifying information.

EXAMPLE 2

```
PROGRAM EXAMP2
REAL A,X
READ*,A,X
X = FUNCT1(A,X)
PRINT*,A,X
END
FUNCTION FUNCT1(X)
REAL X
FUNCT1 = X + X**2 + X**3
END
```

An error message results in this case. When FUNCT1 is called into action in the calling program, it is called with two actual arguments A and X. But only one formal argument X occurs in the FUNCTION line of the subprogram.

EXAMPLE 3

```
INTEGER A(10,3)              Main program
.
.
.
CALL SUB2(A,A(10,1),B)
.
.
.
END
SUBROUTINE SUB2(X,Y,Z)       Subprogram
INTEGER X(10,3)
.
.
.
RETURN
```

This example demonstrates the handling of arrays in subprograms. Note that in the CALL statement the array name A appears without subscripts in the list of arguments. The address of the first member of array A is thus passed to SUB2 so that all 30 computer words of array A are available to both the main program and the subprogram.

In the subprogram the first argument is an array and should be properly defined as an array, as it is in this example. The form of array X in subroutine SUB2 is exactly the same as that of array A in the main program. Although not necessary, it is good programming practice to declare corresponding arrays in the main program and subprograms to be of identical form and size.

The second argument in the CALL statement is A(10,1) and in the SUBROUTINE statement it is Y. Thus, whatever operations involve Y in the subprogram will use the value stored in A(10,1) from the main program. Similarly, B in the main program will contain whatever the subprogram puts in its variable Z after completion of subprogram SUB2.

EXAMPLE 4

Main program

```
      PROGRAM EXAMP4
      REAL A(10)
      INTEGER N
      READ*,A
      N = 10
      CALL SUB3(N,A)
      IF (N .NE. 0) THEN
          PRINT*,N, ' IS THE ROUNDED SUM OF THE ELEMENTS OF A.'
      ELSE
          PRINT*,' THE SUM OF THE ELEMENTS OF A IS ZERO'
      ENDIF
      END
```

Subprogram

```
      SUBROUTINE SUB3(N,B)
      REAL B(10), SUM
      INTEGER I,N
      SUM = 0
      I = 1
10    IF (I .GT. N) GO TO 20
          SUM = SUM + B(I)
          I = I+1
      GO TO 10
20    N = SUM + .5
      RETURN
      END
```

The simple variable N and the array A are passed to SUB3—see the arguments in the CALL statement.

In the subprogram, N is equivalent to N and array B to array A.

The sum of the elements in the array is computed and the rounded value of the sum is returned to the main program with the name N. Here is an example of using an argument both for passing data *to* the subprogram and for passing a result back from the subprogram.

Although FORTRAN permits this double use of arguments it is not good programming style. Understanding the use of arguments is clearer when each argument has only one purpose.

Array A in the main program was used by the subprogram but its values were not affected.

Passing arrays as arguments. Note in the examples that you must take care when passing arrays as arguments between the calling program and the subprogram. The following guidelines are worth remembering:

1. When entire arrays are passed as arguments, only the array names, without subscripts, appear in the list of arguments.

2. When arrays or individual array elements are passed as arguments, it is easier to keep track of what is happening if the dimensions of arrays are declared identically in the calling program and in the subprogram.

   Although such identical declaration is not required by the FORTRAN compiler, the correspondence of storage locations between calling program and subprogram is simpler to follow than when the declarations are different.

3. Any formal argument may be used both for passing information to a subprogram and back from it, unless the corresponding actual argument is an expression or a constant. In this case only the value of the expression or constant is passed to the subprogram.

   Since the limitation on number of arguments is not very restrictive, we recommend that certain arguments be used for passing data *to* the subprogram and different arguments be used to receive results *from* the subprogram.

4. The same memory location is used by the program for a formal argument and the corresponding actual argument.

The COMMON statement. In addition to using arguments for making information available to main programs and subprograms, FORTRAN provides the COMMON statement. This is a nonexecutable statement that sets aside specified portions of computer memory and makes those portions available to all subprograms as well as to the main program. It literally specifies portions of memory that are shared in common by the main program and by all subprograms in which appropriate COMMON statements appear. Here is its general form:

```
COMMON VAR1,VAR2, . . . ,VARN
```

where VAR1,VAR2, . . . ,VARN represent any acceptable FORTRAN variables or arrays.

If any of the variables in the COMMON statement is an array, the COMMON statement may also specify the dimension of the variable. If, however, you place a subscripted variable in both a type declaration or DIMENSION statement and in a COMMON statement, the variable may appear with subscripts in only one of the statements.

Here is an example of the use of the COMMON statement:

EXAMPLE

```
INTEGER A,N
REAL B
CHARACTER X
COMMON A, B, N
READ *,N
.
.
.
X=FUNC2
.
.
.
END
CHARACTER FUNCTION FUNC2
INTEGER X,M
REAL B
COMMON X, B, M
IF(M .GT. 0)FUNC2='P'
IF(M .EQ. 0)FUNC2='Z'
IF(M .LT. 0)FUNC2='N'
RETURN
END
```

When this program and function subprogram are executed, a variable called A in the main program and X in the subprogram occupies the first location of common storage. A variable called B in both main program and subprogram occupies the second location in common storage, and a variable called N in the main program and M in the subprogram occupies the third location.

The first two variables here are not used by the subprogram, though they are available to it because they are specified in a COMMON statement. The only variable stored in common that is used is the variable called M in the subprogram and N in the main program. The value of M determines whether FUNC2 is assigned the character value 'P', 'Z' or 'N', and one of these values is then assigned to variable X in the main program.

Although here we use different names for the variables in the COMMON statements in the main program and subprogram, we recommend against such a practice unless there is an overriding reason. The COMMON statement is meant to make values available in both the main program and subprograms, and it is normally expected that such shared information is called by the same name wherever it appears.

For example, if a variable is called SALARY in the main program, it should also be called SALARY in any subprogram that references it. Consequently, it's good practice to duplicate in any subprogram that requires the use of shared values the applicable COMMON statements that appear in the main program.

Exercises 6.1

1. Indicate which of the following statements are true and which are false. Recall that a statement must be considered false if any part of it is false. Be prepared to make changes in those that are false so that they will be true.

a. A COMMON statement must appear in a program after any type declaration statements.

b. A DATA statement serves the purpose of assigning values to the elements of the array.

c. When COMMON statements appear in the main program and in subprograms, any array appearing in such COMMON statements must have identical dimensions wherever it appears.

d. The statement

```
DATA A(10)/10*0/
```

will set A(1) through A(10) to zero.

e. The following statement is syntactically correct:

```
DATA A/5.2/, B/6.7/
```

f. Any INTEGER statements in a program must follow all COMMON statements.

g. A FUNCTION statement may appear only in the main program and cannot be in any subprogram.

h. SUBROUTINE subprograms must have at least one argument.

i. A variable appearing in a COMMON statement of the main program may be an argument of a FUNCTION subprogram as long as there is no COMMON statement in the subprogram.

j. Any given program may have no more than one COMMON statement.

k. Any variable that appears in a COMMON statement of a subprogram must also appear in a COMMON statement in the main program.

l. A function defined by a FUNCTION statement must have no arguments.

m. A FORMAT statement in the main program may be referenced by an input or output statement in a subprogram.

n. All complete FORTRAN programs must have exactly one main program but may have as many subprograms as desired.

o. A FUNCTION statement must not appear in a function subprogram.

p. If a FUNCTION statement is to appear in a program it must precede the first executable statement in that program.

q. A function defined in a FUNCTION statement may appear as an argument of a subprogram.

r. One difference between a SUBROUTINE subprogram and a FUNCTION subprogram is that the FUNCTION subprogram returns a value to a memory location identified by the function's name and, therefore, the function name may be included in an arithmetic expression.

s. A variable name may appear in more than one COMMON statement of a given program.

t. Suppose the following statement is the first line of a SUBROUTINE subprogram:

```
SUBROUTINE SUB(N,X)
```

Then the statement

```
CALL SUB(1,SIN(X))
```

could be a valid statement for calling the subprogram into action.

u. Suppose the following statement is the first line of a SUBROUTINE subprogram:

```
SUBROUTINE SUB1(A,B,I,C,J)
```

Then the statement

```
CALL SUB1(X, 1, K, A, 4)
```

could be a valid statement for calling the subprogram.

v. If the statement

```
FUNC(X,Y) = X * Y
```

appears in a program, then the statement

```
A=FUNC(B,B)
```

is a valid statement as long as it does not precede the first statement above.

w. A FUNCTION subprogram can only return one value to the calling program and that only through the subprogram name.

x. If an array A is to be included in a COMMON statement, it must appear in a DIMENSION statement previous to its appearance in the COMMON statement.

2. Some of the following FORTRAN statements are correct, others incorrect. Assume that all variables that appear in any statement have been properly defined in the program before the appearance of the given statement. Identify the incorrect statements and suggest changes that would make them valid.

a. `COMMON A, B(10), I OR J`

b. `COMMON A, A(100), B`

c. `COMMON DATA, OR, DIM`

d. `SUBROUTINE NAME = (3 * G)/X`

e. `FUNCTION F1(A, B, X)`

f. `F3(X, Y) = X * SIN(X) + Y * SIN(Y)`

g. `SUBPROGRAM S2(A, B, C)`

h. `CALL S2(2.5, R, S)`

i. `CALL SUB(X+Y, 5)`

j. `X = FUNCT(5, B)`

k. `COMMON A, B(5), X(20)`

3. Identify all syntax errors in each of the following program segments. Assume the default data type based on first letter of name unless otherwise declared.

a.

```
F(X) = SIN(X) + COS(X)
G(X) = SIN(X) - COS(X)
READ *, X
PRINT *, X, F(X), G(X), SIN(X), COS(X)
```

b.

```
COMMON A, B
DIMENSION A(10)
.
.
.
SUBROUTINE XX(I)
COMMON A, B, C(9)
DATA A, B,/ 2.3, 7.1/
DATA C/ 9*0/
```

c.

```
CALL SUB(S)N(X)
.
.
.
SUBROUTINE SUB(X)
IF (X .GT. 0) PRINT *, 'RIGHT'
IF (X .LE. 0) PRINT *, 'LEFT'
X = X+1
CALL SUB(X)
```

d.

```
CALL SUB(F(X))
.
.
.
SUBROUTINE SUB(X)
F(X) = X*X+2*X+1
```

e.

```
READ *, X, Y
F(X) = X*X+Y
CALL SUB(F(X),Y)
.
.
.
SUBROUTINE SUB(G(X))
```

f.

```
COMMON A,B
DATA A,B/10,-10/
CALL SUB(A,B,A+B)
.
.
.
SUBROUTINE SUB(A,B,J)
```

Problem 6.1
Calculating Airflow Effects

SITUATION As part of a computer-aided design CAD system to be used for designing aircraft, your firm is developing a simple *descriptor language*, a definition of the common terminology and mathemetics of aeronautics in the FORTRAN language. Your particular task is to describe the vector functions commonly used in calculating the effects of airflow over a surface. These include

1. The *dot product* or inner product that defines the work that must be done to maintain course in a given wind.
2. The functions *vector length*, *unit vector*, and *angle* that convert information about forces into polar coordinate form so they are easier to understand and to use in a variety of functions.

3. *Sum* and *difference*, the vectors used to find, among other things, the resultant forces of wind plus airspeed across a wing surface.

OBJECTIVE The general problem is as follows: Develop an algorithm and a FORTRAN program that read the coordinates of two vectors, $\vec{a}$ and $\vec{b}$, and perform any or all of the vector operations just discussed.

DEFINITION Suppose $\vec{a}$ and $\vec{b}$ are two N-dimensional vectors represented by their coordinates as follows:

$$\vec{a} = (A1, A2, \ldots, AN)$$
$$\vec{b} = (B1, B2, \ldots, BN)$$

We can then state the following definitions:

1. The *inner product* or *dot product* of $\vec{a}$ and $\vec{b}$ is
$$\vec{a} \cdot \vec{b} = (A1*B1 + A2*B2 + \ldots + AN*BN)$$
2. The *length* of vector $\vec{a}$ is
$$|\vec{a}| = \sqrt{A1^2 + A2^2 + A3^2 + \ldots + AN^2}$$
3. The *unit vector* that has the same direction as $\vec{a}$ is
$$\left(\frac{A1}{|\vec{a}|}, \frac{A2}{|\vec{a}|}, \ldots, \frac{AN}{|\vec{a}|}\right)$$
4. The *sum* of $\vec{a}$ and $\vec{b}$ is given by
$$\vec{a} + \vec{b} = (A1+B1, A2+B2, \ldots, AN+BN)$$
5. The *difference* of $\vec{a}$ and $\vec{b}$ is
$$\vec{a} - \vec{b} = (A1-B1, A2-B2, \ldots, AN-BN)$$
6. The *angle* θ between the two vectors $\vec{a}$ and $\vec{b}$ is defined by
$$\cos\theta = \frac{\vec{a} \cdot \vec{b}}{|\vec{a}| \cdot |\vec{b}|}$$

ANALYSIS Let us assume N, the number of coordinates in a vector, to be less than or equal to 100. And we'll have the vector operations determined from the user's choice on a menu similar to the following:

```
1) Enter vector A or B.
2) Compute the inner product of A and B.
3) Compute the length of vector A or B as specified.
4) Compute the unit vector for A or B as specified.
5) Compute the sum of vectors A and B.
6) Compute the difference of vectors A and B.
7) Compute the cosine of the angle between A and B.
8) Quit processing.
```

The program should check for any reasonable error in input or in processing. For example, coordinate values for both vectors $\vec{a}$ and $\vec{b}$ must have been entered before algorithm steps 2, 5, 6, or 7 can be performed, and the coordinate values for the vector named in choices 3 or 4 must have been entered before computation for the choice is attempted.

MODULES The solution is designed in modular fashion.

MAIN The main module sets up the menu and requests a selection from the user. Based on the selection, the appropriate module will be called, after which control will return to the main module for further selection until the QUIT option is selected, upon which program execution will terminate.

PRODUCT The PRODUCT module computes the inner product of vectors $\vec{a}$ and $\vec{b}$ and reports it.

LENGTH The LENGTH module computes the unit vector for the specified vectors and stores the results in UA or UB, or both. Coordinates for specified unit vectors are reported.

SUM The SUM module computes and reports the sum of the two vectors.

DIFF The DIFF module computes and reports the difference of the two vectors.

ANGLE The ANGLE module computes and reports the angle between the positive directions of the two vectors.

ALGORITHM We will write the algorithms by module:

MAIN

1. Declare appropriate variables and arrays for vectors A, B, UA, UB.
2. Display the menu.
3. If DONE then stop.
4. Read the user's choice.
5. If CHOICE = 1 then call INPUT module,
   Else if CHOICE = 2 then call PRODUCT module,
   Else if CHOICE = 3 then call LENGTH module,
   Else if CHOICE = 4 then call UNIT module,
   Else if CHOICE = 5 then call SUM module,
   Else if CHOICE = 6 then call DIFF module,
   Else if CHOICE = 7 then call ANGLE module,
   Else assign the value TRUE to DONE.
6. Go to step 3.
7. End

INPUT

1. Read the dimension of the vector whose coordinates are to be entered.
2. If dimension > 0 and dimension ≤ 100, then read coordinates.
3. Return the vector just read together with its dimension.
4. End.

PRODUCT

1. If vectors A and B are not yet defined or their dimensions are not equal, display an appropriate message and return to main module.
2. Compute PROD = A1*B1 + A2*B2 + . . . + AN*BN, where N is the dimension of both vectors.
3. End.

LENGTH

1. Compute LENGTH = $A1^2 + A2^2 + \ldots + AN^2$ or LENGTH = $B1^2 + B2^2 + \ldots + BN^2$
2. Compute LENGTH = SQRT(LENGTH)
3. End.

UNIT

1. Compute the length of the designated vector by calling the LENGTH module.
2. Compute UA or UB by dividing each coordinate of the specified vector by its length.
3. Return UA or UB to the main module.
4. End.

SUM

1. If both vectors A and B are defined and are of the same dimension SUM = (A1+B1, A2+B2, . . . , AN+BN).
2. If either or both of vectors A and B are undefined or if their dimensions are unequal, display an appropriate message and return to the main module.
3. End.

DIFF

1. If both vectors A and B are defined and have the same dimension, compute and report DIFF = (A1–B1, A2–B2, . . . , AN–BN). Return to the main module.
2. If either or both vectors are undefined or their dimensions are unequal, display an appropriate message and return to the main module.
3. End.

ANGLE

1. Call LENGTH module to compute the length of vector A.
2. Call LENGTH module to compute the length of vector B.
3. Call PRODUCT module to compute the inner product.
4. Compute COSTH = PRODUCT(A, B) / (LENGTH(A) * LENGTH(B))
5. Report the cosine and the angle using the ACOS function and return to the main module.
6. End.

FORTRAN PROGRAM

```
      PROGRAM VECTOR
C*    VARIABLE DEFINITIONS
C*    A(100) IS AN ARRAY OF REALS TO STORE COORDINATES OF VECTOR A.
C*    B(100) IS AN ARRAY OF REALS TO STORE COORDINATES OF VECTOR B.
C*    UA(100) IS AN ARRAY OF REALS TO STORE THE UNIT VECTOR FOR A.
C*    UB(100) IS AN ARRAY OF REALS TO STORE THE UNIT VECTOR FOR B.
C*    SIZEA IS AN INTEGER TO STORE THE DIMENSION OF VECTOR A.
C*    SIZEB IS AN INTEGER TO STORE THE DIMENSION OF VECTOR B.
C*    CHOICE IS AN INTEGER TO STORE THE USER'S CHOICE FROM MENU.
C*    NAME IS A CHARACTER FOR STORING THE VECTOR'S NAME.
C*    DONE IS A LOGICAL VARIABLE WHICH IS TRUE IF USER CHOOSES TO STOP
C*        FURTHER PROCESSING.
C*
      REAL A(100), B(100), UA(100), UB(100)
      INTEGER SIZEA, SIZEB, CHOICE
      CHARACTER NAME
      LOGICAL DONE
      CALL INIT(A, B, UA, UB, SIZEA, SIZEB, DONE)
 1    IF (DONE) STOP
          PRINT *, '1) ENTER VECTOR A OR B'
          PRINT *, '2) COMPUTE THE INNER PRODUCT OF A AND B'
          PRINT *, '3) COMPUTE THE LENGTH OF VECTOR A OR B'
          PRINT *, '4) COMPUTE THE UNIT VECTOR FOR A OR B'
          PRINT *, '5) COMPUTE THE SUM OF A AND B'
          PRINT *, '6) COMPUTE THE DIFFERENCE OF A AND B'
          PRINT *, '7) COMPUTE COSINE OF ANGLE BETWEEN A AND B'
          PRINT *, '8) QUIT PROCESSING'
          PRINT *
          PRINT *, 'ENTER YOUR CHOICE, 1 TO 8'
          READ *, CHOICE
          IF (CHOICE .EQ. 1) THEN
              PRINT *, 'ENTER VECTOR NAME'
              READ *, NAME
              IF (NAME .EQ. 'A') THEN
                  CALL INPUT (A, SIZEA)
              ELSE
                  CALL INPUT(B, SIZEB)
              ENDIF
```

```
          ELSEIF (CHOICE .EQ. 2) THEN
              PRINT *, PROD(A, B, SIZEA, SIZEB)
          ELSEIF (CHOICE .EQ. 3) THEN
              PRINT *, 'ENTER VECTOR NAME'
              READ *, NAME
              IF (NAME .EQ. 'A') THEN
                  PRINT *, LENGTH(A, SIZEA)
              ELSE
                  PRINT *, LENGTH(B, SIZEB)
              ENDIF
          ELSEIF (CHOICE .EQ. 4) THEN
              PRINT *, 'ENTER VECTOR NAME'
              READ *, NAME
              IF (NAME .EQ. 'A') THEN
                  CALL UNIT(A, UA, SIZEA)
              ELSE
                  CALL UNIT(B, UB, SIZEB)
              ENDIF
          ELSEIF (CHOICE .EQ. 5) THEN
              CALL SUM (A, B, SIZEA, SIZEB)
          ELSEIF (CHOICE .EQ. 6) THEN
              CALL DIFF(A, B, SIZEA, SIZEB)
          ELSEIF (CHOICE .EQ. 7) THEN
              CALL ANGLE(A, B, SIZEA, SIZEB)
          ELSEIF (CHOICE .EQ. 8) THEN
              DONE = .TRUE.
          ENDIF
      GO TO 1
      END
C***************************************************************************
      SUBROUTINE INIT(A, B, UA, UB, SIZEA, SIZEB, DONE)
      REAL A(100), B(100), UA(100), UB(100)
      INTEGER SIZEA, SIZEB
      LOGICAL DONE
      DATA A, B, UA, UB/400*0/
      DATA SIZEA, SIZEB/0,0/
      DONE = .FALSE.
      END
C***************************************************************************
      SUBROUTINE INPUT(X, N)
      REAL X(100)
      INTEGER N, I
      PRINT *, 'ENTER THE NUMBER OF COORDINATES IN THE VECTOR'
      READ *, N
      PRINT *, 'ENTER ' ,N, ' NUMBERS FOR YOUR COORDINATES'
      READ *, (X(I), I = 1, N)
      END
```

```
C***********************************************************************
      REAL FUNCTION PROD(A, B, SIZEA, SIZEB)
      REAL A(100), B(100), SUM
      INTEGER SIZEA, SIZEB, I
      SUM = 0
      IF (SIZEA .NE. SIZEB) THEN
          PRINT *, 'THE VECTORS HAVE DIFFERENT DIMENSIONS'
          RETURN
      ELSEIF (SIZEA .EQ. 0) THEN
          PRINT *, 'VECTOR A IS NOT YET DEFINED'
          RETURN
      ELSEIF (SIZEB .EQ. 0) THEN
          PRINT *, 'VECTOR B IS NOT YET DEFINED'
          RETURN
      ELSE
          DO 10 I = 1, SIZEA
              SUM = SUM + A(I) * B(I)
 10       CONTINUE
      ENDIF
      PROD = SUM
      END
C***********************************************************************
      REAL FUNCTION LENGTH (X, N)
      REAL X(100), SUM
      INTEGER N, I
      SUM = 0
      IF (N .EQ. 0) THEN
          PRINT *, 'VECTOR IS UNDEFINED'
      ELSE
          DO 10 I = 1, N
              SUM = SUM + X(I) * X(I)
 10       CONTINUE
          LENGTH = SQRT(SUM)
      ENDIF
      END
C***********************************************************************
      SUBROUTINE UNIT(X, UX, N)
      REAL X(100), UX(100), Z
      INTEGER N, I
      Z = LENGTH(X, N)
      DO 10 I = 1, N
          UX(I) = X(I)/Z
 10   CONTINUE
      END
```

```
C**************************************************************************
      SUBROUTINE SUM(A, B, SIZEA, SIZEB)
      REAL A(100), B(100)
      INTEGER SIZEA, SIZEB, I
      IF (SIZEA .NE. SIZEB) THEN
          PRINT *, 'THE VECTORS HAVE DIFFERENT DIMENSIONS'
      ELSEIF (SIZEA .EQ. 0) THEN
          PRINT *, 'VECTOR A IS NOT YET DEFINED'
      ELSEIF (SIZEB .EQ. 0) THEN
          PRINT *, 'VECTOR B IS NOT YET DEFINED'
      ELSE
          PRINT *, ((A(I) + B(I)), I = 1, SIZEA)
      ENDIF
      END
C**************************************************************************
      SUBROUTINE DIFF(A, B, SIZEA, SIZEB)
      REAL A(100), B(100)
      INTEGER SIZEA, SIZEB, I
      IF (SIZEA .NE. SIZEB) THEN
          PRINT *, 'THE VECTORS HAVE DIFFERENT DIMENSIONS'
      ELSEIF (SIZEA .EQ. 0) THEN
          PRINT *, 'VECTOR A IS NOT YET DEFINED'
      ELSEIF (SIZEB .EQ. 0) THEN
          PRINT *, 'VECTOR B IS NOT YET DEFINED'
      ELSE
          PRINT *, ((A(I), - B(I)), I = 1, SIZEA)
      ENDIF
      END
C**************************************************************************
      SUBROUTINE ANGLE(A, B, SIZEA, SIZEB)
      REAL A(100), B(100), COSTH
      INTEGER SIZEA, SIZEB
      IF (SIZEA .NE. SIZEB) THEN
          PRINT *, 'THE VECTORS HAVE DIFFERENT DIMENSIONS'
      ELSEIF (SIZEA .EQ. 0) THEN
          PRINT *, 'VECTOR A IS NOT YET DEFINED'
      ELSEIF (SIZEB .EQ. 0) THEN
          PRINT *, 'VECTOR B IS NOT YET DEFINED'
      ELSE
          COSTH = PROD(A, B, SIZEA, SIZEB) / (LENGTH(A, SIZEA) *
     +        LENGTH(B, SIZEB))
          PRINT *, 'THE COSINE OF THE ANGLE BETWEEN A AND B IS ', COSTH
          PRINT *, 'THE ANGLE BETWEEN A AND B IS ', ACOS(COSTH)
      ENDIF
      END
C**************************************************************************
```

CHANGE 1 Two definite improvements can be made in this program. The first has to do with testing for errors in the data related to the vectors. Instead of checking the dimensions and existence of the vectors each time that information is needed, we can use a subprogram to check all data once. We'll call it the function ERROR:

SUBPROGRAM ERROR

```
LOGICAL FUNCTION ERROR(A, B, SIZEA, SIZEB)
REAL A(100), B(100)
INTEGER SIZEA, SIZEB
IF (SIZEA .NE. SIZEB) THEN
    PRINT *, 'THE VECTORS HAVE DIFFERENT DIMENSIONS'
    ERROR = .TRUE.
ELSEIF (SIZEA .EQ. 0) THEN
    PRINT *, 'VECTOR A IS NOT YET DEFINED'
    ERROR = .TRUE.
ELSEIF (SIZEB .EQ. 0) THEN
    PRINT*, 'VECTOR B IS NOT YET DEFINED'
    ERROR = .TRUE.
ELSE
    ERROR = .FALSE.
ENDIF
END
```

We now invoke function ERROR in function PROD and in subroutines SUM, DIFF, and ANGLE with a statement like this:

```
IF (ERROR(A, B, SIZEA, SIZEB)) RETURN
```

This statement is the first executable statement in each subprogram.

CHANGE 2 The second improvement is to combine subroutines SUM and DIFF. In the combined subroutine, note that a fifth argument P has been added. When the sum of the vectors is to be computed, P is set to 1, whereas if the difference is to be computed, P is set to −1.

COMBINED SUBROUTINE SUBDIFF

```
SUBROUTINE SUMDIF(A, B, SIZEA, SIZEB, P)
REAL A(100), B(100)
INTEGER SIZEA, SIZEB, P
IF (ERROR(A, B, SIZEA, SIZEB)) THEN
    RETURN
ELSE
    PRINT *, ((A(I) + P*B(I)), I=1, SIZEA)
ENDIF
END
```

Programming applications to matrices. Matrix operations apply to a great many situations in the field of science. Since FORTRAN was designed primarily for use in mathematics, statistics, and the natural sciences, the FORTRAN programmer is likely to come up against the need to program applications to matrices.

Some programming languages like BASIC provide matrix operations using system library functions. FORTRAN does not, but software enhancements can be purchased that allow FORTRAN programmers to use techniques like those associated with system library functions.

Even with unenhanced FORTRAN, there is some capability to handle matrix operations, which we will explore using examples. But first let's develop a few definitions we'll need.

Matrix definitions. These are the basic terms used in describing and dealing with matrices.

1. An arrangement of numbers in m rows and n columns is called a ***matrix***. If we let the capital letter A represent the matrix and the small letter a with subscripts represent individual numbers in the matrix, the result is as follows:

$$A = \begin{pmatrix} a_{11} & a_{12} & \cdots & a_{1n} \\ a_{21} & a_{22} & \cdots & a_{2n} \\ \cdot & & & \\ \cdot & & & \\ \cdot & & & \\ a_{m1} & a_{m2} & \cdots & a_{mn} \end{pmatrix}$$

   where the brackets are used to enclose the members of the matrix.

   Note that the first in each pair of subscripts specifies the row in which a member appears and the second the column.

2. A matrix is called a ***square matrix*** if the number of rows and columns are equal.

3. The ***transpose*** of matrix A is matrix B where the rows of B are the columns of A and the columns of B are the rows of A, all in the same order as in matrix A. Note that if A is an mxn matrix, then B is an nxm matrix.

4. If A and B are both mxn matrices, then the matrix C, whose elements, c_{ij}, are determined by adding corresponding elements a_{ij} and b_{ij} of A and B, is called the ***sum*** of matrices A and B. We write C = A + B, where $c_{ij} = a_{ij} + b_{ij}$.

5. Similarly, the matrix D obtained by subtracting corresponding elements of A and B is called the ***difference*** of A and B. We write D = A − B, where $d_{ij} = a_{ij} - b_{ij}$.

6. If A is a matrix whose elements a_{ij} are numbers, and k is a number like the elements of A, then the ***scalar product*** of k and A is the matrix P, whose elements, p_{ij} are the products of the number k and the elements of A. We write P = kA, where $p_{ij} = ka_{ij}$.

Problem 6.2 Manipulating a Matrix

OBJECTIVE Write a program to do the following:

1. *Input* one or two matrices, A and B, whose dimensions are MXN, where M and N are both less than 20;
2. Find the *sum* of the matrices input if there are two of them;
3. Find the *difference* of the matrices input if there are two of them;
4. Find the *scalar product* of matrix A and number K.
5. Find the *transpose* of matrix A.

OPERATIONS Write the program so that the user can accomplish one or more of these objectives by specifying the desired operations as follows:

1. `INPUT (A or B)M,N`

   One letter, either A or B, follows INPUT. This causes input into array A or array B.
   Next are the two positive integers M and N, specifying the number of rows and columns.
   The M x N members of the array follow, separated by at least one blank space. The numbers may take more than one line if necessary.

2. `ADD`

   The sum of arrays A and B is computed and stored in array C. The elements of C are printed.

3. `SUB`

   The difference of arrays A and B is computed and stored in array C. The elements of C are printed.

4. `MULT (A or B)K`

   One letter, either A or B, follows MULT. The scalar product of K and A or B is computed and stored in array C. The elements of C are printed.

5. `TRANSP (A or B)`

   One letter, either A or B, follows TRANSP. The transpose of the specified array is stored in array C. The elements of C are printed.

6. `TRANSF (A or B)`

   One letter, either A or B, follows TRANSF. A copy of array C is stored in the specified array.

7. `FINISH`

   Terminates processing.

ALGORITHM The elements of the solution are divided into subprogram modules. Note also how this solution uses iteration structures.

MAIN

M.1 Input the process code CODE and array identifier NAME, if any.

M.2 If CODE is FINISH, terminate processing.

M.3 If CODE is INPUT, call subprogram INPUT.

M.4 If CODE is ADD, call subprogram ADDSUB.

M.5 If CODE is SUB, call subprogram ADDSUB.

M.6 If CODE is MULT, call subprogram MULT.

M.7 If CODE is TRANSP, call subprogram TRANSP.

M.8 If CODE is TRANSF, call subprogram TRANSF.

M.9 If CODE is none of the above, print message about incorrect process code.

M.10 Repeat the process from step M.1.

INPUT The argument NAME for subprogram INPUT identifies the array name.

I.1 Read M and N, the number of rows and columns in the array to be read.

I.2 If either M or N is negative or is greater than 20, then return to the calling program.

I.3 If NAME is 'A', then read M rows of N values per row to array A and return the number of rows in A to variable MA and the number of columns in A to variable NA.

Otherwise, read M rows of N values per row to array B and return the number of rows to variable MB and the number of columns to variable NB.

I.4 Return to the calling program.

ADDSUB The argument L for subprogram ADDSUB is +1 for addition, –1 for subtraction.

A.1 If MA or NA ≤ 0, print appropriate message and return to the calling program.

A.2 If MB or NB ≤ 0, print appropriate message and return to the calling program.

A.3 If MA ≠ MB or NA ≠ NB, print appropriate message and return to the calling program.

A.4 Compute C, the sum or difference array, using the formula C(I, J) = A(I, J) + L*B(I, J) for each of the elements in arrays A and B.

A.5 Return to the calling program.

MULT The argument NAME of subprogram MULT identifies the array name.

P.1 Read the number K to be used as the multiplier.

P.2 If NAME is 'A', compute the product array C according to the formula C(I, J) = K*A(I, J) for each of the elements in array A.

P.3 If NAME is not 'A', compute the product array C according to the formula C(I, J) = K*B(I, J) for each of the elements in array B.

P.4 Print array C.

P.5 Return to the calling program.

TRANSP The argument NAME of subprogram TRANSP identifies the array name.

T.1 If NAME is 'A', then

T.2 If MA or NA ≤ 0, report the message that array A has not been defined; then return to calling program.

T.3 Compute transpose array C according to the equation C(I, J) = A(J, I) for each of the elements in array A.

T.4 Set MC = MA and NC = NA and proceed to step T.8.

T.5 If MB or NB ≤ 0, report the message that array B has not been defined and return to the calling program.

T.6 Compute transpose array C according to the equation C(I, J) = B(J, I) for each of the elements in array B.

T.7 Set MC = MB and NC = NB.

T.8 Output array C.

T.9 Return to calling program.

TRANSF The argument NAME of subprogram TRANSF identifies the array name.

F.1 If NAME is 'A', perform steps F.2 and F.3. Otherwise perform steps F.4 and F.5.

F.2 Transfer array C to array A by setting A(I, J) = C(I, J) for each element C(I, J) in C.

F.3 Set MA = MC and NA = NC and proceed to step F.6.

F.4 Transfer array C to array B by setting B(I, J) = C(I, J) for each element C(I, J) in C.

F.5 Set MB = MC and NB = NC and proceed to step F.6.

F.6 Output the resulting array C.

F.7 Return to calling program.

FORTRAN PROGRAM

```
      PROGRAM MATRIX
C***********************************************************************
C*                          PROGRAM DEFINITION                         *
C*    THIS PROGRAM IS TO CARRY OUT ANY OF SIX OPERATIONS WITH ONE      *
C*    OR TWO MATRICES DEPENDING ON THE INPUT DATA. THE OPERATIONS ARE: *
C*    1. INPUT A MATRIX INTO ARRAY A OR B.                             *
C*    2. ADD MATRICES A AND B.                                         *
C*    3. SUBTRACT MATRIX B FROM MATRIX A.                              *
C*    4. MULTIPLY MATRIX A.                                            *
C*    5. TRANSPOSE MATRIX A.                                           *
C*    6. TRANSFER MATRIX C INTO MATRIX A OR B.                         *
C***********************************************************************
C*                          VARIABLE DEFINITION                        *
C*    A, B, C ARE THREE ARRAYS TO HOLD THE TWO POSSIBLE INPUT          *
C*        MATRICES AND THE RESULT MATRIX.                              *
C*    MA, MB, MC ARE NUMBER OF ROWS OF MATRICES A, B, C, RESPECTIVELY. *
C*    NA, NB, NC ARE NUMBER OF COLUMNS OF MATRICES A, B, C.            *
C*    F IS FACTOR TO MULTIPLY MATRIX, DEFINED IN SUBROUTINE MULT.      *
C*    CODE INDICATES ONE OF THE SIX OPERATIONS TO BE PERFORMED.        *
C*    NAME IS THE NAME OF THE MATRIX, A OR B, USED IN THE OPERATION.   *
C***********************************************************************
C*                          LIST OF SUBPROGRAMS                        *
C*    INPUT ENTERS ONE OR TWO MATRICES INTO ARRAYS A AND B.            *
C*    ADDSUB ADDS OR SUBTRACTS TWO MATRICES.                           *
C*    MULT FINDS THE SCALER PRODUCT OF A NUMBER AND A MATRIX.          *
C*    TRANSP FINDS THE TRANSPOSE OF A MATRIX.                          *
C*    TRANSF PLACES A COPY OF ONE MATRIX INTO ANOTHER.                 *
C***********************************************************************
C*                          START OF THE MAIN PROGRAM                  *
C*    THE MAIN PROGRAM READS THE CODE AND THE NAME OF THE MATRIX       *
C*    AND CALLS APPROPRIATE SUBROUTINE INTO ACTION.                    *
C***********************************************************************
C*
      REAL A(20,20),B(20,20),C(20,20)
      INTEGER MA, NA, MB, NB, MC, NC
      CHARACTER CODE*6, NAME
      COMMON A,B,C,MA,NA,MB,NB,MC,NC
C*
      CODE = '      '
 1    IF (CODE .EQ. 'FINISH') GOTO 100
         PRINT*,'ENTER OPERATION CODE ENCLOSED BY SINGLE QUOTES. '
         PRINT*,'ACCEPTABLE CODE WORDS ARE FINISH, INPUT, ADD, '
         PRINT*,'SUB, MULT, TRANSP, TRANSF.'
         PRINT*,'FOLLOWING OPERATION CODE ENTER BLANK SPACE '
         PRINT*,'FOLLOWED BY A OR B ENCLOSED BY SINGLE QUOTES.'
         READ*,CODE,NAME
         IF (CODE .EQ. 'INPUT') THEN
             CALL INPUT(NAME)
         ELSEIF (CODE .EQ. 'ADD') THEN
             CALL ADDSUB(1)
         ELSEIF (CODE .EQ. 'SUB') THEN
             CALL ADDSUB(-1)
```

```
          ELSEIF (CODE .EQ. 'MULT') THEN
              CALL MULT(NAME)
          ELSEIF (CODE .EQ. 'TRANSP') THEN
              CALL TRANSP(NAME)
          ELSEIF (CODE .EQ. 'TRANSF') THEN
              CALL TRANS(NAME)
          ELSE
              PRINT*,'INVALID CODE: ', CODE
          ENDIF
      GOTO 1
 100  STOP
      END
C*
C*                          SUBROUTINE TO READ A MATRIX
C*
      SUBROUTINE INPUT(NAME)
      REAL A(20,20),B(20,20),C(20,20)
      INTEGER M,N
      CHARACTER NAME
      COMMON A,B,C,MA,NA,MB,NB,MC,NC
C*
      PRINT*,'ENTER MATRIX ROWS AND COLUMNS'
      MA = 0
      NA = 0
      MB = 0
      NB = 0
      READ*,M,N
      IF (M.LE.0 .OR. M.GT.20 .OR. N.LE.0 .OR. N.GT.20) THEN
          PRINT*,'ERROR IN MATRIX SIZE: ', M, N
          RETURN
      ENDIF
      PRINT*,'ENTER YOUR MATRIX ROW BY ROW'
C*
      IF (NAME .EQ. 'A') THEN
          READ*,((A(I,J),J=1,N),I=1,M)
          MA = M
          NA = N
      ELSE
          READ*,((B(I,J),J=1,N),I=1,M)
          MB = M
          NB = N
      ENDIF
      RETURN
      END
C*
C*                          SUBPROGRAM ADDSUB
C*    THE ARGUMENT L IS 1 FOR ADDITION, -1 FOR SUBTRACTION.
C*
      SUBROUTINE ADDSUB(L)
      REAL A(20,20),B(20,20),C(20,20)
      COMMON A,B,C,MA,NA,MB,NB,MC,NC
```

```
C*
      IF (MA.LE.0 .OR. NA.LE.0) THEN
          PRINT*,'ARRAY A IS NOT DEFINED'
          RETURN
      ELSEIF (MB.LE.0 .OR. NB.LE.0) THEN
          PRINT*,'ARRAY B IS NOT DEFINED'
          RETURN
      ELSEIF (MA.NE.MB .OR. NA.NE.NB) THEN
          PRINT*,'A AND B ARE NOT THE SAME SIZE'
          RETURN
      ELSE
          DO 40 J=1, MA
              DO 30 K=1, NA
                  C(J,K) = A(J,K) + L*B(J,K)
 30           CONTINUE
          PRINT*,'ROW ',J
          PRINT*, (C(J,K),K=1,NA)
 40       CONTINUE
      ENDIF
      MC = MA
      NC = NA
      RETURN
      END
C*
C*                               SUBPROGRAM MULT
C*
      SUBROUTINE MULT(NAME)
      CHARACTER NAME
      REAL A(20,20),B(20,20),C(20,20)
      COMMON A,B,C,MA,NA,MB,NB,MC,NC
C*
      PRINT*,'ENTER FACTOR'
      READ*,K
      IF (NAME .EQ. 'A') THEN
          DO 60 I=1, MA
              DO 70 J=1, NA
                  C(I,J) = K*A(I,J)
 70           CONTINUE
 60       CONTINUE
          MC = MA
          NC = NA
      ELSE
          DO 90 I=1, MB
              DO 80 J=1, NB
                  C(I,J) = K*B(I,J)
 80           CONTINUE
 90       CONTINUE
          MC = MB
          NC = NB
      ENDIF
```

```
C*
      DO 100 I=1, MC
          PRINT*,'ROW ', I
          PRINT*, (C(I,J,),J=1,NC)
 100  CONTINUE
      RETURN
      END
C*
C*                         SUBPROGRAM TRANSP
C*
      SUBROUTINE TRANSP(NAME)
      CHARACTER NAME
      REAL A(20,20),B(20,20),C(20,20)
      COMMON A,B,C,MA,NA,MB,NB,MC,NC
C*
      IF (NAME .EQ. 'A') THEN
          IF (MA.LE.0 .OR. NA.LE.0) THEN
              PRINT*,'ARRAY A IS NOT DEFINED'
              RETURN
          ELSE
              DO 20 I=1, MA
                  D0 15 J=1, NA
                      C(J,I) = A(I,J)
 15               CONTINUE
 20           CONTINUE
              NC = MA
              MC = NA
          ENDIF
      ELSE
          IF (MB.LE.0 .OR. NB.LE.0) THEN
              PRINT*,'ARRAY B IS NOT DEFINED'
              RETURN
          ELSE
              DO 30 I=1, MB
                  DO 25 J=1, NB
                      C(J,1) = B(I,J)
 25               CONTINUE
 30           CONTINUE
          NC = MB
          MC = NB
          ENDIF
      ENDIF
C*
      DO 40 I=1, MC
          PRINT*,'ROW ', I
          PRINT*, (C(I,J),J=1,NC)
40    CONTINUE
      RETURN
      END
```

```
C*
C*                                  SUBPROGRAM TRANSF
C*
      SUBROUTINE TRANSF(NAME)
      CHARACTER NAME
      REAL A(20,20),B(20,20),C(20,20)
      COMMON A,B,C,MA,NA,MB,NB,MC,NC
C*
      IF (NAME .EQ. 'A') THEN
          DO 300 I=1, MC
              DO 310 J=1, NC
                  A(I,J) = C(I,J)
 310          CONTINUE
 300      CONTINUE
          MA = MC
          NA = NC
      ELSE
          DO 330 I=1, MC
              DO 320 J=1, NC
                  B(I,J) = C(I,J)
 320          CONTINUE
 330      CONTINUE
          MB = MC
          NB = NC
      ENDIF
C*
      DO 350 I=1, MC
          PRINT*,'ROW ', I
          PRINT*, (C(I,J),J=1,NC)
 350  CONTINUE
      RETURN
      END
```

COMMENTS This program does not edit all input data as well as it might. In particular, the name of an array to be processed is always assumed to be A and B. We check only to see if the name is A—if it is not A, we assume it is B. If the name were *also not* B, this program would not detect the error.

Another weakness of this program is that it always produces output showing the results of the matrix operation being done. There may be times when such output could cause confusion, depending on the sequence of matrix operations requested. Here is an example.

Suppose matrix A is given by

$$A = \begin{pmatrix} 3 & 5 & 10 \\ 8 & -2 & 6 \\ 2 & 7 & 1 \end{pmatrix}$$

and A is to be added to the transpose of A by means of the previous program. Following are the input lines needed to accomplish these tasks, including at the left, the order of reading of each line:

```
1 'INPUT', 'A'
2 3,3
3 3,5,10
4 8,-2,6
5 2,7,1
6 'TRANSP','A'
7 'TRANSF','B'
8 'ADD'
```

The first 5 lines result in array A being properly stored.

Line 6 causes the transpose of A to be computed and stored in array C. Also the transpose array is printed. This may cause confusion because the user does not need this result, only the final sum of array A and its transpose.

Line 7 causes the transpose array in array C to be transferred to array B. Again, unnecessary output is produced, possibly causing confusion.

Finally, with the reading of line 8, the sum of array A and its tranpose in array B is computed and stored in array C as well as being printed.

REVISION

As you can tell, the original program can be improved; we leave it as an exercise to the interested reader. You may also include provisions for interactive communication. Readers with adequate background in linear algebra may find it interesting to enlarge the program to include matrix multiplication.

PROGRAM DESIGN ISSUES

A common problem in many firms is that a simplified or good enough program developed for one particular use may be borrowed later by people who need it for more precise work, or to handle data outside the range for which it was designed. Thus, even if you have no thought of reusing your code, it is best to make sure that a potential naive user, perhaps years in the future, will have adequate documentation and a reasonable assurance that the program is reliable. Some issues to consider include these:

Are variables named using standard mathematical notation? If not, be sure to define each one carefully in the comments.

Are the procedures general? One advantage of using subprograms, as here, is that each module can be written to solve a specific, closely defined general problem—and then be available when the same problem arises elsewhere. But you need to be careful to look beyond current specifics. If there are undefined cases, are there adequate input and output filters? Does the program give an intelligible warning when unusable data is identified?

Is the exact method of computation specified in the comments? This information may be vital in cases where there is a sensitive dependence on initial conditions. Whoever uses or modifies the code will benefit by having the method clearly explained: Is it iterative, simply building an actual sum, or does it find the limit of a sum? Does it compute a derivative directly, or does it find the delta for increasingly small intervals?

Problem 6.3 Designing a Commuter Airline

SITUATION Your firm has been hired to do the market and feasability studies for a new commuter airline and to develop aircraft design goals. The key question is, Where should the planes be able to fly? Small differences in range may have large impact on fuel requirements, and thus on the corresponding passenger and freight capacities, and also on the absolute ability to fly certain direct routes between cities.

Especially with a commuter airline flying out of small airports, it is important to be able to offer flights to a range of airports, not just to one nearby large airport. So commuters from San Luis Obispo may want to go to Los Angeles in the morning but require afternoon flights to San Francisco or Phoenix. And sometimes scheduling may require a plane to fly San Luis–Phoenix, then directly to Los Angeles for a return to San Luis.

One plane can thus fly trips of varying distances in the same day. And a plane with the necessary range could be based anywhere within a triangle of international airports and fly any combination of trips among those airports and the base.

OBJECTIVE This program module is to solve key geometric questions relating to range. As always, we begin by generalizing the statement of the problem to work within any coordinate system.

Assume a set of three 2–dimensional geometric objects: a point, a triangle and a circle. The point, a general representation of an aircraft base, is defined by a single pair of coordinates. The triangle, which represents the set of major airports, is defined by the coordinates of its vertices. The circle is defined by the length of its radius, which is the range of the aircraft in question, and the coordinates of its center. Given any two of these objects, determine whether or not object 1 encloses object 2.

ANALYSIS Note that object 1 encloses object 2 if all points on the boundary of object 2 are inside of or on the boundary of object 1. This definition is not reasonable if object 1 is a point and object 2 is either a triangle or a circle, but in all other combinations the definition is meaningful. Following is a list of the reasonable possibilities:

1. Circle enclosing a point.
2. Circle enclosing a triangle.
3. Circle enclosing a circle.
4. Triangle enclosing a point.
5. Triangle enclosing a triangle.
6. Triangle enclosing a circle.
7. Point enclosing a point, meaning the points coincide.

Let's consider how to test for each of these possibilities. Note that the program we develop uses subroutines to accomplish most of the checking required for each of the cases.

CASE 1 Suppose that the coordinates of the point are *Px* and *Py*, the coordinates of the center of the circle are *Cx* and *Cy*, and the length of the radius of the circle is *R*. The distance from the center of the circle to the point is given by the following equation:

$$CP = \sqrt{(Cx - Px)^2 + (Cy - Py)^2}$$

If *CP* is less than or equal to *R*, the point is enclosed by the circle.

CASE 2 Since a triangle is defined by the coordinates of its 3 vertices, if all of the vertices are enclosed by the circle, using the test described in case 1 for each vertex, then the circle encloses the triangle.

CASE 3 Circle *C*1 with radius *R*1 encloses circle *C*2 with radius *R*2 if and only if the distance between centers is less than the absolute value of the difference between radii. Note that only the circle with the larger radius may enclose the other circle. Assume that center *C*1 has coordinates *C*1*x* and *C*1*y*, and that center *C*2 has coordinates *C*2*x* and *C*2*y*. Also assume that $R1 > R2$. Then

$$\textit{Distance between centers} = C1\,C2 = \sqrt{(C1x - C2x)^2 + (C1y - C2y)^2}$$

And *C*1 encloses *C*2 if $R1 - R2 \geq C1\,C2$.

CASE 4 To determine if a point is inside a triangle, we must first know the coordinates of the center of the triangle. If the line segment joining the point with the center of the triangle does not intersect any of the 3 sides of the triangle, the point is enclosed by the triangle.

To make this concept precise, assume the coordinates of the point are *Px* and *Py*. Assume that the vertices of the triangle are *V*1 and with coordinates *x*1 and *y*1, *V*2 with coordinates *x*2 and *y*2, and *V*3 with coordinates *x*3 and *y*3. The the center of the triangle, at coordinates, *Cx* and *Cy*, is defined by the following equations:

$$Cx = \frac{x1 + x2 + x3}{3}$$

$$Cy = \frac{y1 + y2 + y3}{3}$$

In order to determine whether or not the line segment joining the point at coordinates *Px* and *Py* to the center of the triangle at coordinates *Cx* and *Cy*, we recall some computations from geometry:

1. For side *V*1*V*2 compute

   $A1 = y2 - y1$
   $B1 = x1 - x2$
   $C1 = y1x2 - y2x1$

2. For side *V*2*V*3 compute

   $A2 = y3 - y2$
   $B2 = x3 - x2$
   $C2 = y2x3 - y3x2$

3. For side *V*3*V*1 compute

   $A3 = y3 - y1$
   $B3 = x3 - x1$
   $C3 = y3x1 - y1x3$

Now compute distance to determine if the point is enclosed by the triangle:

$$Si = (Ai^*Px + Bi^*Py + Ci) * (Ai^*Cx + Bi^*Cy + Ci)$$

for *i*=1, 2, 3
where *Ai*, *Bi*, and *Ci* are defined by the preceding equations.

If *S*1>0 and *S*2>0 and *S*3>0, then the point is enclosed by the triangle.

CASE 5 In order to determine if triangle *V*1*V*2*V*3 encloses triangle *KLM*, we use with each of the three vertices *K*, *L* and *M* the process described in case 4 for a single point.

We use the computations above for *Ai*, *Bi*, and *Ci* (*i*=1, 2, 3) and assume that vertex *K* has coordinates *Kx* and *Ky*, vertex *L* has coordinates *Lx* and *Ly*, and vertex *M* has coordinates *Mx* and *My*. In order to have triangle *V*1*V*2*V*3 enclose triangle *KLM*, it must be shown that

$$(Ai^*Kx + Bi^*Ky + Ci) * (Ai^*Lx + Bi^*Ly + Ci) * (Ai^*Mx + Bi^*My + Ci)$$

is greater than zero.

CASE 6 For a triangle to enclose a circle with its center at coordinates *Cx* and *Cy*, and radius *R*, it must be determined that

1. The center of the circle is inside the triangle, and
2. The perpendicular distance from each side of the triangle to the center of the circle is greater than or equal to *R*.

The first condition may be verified in the same manner as described in case 4 of a triangle enclosing a point. To check for the second condition, compute *Ai, Bi,* and *Ci* for $i = 1, 2,$ and 3 as in case 4. Then the equations for the three sides of the triangle are

$$A1*x + B1*y + C1 = 0$$
$$A2*x + B2*y + C2 = 0$$
$$A3*x + B3*y + C3 = 0$$

And the perpendicular distance from each of the three sides may be computed as follows:

$$H1 = \frac{|\, A1 * Cx + B1 * Cy + C1 \,|}{\sqrt{A1^2 + B1^2}}$$

$$H2 = \frac{|\, A2 * Cx + B2 * Cy + C2 \,|}{\sqrt{A2^2 + B2^2}}$$

$$H3 = \frac{|\, A3 * Cx + B3 * Cy + C3 \,|}{\sqrt{A3^2 + B3^2}}$$

Note that the numerators are absolute values, hence non-negative. The second condition is true if *H*1, *H*2, and *H*3 are all greater than *R*.

CASE 7 For a point *P* with coordinates *Px* and *Py* to enclose a point *Q* with coordinates *Qx* and *Qy*, we need only to check if the points coincide, that is, if *Px*=*Qx* and *Py*=*Qy*.

FORTRAN PROGRAM

```
      PROGRAM ENCLOS
C***
C***  THE MAIN PROGRAM READS A DIGIT SPECIFYING WHICH OF THE 7
C***  CASES OF ENCLOSING IS TO BE CHECKED. THE USER ENTERS 8
C***  IF NO MORE CASES ARE TO BE RUN.
C***  INTEGER SELECT
      SELECT = 0
```

```
 100  IF (SELECT .EQ. 8) GOTO 300
          PRINT *, 'ENTER YOUR CHOICE OF DIGIT AS FOLLOWS:'
          PRINT *, '1 IF CIRCLE ENCLOSING POINT.'
          PRINT *, '2 IF CIRCLE ENCLOSING TRIANGLE.'
          PRINT *, '3 IF CIRCLE ENCLOSING CIRCLE.'
          PRINT *, '4 IF TRIANGLE ENCLOSING POINT.'
          PRINT *, '5 IF TRIANGLE ENCLOSING TRIANGLE.'
          PRINT *, '6 IF TRIANGLE ENCLOSING CIRCLE.'
          PRINT *, '7 IF POINT ENCLOSING POINT.'
          PRINT *, '8 TO TERMINATE PROGRAM.'
          READ *, SELECT
 150      IF (SELECT.LE.8 .AND. SELECT.GE.1) GOTO 200
              PRINT *, 'PLEASE ENTER A DIGIT BETWEEN 1 AND 8.'
              READ *, SELECT
          GOTO 150
 200      IF (SELECT .EQ. 1) THEN
              CALL CIRPNT
          ELSEIF (SELECT .EQ. 2) THEN
              CALL CIRTRI
          ELSEIF (SELECT .EQ. 3) THEN
              CALL CIRCIR
          ELSEIF (SELECT .EQ. 4) THEN
              CALL TRIPNT
          ELSEIF (SELECT .EQ. 5) THEN
              CALL TRITRI
          ELSEIF (SELECT .EQ. 6) THEN
              CALL TRICIR
          ELSEIF (SELECT .EQ. 7) THEN
              CALL PNTPNT
          ENDIF
      GOTO 100
 300  STOP
      END
C***
C***  THIS SUBROUTINE CHECKS FOR A CIRCLE ENCLOSING A POINT.
C***  INPUT DATA CONSISTS OF THE COORDINATES OF THE CENTER OF THE CIRCLE,
C***  THE RADIUS OF THE CIRCLE, AND THE COORDINATES OF THE POINT.
C***
      SUBROUTINE CIRPNT
      REAL CX, CY, R, PX, PY, DIST
      PRINT *, 'ENTER THE COORDINATES OF THE CIRCLE CENTER.'
      READ *, CX, CY
      PRINT *, 'ENTER THE RADIUS OF THE CIRCLE.'
      READ *, R
      PRINT *, 'ENTER COORDINATES OF THE POINT.'
      READ *, PX, PY
      DIST = SQRT ((CX-PX)**2 + (CY-PY)**2)
      IF (DIST .LT. R) THEN
          PRINT *, 'THE CIRCLE WITH CENTER ', CX, CY,
     +        ' AND RADIUS ', R
          PRINT *, 'ENCLOSES THE POINT ', PX, PY
```

```
      ELSE
          PRINT *, 'THE CIRCLE WITH CENTER ', CX, CY,
     +        ' AND RADIUS ', R
          PRINT *, 'DOES NOT ENCLOSE THE POINT ', PX, PY
      ENDIF
      END
C***
C***  THIS SUBROUTINE CHECKS FOR A CIRCLE ENCLOSING A TRIANGLE.
C***  INPUT DATA CONSISTS OF THE COORDINATES OF THE CENTER OF THE
C***  CIRCLE, THE RADIUS OF THE CIRCLE, AND THE COORDINATES OF THE
C***  3 VERTICES OF THE TRIANGLE.
C***
      SUBROUTINE CIRTRI
      REAL V1X, V1Y, V2X, V2Y, V3X, V3Y, CX, CY, R
      PRINT *, 'ENTER THE COORDINATES OF THE CENTER.'
      READ *, CX, CY
      PRINT *, 'ENTER THE RADIUS OF THE CIRCLE.'
      READ *, R
      PRINT *, 'ENTER THE PAIRS OF COORDINATES OF THE VERTICES'
      PRINT *, 'OF THE TRIANGLE, ALL 3 PAIRS ON ONE LINE.'
      READ *, V1X, V1Y, V2X, V2Y, V3X, V3Y
      DIST1 = SQRT ((CX-V1X)**2 + (CY-V1Y)**2)
      DIST2 = SQRT ((CX-V2X)**2 + (CY-V2Y)**2)
      DIST3 = SQRT ((CX-V3X)**2 + (CY-V3Y)**2)
      IF (DIST1.LE.R .AND. DIST2.LE.R .AND. DIST3.LE.R) THEN
          PRINT *, 'THE CIRCLE WITH CENTER AT ', CX, CY
     +        ' AND RADIUS ', R
          PRINT *, 'ENCLOSES THE TRIANGLE WITH VERTICES'
          PRINT *, '(', V1X, V1Y, '), (', V2X, V2Y, '), (', V3X, V3Y, ').'
      ELSE
          PRINT *, 'THE CIRCLE WITH CENTER AT ', CX, CY
     +        ' AND RADIUS ', R
          PRINT *, 'DOES NOT ENCLOSE THE TRIANGLE WITH VERTICES'
          PRINT *, '(', V1X, V1Y, '), (', V2X, V2Y, '), (', V3X, V3Y, ').'
      ENDIF
      END
C***
C***  THIS SUBROUTINE CHECKS FOR A CIRCLE ENCLOSING ANOTHER CIRCLE.
C***  INPUT DATA CONSISTS OF THE COORDINATES OF THE CENTERS OF THE
C***  TWO CIRCLES AND THE RADIUS OF EACH OF THEM.
C***
      SUBROUTINE CIRCIR
      REAL C1X, C1Y, R1, C2X, C2Y, R2, DIST
      PRINT *, 'ENTER THE COORDINATES FOR THE CENTER OF THE ',
     +    'LARGER CIRCLE.'
      READ *, C1X, C1Y
      PRINT *, 'ENTER THE RADIUS OF THE LARGER CIRCLE.'
      READ *, R1
      PRINT *, 'ENTER THE COORDINATES FOR THE CENTER OF THE ',
     +    'SMALLER CIRCLE.'
      READ *, C2X, C2Y
      PRINT *, 'ENTER THE RADIUS OF THE SMALLER CIRCLE.'
```

```
      READ *, R2
      DIST = SQRT ((C1X-C2X)**2 = (C1Y-C2Y)**2)
      IF (DIST .LE. (RI-R2)) THEN
          PRINT *, 'THE CIRCLE WITH RADIUS ',R1,
     +        ' AND CENTER ', C1X, C1Y
          PRINT *, 'ENCLOSES THE CIRCLE WITH RADIUS ', R2
     +        ' AND CENTER ', C2X, C2Y
      ELSEIF (DIST .LE. (R1-R2)) THEN
          PRINT *, 'THE CIRCLE WITH RADIUS ', R1,
     +        ' AND CENTER ', C1X, C1Y
          PRINT *, 'DOES NOT ENCLOSE THE CIRCLE WITH RADIUS ', R2,
     +        ' AND CENTER ', C2X, C2Y
      ELSE
          PRINT *, 'NEITHER CIRCLE ENCLOSES THE OTHER.'
      ENDIF
      END
C***
C***  THIS SUBROUTINE CHECKS FOR A TRIANGLE ENCLOSING A POINT.
C***  INPUT DATA CONSISTS OF THE COORDINATES OF THE POINT AND THE
C***  COORDINATES OF THE VERTICES OF THE TRIANGLE.
C***
      SUBROUTINE TRIPNT
      LOGICAL INSIDE
      REAL PX, PY, V1X, V1Y, V2X, V2Y, V3X, V3Y
      COMMON V1X, V1Y, V2X, V2Y, V3X, V3Y
      PRINT *, 'ENTER THE COORDINATES OF THE POINT.'
      READ *, PX, PY
      PRINT *, 'ENTER 3 PAIRS OF COORDINATES FOR THE 3 VERTICES'
      PRINT *, 'OF THE TRIANGLE, ALL 3 PAIRS ON ONE LINE.'
      READ *, V1X, V1Y, V2X, V2Y, V3X, V3Y
      CALL TRCHEK (INSIDE, PX, PY)
      IF (INSIDE) THEN
          PRINT *, 'THE POINT WITH COORDINATES ', PX, PY
          PRINT *, 'IS ENCLOSED BY THE TRIANGLE WITH VERTICES'
          PRINT *, '(', V1X, V1Y, '), (', V2X, V2Y, '), (', V3X, V3Y, ').'
      ELSE
          PRINT *, 'THE POINT WITH COORDINATES ', PX, PY
          PRINT *, 'IS NOT ENCLOSED BY THE TRIANGLE WITH VERTICES'
          PRINT *, '(', V1X, V1Y, '), (', V2X, V2Y, '), (', V3X, V3Y, ').'
      ENDIF
      END
C***
C***  THIS SUBROUTINE CHECKS FOR ONE TRIANGLE ENCLOSING ANOTHER
C***  TRIANGLE. INPUT DATA CONSISTS OF THE COORDINATES OF THE
C***  VERTICES OF THE LARGER TRIANGLE AND THE COORDINATES OF THE
C***  VERTICES OF THE SMALLER TRIANGLE.
C***
      SUBROUTINE TRITRI
      LOGICAL INSID1, INSID2, INSID3
      REAL V1X, V1Y, V2X, V2Y, V3X, V3Y
      REAL W1X, W1Y, W2X, W2Y, W3X, W3Y
      COMMON V1X, V1Y, V2X, V2Y, V3X, V3Y
```

```
      PRINT *, 'ENTER THE COORDINATES OF THE VERTICES OF THE',
      PRINT *, 'LARGER TRIANGLE, ALL 3 PAIRS ON ONE LINE.'
      READ *, V1X, V1Y, V2X, V2Y, V3X, V3Y
      PRINT *, 'NOW ENTER THE COORDINATES OF THE VERTICES OF'
      PRINT *, 'THE SMALLER TRIANGLE, ALL 3 PAIRS ON ONE LINE.'
      READ *, W1X, W1Y, W2X, W2Y, W3X, W3Y
      CALL TRCHEK (INSID1, W1X, W1Y)
      CALL TRCHEK (INSID2, W2X, W2Y)
      CALL TRCHEK (INSID3, W3X, W3Y)
      IF (INSID1 .AND. INSID2 .AND. INSID3) THEN
          PRINT *, 'THE LARGER TRIANGLE ENCLOSES THE SMALLER ONE.'
      ELSE
          PRINT *, 'THE LARGER TRIANGLE DOES NOT ENCLOSE THE SMALLER.'
      ENDIF
      END
C***
C***  THIS SUBROUTINE CHECKS FOR A TRIANGLE ENCLOSING A POINT.
C***  THERE ARE 3 PARAMETERS FOR THIS SUBROUTINE. THE FIRST ONE IS
C***  RETURNED BY THIS SUBROUTINE AND INDICATES WHETHER OR NOT THE
C***  POINT IS INSIDE THE TRIANGLE. THE NEXT TWO PARAMETERS ARE THE
C***  COORDINATES OF THE POINT TO BE CHECKED. THE COORDINATES OF THE
C***  TRIANGLE TO BE USED IN THIS CHECK ARE AVAILABLE TO THE
C***  SUBROUTINE IN THE COMMON AREA.
C***
      SUBROUTINE TRCHEK (INSIDE, PX, PY)
      LOGICAL INSIDE
      REAL PX, PY
      COMMON V1X, V1Y, V2X, V2Y, V3X, V3Y
C***
C***  FIRST COMPUTE THE COORDINATES OF THE CENTER OF THE TRIANGLE.
C***
      CX = (V1X + V2X + V3X) / 3
      CY = (V1Y + V2Y + V3Y) / 3
C***
C***  COMPUTE COEFFICIENTS OF THE EQUATIONS OF THE 3 LINES JOINING
C***  THE 3 VERTICES OF THE TRIANGLE.
C***
C***  THE SIDE FORMED BY JOINING VERTICES V1 AND V2
      A1 = V2Y - V1Y
      B1 = V2X - V1X
      C1 = V1Y*V2X - V2Y*V1X
C***  THE SIDE FORMED BY JOINING VERTICES V2 AND V3
      A2 = V3Y - V2Y
      B2 = V3X - V2X
      C2 = V2Y*V3X - V3Y*V2X
C***  THE SIDE FORMED BY JOINING VERTICES V1 AND V3
      A3 = V3Y - V1Y
      B3 = V3X - V1X
      C3 = V3Y*V1X - VIY*V3X
```

```
C***  NOW DETERMINE IF THE POINT IS INSIDE THE TRIANGLE.
      S1 = (A1*PX + B1*PY + C1) * (A1*CX + B1*CY + C1)
      S2 = (A2*PX + B2*PY + C2) * (A2*CX + B2*CY + C2)
      S3 = (A3*PX + B3*PY + C3) * (A3*CX + B3*CY + C3)
      IF (S1.GT.0 .AND. S2.GT.0 .AND. S3.GT.0) THEN
          INSIDE = .TRUE.
      ELSE
          INSIDE = .FALSE.
      ENDIF
      END
C***
C***  THIS SUBROUTINE CHECKS FOR A TRIANGLE ENCLOSING A CIRCLE.
C***  INPUT DATA CONSISTS OF THE COORDINATES OF THE VERTICES OF THE
C***  TRIANGLE, THE COORDINATES OF THE CENTER OF THE CIRCLE, AND THE
C***  LENGTH OF THE RADIUS OF THE CIRCLE.
C***
      SUBROUTINE TRICIR
      LOGICAL INSIDE
      COMMON V1X, V1Y, V2X, V2Y, V3X, V3Y
      REAL CX, CY, R, A1, A2, A3, B1, B2, B3, C1, C2, C3
      REAL H1, H2, H3
      PRINT *, 'ENTER THE COORDINATES FOR THE TRIANGLE VERTICES, '
      PRINT *, 'ALL 3 PAIRS ON ONE LINE.'
      READ *, V1X, V1Y, V2X, V2Y, V3X, V3Y
      PRINT *, 'ENTER THE COORDINATES OF CENTER OF CIRCLE.'
      READ *, CX, CY
      PRINT *, 'ENTER THE LENGTH OF RADIUS OF CIRCLE.'
      READ *, R
C***
C***  COMPUTE THE COEFFICIENTS OF THE EQUATIONS OF THE 3 LINES
C***  JOINING THE 3 VERTICES OF THE TRIANGLE.
C***
C***  THE SIDE JOINING VERTICES V1 AND V2
      A1 = V2Y - V1Y
      B1 = V2X - V1X
      C1 = V1Y*V2X - V2Y*V1X
C***  THE SIDE JOINING VERTICES V2 AND V3
      A2 = V3Y - V2Y
      B2 = V3X - V2X
      C2 = V2Y*V3X - V3Y*V2X
C***  THE SIDE JOINING VERTICES V1 AND V3
      A3 = V3Y - V1Y
      B3 = V3X - V1X
      C3 = V1Y*V3X - V3Y*V1X
C***
C***  COMPUTE THE DISTANCES FROM EACH OF THE 3 TRIANGLE SIDES TO
C***  THE CENTER OF THE CIRCLE.
C***
      H1 = ABS(A1*CX + B1*CY + C1) / SQRT(A1**2 + B1**2)
      H2 = ABS(A2*CX + B2*CY + C2) / SQRT(A2**2 + B2**2)
      H3 = ABS(A3*CX + B3*CY + C3) / SQRT(A3**2 + B3**2)
C***
```

```
C***   CHECK IF THE CIRCLE'S CENTER IS INSIDE THE TRIANGLE.
C***
       CALL TRCHEK (INSIDE, CX, CY)
C***
C***   FOR THE CIRCLE TO BE INSIDE THE TRIANGLE, H1, H2, H3
C***   MUST ALL BE GREATER THAN R.
C***
       IF (INSIDE .AND. H1.GT.R. .AND. H2.GT.R .AND. H3.GT.R) THEN
           PRINT *, 'THE TRIANGLE ENCLOSES THE CIRCLE.'
       ELSE
           PRINT *, 'THE TRIANGLE DOES NOT ENCLOSE THE CIRCLE.'
       ENDIF
       END
C***
C***   THIS SUBROUTINE CHECKS IF POINTS P AND Q COINCIDE.
C***   INPUT DATA CONSISTS OF THE COORDINATES OF THE 2 POINTS.
C***
       SUBROUTINE PNTPNT
       REAL PX, PY, QX, QY
       PRINT *, 'ENTER THE COORDINATES OF THE FIRST POINT.'
       READ *, PX, PY
       PRINT *, 'ENTER THE COORDINATES OF THE SECOND POINT.'
       READ *, QX, QY
       IF (PX.EQ.QX .AND. PY.EQ.QY) THEN
           PRINT *, 'POINT P ENCLOSES POINT Q.'
       ELSE
           PRINT *, 'POINT P DOES NOT ENCLOSE POINT Q.'
       ENDIF
       END
```

Summary

The general form of a ***FUNCTION statement*** is:

```
NAME(ARG1,ARG2, . . . ,ARGN) = Definition
```

where NAME is a function name that complies with the usual rules for variable names,
ARG1,ARG2, . . . ,ARGN are formal arguments, of which there must be at least one, and
Definition is any arithmetic, logical, or string expression.

The general form of a ***FUNCTION subprogram*** is:

```
Type FUNCTION NAME(ARG1,ARG2,  . . . ,ARGN)
       Statement 1
       Statement 2
       .
       .
       .
       Statement N
RETURN
END
```

where Type is one of the variable data types available in FORTRAN (Type may be omitted, in which case NAME specifies the type as integer or real according to its first letter),
NAME is a function name that complies with FORTRAN rules for variable names,
ARG1, ARG2, . . . , ARGN are formal arguments, of which there must be at least one and no more than 63,
Statement 1, Statement 2, . . . , Statement N represent acceptable FORTRAN statements,
RETURN may appear none, one, or more times, and
END must be the last statement in the function.

The general form of a ***SUBROUTINE subprogram*** is:

```
SUBROUTINE NAME (ARG1,ARG2,  . . . ,ARGN)
Statement 1
Statement 2
.
.
.
Statement N
RETURN
END
```

where NAME represents the subprogram name and must comply with the usual rules for FORTRAN variables,
ARG1,ARG2, . . . ,ARGN represent formal arguments,
Statement 1, Statement 2, . . . , Statement N represent any acceptable FORTRAN statements,
RETURN should appear at least once in the subroutine, and
END must be the last statement in the subroutine.

The general form of a ***CALL statement*** is:

```
CALL NAME(ARG1,ARG2,  . . . ,ARGN)
```

where NAME represents the name of a subroutine subprogram, and ARG1,ARG2, . . . ,ARGN represent the arguments of the subroutine subprogram; the arguments and parentheses enclosing them may be omitted if the subroutine being called has no formal arguments.

The ***COMMON statement*** is a means of making information available to more than one module in a given program. Its general form is:

```
COMMON VAR1,VAR2, . . . ,VARN
```

where VAR1,VAR2, . . . ,VARN represent variable names of simple or array variables.

End of Chapter Exercises

1. Write a program to make an ordinary terminal or line printer act as a plotter. The output will be a graph that looks something like this:

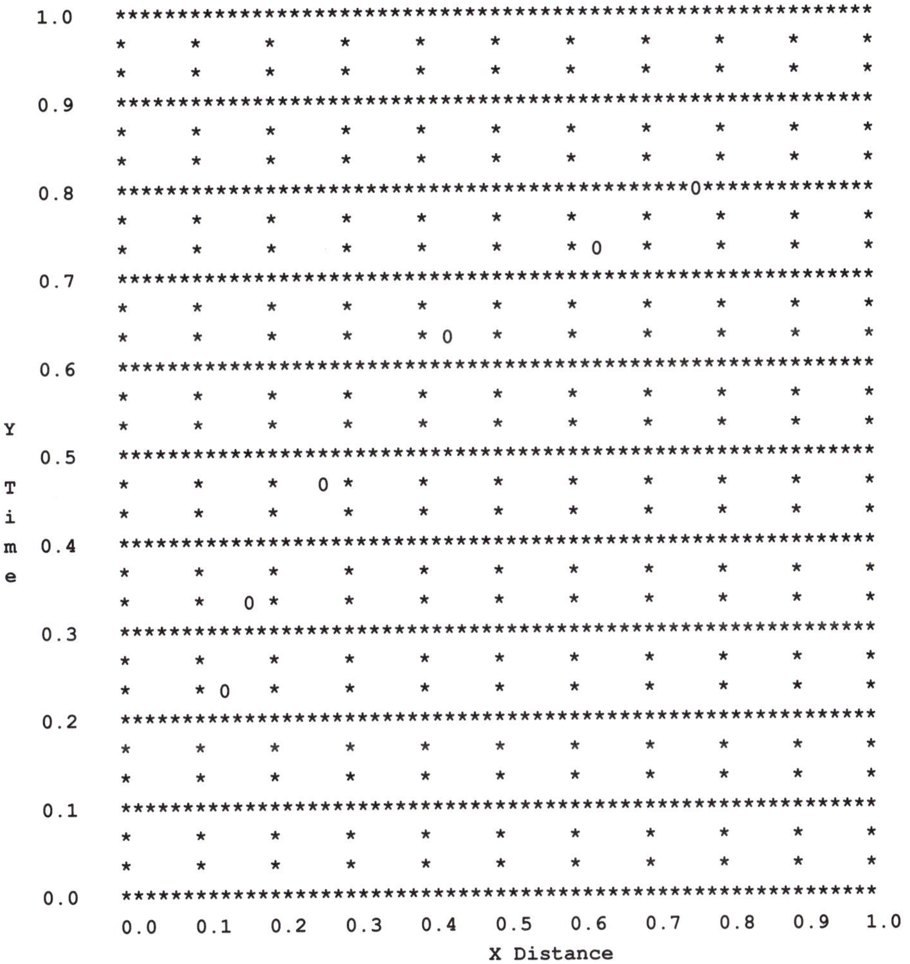

Note that this is a 10x10 grid. The Y axis runs vertically along the left edge of the grid and the X axis runs horizontally along the bottom edge of the grid. Note also the labels printed along these axes. The zeroes on the grid indicate points on the function being graphed.

The main program is to be stored in an array X, and N real values are to be stored in an array Y. Also to be read using a format are labels, not to exceed 16 characters each, to be printed along the X and Y axes as shown. Assume that all values for X and Y are not less than 0 nor greater than 1.

The main program calls a subroutine subprogram GRAPH which is to produce an output array whose elements contain the exact characters to be printed on the graph. For example, in the sample there are 68 spaces from left to right starting at the column that contains the label for the Y axis, and 32 spaces from top to bottom counting from the top row of asterisks to the bottom row that contains the label for the X axis. That is a total of 68 times 32, or 2176 spaces in the output array. Thus the characters stored in the first row of the output array, let's call it OUTPUT, are as follows:

OUTPUT(1,1) and OUTPUT(1,2) contain blank spaces.
OUTPUT(1,3) contains 1.
OUTPUT(1,4) contains a period.
OUTPUT(1,5) contains 0.
OUTPUT(1,6) contains blank space.
OUTPUT(1,7) through OUTPUT(1,68) contain asterisks.

Similarly, the contents of row 2 and subsequent rows in array OUTPUT are blank spaces and asterisks.

Subprogram GRAPH calls a subprogram GRID, which stores all necessary characters in appropriate cells of array OUTPUT to later print out the asterisks of the grid and the labels for the axis.

After subprogram GRID has been called, subprogram POINTS is called by GRAPH. The function of POINTS is to store zeroes in the cells of array OUTPUT that correspond to the points whose coordinates are given by the values stored in arrays X and Y. Remember that everything stored in array OUTPUT must be stored as a character.

2. Let F be the focal length of a lens, let A be the distance from the lens to the object Q and let B be the distance from Q to the image of Q produced by the lens. Then the following equation holds:

$$1/A + 1/B = 1/F$$

If $B > 0$ then the image is a real image. If $B < 0$ the image is said to be a virtual image. If $1/B = 0$, B approaches infinity and we say that there is no image.

Write a program to tabulate the image distance B for all values of $A = 1, 2, \ldots, N$ and for all values of $F = 1, 2, \ldots, M$ where M and N are input values to the program. Output appropriate messages, based on the value of B, resulting from the given situation.

3. Write a program to study each of the following limits. A starting value for the variable is provided in each case as is the equation for obtaining the succeeding values.

a.

$$\lim_{t \to 0} \left[\cos 2t \frac{1}{t^2} \right]$$

a.1 Use $t_0 = -1$ and $t_n = t_{n-1} + 0.01$

a.2 Use $t_0 = 1$ and $t_n = t_{n-1} - 0.01$

b.

$$\lim_{t \to 0} \left[\frac{1 + t}{t} - \frac{1}{\log(1 + t)} \right]$$

Use $t_0 = 1$ and $t_n = t_{n-1} - 0.01$
Stop when $t = 0$

c.

$$\lim_{t \to \infty} \left[\frac{3t^3 - 2t + 4}{2 - 3t^2 - 2t^3} \right]$$

Use $t_0 = 1$ and $t_n = t_{n-1} + 10$
Stop when $t = 10{,}000$

d.

$$\lim_{t \to \infty} \left[\frac{1 + \frac{1}{n^2}}{1 + \frac{1}{n}} \right]^{0.5}$$

Use the same initial value for t and the same formula for computing succeeding values as in part c.

4. Under ideal conditions, a bullet fired into the air with an initial velocity of v and an angle of inclination θ will travel a distance d as given by the following equation:

$$d = \frac{v^2 \sin 2\theta}{g}$$

during time $t = (2v \sin 2\theta)/g$ where $g = 9.8$ meters/sec/sec.

Develop a program to read a value for v, then produce as output a table of values for d, t, and θ where $\theta = 1, 2, 3, \ldots, 90$.

PROGRAM DESIGN ISSUES

In the very early days of computing, problems like Exercises 2 and 4 were believed to be the most important types of problems for computers. Before the electronic calculator, such complex computations usually involved looking up values in tables. An artillery officer would rely on paper copies of this Exercise 4 matrix; a telescope designer would use the matrix from Exercise 2.

We now find it more effective to provide engineers with computers than to provide them with computer-generated tables. But recent technological advances have caused a renewed interest in such problems. Parallel architecture, the basic design of supercomputers and of neutral nets, has accelerated processing so much that if a given function is often needed, it may actually be faster to have the computer look it up, or to look up two values and interpolate between them, than to do the calculation each time.

In writing these matrix-building programs, consider the following issues:

Does this function have regions where its values change very rapidly? If yes, use closer intervals in those areas for greater accuracy. An example of a critical area are the tangents for values very close to $\pi/2$.

Is the table symmetrical? For example, does $t(x, y) = t(y, x)$? Or, in a slightly more complex relation, does $t(x, y) = 1/t(y, x)$? If so, processing can be simplified by using the symmetry to obtain some values and reducing the number of times that a complicated function must be calculated from scratch.

Are values used in ratios? If so, remember that the accuracy of a function of several values falls off much more rapidly than the accuracy of the individual values. For example, even if x and y are accurately specified to four digits, the function $1/(x - y)$ is wildly inaccurate any time x and y are within .0001 of each other. At that range, the margin of error can exceed the actual remainder. To ensure accuracy, it is sometimes necessary to compute table values to a large number of digits.

5. Suppose that a function F(X) is continuous in the interval [A,B] and is known to have a single maximum value in that interval. Write a program to find X_0 in the interval such that F(X0) is approximately the maximum of F(X) in the interval [A,B]. You may want to use the following algorithm:

1. Divide the interval [A,B] into 4 equal subintervals [A,C], [C,M], [M,D] and [D,B].
2. Compute F(A), F(C), F(M), F(D) and F(B). If F(C) > F(M) then X0 is in [M,B]. Otherwise X0 is in [C,D]. Repeat these steps until the interval containing X0 is no longer than some specified value E.

Write your program to find the maximum of F where F(X) = 2X – X**3 , A = 0, B = 1, and E = 0.00005

6. Let F(X) be a continuous function in the interval [A, B]. If the product of F(A) and F(B) is negative, then there exists a point, X0, in [A, B] such that F(X0) = 0. In this case X0 is called a root of F(X). It is possible to compute a value for X0 such that |F(X0)| ≤ E for any arbitrary positive number, E. One algorithm for computing X0 is known as the bisection method, which goes as follows:

1. Let X0 = (A + B)/2.
2. Compute F(A) * F(X0) and F(X0) * F(B).
3. If F(A) * F(X0) < 0 then the root of F(X) is in the interval [A, X0].

   If F(X0) * F(B) < 0 then the root is in [X0, B].
4. Next compute X1 = (A + X0)/2 or X1 = (X0 + B)/2 depending on which interval is known to contain the sought-after root.
5. Now let X1 be the X0 of the bisection algorithm as just described and compute a new value for F(X0). This algorithm may be continued until |X1 − X0| ≤ E for any given positive number E.

   Write a program that implements the bisection method.

Chapter 7

Input/Output Options

The programs with which we have been working so far take in lists of data from the keyboard, process the data according to the program statements, and produce results on a video screen or printer.

But there are other ways to provide data to a FORTRAN program, both from other sources, like data files stored on magnetic or optical disks, and in formats other than simple lists. And you may want the program output to go somewhere besides your screen or printer, like back to a magnetic file, or to be presented in a particular layout. In this chapter, we discuss the use of data files for input and output, and then the use of formatted READ, WRITE, and PRINT statements and format specifications.

Data Files

When data are stored in primary memory, they are lost when the computer is shut off. Data in primary memory are thus available only to the program that places the data in memory, and only at the time that the program is executed. Even when running the same program at a different time, the data must be reentered. Similarly with output generated on screen. When the screen displays a new image, the old image is gone forever. To recover the data, the program must be run again. And when output is printed, it remains on the paper, but is impossible to modify or to use in that form as part of another program.

These problems can be solved by using *secondary storage devices*, primarily the magnetic or optical disk, with a programming concept called a *file*. When data are stored in a file on a disk, they are available for use whenever the user calls. Furthermore, disk files may be read as input by other programs, then modified and stored in modified form into the same or a new disk file.

Records and files. We begin our discussion of files with a concept called the *record*. A record in computer context is a collection of related data items. For example, a structural engineer might keep the following data about different types of reinforcing steel bars, or rebar:

```
TYPE
IDENTIFICATION NUMBER
SUPPLIER
AVAILABILITY
COMPOSITION
GAUGE
TENSILE STRENGTH
EXPANSION FACTOR
CROSS SECTION
```

These items of information are all data about a single variety of rebar. Such a collection of related information is often referred to as a *record*. Two or more related records are called a *file*.

Data files are usually assigned names for the purpose of easily identifying the correct file. For example, a data file containing the rebar records might be assigned the name RBFILE. The rules for naming files are dependent on the FORTRAN compiler used or the computer system on which processing takes place.

Accessing files. Three FORTRAN statements are necessary to open a data file, position the pointer at the beginning of the file, and close the file: OPEN, REWIND, and CLOSE.

The OPEN statement. This statement prepares a file either to be read from or to be written into. It is discussed in detail in Chapter 9, but a somewhat restricted form is adequate for our current needs:

```
OPEN (U,FILE='Filename',STATUS=('OLD' or 'NEW'))
```

where U is the unit number assigned to the file,
Filename is the name of the file, and
STATUS is OLD if the file already exists in the system and NEW if the file is just being created.

Open a NEW file to use with a WRITE statement to produce output. If you open an OLD file to use with a WRITE statement for output, ***you lose the information*** that is stored in the file—the WRITE process in effect erases the stored information as it is written to the output device. You usually open an OLD file to use with a READ statement for input, in which case you bring stored information into the computer for use in the current program.

Here are two examples of the OPEN statement:

EXAMPLE 1

```
OPEN(1,FILE='STFILE',STATUS='OLD')
```

The existing file STFILE is associated with unit 1 and is prepared for input or output.

EXAMPLE 2

```
OPEN(3,FILE='TEMP',STATUS='NEW')
```

File TEMP is made ready for output. It is a new file, created for the first time, and is associated with unit 3.

The REWIND statement. This statement positions a data file at its starting point so that the first record is ready for input or output. The form is

```
REWIND U        or        REWIND(U)
```

where U is the unit number associated with the file.

EXAMPLE 1

```
REWIND 3
```

Unit 3 is positioned so that the first record of the data file is ready for reading or writing.

EXAMPLE 2

```
REWIND(4)
```

This example does the same for the data file associated with unit 4.

The CLOSE statement. This statement closes a file that is no longer needed by the program. Every file used by a program should be closed before the program ends. Otherwise the file is not properly disconnected and data corruption, computer malfunction, or even the loss of the file may result. The general form of the statement is

```
CLOSE(UL,U2, . . . ,UK)
```

where Ul,U2, . . . ,UK are one or more different unit numbers.

Here are examples:

EXAMPLE 1

```
CLOSE(1)
```

Properly disconnects the file on unit 1.

EXAMPLE 2

```
CLOSE(3,7,8)
```

Properly disconnects the three files 3, 7, and 8.

Reading from a file. The three common methods of organizing data files are *sequential*, *indexed sequential*, and *direct*. We discuss only sequential files here, in which records are read or written one after another. To read or write record N it is necessary for the program to first process in some way all N–1 records that sequentially precede it in the file. A program may simply bypass the previous records to get to the object datum, but there is no way in sequential file organization to skip directly to a particular record.

To read data from a file, use the following form of the READ statement:

```
READ(U,*,END=N) Var-list
```

where U is the unit number associated with the file,
* refers to unformatted input,

N is the reference number of the statement to be executed next when the end of the file is reached, and
Var-list refers to the list of variables into which data are to be read.

The END statement is not required, but if it is omitted and the computer attempts to read beyond the end of the file, an error results, terminating the program.

Here are three specific examples of READ statements:

EXAMPLE 1

```
READ(2,*,END=20) A,B
```

One record from the file associated with unit 2 is accessed and two data elements are read, the first into variable A and the second into variable B.

If reading is attempted when the last record of the file has been passed, program control transfers to statement number 20 (END=20).

EXAMPLE 2

```
READ(7,*,END=30) NAME,ADDRES
```

One record from the file associated with unit 7 is accessed and two data elements are read, the first into variable NAME and the second into variables ADDRES.

If reading is attempted past the last record in the file, program control transfers to statement 30.

EXAMPLE 3

```
READ(1,*) X,Y,Z
```

One record from the file associated with unit 1 is read and three data elements are stored, one in variable X, one in variable Y, and the third in variable Z.

Note that we omit the optional END. If reading is attempted past the last record of the file, an error results and the program is terminated.

Keyboard input. Unit 5 is reserved on most computer systems for the primary input device, either the keyboard or terminal depending on the type of system. Therefore the statements

`READ(5,*)A` *and* `READ*,A`

both read the value of A from a keyboard or terminal.

Writing to a file. The general form of a statement to write one record into a data file is the following:

```
WRITE(U,*) Out-list
```

where U and * are as described for the READ statement, and
Out-list refers to constants or variables to be output to the data file associated with unit U.

Here are two specific examples, both using the familiar unformatted WRITE statement:

EXAMPLE 1 `WRITE(3,*) NAME,STREET,CITY,STATE,ZIP`

One record of 5 data elements is output to the data file associated with unit 3.

EXAMPLE 2 `WRITE(1,*) HOURS`

One record of 1 data element is output to the data file associated with unit 1.

Problem 7.1
Classifying Shift Malfunctions

SITUATION The automobile company for which you work has received several disturbing reports involving their new, high-end sports model. Occasionally, in passing and emergency situations involving rapid acceleration, those models of the car equipped with a new intelligent shift transmission have suddenly stalled.

The intelligent shift transmission employs a small computer to control the shifting of gears so the engine always runs at the optimum torque for the combination of rpm, airflow, and engine temperature.

After much research, the company engineers have arrived at one possible cause for the problem. It is possible that, in the turbocharged model, vibration from the turbocharger may loosen the contact for the ground connection of the tachometer that feeds data to the intelligent shift computer. This may make the tachometer slightly slow in its response, so during sudden acceleration it may first undershift, placing the car in too low a gear, and then, as rpm rapidly climbs, overshift into too high a gear, stalling the engine.

The original test data for the car were not organized to track this possibility. So it is now necessary to take the archived data from storage, identify the test cars that may have exhibited even a mild form of the problem, and then reanalyze that data to check for over- and undershifting under extreme acceleration.

OBJECTIVE Write a program that identifies the road test records that should be reanalyzed, and creates a file that contains the identifiers of those records.

ANALYSIS Each test vehicle is identified by a number, stored in a field called RUNID. If the vehicle had a turbocharger, variable TURBO is set to 1; otherwise it is 0. If the vehicle had an intelligent shift, the variable SMRTSH (for smart shift) is set to 1; otherwise it is 0. The maximum acceleration recorded in each test is stored in the variable TOPACC (for top acceleration) as a real number in feet/sec^2. For the purposes of this reassessment, accelerations of over 11, the acceleration needed to go from 0 to 60 mph in about 8 seconds, are defined as high.

Each record must be checked for the presence of all three conditions TURBO = 1, SMRTSH = 1, and TOPACC ≥ 11, and the identifiers for the records that meet the criteria written to a new file.

FORTRAN PROGRAM

```
      PROGRAM SHIFT
C*    FILE TVHCLE CONTAINS DATA IDENTIFYING VEHICLES BY
C*    THE FOLLOWING CHARACTERISTICS:
C*    RUNID IS A UNIQUE IDENTIFICATION NUMBER.
C*    TURBO IS 1 IF THE VEHICLE HAS TURBO POWER, 0 IF NOT.
C*    SMRTSH IS 1 IF IT HAS INTELLIGENT SHIFT, 0 IF NOT.
C*    TOPACC IS THE TOP ACCELERATION OF THE VEHICLE.
C*
C*    FILE ACCVH IS EMPTY AT THE BEGINNING OF RUNNING THIS PROGRAM
C*    BUT AT TERMINATION IT WILL CONTAIN VEHICLE IDENTIFICATION NUMBERS
C*    FOR ALL VEHICLES SHOWN BY THE DATA IN FILE TVHCLE TO BE EQUIPPED
C*    WITH BOTH TURBO POWER AND INTELLIGENT SHIFT WITH TOPACC > 11.
C*
      INTEGER RUNID,TURBO,SMRTSH
      REAL TOPACC
      OPEN (1, FILE='TVHCLE', STATUS='OLD')
      OPEN (2, FILE='ACCVH', STATUS='NEW')
 10   READ (1,*,END=20) RUNID,TURBO,SMRTSH,TOPACC
      IF ((TURBO*SMRTSH .EQ. 1) .AND. (TOPACC .GE. 11)) WRITE (2,RUNID)
      GOTO 10
 20   CLOSE (1,2)
      END
```

Formatted Input/Output

We have so far been using unformatted READ, PRINT, and WRITE statements. These are called *unformatted* because there is no way for the programmer to specify the format of the columns into which data are to be read from input lines or to prescribe the columns across the page or screen in which output is to be printed or written. The layout of both input and output is specified by default values in the computer system. Because data are provided to and retrieved from such statements in the form of a raw, unformatted list, such statements are also called *list directed* statements.

A major benefit of list directed input/output is that the programmer need not be concerned about their precise organization. This relieves you of some of the drudgery of programming. But of course, in many situations it's the organization of the data that makes random fact into useful information. Format might be essential for understanding a report. It may be that data are prepared in certain fields and we want to be able to read only some of those fields without looking at all the columns of data. In situations like these, FORTRAN makes available ways of using *formatted* input and output.

The formatted READ statement. The formatted READ has two general forms:

FORM A When input takes place from a keyboard:

```
READ F,V1,V2, . . . ,VN
```

FORM B When input occurs from an electronically stored file:

```
READ(U,F,END=N)V1,V2, . . . ,VN
```

where in both forms F is either a format specification string or the reference number of a FORMAT statement—discussed in the next section—that specifies the format,
V1,V2, . . . ,VN is the list of variables into which data are being read, separated by commas;
and in form 2 U is the number of the logical unit number from which the formatted data are being read, and
END=N tells the program, if an end-of-file mark is encountered, to proceed to the statement with reference number N. END=N is optional.

The formatted PRINT statement. The general form is

```
PRINT F,Out-list
```

where F again is the format specification string or the reference number of the associated FORMAT statement, and
Out-list is the list of output to be produced, with items separated by commas.

The comma that separates the number F from the output list and the commas used to separate the entries in the output list from each other are required here just as in the formatted READ statement above.

The output list in a formatted PRINT statement may consist of variables, numeric constants, string constants, or arithmetic expressions, the same as with the unformatted PRINT statement. The formatted PRINT statement always causes output to occur on a printer or a video display monitor. Here is an example:

EXAMPLE

```
PRINT 10,A,B,A+B, 'THIS IS OK.'
```

where 10 is the reference number of the associated FORMAT statement elsewhere in the program,

A and B are previously defined variables,
A+B is an arithmetic expression, and
'THIS IS OK.' is a character string.

The formatted WRITE statement. As with the unformatted WRITE statement, output can be either to a printing device or a video display monitor, as with PRINT statements, or to a disk file. The general form is

```
WRITE(U,F)Out-list
```

where U is the number of the logical unit where output is to occur—logical unit 6 is commonly used to designate the screen—
F represents the format specification string or the reference number of the associated FORMAT statement, and
Out-list is the list of outputs to be produced; this list may be blank.

If you have a blank output list, the WRITE statement produces at least one blank line of output.

The FORMAT Statement and Format Specifications

The FORMAT statement is at the heart of formatted input and output in FORTRAN. In addition to the statement itself, there are several different standard format specifications. A format may be provided to a READ, PRINT, or WRITE statement in two equivalent ways:

1. As a character string within the input or output statement bounded by a pair of single quotes and parentheses. This string specifies the spacing and form of the input or output data.
2. As the reference number of an available FORMAT specification. In this case, the FORMAT statement specifies the spacing and form information in parentheses.

EXAMPLE 1A

```
      PRINT '(I2,I7)',M,N
```

Using the character string; or

EXAMPLE 1B

```
      PRINT 10,M,N
   10 FORMAT(I2,I7)
```

Using the format at reference 10

EXAMPLE 2A

```
      PRINT '(I4,1X,I6)',A,B
```

Using the character string; or

EXAMPLE 2B

```
      PRINT 20,A,B
   20 FORMAT(I4,1X,I6)
```

Using the format at reference 20

Note that the format specifications that appear in the input or output line itself may alternatively appear in a separate FORMAT statement on another line. The advantage of the separate FORMAT statement is that it may be referenced by many lines in the same program, rather than always having to insert the character string into the input or output statement.

The FORMAT statement is nonexecutable. It specifies or modifies the action resulting from a READ, PRINT, or WRITE statement.

Every FORMAT statement has a unique reference number that appears in the READ, PRINT or WRITE statement using it. Of course, this reference number may not be assigned to any other statement. However, many READ, PRINT, and WRITE statements in the program may reference the same FORMAT.

Following the word FORMAT is at least one pair of parentheses inside of which appear the numbers that determine the spacing and form of the information.

EXAMPLE 3 This simple program illustrates the use of FORMAT and the format string:

```
       PROGRAM SIMPLE
       INTEGER M,N
       READ '(I3,I7)',M,N
       WRITE(6,20)M,N,M+N
 20    FORMAT(1X,I3,1X,I7,1X,I9)
       END
```

The READ statement reads two integers M and N in the form and spacing specified in the format string immediately following the word READ: I3 and I7 in parentheses.
The letter I requires that the numbers input be integers and be stored internally as integers. This is called I format, and is discussed further below with other format specifications.
The number 3 specifies that the integer input for M occupies 3 spaces when entered from a keyboard. Similarly, 7 spaces are used for N.

Note that the READ statement has two items in its data list and the associated format string has two specifications. These should always match.

The WRITE statement has a 6 for the unit number associated with the output, followed by 20 as the reference number of the associated FORMAT.
The FORMAT with reference number 20 has 3 I specifications and three X specifications. The number of I specifications is the same as the number of values to be output.
The X specifications designate blank spaces.
So FORMAT 20 applied to the WRITE statement begins with an integer (including sign if it is negative) in positions 1 through 3, one blank space in position 4, an integer in positions 5 through 11, yet another blank space in position 12, and an integer in positions 13 through 21. The first 1X specifies a carriage control character that regulates the line on which the WRITE operates. Carriage control characters are discussed later in this chapter.

Now we discuss format specifications permitted in FORMAT statements or format strings. As we do so you will realize how much control the programmer gains over the form and spacing of input and output through the use of formatting. In fact, the control is complete. Therefore it is most important to learn how to apply FORMAT statements appropriately.

The I format. The *integer* format specification designates the data type as INTEGER and sets the number of spaces in the field. The number to the right of the I specifies the total number of positions set aside for a value to be read to or printed from a given memory location. The general form of the I format is as follows:

```
IW
```

where I designates that the datum processed is an integer, and
W is a positive integer specifying the width of the field allowed for input or output. If there is a sign associated with the integer it must be included in the designated width.

The integer is always assumed to be right justified in its field, that is, with the units digit in the rightmost space of the field. If a number shorter than the field is entered from the left with blanks entered to the right of the number, the blank spaces are assumed to be zeros. For example,

EXAMPLE 1

```
      READ 10,N
 10   FORMAT(I5)
```

Suppose that the line in which the value of N is entered looks like this, where the underlines represent blank spaces:

```
5 0 _ _ _
```

The value input for variable N is 50000. The blanks in positions 3, 4, and 5 are interpreted as zeros in conjunction with the I5 format specification.

The same principle operates when information is printed. The units digit is positioned at the right of its designated field.

EXAMPLE 2 Here is a complete program to further illustrate the I format.

```
1         PROGRAM TEST
2         INTEGER NUM1, NUM2, NUM3
3         READ(5,10)NUM1, NUM2, NUM3
4         WRITE(6,15)NUM1, NUM2, NUM3
5   10    FORMAT(I2,I5,I4)
6   15    FORMAT(1X,I5,I8,I7)
7         END
```

Line 3 causes the reading of three pieces of information from logical unit 5—the keyboard—in compliance with FORMAT 10 (line 5) that specifies the spacing to be used for the three integers being read. NUM1 is read from positions 1 and 2, NUM2 from positions 3–7, and NUM3 from positions 8–11.

Line 4 causes printing on logical unit 6 (screen) in compliance with FORMAT 15, that reserves positions 1–5 for NUM1, the next 8 spaces for NUM2, and the next 7 spaces for NUM3.

Line 7 signals the end of processing.

CASE A Suppose this program is run and that the data are entered as follows:

```
_6_-210__13
```

The READ and FORMAT statements cause the value 6 to be stored in NUM1, the value –210 to be stored in NUM2, and the value 13 to be stored in NUM3.

Note that fields on the input lines exactly match the I format specifications in FORMAT statement 10. Columns 1 and 2 are the two columns called for with I2, columns 3–7 are the five columns for I5, and columns 8–11 are the four columns for I4.

CASE B Assume that the preceding program is executed and that the data are entered as follows:

```
17234152
```

The value stored in NUM1 is determined by the specification I2, so the first two digits constitute this value, namely I7.

NUM2 is read according to specification I5, so the next 5 digits, 23415, make up the value stored in NUM2.

Finally, NUM3 is read with the specification I4 so the next 4 digits constitute the value stored in NUM3. Since only one digit remains of the eight entered as input, the program assumes the other 3 digits of the 4 needed to satisfy the I4 specification are zeros. The value stored in NUM3 is 2000.

CASE C If the user of the program intended NUM3 to have the value 2, the input should have been entered like this:

```
1723415___2
```

with the digit 2 aligned at the right of its 4-space field.

If the program is executed with this input, the output is as follows:

```
___17___23415______2
```

The X format. The X format specification designates the number of *blank spaces* to be inserted. The number preceding the X specifies the total number of blanks. The general form of the X format is

NX

where N is a positive integer that indicates the number of spaces, and
X identifies the input or output as blank spaces.

As with the I format, X format can be used for both input and output. When used in conjunction with a formatted READ, the X format causes the designated number of characters to be treated as blank spaces. In formatted output, X format causes the designated number of blank spaces to be produced on the output device.

EXAMPLE

```
1        PROGRAM EXAMPL
2        INTEGER N, M
3        READ 100, N, M
4   100  FORMAT(2X,I3,1X,I4)
5        PRINT 100, N, M
6        END
```

CASE A Suppose this program is executed using the input

```
23567,2381
```

Format specification 2X in line 4 causes the first 2 characters of input to be ignored.

Format specification I3 causes the next 3 digits 567 to be stored in variable N.

Format specification 1X causes the next character input, the comma, to be ignored.

Finally, the specification I4 causes the four digits 2381 to be stored as the value of M.

In this case the output is

```
_567_2381
```

First, the 2X specifies 1 blank space for the carriage control character and causes 1 blank space to be output.

I3 causes the contents of N, 567, to be printed.

Next, 1X causes one blank space.

Finally, I4 causes the contents of M, 2381, to be printed. Since the number of positions allotted in I4 is exactly the same as the number of digits in M, no extra blank spaces are output to the left of the 2381—we have only the one blank space produced by the previous 1X specification.

For practice in the use of I and X formats, consider the following different input data to the preceding program:

CASE B `3681275100`

CASE C `1-812.51`

CASE D `2-812*51`

verify that in all three cases the output is

```
812 5100
```

The F format. The *floating point*, or *real* format specification designates the data type as REAL and sets the number of spaces in the field and the number of decimal digits. (When FORTRAN was developed, real numbers were called floating point numbers.) The general form of the F format is as follows:

```
FW.D
```

where F indicates that the value to be read or printed is a real number,
W specifies the total width of the field, including sign and decimal point if they are included in the data, and
D specifies the number of decimal digits in the input or output.

The decimal point is required in the F format specification. As the examples show, decimals in input data override the D value.

F format for output. Consider these three programs and realize that they all perform the same tasks and produce the same output. They differ only in the use of format specifications.

EXAMPLE 1

```
      PROGRAM P1
      REAL A, B
      A = 26.812
      B = 17
      PRINT 15, A, B
 15   FORMAT(3X,F6.2)          Uses a FORMAT statement to specify output form.
      END
```

First, the value 26.812 is stored in variable A and the value 17 is stored in variable B.

The PRINT statement calls the FORMAT statement at reference 15 and causes 2 blank spaces (3X provides 1 blank space for carriage control and 2 in the actual output.) followed by a field of 6 positions (F6.2) to contain the value of A—but the F specification allows only two decimal digits. The output value of A is thus correctly rounded to two decimal digits, and this prints 26.81. This is only 5 characters including the decimal point, so the sixth space is left blank and positioned at the left.

The PRINT statement causes two variables A and B to be output, but there is only one real number specification in the FORMAT statement. The compiler thus repeats the format instructions for the second variable. When the statement is repeated it includes the parentheses. When the program encounters the parenthesis before the second output format specification, it inserts a new line. So variable B is printed right aligned in 6 spaces on the second line.

The other two programs are similar. Compare them to see how they work. All three programs produce the output

```
___26.81
____17.00
```

EXAMPLE 2

```
PROGRAM P2
REAL A, B
A = 26.812
B = 17
PRINT '(3X,F6.2)', A, B        Uses a format string in the PRINT statement.
END
```

EXAMPLE 3

```
PROGRAM P3
REAL A, B
CHARACTER FMT*9                Uses CHARACTER variable FMT.
A = 26.812
B = 17
FMT  = '(3X,F6.2)'
PRINT FMT, A, B
END
```

Duplicating format specifications. When the number of variables in an input or output statement does not match the number of format specifications, the given specifications are repeated beginning with the rightmost right facing parenthesis. If the closing parenthesis in the FORMAT statement is encountered before all items in the input or output statement have been entered or output, a new line is produced before any more output occurs.

In a PRINT or WRITE statement, this produces extra lines of output. With a READ statement, input data for the additional variables will not be read unless they are entered on a new line.

F format for input. When the F format specification is used in conjunction with a READ statement, the results vary according to the situation. Note especially that the decimal position is treated differently for input than for output.

CASE A

Data entered from the keyboard or data file include no decimal points. The F specification causes the data to be stored with the number of fractional digits indicated. The decimal point is not counted as one of the digits.

EXAMPLE 1

```
      READ 100,A,B
100   FORMAT(F6.2,F8.4)
```

If these lines are executed as part of a complete program and input data are entered as follows:

```
12345612345678
```

The value stored in variable A is 1234.56; in this case, the specification F6.2 causes 6 characters to be read and stored with a decimal point and 2 fractional digits.

Similarly, the number in variable B is 1234.5678 because F8.4 causes the next 8 characters to be read and stored with a decimal and 4 fractional digits.

CASE B Input data include decimal points. The placement of the decimal point in a given datum overrides the F specification and determines the number of fractional digits stored. The decimal point is counted in the number of digits allowed.

EXAMPLE B

```
      READ 100,A,B
100   FORMAT(F6.3,F8.0)
```

Suppose this program segment is executed with the following input data:

```
123.45123.4567
```

The value stored in variable A is 123.45. The specification F6.3 causes 6 characters to be stored, including the decimal point and the *two* fractional digits to its right. The decimal point in the input data overrides the specification in the F format. Because the decimal is included as one of the 6 allowable characters, only 5 digits are available to store the number read. Notice in case A, that the format specification automatically inserts the decimal and 6 digits are stored.

Similarly, the value stored in variable B is 123.4567. Although F8.0 specifies 8 characters, the decimal point in the input data overrides this specification, and the program stores the equivalent of a decimal point and 7 digits, including 4 fractional digits.

The E format. The *exponential* format specification designates the total number of spaces in the field and sets the number of digits that are occupied by the real number. Input values include a real number, with or without a decimal point, the E for exponentiation, and the exponent. The E specification is used to read or print data in exponential form. Its general form is

```
EW.D
```

where W is the total width of the input or output field and
D is the number of fractional digits that appear to the left of the E.
As with the F format, a decimal point in the data overrides the number of digits specified by D.

EXAMPLE 1

`E8.4`	*Format specification*
`13562E05`	*Number input*
`1.3562X10**5`	*Value stored*

Recall that the D in EW.D specifies the number of fractional digits in the real number to the left of E, and W specifies the number of positions in the entire field in which the number appears.

EXAMPLE 2

`E8.3`	*Format specification*
`1.3562E5`	*Number input, including decimal*
`1.3562x10**5`	*Value stored*

In this case, the real part of the number in exponential form contains a decimal point that overrides the D value in the format specification.

As in other format specifications, an input decimal also takes one of the specified field positions. This number has 8 positions and stores 5 digits in the real value and a 1 digit exponent; the other 2 positions are taken by the E and the decimal point.

E format for output. Because of the way format statements treat decimal points, negative signs, and exponents, one must be especially careful when specifying the spaces available for output of an expoenetial number. The form of the output is always

```
±0.XXXXE±XX
```

Notice that there are 7 possible non-integer characters in the output:

1 A sign preceding the integer, printed if it is negative,
2 a 0, printed if there is no datum before the decimal point,
3 the decimal point itself,
4 the E for exponent,
5 a sign preceding the exponent, printed if it is negative and left as a blank space if it is positive, and
6,7 two digits for the exponent itself.

To be sure to have enough space for the number to be printed, the value of W in specification EW.D, representing the total number of available spaces, must be at least 7 greater than the value of D, representing the desired number of decimal integers.

EXAMPLE This program is an example of the correct use of E format specifications:

```
      PROGRAM EXAMPL
      REAL A, B
      READ 10, A, B
      PRINT 20, A, B
10    FORMAT (E7.4,F9.2)
20    FORMAT (1X,E13.6,E9.2)
      END
```

You may be interested in checking carefully the relationship between input data and output as they relate to format specifications.

The A format.

The A format. The *alphabetical* format specification designates the data type as CHARACTER and sets the number of spaces in the field. The number to the right of the A specifies the total number of positions set aside for a value to be read to or printed from a given memory location. The general form of the A format is as follows:

```
AW
```

where W is the width of the field being read or printed.

When the variable being read or printed has already been declared as a character variable of size W, it is not necessary to include W in the A specification unless your version of FORTRAN requires it. With W omitted, the input or output operation processes all characters. We recommend, however, in the interest of program clarity, that you specify W.

- *It is simply good programming practice to always specify W.*

Format and data widths. Three basic situations may arise when using the A format:

CASE A **W = M**

where, in each case, W is the width of the field as specified in the A format, and
M is the declared size of the character variable to which it applies.

In this case, the situation is as already described.

CASE B **W > M**

When used with input, only the M leftmost characters from the field of width W are stored. The remaining W – M characters of the input field are not stored. When the variable is output, W – M blank spaces are placed at the left of the M characters of the character variable.

CASE C **W < M**

When used with input, W characters are stored from the left of the field; the rightmost M – W characters of the variable are filled with blanks. When output, the program displays only the W leftmost characters of the M characters available. The remaining W – M characters are not displayed.

EXAMPLE

```
PROGRAM ONE
CHARACTER ST*10
ST = 'ABCDEFGHIJ'
PRINT '(1X,A)' ,ST
PRINT '(1X,A2)' ,ST
PRINT '(1X,A12)' ,ST
END
```

The output is:

```
ABCDEFGHIJ
AB
  ABCDEFGHIJ
```

The first PRINT statement has no W in the A format specification, so all 10 characters of ST are printed.

The second PRINT statement has W = 2, and only the leftmost 2 characters of ST are printed.

The final PRINT statement calls for 12 characters to be printed, W = 12. Only 10 characters are available, so 2 blank spaces are printed at the left of the 10-character string.

Problem 7.2 Registering Complaints

SITUATION While your company is still studying the intelligent shift stalling problem described in Problem 7.1, the television news crews hear of the story. Suddenly the company is inundated with complaints of stalling during acceleration. While this is a major problem for public relations, the engineers are pleased. If the acceleration incidents that are related to the problem under study can be separated out from false claims and incidents caused by other problems, there will be relevant new data to help pinpoint the trouble.

Because the reports of trouble did not specify that the problem existed only in turbocharged intelligent shift cars, owners of many other models are entering acceleration complaints as well.

OBJECTIVE You have been asked to write a program to take the automobile's serial number from the warranty complaint file, find the description of the model from the dealer order file, and determine whether or not that model is turbocharged with an intelligent shift; that is, whether it could have the problem under study.

The output is to be a file listing each automobile about which a complaint has been made, with a code indicating whether the complaint could be caused by the problem under study.

ANALYSIS The company has three different kinds of distributorships, each listed in one of three files. The dealer records are identified with a unique code that is the same in the dealer files and in the warranty file.

The following information is needed to solve the problem:

WARRANTY FILE Acceleration complaints are code 00047. Complaint codes are entered in positions 29–33 of each record.

Automobile serial numbers, containing both letters and numbers, appear in positions 8–16.

The dealer codes in positions 52–61 contain the following, depending on the type of dealer:
3 letters, 4 digits, and 3 blanks if the dealership is wholly owned;
5 letters and 5 digits if the dealership is franchised; and
7 digits and 3 blanks if the dealership is independent.

DEALER FILES ***Wholly owned dealer file***. Serial numbers are in the first 9 positions;
if turbocharged, TURBO appears in positions 98–102;
if intelligent shift, SMARTSHIFT appears in positions 155–164.

Franchised dealer file. Serial numbers are in positions 11–19; if turbocharged, 1 appears in position 32; if intelligent shift, 3 appears in position 62.

Independent dealer file. Serial numbers are in the first 9 positions; turbocharged and intelligent shift ordered only in packages ZEPHYR, BREEZE, CHINOOK, GUST, and TORNADO, named in positions 78–90, with shorter names left justified in the field.

This sort of problem frequently arises when data collected for one purpose must be pressed into service for another use. The basic objective is to get material from the proper files, categorize it, select the correct output, and write the output to a file.

ALGORITHM

1. Read the serial number, dealer identifier, and complaint type from the warranty file.
2. If the complaint type is not 00047, reject this case and go on to the next.
3. If the complaint is 00047, then
   - 3.1 If the dealer type has letters in positions 4–5, then
     - 3.1.1 Look up the record by serial number in the franchised dealer file.
     - 3.1.2 If postion 32 = 1 and position 62 = 3, then set the evaluation to CONFRM; otherwise set to OTHER.
   - 3.2 If the dealer type has a letter in position 1 and a digit in position 4, then
     - 3.2.1 Look up the record by serial number in the wholly owned dealer file.
     - 3.2.2 If TURBO appears in positions 98–102 and SMARTSHIFT in positions 155–164, then set the evaluation to CONFRM; otherwise set the evaluation to OTHER.
   - 3.3 If the dealer type has a digit in position 1, then
     - 3.3.1 Look up the record by serial number in the independent dealer file.
     - 3.3.2 If ZEPHYR, BREEZE, CHINOOK, GUST, or TORNADO appears in positions 78–90, then set the evaluation to CONFRM; otherwise set the evaluation to OTHER.
4. Write the serial number and the evaluation to the output file.

FORTRAN PROGRAM

```
      PROGRAM COMPL
C*    THIS PROGRAM READS FROM THE WARRANTY FILE WFILE THE DATA
C*    SNUMB, THE SERIAL NUMBER OF THE VEHICLE;
C*    DLRID, THE DEALER IDENTIFICATION NUMBER; AND
C*    CCODE, THE COMPLAINT CODE.
C*
C*    IF CCODE = 00047 THE PROGRAM READS AN APPROPRIATE DEALER FILE
C*    TO DETERMINE IF THE COMPLAINT IS FOR A TURBOCHARGED VEHICLE WITH
C*    INTELLIGENT SHIFT. IF SO, THE VEHICLE SERIAL NUMBER AND THE WORD
C*    'CONFIRM' ARE REPORTED TO THE OUTPUT FILE. OTHERWISE THE SERIAL
C*    NUMBER AND THE WORD 'OTHER' ARE REPORTED.
C*
C*    FILENAME DEFINITIONS:
C*    WFILE IS THE WARRANTY FILE.
C*    OWFILE CONTAINS INFO FOR WHOLLY OWNED DEALERS.
C*    FRFILE CONTAINS INFO FOR FRANCHISED DEALERS.
C*    INDFIL CONTAINS INFO FOR INDEPENDENT DEALERS.
C*    OUTFIL IS THE OUTPUT FILE.
C*    SEE PROBLEM STATEMENT FOR DEFINITION OF DEALER FILES.
C***********************************************************************
      CHARACTER SNUMB*9, DLRID*10, CCODE*5, CODE*8
      OPEN (10, FILE='OUTFIL', STATUS='NEW')
      OPEN (1, FILE='WFILE', STATUS='OLD')
      OPEN (2, FILE='OWFILE', STATUS='OLD')
      OPEN (3, FILE='FRFILE', STATUS='OLD')
      OPEN (4, FILE='INDFIL', STATUS='OLD')
 1000 FORMAT (7X, A9, 12X, A5, 19X, A10)
 1010 FORMAT (1X, A9, 1X, A8)
 1020 FORMAT (2X, A9, 2X, 'IS NOT IN DEALER FILE')
C*
 100  READ (1, 1000, END=110) SNUMB, CCODE, DLRID
      IF (CCODE .EQ. '00047') THEN
          IF (DLRID(5:5) .LE. 'Z') CALL READFR(SNUMB,CODE)
          IF ((DLRID(1:1) .LE. 'Z') .AND. (DLRID(4:4) .GT. 'Z')
     +        CALL READOW(SNUMB,CODE)
          IF (DLRID(1:1) .GT. 'Z') CALL READIN(SNUMB,CODE)
          IF (CODE .NE. 'NOTFOUND') THEN
              WRITE (10, 1010) SNUMB, CODE
          ELSE
              PRINT 1020, SNUMB
          ENDIF
      ENDIF
      GOTO 100
 110  CLOSE (1,2,3,4,10)
      END
C***********************************************************************
```

```
      SUBROUTINE READOW(SNUMB,CODE)
      CHARACTER NUMB*9, SNUMB*9, CODE*8, T*5, S*10
      REWIND (2)
      CODE = 'NOTFOUND'
 300  READ (2, 320, END=310) NUMB, T, S
          IF (SNUMB .EQ. NUMB) THEN
              IF ((T .EQ. 'TURBO') .AND. (S .EQ. 'SMARTSHIFT')) THEN
                  CODE = 'CONFIRM'
              ELSE
                  CODE = 'OTHER'
              ENDIF
              RETURN
          ENDIF
      GOTO 300
 310  RETURN
 320  FORMAT (A9, 89X, A5, 53X, A10)
      END
C***************************************************************************
      SUBROUTINE READFR(SNUMB,CODE)
      CHARACTER NUMB*9, SNUMB*9, CODE*8
      INTEGER T,S
      REWIND (3)
      CODE = 'NOTFOUND'
 200  READ (3, 220, END=210) NUMB, T, S
          IF (SNUMB .EQ. NUMB) THEN
              IF (T.EQ.1 .AND. S.EQ.3) THEN
                  CODE = 'CONFIRM'
              ELSE
                  CODE = 'OTHER'
              ENDIF
              RETURN
          ENDIF
      GOTO 200
 210  RETURN
 220  FORMAT (10X, A9, 12X, I1, 29X, I1)
      END
C***************************************************************************
      SUBROUTINE READIN(SNUMB,CODE)
      CHARACTER NUMB*9, SNUMB*9, TYPE*13, CODE*8
      REWIND (4)
      CODE = 'NOTFOUND'
```

```
400   READ (4, 420, END=410) NUMB, TYPE
          IF (SNUMB .EQ. NUMB) THEN
              IF ((TYPE .EQ. 'ZEPHYR') .OR. (TYPE .EQ. 'BREEZE')
     +            .OR. (TYPE .EQ. 'CHINOOK') .OR. (TYPE .EQ. 'GUST')
     +            .OR. (TYPE .EQ. 'TORNADO')) THEN
                  CODE = 'CONFIRM'
              ELSE
                  CODE = 'OTHER'
              ENDIF
              RETURN
          ENDIF
      GOTO 400
410   RETURN
420   FORMAT (A9, 69X, A13)
      END
```

Using quote marks. Recall that in the unformatted PRINT or WRITE statement, we are able to use a string constant as a data element to be printed. The same procedure is possible with formatted PRINT and WRITE statements by including the string constants in a format specification. Any character constant appearing between a pair of single quotation marks in a FORMAT statement will be output in the order it appears in the FORMAT. For example:

EXAMPLE 1

```
      PRINT 10, N
10    FORMAT (1X,'TOTAL=',I3)
```

First the string consisting of the 6 characters TOTAL= is printed, followed by the value stored at N in I3 format.

EXAMPLE 2

```
      PRINT 20, A, '+', B, A+B
20    PRINT (1X,F6.2,A1,F6.2,'=',F7.2)
```

Output consists of the value of A, the character +, the value of B, the character =, and the sum of A and B.

The FORMAT statement has an F6.2 specification for the value of A, an A1 specification for the character +, an F6.2 specification for the value of B, and an F7.2 specification for the sum A+B.

Each item in the output list has a corresponding format specification. In addition, the character = appears in the FORMAT statement, causing an equal sign to be output between the value for B and the value for A+B.

EXAMPLE 3

```
      WRITE(6,10)
10    FORMAT(5X,'NAME',5X,'NUMBER',1X,'CODE')
```

This is a typical method for printing a heading.

There is no output list in the WRITE statement. Everything to be printed is specified in the FORMAT, including spacing.

The* H *format alternative. In older versions of FORTRAN, character strings were output with the H format instead of using quote marks. The general form is

```
NHString
```

where N is the number of characters to be printed, and
String is exactly N characters long, N being a positive integer.

This older method for treating character strings is not as convenient as the single quotation style, although the H format specification is still accepted by FORTRAN 77.

- *We recommend you use quotation marks, not the* H *format.*

EXAMPLE

```
      PRINT 10,AVG
10    FORMAT(1X,22HTHE AVERAGE WEIGHT IS ,F6.2)
      PRINT 15,A,B,A+B
15    FORMAT(1X,F6.2,1H+,F6.2,1H=,F8.2)
```

The format with statement number 10 causes the 22 characters immediately following the letter H to be printed, followed by the value of AVG in F6.2 format.

In FORMAT 15, F6.2 formats the output for the value of A, then a plus sign is printed followed by the value of B, again in F6.2 format. Next is printed the single character =, after which the sum of A and B is output in F8.2 format. Compare this with the same pattern printed in Example 2 above.

Control of vertical spacing.

On a video screen or printer, the execution of each unformatted PRINT or WRITE statement causes one line of output. The output device vertically spaces the output, moving one line with each statement executed. If you have a multiline message, do not just continue the message from line to line of the program—in that case, it will try to print all on one output line. You need to repeat the PRINT or WRITE statement for each new line of output.

Sometimes you may want to space immediately to a new page, double space the output, or print two lines on top of each other with no vertical spacing at all. Such control of vertical spacing is called *carriage control*, from the carriage that vertically positions the paper in a printer.

The carriage control character. In formatted output, carriage control is not automatic. The first character of every line of formatted output controls the movement of the paper carriage. Therefore, the first character specified for output by a FORMAT statement is the carriage control character, selected from the list in Table 7.1.

This carriage control character is not printed on the output page—it simply transmits the appropriate vertical spacing command. The second character in the FORMAT specification is printed in the first space on the output.

TABLE 7.1 *Carriage control characters*

Character	*Effect on paper carriage*
Blank	Single line forward, the most common character.
0	Double line forward, causes output to skip one line.
1	Move to the top of a new page or screen.
+	Print on the same line as previous output, suppresses normal spacing.

EXAMPLE

```
      PRINT 20
 20   FORMAT('1',10X,'NAME',10X,'ID#',5X,'WAGE')
      PRINT 30,NAME,EMPLID,WAGE
 30   FORMAT(' ',2X,A22,1X,A6,1X,F5.2)
```

The FORMAT accompanying the first PRINT starts with '1', causing the following heading line to be displayed at the top of a new page or screen.

The FORMAT accompanying the second PRINT starts with a blank, causing the values for NAME, EMPLID and WAGE to be displayed on the line directly below the heading. The output device moves a single line space before displaying each new item.

Previous code samples use the single space carriage control character *blank* represented in the FORMAT line by 1X. When this character appears at the beginning of the FORMAT statement, it places the following output on a new line. Later in the statement, as in FORMAT 30 above, the 1X simply leaves a blank space. You may use either the *blank* character or the 1X character for single space carriage control in FORTRAN 77.

The slash. The format specifier that causes input or output to advance to a new line is the slash /. When used in a FORMAT statement referenced by a PRINT or WRITE, the slash indicates that the character of output specified to the right of the slash is to appear on a new line. A double slash indicates to advance two lines. Here is a simple example:

EXAMPLE Suppose values sorted at A, B, and C are 20575, 30.5, and .752 respectively. Consider these program statements for printing those values:

```
      PRINT 20,A,B,C
 20   FORMAT (//1X,F10.2,/1X,F10.2,1X,F10.2)
```

The output produced by these two lines of program is

```
_____20.58
_____30.50________.75
```

The first two slashes cause two blank lines and position the print mechanism to be ready for printing on the third line.

The 1X to the right of the second slash produces the blank space carriage control character, while F10.2 causes the value of A (20.575) to be rounded to two decimal places and printed right justified in the leftmost 10 spaces on the line.

The third slash causes a new line to begin; again 1X produces the carriage control character; F10.2 causes the value of B to be printed with two fractional digits right justified in the leftmost 10 spaces on the second line; 1X causes one blank space; and the last F10.2 causes the value of C to be printed with two rational digits in the next 10 spaces.

If a slash appears in a FORMAT referenced by a READ statement, it causes the current line of input to be skipped and input taken from the next line or record. Consider the following partial program:

EXAMPLE

```
      READ 10,A,B,C
10    FORMAT(F8.3//F8.2,F6.1)
```

Assume these lines of input data are provided:

```
___305____29_6
__175_4__472_50
____2557__6045
```

The value stored in A is 30.5 from the leftmost 8 positions of line 1.

The rest of line 1 and all of line 2 is skipped because of the two slashes in FORMAT 10.

The leftmost 8 columns of line 3 are used to provide a value for B. Since two decimal digits are specified in F8.2, the value stored in B is 25.57.

The next 6 columns of line 3 are used to provide a value for C. Since one decimal digit is specified in F6.1, the value stored in C is 604.5.

Problem 7.3 Updating Turbine Records

SITUATION An electric utility in a major city operates 38 gas turbine generators at 5 different facilities as backup generators to meet peak load demands. These generators need to be brought on line quickly during the hours of highest need, and shut down quickly when no longer needed. Gas turbines are used for this task because, although they are expensive to run, they can be brought up quickly and they are relatively low polluters.

The utility records system has, unfortunately, not been updated since the gas turbines, all the same model, replaced the older coal- and oil-fired steam generators. For the old generators, each custom built and with its own set of maintenance needs, data on breakdowns and malfunctions are stored in records divided as follows:

> Characters 1–15 designate the generator,
> characters 16–19 designate the year of the record,
> 15-digit sets of repeated fields: 2 digits for the month, 2 digits for the day, 4 digits for the malfunction code, and 7 digits for the cause of malfunction code.

These records could store up to 15 malfunctions per year, many more than were normally expected, and records for any one generator were always readily available. But the system was not set up to allow comparison of malfunctions among generators; in fact, many of the machines had unique malfunction codes.

But now, the engineers have noticed an unsettling frequency of certain types of malfunction. In fact, the performance and reliability of the turbines has fallen below the manufacturer's contract guarantee of fleet reliability. Fewer than the specified percentage of the turbines are available to go on line at any time, and the work-hours needed to maintain the turbines is far above that allowed by the contract.

OBJECTIVE In order to document the unsatisfactory level of fleet reliability, the company needs you to take the separate maintenance records with one record for each turbine and convert them to a single file with one record per malfunction.

ANALYSIS One of the simplest ways to do this is to take each record in the old form

```
GEN YEAR MAL1 MAL2 . . . MAL15
```

> where GEN is the 15 digit generator code,
> YEAR is the year of the record, and
> MALN includes the month MMON, date MDAY, malfunction code MCOD, and malfunction cause CAUS.

and convert it into a form that will write 15 separate records from each original record, one record per malfunction, duplicating GEN and YEAR in each. This produces an intermediate file, with many blanks for extra malfunction spaces. The final version of the file can be assembled by scanning for and deleting records with blank MCOD.

ALGORITHM

1. Create the intermediate file.

1.1 Read each record from the old file.

1.2 Write individual records to the intermediate file in the form

```
MCOD1 CAUS1 (MMON1 MDAY1, YEAR) GEN
MCOD2 CAUS2 (MMON2 MDAY2, YEAR) GEN
.
.
.
MCOD15 CAUS15 (MMON15 MDAY15, YEAR) GEN
```

Each original record results in 15 new records, each duplicating the original values for YEAR and GEN.

2. Create the new file.

2.1 Read each record from the intermediate file.

2.2 If MCODN is blank, go to the next record.

2.3 If MCODN is not blank, write the record to the new file and go on to the next record.

FORTRAN PROGRAM

```
      PROGRAM MFUNCT
C*    DEFINITION OF VARIABLES:
C*        YEAR IS YEAR OF MALFUNCTION OCCURENCE.
C*        MMON IS MONTH OF MALFUNCTION OCCURENCE.
C*        MDAY IS DAY OF MONTH OF MALFUNCTION OCCURENCE.
C*        MCOD IS MALFUNCTION CODE.
c*        CAUS IS THE MALFCUNTION CAUSE.
C*        GEN IS GENERATOR IDENTIFICATION NUMBER.
C*    DEFINITION OF FILES:
C*        MFFILE IS RECORD OF PREVIOUS MALFUNCTIONS.
C*        NEWF IS THE NEW FILE OF MALFUNCTIONS.
C*        TEMP IS A SCRATCH FILE USED BY THIS PROGRAM.
C*
      CHARACTER GEN*15
      INTEGER YEAR,MMON(15),MDAY(15),MCOD(15),CAUS(15)
      OPEN (1, FILE='MFFILE', STATUS='OLD')
      OPEN (2, FILE='NEWF', STATUS='NEW')
      OPEN (3, FILE='TEMP', STATUS='NEW')
 100  READ (1,210,END=200) GEN,YEAR,(MMON(I),MDAY(I),MCOD(I),
     +    CAUS(I), I=1,15)
          DO 110 I=1,15
             WRITE (3,230) GEN,YEAR,MMON(I),MDAY(I),MCOD(I),CAUS(I)
 110      CONTINUE
      GOTO 100
 200  CLOSE (3)
      OPEN (3, FILE='TEMP', STATUS='OLD')
 240  READ (3,230,END=300) GEN,YEAR,MMON(1),MDAY(1),MCOD(1),CAUS(1)
          IF (MCOD(1) .NE. 0) WRITE (2,230) GEN,YEAR,MMON(1),MDAY(1),
     +        MCOD(1),CAUS(1)
      GOTO 240
 300  CLOSE (1,2,3)
 210  FORMAT (A15, I4, (I2, I2, I4, I7))
 230  FORMAT (A15, I4, I2, I2, I4, I7)
      END
```

Repeating format specifications. When repeated patterns of format specifications occur, you don't have to rewrite the pattern each time, as often as it occurs. FORTRAN allows you to specify repeating patterns by placing the specifications in parentheses and preceding the parentheses with an integer that indicates the number of repetitions. When the repeat pattern consists of only one specification, the parentheses are optional. For example, suppose this FORMAT statement occurs in a program:

EXAMPLE 1A
```
FORMAT(1X,F10.4,1X,F10.4,1X,F10.4)
```

Obviously, the repeated pattern is 1X,F10.4. Therefore, we could write:

EXAMPLE 1B
```
FORMAT(3(1X,F10.4))
```

EXAMPLE 2A Here is another example:

```
FORMAT(1X,I10,I10,I10,I10,A2,F10.2,F10.2)
```

For which we could substitute:

EXAMPLE 2B
```
FORMAT(1X,3I10,A2,2F10.2)
```

Notice that the repeated I10 and F10.2 need be written only once preceded by an integer indicating the number of times each is repeated. In this case, no parentheses are required.

Reconciling input/output lists. We have discussed the need for making sure that the items in the list of a READ, PRINT, or WRITE statement correspond in data type to the specifications in the associated FORMAT statement. It is also important that there be the same *number* of format specifications as there are items in the associated input/output list.

If there are more format specifications than items in the list, there is no problem. If there are more items in the input/output list, these general rules apply:

1. Each item in the input/output list is matched to the format specifications until all formats have been assigned.
2. If there are still list items to be processed, the format specifications are repeated, beginning with the replication number, if any, in front of the rightmost right-facing parenthesis, until all formats have been assigned.

Remember, when a program repeats format specifications in this way, the formatted input or output appears on a new line.

When a program is forced to repeat format specifications, it is difficult to keep track of the data types needed, and the data type of the item to be input or output often may not match that of the specification.

Unless repeat use is carefully and intentionally designed, data type incompatibility can cause errors.

Here are two examples:

EXAMPLE 1

```
      REAL A,B,X
      INTEGER K
      READ 10,A,B,K,X
10    FORMAT(F10.5,F6.2,I3)
```

The first three items in the data list of the READ correspond correctly to the first three specifications in the FORMAT.

Repeated use of format specifications begins with the rightmost right-facing parenthesis, so the fourth item in the input list of the READ is associated with specification F10.5. No mismatch of mode occurs between data list items and format specifications, and no error message is generated.

Note, however, that the value of X will be taken from the first 10 columns of the *second* input line. Repeating format specifications always causes a move to a new line.

EXAMPLE 2 This example presents one READ statement with four alternate FORMAT statements and discusses the effect of each combination:

```
      REAL A,K
      INTEGER K,J
      READ N,A,K,X,J
```

N=10

```
10    FORMAT(F10.2,I6)
```

Variable A is read with the specification F10.2 and variable K with specification I6.

Since there are no more format specifications, an automatic return to the rightmost right-facing parenthesis occurs. Specifications are repeated from that point, and a new line is read.

Therefore, variable X is read with F10.2 specification and variable J with specification I6. Remember that values for A and K are read from the first input line and X and J from the second input line.

N=20

```
20    FORMAT(2(F10.2,I6)
```

The specifications F10.2 followed by I6 are repeated twice. Thus variable A is read with F10.2, variable K with format I6, variable X with format F10.2, and variable J with I6. input data are all taken from the same line.

N=30

```
30    FORMAT(F10.2,F10.2,I6)
```

This statement has exactly the same effect as FORMAT 20. The specification pattern is simply repeated instead of being called twice.

N=40

```
40    FORMAT(F10.2,I6,F10.2,I6,2A5)
```

Variable A is read according to format F10.2, variable K according to format I6, variable X according to format F10.2, and variable J according to format I6. The remaining format specifications (2A5) are not used by the given READ statement but cause no errors.

Problem 7.4
Ranking Stopsign Locations

We conclude with a problem typical of a real life situation where data needed to solve the problem must be assembled from a variety of sources.

SITUATION You are city engineer of a small city. The city has just received a matching fund grant from the state department of transportation that will help put up 24 stopsigns at previously unmarked intersections.

OBJECTIVE Choose which 24 of the 280 unmarked intersections in the city would most benefit from stopsigns.

ANALYSIS You have the following material at your disposal:

Police files of accident reports, transcribed from the microcomputer in the police department, in the following form:

Street address in front of or near which the accident occurred, in the form

NUM_STNAME,
Number of moving vehicles,
Drinking? Y or N,
Excessive speed? Y or N,
Failure to yield right of way? Y or N,
{ Several other irrelevant variables },
{ Text description of the accident },
/** (the indicator for the end of the record)

City street directory, that lists for each intersection

North-south street name,
East-west street name,
Begins which N–S block number,
Begins which E–W block number,
UNM if corner is unmarked (or code for marked corners),
{ Other data not relevant }

There are several things you want to know:

1. Which unmarked corners are associated with the most multiple-car accidents?
2. Of these corners, which are associated with the most accidents related to speed or failure to yield, problems that might be solved by a stopsign?
3. Do any adjacent corners have a worse record? A stopsign at an adjacent corner may solve the problem at this corner, thus freeing a stopsign for another location.

As the accident data are developed, we associate an accident with an intersection if it occurs within one block of that intersection. Each accident thus counts for both of the two adjacent intersections. That does not change the results: A truly dangerous intersection is adjacent to four such blocks, while the four less dangerous adjacent intersections each adjoins only one dangerous block.

SOLUTION First screen out unwanted data by using a filter to eliminate solo accidents and all accidents associated with marked intersections. Then construct an array using the remaining data.

For each unmarked intersection, keep count of the following:

1. Total multicar accidents.
2. Total accidents involving excessive speed or failure to yield.
3. Total drunk driving accidents. This will be a disqualifying entry; we don't want to waste a stopsign on an intersection made dangerous by drunk drivers, who are not likely to stop anyway.
4. The ratings in each of these 3 categories held by the 4 neighboring intersections.

The final output is to include the following data on each unmarked intersection:

N–S street name NSSTRT,
E–W street name EWSTRT,
Total multicar accidents TACC,
Accidents involving speed or failure to yield SYACC,
Drunk driving accidents DDACC,
TACC for the intersection to the north NOR,
SYACC for NOR,
DDACC for NOR,
TACC for the intersection to the south SOU,
SYACC for SOU,
DDACC for SOU,
TACC for the intersection to the east EAS,
SYACC for EAS,
DDACC for EAS,
TACC for the intersection to the west WES,
SYACC for WES,
DDACC for WES.

FORTRAN PROGRAM The reader is urged to write an algorithm and a FORTRAN program that comply with this solution.

There are many more intricacies that occur in the use of FORMAT statements. However, there is probably no satisfactory method of discussing most of them until they are encountered in actual situations—practice is the best teacher. In Chapter 9, we discuss special cases in the use of FORMAT and explain the effects.

Summary

In this chapter we discuss using data files and formatted input and output.

File processing.

```
OPEN (UNIT=U,FILE='Filename',STATUS='Status')
```

where U, an unsigned integer, is the unit number of the file,
Filename is the programmer's name for the file, and
Status is the status of the file: OLD, NEW, or UNKNOWN, default UNKNOWN.

```
REWIND U
```

where U is the unit number of the file that appeared in a previously executed OPEN statement.

```
CLOSE(U)
```

where U is a unit number or a list of unit numbers separated by commas that appeared in a previously executed OPEN statement.

Formatted input.

```
READ F,V1,V2, . . . ,VN
```

where F is the reference number of the associated FORMAT statement or the format specification itself, and
V1,V2 . . . ,VN are variables into which information is to be stored.

```
READ(U,F,END=N)V1,V2, . . . ,VN
```

where U is an integer specifying logical unit number,
F is the reference number of the associated FORMAT statement or the format specification string itself,
the first N is the reference number of the statement to be executed when an end-of-file message is encountered, and
V1,V2, . . . ,VN are variables into which information is stored.

Formatted output.

```
PRINT F,Out-list
```

where F is the reference number of the associated FORMAT statement or the format specification itself, and
Out-list is the list of output items.

```
WRITE(U,F)Out-list
```

where U is an integer specifying logical unit number,
F is the reference number of the associated FORMAT statement or the format specification string itself, and
Out-list is the list of output items.

The FORMAT statement and format specifications.

```
R    FORMAT(S1,S2, . . . ,SN)
```

where R is the reference number, and
S1,S2, . . . ,SN are format specifications:

I format for integer input/output.

```
IW
```

where W is the maximum number of digits allowed in the integer, including the sign, if any.

X format for blank spaces.

```
NX
```

where N is the number of blank spaces to be output or spaces to be skipped in the input record.

F format for real numbers.

```
FW.D
```

where W is the width of the input or output field and
D is the number of decimal digits to the right of the decimal point in the input or output.

E format for exponential form of real numbers.

```
EW.D
```

where W is the total width of the input or output field and
D is the number of fractional digits in the coefficient that appears to the left of the E.

A format for character data.

```
AW
```

where W is the number of characters being input or output.

Character strings may be included in an output format specification string by enclosing them in single quote marks. The string is then displayed in position exactly as entered.

Carriage control. Vertical spacing is controlled by the first character of the specification in FORMAT statements, according to the table presented in text. Vertical spacing may also be controlled by using the slash to cause the input or output device to perform the next operation on a new line. Slashes may appear in multiples.

Repeating format specifications. Patterns of format specifications are repeated if they are preceded by an integer. The integer is the number of repetitions. If there is more than one specification, they must be enclosed in parentheses.

End of Chapter Exercises

1. Indicate whether the following statements are true or false. Remember that a statement must be considered false if any part of it is false. Be able to make changes in those that are false so that they will be true.

a. It is impossible to write a complete FORTRAN program without using a FORMAT statement.

b. A FORMAT statement must appear in the program immediately following the input or output statement that references it.

c. A FORMAT referenced by a READ statement cannot be referenced by a WRITE statement.

d. It is not permissible to use both the A format specification and quotation marks in the same FORMAT statement.

e. Every FORMAT statement must have a reference number.

f. it is possible to have a READ statement that results in no input taking place.

g. A single READ statement may cause the input of more than one record.

h. Every WRITE statement will cause the printing of at least some information on the printer.

i. Every READ statement causes the input of exactly one record of data.

j. A READ statement need not reference a FORMAT statement.

k. A single FORMAT statement may be referenced by more than one READ statement.

l. Whenever a slash occurs in a FORMAT referenced by a READ statement, reading will occur from the next record of data.

m. If a slash occurs as the last character within the parentheses of a FORMAT that is referenced by a PRINT statement, the result is the printing of one blank line.

n. One way of printing a blank line of output is to include a PRINT statement with no output list.

o. The output list of a formatted PRINT statement cannot include any character strings.

p. The following is a correct FORTRAN statement:

```
FORMAT(A10,2X)
```

q. The following statement would cause the printing of the value of A on one line and the value of B on the next line:

```
PRINT*,A,'/',B
```

r. The X format specification can only be used in FORMAT statements that are referenced by output statements.

s. The following is a correct FORTRAN statement:

```
 10   READ(1,10)A,B
```

t. If a variable defined as real appears in a READ statement input list corresponding to an I specification in the associated FORMAT statement, only the integer part of the data will be input.

u. If a variable contains string data, that information can be printed using either an A or F format specification.

v. FORMAT statement 10 as referenced in the PRINT statement

```
PRINT 10,A,B,'BE CAREFUL'
```

need only include format specifications for the variables A and B.

w. The statement

```
READ 10,A
```

could never cause the input of more than one data line.

x. The statement

```
READ* ,A,B
```

will cause the input of exactly one data line.

y. If NAME is a variable into which data are correctly read using I6 as the format specification, it is possible to output the contents of NAME correctly using A6 as the format specification, without creating an error message.

z. The number of records input or output by a READ or PRINT statement depends on the referenced FORMAT statement.

2. Determine which of the following FORTRAN statements or groups of statements are correct and which contain errors. For those that are incorrect, make the changes needed to correct them. Assume all numeric variables have been declared as real.

.1
```
READ 23
```

.2
```
READ*,'A',A
FORMAT(1X,F6.2)
```

.3
```
READ*,PRINT,WRITE,READ
```

.4
```
      READ 10,READ 20
 10   FORMAT(F6.2)
 20   FORMAT(I6)
```

.5
```
      READ 10,A,B,C
 10   FORMAT('1',3F6.2)
```

```
.6    READ,10,A,B,C
 10   FORMAT(3F6.2)
.7    READ 10,A,B,C
 10   FORMAT(1X,F10.2)
.8    READ 10,A,B,C
 10   FORMAT(1X,2F10.6)
.9    READ 10,A,B,C
 10   FORMAT(1X,F4.6,F6.4)
.10   READ 20,THIS,IS,GOOD
 20   FORMAT(A4,A2,F6.2)
.11   READ 20,THIS,IS,BAD
 20   FORMAT(A4,I6)
.12   READ 20,THINK,BRIGHT
 20   FORMAT('NOT NOW',A5,A6)
.13   READ(1,10,END=10)A,B
 10   FORMAT(2F6.2)
.14   READ(1,10)A,B,C
 10   FORMAT(F6.2,2*(1X,F6.2))
.15   READ(5,10,END=100)
 10   FORMAT(1X,/)
.16   READ(5,*,END=100)PRINT
 5    FORMAT(2X,F6.2)
.17   READ(10,10,END=7)A,B
 10   FORMAT(F.2)
.18   READ(10,10)A1,A2,A3,A4
 10   FORMAT(1X,A6,2(A6,F6.2))
.19   READ(1,100,END=100A,B
.20   PRINT 20,READ 30
 20   FORMAT(2X,A8)
.21   PRINT(6,20)A,B
 20   FORMAT(A6,2X,F6.2)
.22   PRINT,20,A,B
 20   FORMAT('IS THIS A',A6,)
.23   PRINT 20,A,B
 20   FORMAT(5X,A,F6.2)
.24   PRINT,PRINT
.25   PRINT,PRINT5,READ5
 5    FORMAT(A6,A6)
.26   PRINT(6,20,END=10)A,B
 20   FORMAT(A6,A6)
.27   X=10
      PRINT 10,X
 10   FORMAT(I3)
```

.28
```
    X=Y=10
    PRINT 10,X,Y,X+Y
10  FORMAT(F6.2/F6.2/12X,F6.2)
```

.29
```
    READ 10,A,B
    PRINT 10,A,B,A+B
10  FORMAT(F6.2,F6.2,'A+B=',F6.2)
```

.30
```
    READ 10,FORMAT,NOT
10  FORMAT (2A3,I6)
    PRINT 10,NOT,FORMAT
```

.31
```
    READ 10,ONE,TWO,THREE
10  FORMAT(1X,2(A3,1X),A4)
    PRINT 10,ONE,TWO,THREE,ONE+TWO
```

.32
```
    A=10.0
    B='AB'
    PRINT,A,A+B
```

.33
```
    A=10.0
    B=A*2
    PRINT A,B,A/B
```

.34
```
    READ(6,10,END=30)A,B
    WRITE(1,30)A,A+B,B
10  FORMAT(2F10.4)
30  FORMAT(3F10.4)
```

.35
```
    WRITE(6,10)
10  FORMAT(A,B,C)
    READ 10,A,B,C
```

.36
```
    WRITE(6,10)A,A+B,'A*B'
10  FORMAT(3F10.6)
```

.37
```
    READ 10,A,B
    X=A/B
    PRINT,10,X,B
10  FORMAT(1X,2F6.2)
```

.38
```
    READ 20
    WRITE(6,20)
20  FORMAT('THIS IS A HEADLINE',/)
```

.39
```
    WRITE(6,20)
20  FORMAT('0',200('*'))
```

.40
```
    WRITE(6,20)
20  FORMAT('1*',131(*)/'*',130' ')
```

.41
```
    WRITE(6,20)
20  FORMAT(1X,A6,//)
```

.42
```
    WRITE(6,20,END=5)A,B
20  FORMAT(2F6.2)
```

.43
```
    I=2
    X=I*2.5
    WRITE(6,10)I,X,I
10  FORMAT(I4,F6.2,A1)
```

3. Write an appropriate program segment for each of the following actions using FORMAT statements.

a. Print the value of A at about the middle of the second line where each line is 132 spaces wide.

b. Print on eleven different lines the values for

I, I*10, I*10^2, I*10^3 , . . . , I*10^{10}

c. Use FORMAT and PRINT statements (and maybe others) to draw a square with 60 asterisks along each of it sides.

d. Use FORMAT and PRINT statements (and maybe others) to draw a square of 60 asterisks and its diagonals with asterisks.

e. Use FORMAT and PRINT statements to print your name with asterisks.

f. With FORMAT and PRINT statements (and maybe others) draw a circle with a radius of 10 spaces and a horizontal diameter.

g. Print the following headings:

```
NAME  STREET  CITY  STATE  TELEPHONE
```

h. Print the following heading:

```
EXAMPLE OF HEADING
| DATA   | DATA   | DATA   | DATA   | DATA   | DATA   | TOTAL |
| ONE    | TWO    | THREE  | FOUR   | FIVE   | SIX    | DATA  |
```

4. Describe the output produced by each of the following program segments. Assume default data types based on the first letter of the variable name.

a.

```
      CHARACTER*6 B
      A=25
      B='TOTAL'
      PRINT 10,A,B
10    FORMAT('1',2X,F4.0,1X,'IS THE',1X,A6)
```

b.

```
      I=10
      J=I*2.98
      PRINT 10,I,J,I*J
10    FORMAT('1',2X,I3/3X,I3/3X,'  *'/3X,I6)
```

c.

```
      READ 10,A,B
      PRINT 20,A,B
20    FORMAT('1',F6.2)
10    FORMAT(2F6.3)
```

d.

```
5     READ 10,A,B
      IF(A .EQ. B)STOP
      PRINT 20,A,B,A/(A+B)
20    FORMAT('1',3F6.2)
      GO TO 5
```

e.

```
     A=0
     PRINT 10
 10  FORMAT('I')
 15  A=A+1
     PRINT 20,A,A, A*A, A*A*A
 20  FORMAT(2X,3(F6.2,2X))
     IF(A .LT. 100)GO TO 15
```

f. Use your own name as input data.

```
     CHARACTER*6 B,LNAME,FNAME,INIT
     B= 'NAME'
     READ 10,LNAME,FNAME,INIT
 10  FORMAT(3A6)
     PRINT 10,B,LNAME,FNAME,INIT
     PRINT 20,B,LNAME,FNAME,INIT
 20  FORMAT(2X,A6,1X,3A6)
```

g.

```
     CHARACTER *12 FNAME
     PRINT*,'WHAT IS YOUR FIRST NAME?'
     READ 10,FNAME
 10  FORMAT(A12)
     PRINT 20,FNAME
 20  FORMAT(1X,'WHAT IS YOUR AGE',A12,'?')
     READ*,IAGE
     PRINT 30,FNAME,IAGE
 30  FORMAT(1X,A12,1X,'YOU MUST BE',I3,1X,'YEARS OLD')
```

h.

```
     CHARACTER *12 NAME1
     PRINT*,'HI, I AM JOE COMPUTER. WHO ARE YOU?'
     READ 10,NAME1
 10  FORMAT(A12)
     A=15.6
     R=2.3
     PRINT 20,NAME1,A,B
 20  FORMAT(1X,2A6,'CAN YOU ADD',F4.1,'AND',F4.1,'?')
     PRINT*,'WHAT IS YOUR ANSWER?'
     READ* ,ANS
     IF(ANS .EQ. A+B)THEN
         PRINT,'CORRECT'
     ELSE
         PRINT*,'YOU ARE WRONG.'
     ENDIF
```

5. Identify the compile-time errors and the run-time errors, if any, in the following program segments. In parts a–d, assume all numeric variables are declared REAL.

a.

```
     READ*,A,B
     PRINT 20,A,B,A*B
 20  FORMAT(1X,F6.2,A6,F6.2)
```

b.

```
     A=45.6
     B=A*10
     C=B
     IF(C .EQ. 456)PRINT*,C
```

c.

```
      I=1
      ISUM=0
10    ISUM=ISUM+1
         PRINT 10,I,ISUM
         I=I+3
      GO TO 10
10    FORMAT(1X,'THE SUM OF ODD INTEGERS FROM 1 TO',I8,'IS',I10)
```

d.

```
      READ*,A,B,C
      DELTA=B*B-4.*A*C
      IF(DELTA .LT. 0)THEN
         PRINT*,'THERE IS NO ANSWER FOR'
         PRINT 10,A,B,C
10       FORMAT(1X,F6.2,'*X*X+(',F6.2,')*X+(',F6.2,')=0')
      ELSEIF(DELTA .EQ. 0)THEN
         X1=-B/2
         PRINT*,X1
         PRINT*,'IS THE ONLY ANSWER FOR'
         PRINT 10,A,B,C
      ELSE IF(DELTA .GT. 0)THEN
         X1=-B/2+DELTA**.5
         X2=-B/2-DELTA**.5
         PRINT*,X1,X2
         PRINT*,'ARE THE TWO ANSWERS FOR'
         PRINT 10,A,B,C
      ENDIF
```

- *In parts e and f assume all numeric variables are declared as* INTEGER.

e.

```
      CHARACTER*6 NUM,NAME1,NAME2,NAME3
      PRINT 10
 5    READ(5,20)NUM,NAME1,NAME2,NAME3
      IF (A .EQ. 0)STOP
      PRINT(6.30)NUM,NAME1,NAME2,NAME3
      GO TO 5
10    FORMAT(1X,'STUDENT NO.      NAME')
20    FORMAT(4A6)
30    FORMAT(1X,A6,7X,3A6)
```

f.

```
      PRINT*,'INPUT A POSITIVE INTEGER'
10    READ*,N
      IF(N .LE. 0)THEN
         PRINT*,'YOUR NUMBER MUST BE POSITIVE. TRY AGAIN.'
         GO TO 10
      ELSE
20       ISUM=ISUM+N
         N=N-1
         IF(N .GT. 0)GO TO 20
         PRINT 30,N,ISUM
      ENDIF
30    FORMAT(1X, '1+2+ . . . + ' ,I4, ' = ' ,I6)
```

6. Develop an algorithm and an interactive program that prints a geometric figure and asks the user to identify it. We suggest you use the following figures and corresponding codes: 1 = circle, 2 = square, 3 =

rectangle, 4 = star, 5 = triangle. The program should output any one of these figures and then ask the user to enter the digit 1 if the user recognizes the figure as a circle, 2 if the figure is recognized as a square, and so on. If the user enters something other than 1–5, output a message asking the user to enter a code within the specified range.

If the user identifies the figure incorrectly, give another chance, up to three chances, then give the correct response. When a correct answer is given, the program should respond with an encouraging comment and ask if the user wants to continue. If no, output the record of number of correct guesses on first try, second try, and third try, and the number wrong. If yes, randomly select another figure to output and proceed as described previously.

Your program should include the following:

a. Output messages telling the use about the code for each figure.

b. Output messages clearly describing the response expected from the user.

c. Output messages indicating correct or incorrect answer, and on which attempt it occurred.

d. Output a summary of the user's final score.

7. Develop an algorithm and a program to input a value for N, followed by N pairs of numbers where for each pair the numbers are denoted X and Y. Compute all of the following:

$$\text{SUMX} = \sum_{i=1}^{N} X_i$$

$$\text{SUMY} = \sum_{i=1}^{N} Y_i$$

$$\text{SUMXY} = \sum_{i=1}^{N} X_i Y_i$$

$$\text{SUMX2} = \sum_{i=1}^{N} X_i^2$$

$$\text{SUMY2} = \sum_{i=1}^{N} Y_i^2$$

```
XMEAN = SUMX / N

YMEAN = SUMY / N

XVAR = SUMX2 / N - XMEAN*XMEAN

YVAR = SUMY2 / N - YMEAN*YMEAN

XSTD = SQRT(XVAR)

YSTD = SQRT(YVAR)
```

```
B = (SUMXY - N*XMEAN*YMEAN) / (SUMX2 - N*XMEAN*XMEAN)

A = YMEAN - B*XMEAN
```

Print the following equation where, instead of A and B as shown, the values for A and B computed above are printed.

```
Y = A * X + B
```

Use the following data that correspond to a random sample of fifteen males participating in a research project:

```
X = AGE          = 45 43 46 49 50 37 34 30 31 26 22 58 60 52 27
Y = HDL COUNT    = 30 52 45 38 62 55 25 30 40 17 28 44 61 58 45
```

8. Develop an algorithm and a program to compute the area of any of a selected number of geometric figures. The program is to be interactive in the sense that conversational kinds of comments and questions are presented to the user for his or her response. Also include output that describes for the user what choices of figures are available, and exactly what input is expected from the user once he or she has selected the figure of which area is to be computed. When processing for one figure is complete, have the program ask if the user wants to stop or continue. If the choice is to continue, present to the user the compute list of options each time.

9. Develop an algorithm and a computer program that converts the common units of English measure into corresponding unit of metric measure. The program is to be interactive in the sense that conversational kinds of comments and questions are presented to the user for response. Also include output that describes for the user what choices of measures are available, and exactly what input is expected from the user once the option to be used has been selected. The output resulting from the conversion form the English units to the metric might look something like this:

```
XX.X DEGREES FAHRENHEIT = XX.X DEGREES CELSIUS
XX.X MILES = XXX.X KILOMETERS
```

The program should produce output that asks the user whether or not to stop the program or continue processing other cases.

10. Develop an algorithm and write a program to read a number and determine its value rounded to the Nth decimal place. We define the Nth decimal place as positive to the right of the decimal point and negative to the left of the decimal point. For example, the number 6532.15 rounded to the –2 position would be 6500. The same number rounded to the 1 position is 6532.2. The output need only be the rounded value.

11. Develop an algorithm and write a program to read any letter of the alphabet and print the same letter 2 inches high and about 1.2 inches wide. Letters like W and M may need to be wider; letters like I may look best if narrower. You these large characters from a pattern of small characters arranged so that the result has the appearance of the letter desired. The first step is the drawing on squared paper of all 26 letters in the specified size so that you know where characters must be printed to draw each letter. Draw each letter using small letters of the same kind; for example, a large A is made of small As printed in the appropriate pattern.

12. Develop an algorithm and a program that accepts as input one of the expressions

```
A*B, A**B, A / B, A - B, A + B
```

and produces as output the corresponding phrase like one of these:

```
A MULTIPLIED BY B
A RAISED TO THE POWER B
A DIVIDED BY B
B SUBTRACTED FROM A
B ADDED TO A
```

13. Develop an algorithm and a FORTRAN program to draw the curve for the trigonometric functions sin(x) and cos(x) on an x–y coordinate axes such that the range for x is $-\pi$ to $+\pi$ and the range for y is –1 to +1. Use a lower-case *s* to represent the points of the sine curve and lower-case *c* for the points of the cosine curve. Plot 50 points in the interval from $-\pi$ to $+\pi$. If the printer available to you has graphics capability, use dots to represent the plotted points and make 500 of them in the interval from $-\pi$ to $+\pi$.

14. Develop an algorithm and a FORTRAN program that will perform the following tasks:

a. Generate a bar graph with a bar for each of two related pieces of information.

b. Interactively request input data such as identification for each bar, values represented by the heights of the bars, and any other necessary data to enable the program to construct the graphs.

c. Label the vertical and horizontal axes of the bar graph. Note that if the input data for the two pieces of information for which graphs are to be constructed are not in the same units, your program will have to adjust the data so that the axes of the graph correctly reflect the truth for both bars.

15. Develop an algorithm and a FORTRAN program to construct a pie graph based on data stored in an array PIE. Each piece of the pie graph should reflect the data at one of the positions of the array.

16. Develop an interactive program to simulate a hand calculator. This will require that input to the program be of the form

```
Operator #
```

where # is a number, and
Operator is one of the arithmetic operators +, –, * or /.

The output of this program will be the numeric result of the arithmetic specified by the input data.

17. Develop a FORTRAN program that produces a circle of some radius, then draws inside the circle a square whose vertices are on the circle, then draws a circle inside the square such that the circle touches each of the 4 sides of the square, then draws another square inside of this circle, then another circle inside of the last square, and so on. Continue this process until the last circle drawn has a radius no more than one-third the initial radius.

Chapter 8

Numerical Computations

In this chapter we present certain algorithms that have been found particularly useful for scientists and engineers over the years. The principal topics are computing zeros of functions, simple integrals, zeros of polynomials of degree greater than 3, and interpolated values of functions. This chapter is not meant to be a rigorous nor complete discussion of numerical methods. We simply present the problem, follow up with one or more algorithms for solving it, and, finally, give one or more FORTRAN programs corresponding to the algorithms.

Although a complete understanding of many of the algorithms requires more mathematics than is normally assumed for the typical student enrolling in this course, our goal is to introduce important basic concepts and show how FORTRAN programs can be developed for using these mathematical tools. You do not need to follow all the mathematics here in order to benefit from the chapter. Engineers and scientists frequently find these programs helpful in solving problems in their own application areas.

Zeros of a Function

Given a function of the form

$$y = f(x)$$

any set of numbers

$$x_0, x_1, \ldots, x_n$$

$$\text{such that } f(x_0) = f(x_1) = f(x_2) = \ldots = f(x_n) = 0$$

is called the *set of zeros* of the function.

If $x_0, x_1, \ldots, x_n$ exist and are distinct, then we say that $f(x)$ has n distinct zeros. Sometimes the computation of these zeros by formal means is difficult or impossible, in which case it is extremely helpful to obtain numerical values close to the exact values. For instance, the function

$$f(x) = x^2 - 3\sqrt{x} + 1$$

has at least one zero between 0 and 1 because $f(0) = 1$ and $f(1) = -1$. If $f(x)$ is a continuous function, there must be some point x_0 between 0 and 1 such that $f(x_0) = 0$. In general, when a continuous function $y = f(x)$ is such that within an interval $f(x)$ changes sign from positive to negative or vice versa, the graph of the function must intercept the x axis in that interval. The point x_0 where this happens is an exact root of $f(x)$, so, $f(x_0) = 0$.

Thus, a general plan for computing a zero of a continuous function is to identify two values, a and b, such that $f(a) * f(b) < 0$. Then somewhere between a and b is a zero of $f(x)$.

Although it may not be difficult to determine a and b, a procedure for computing the zero x_0 to any degree of accuracy is more difficult and less intuitive. The usual notation for representing an arbitrary degree of accuracy is to refer to a computed estimate x_0' and say that, given an arbitrary small number e, if $|f(x_0')| < e$, we have computed a satisfactory estimate for x_0, the exact zero of $f(x)$. The process of computing x_0' is usually iterative; a sequence of values for x_0' is computed until one satisfies $|f(x_0')| < e$.

Bisection method. This is one of the simplest methods for computing a zero of a continuous function $f(x)$, and is represented by the following algorithm:

ALGORITHM

1. Find values for A and B such that F(A) * F(B) < 0. Trial and error is often the only method, unless those values are part of the given information.
2. Set X1 = A and X2 = B.
3. Compute M = (X1 + X2) / 2 and D = F(M).
4. If D = 0 then M is the desired zero, so report M and terminate the algorithm.
5. If D > 0 then set X1 = M.
6. If D < 0 then set X2 = M.
7. If X1 is not a satisfactory approximation for a zero, repeat the process from step 3.
8. Report X1 as a satisfactory approximation for a zero of F(X).
9. End.

This method converges very quickly to a real zero within the interval [A,B]. In fact, at each new iteration, the size of the search interval is half as large as it was on the previous iteration.

You will notice at step 7 that the method for determining if X1 is a satisfactory approximation to a zero is not specified. Generally, one of the following two methods is used for this determination. In either case we assume that the user provides a value for E.

METHOD A 7. If |X1 – X2| > E then repeat the process from step 3, *or*

METHOD B 7. If |F(X1) – F(X2)| > E then repeat the process from step 3.

Method A is used if the accuracy of the result is based on the X value, while method B is used if the accuracy of the computed result is based on the function value.

Now let's apply the bisection algorithm to the function

$$f(x) = x^2 - 3\sqrt{x} + 1$$

in the interval [0,1]. In step 1 of the algorithm A is identified as 0 and B as 1. In step 2, x1 is set to 0 and x2 is set to 1. This table shows the iterations I of steps 3 through 7 needed to arrive at an accuracy of E = 0.0007 as specified by the equation in step 7, method A.

I	*X1*	*X2*	*M = (X1 + X2)/2*	*F(M)*	*|X1 – X2|*
1	0.0	1.0	0.5	–0.873	1.0
2	0.0	0.5	0.25	–0.4375	0.5
3	0.0	0.25	0.125	–0.04503	0.25
4	0.0	0.125	0.625	0.2539	0.125
5	0.0625	0.125	0.03125	0.47064	0.0625
6	0.03125	0.125	0.078125	0.167578	0.09375
7	0.078125	0.125	0.1015625	0.054248	0.046875
8	0.1015625	0.125	0.11328125	0.00311424	0.0234375
9	0.11328125	0.125	0.11914063	–0.021308	0.01171875
10	0.11328125	0.11914063	0.11621094	–0.00918	0.00586
11	0.11328125	0.11621094	0.11474672	–0.00306	0.00293
12	0.11328125	0.11474672	0.11401398	0.00002048	0.00146
13	0.11401398	0.11474672			0.0007

Because the last number in the rightmost column is equal to the specified value for E, the algorithm is terminated. The value reported as the zero for F(X) in the interval [0, 1] is 0.11401398. Even though we had no formal means to compute a zero of the function in question, the bisection algorithm made it possible to compute an *approximation* to a zero.

PROGRAM BISECT

```
      PROGRAM BISECT
C*    This program uses the bisection algorithm to compute a real
C*    zero of the function F(X) in the interval [A,B]. The program
C*    assumes that the user will provide values for A, B, and epsilon.
C*    F(X) is specified in the third program statement following
C*    these comments. If a different function is involved, it
C*    must be specified in this statement function line.
C*
```

```
C*      VARIABLE DEFINITIONS
C*      A is the lower limit of the interval containing a real zero.
C*      B is the upper limit of the interval containing a real zero.
C*      EPS is the desired accuracy for approximating a real zero.
C*      X1 is an approximation to the zero of F(X).
C*      X2 is the next approximation to the zero of F(X).
C*      M is the midpoint of the current search interval.
C*      DONE is a logical variable to be set to TRUE when the search
C*          for a zero is terminated.
C*      The program terminates when ABS(X1-X2) <= EPS.
C*
        REAL A, B, X1, X2, EPS, M
        LOGICAL DONE
C*
C*      Next specify the function for which a zero is computed.
C*
        F(X) = X**2 - 3*SQRT(X) + 1
        PRINT *, 'ENTER LEFT & RIGHT END POINTS OF INTERVAL IN WHICH'
        PRINT *, 'ROOT IS TO BE FOUND. ALSO ENTER ACCURACY.'
        READ *, A, B, EPS
C*
C*      Check to see if A and B are selected correctly.
C*
        IF (F(A)*F(B) .GT. 0) THEN
            PRINT *, 'FUNCTION MAY HAVE NO REAL ZERO WITHIN THE'
            PRINT *, 'INTERVAL [A,B]. EXAMINE INPUT VALUES'
            PRINT *, 'AND RUN THE PROGRAM AGAIN.'
            STOP
        ENDIF
C*
C*      Compute the root of the function.
C*
        DONE = .FALSE.
        X1 = A
        X2 = B
  100   M = (X1+X2)/2
            IF (F(M) .GT. 0) X1 = M
            IF (F(M) .LT. 0) X2 = M
            IF (F(M) .EQ. 0) THEN
                PRINT *, M, ' IS AN EXACT ZERO IN THE INTERVAL.'
                DONE = .TRUE.
            ELSEIF (ABS(X1-X2) .LE. EPS) THEN
                PRINT *, X1, ' IS AN APPROX. ZERO IN THE INTERVAL.'
                DONE = .TRUE.
            ENDIF
        IF (.NOT. DONE) GO TO 100
        END
```

Multiple zeros. It sometimes happens that there are two or more zeros in the specified interval [A,B]. In this case it is important to divide the original interval [A,B] into some number N subintervals so as to find all intervals that contain one zero. Compute H = (B – A)/N, then check each subinterval for zero. The subintervals to check would be [A,A + H], [A + H, A + 2H], . . . , [A + (N – 1)H,B]. The following algorithm shows this process in detail.

ALGORITHM

1. Given a continuous function F(X) and an interval [A,B] compute H = (B – A)/N, where N is also given.
2. If F(A) * F(A + H) = 0 then A + H is a real zero; report it.
3. If F(A) * F(A + H) > 0 then set A = A + H. If the new value for A is less than B, repeat the process from step 2.
4. If F(A) * F(A + H) < 0 then this interval contains a real zero. Call BISECTION routine with A = A and B = A + H.
5. If A < B then repeat the process from step 2.
6. Otherwise terminate processing.

Note that this algorithm does not guarantee finding all the real zeros within a given interval [A,B], since no matter how small each subinterval within [A,B] is there is always a possibility that one or more subintervals may contain more than one real zero. This algorithm simply increases the likelihood that more zeros of F(X) will be found.

FORTRAN PROGRAM

```
      PROGRAM BISCT2
C*    This program reads values for A, B, and N, then computes real
C*    zeros of the continuous function F(X) in intervals [A,A+H],
C*    [A+H,A+2H], . . . , [A+(N-1)H,B], where H = (B-A)/N.
C*    We compute the zeros using the bisection algorithm.
C*
C*    VARIABLE DEFINITION
C*    A is the lower limit of the original search interval.
C*    B is the upper limit of the original search interval.
C*    N is the number of subintervals to compute.
C*    X1 is an approximation to a real zero.
C*    X2 is the next approximation to a real zero.
C*    EPS is the epsilon value used to terminate computation.
C*    DONE is a logical variable to be set TRUE when the search for
C*        a logical within a given subinterval is terminated.
C*
      REAL A, B, EPS
      INTEGER N
      PRINT *, 'ENTER LEFT AND RIGHT ENDPOINTS OF INTERVAL IN'
      PRINT *, 'WHICH ROOT IS TO BE FOUND. ALSO ENTER NUMBER OF'
      PRINT *, 'SUBINTERVALS AND ACCURACY DESIRED.'
      READ *, A, B, N, EPS
      H = (B-A)/N
```

```
 10     IF (A+H .GT. B) GO TO 50
            IF (F(A)*F(A+H) .EQ. 0) PRINT *, A+H, ' IS A ZERO.'
            IF (F(A)*F(A+H) .LT. 0) CALL BISEC(A, A+H, EPS, F)
            A = A+H
        GO TO 10
 50     STOP
        END
C***************************************************************************
C*      The following function makes it possible to invoke the function
C*      whose zeros are being computed in any module of the program.
C*
        REAL FUNCTION F(X)
        REAL X
        G(X) = (Insert definition of function whose zeros are being computed)
        F = G(X)
        END
C***************************************************************************
        SUBROUTINE BISEC (A, B, EPS, F)
C*
C*      Computes a real zero for function F(X) using the bisection method.
C*
        REAL X1, X2, M, A, B, EPS, F
        LOGICAL DONE
        X1 = A
        X2 = B
 100    M = (X1+X2)/2
            IF (F(M) .GT. 0) X1 = M
            IF (F(M) .LT. 0) X2 = M
            IF (F(M) .EQ. 0) THEN
                PRINT *, M, ' IS AN EXACT ZERO.'
                DONE = .TRUE.
            ELSEIF (ABS(X1-X2) .LE. EPS) THEN
                PRINT *, M, ' IS AN APPROXIMATE ZERO.'
                DONE = .TRUE.
            ENDIF
        IF (.NOT. DONE) GO TO 100
        END
```

Iteration method. When an equation $f(x) = 0$ may be written in the form $x = g(x)$, then it is possible to compute an approximate zero of $f(x)$ by a simple iteration method.

Assume $x0$ is a reasonably close approximation to a zero of $f(x)$, and that it is possible to obtain from the equation $f(x) = 0$ an equation of the form $x = g(x)$. Then compute a sequence of approximate zeros (x_1, $x_2, \ldots, x_n$) of $f(x)$ as follows:

$$x_1 = g(x0)$$
$$x_2 = g(x1)$$
$$x_3 = g(x2)$$

.

.

.

$x_n = g(x_{n-1})$

Continue this iterative process until two successive members of this sequence are within the prespecified small number epsilon of each other.

Suppose $f(x) = x^2 - 3\sqrt{x} + 1 = 0$, and epsilon = 0.001. The equation for $f(x)$ may be rewritten in the form

$$x^2 + 1 = 3\sqrt{x}$$

$$(x^2 + 1)^2 = 9x$$

$$x = \left(\frac{x^2 + 1}{3}\right)^2$$, which is in the form $x = g(x)$.

Suppose our first estimate of a zero of $f(x)$ is zero, so $x_0 = 0$. From this first estimate we compute the following sequence of approximations to a zero of $f(x)$:

$$x_1 = g(0) \qquad\qquad = 0.111111$$
$$x_2 = g(0.111111) = 0.113871$$
$$x_3 = g(0.113871) = 0.114011$$
$$x_4 = g(0.114011) = 0.114018$$

If we had been testing the differences between two successive members of the preceding sequence we would have found that $|x4-x3| <$ 0.0007, so we have an approximate zero for $f(x)$ within the epsilon value specified. Note that this method produces a sequence of approximations that converges to a satisfactory zero much faster than the sequence computed by the bisection method.

FORTRAN PROGRAM

```
      PROGRAM INRACT
C*    This program computes approximate zeros of a function F(X) if
C*    and only if the equation F(X)=0 may be written in the form
C*    X=G(X). This iteration method assumes an initial guess X0
C*    reasonably close to actual zero. Once X0 is known, the
C*    sequence X1,X2, . . . ,XN is computed using the equation
C*    X(K)=G(X(K-1)) for K=1,2, . . . ,N.
C*
C*    VARIABLE DEFINITIONS
C*    X0 is an estimate of a zero of F(X).
C*    X1 is the next computed approximation to a zero of F(X).
C*    EPS is the maximum allowable difference between 2 successive
C*        approximations to a zero before computation terminates.
C*    DONE is a logical variable used to terminate computation.
C*
```

```
      REAL X0, X1, EPS
      G(X) = (Insert definition of G(X) from the equation X = G(X))
      PRINT *, 'ENTER INITIAL ESTIMATE AND ACCURACY DESIRED.'
      READ *, X0, EPS
      DONE = .FALSE.
      X1 = G(X0)
10    IF (ABS(X1-X0) .LE. EPS) THEN
          PRINT *, 'AN APPROXIMATE ZERO IS ',X1
          DONE = .TRUE.
      ELSE
          X0 = X1
          X1 = G(X0)
      ENDIF
      IF (.NOT. DONE) GO TO 10
      END
```

EXAMPLE Let's consider another example applying the iteration method. Find a real zero of the function F(X) = X − E**X to 4 digits of accuracy. Assume an initial estimate X0 of 1. Requiring 4 digits of accuracy means that E must be 0.0001. The table shows the computed approximations.

Iteration I	XI	*Iteration* I	XI
0	1.0	10	0.568428
1	0.367879	11	0.566415
2	0.692200	12	0.567556
3	0.500473	13	0.566909
4	0.606243	14	0.567256
5	0.545396	15	0.567079
6	0.579612	16	0.567179
7	0.560115	17	0.567122
8	0.571143	18	0.567155
9	0.564879		

The difference between the approximations computed at iterations 17 and 18 has an absolute value of 0.000033, less than 0.0001, so the acceptable zero is 0.5671. If this value is substituted back into X − E**X, the resulting value is 0.5671 − 0.5671678 = −0.0000678, a number equal to zero in the first 4 decimal positions.

Newton's method. The geometry behind Newton's method involves computing x_{k+1} from the slope of the line tangent to the graph of $f(x)$ at point x_k, which involves computing $f'(x_k)$. When the derivative of a continuous function $f(x)$ is readily computable, then the following formula defines how a sequence of approximate zeros may be computed:

$$x_{k+1} = x_k - \frac{f(x_k)}{f'(x_k)}$$

where $f'(x)$ indicated the first derivative of $f(x)$, and both $f(x)$ and $f'(x)$ are evaluated at x_k.

All that is necessary to begin computing this sequence of approximate zeros is to have an initial value for x_k where $k=0$. Unless it is clear from the definition of $f(x)$ and $f'(x)$ that 0 or 1 cannot be used for x_0, then one of these values is often used.

EXAMPLE

Assume that $f(x) = x - e^{-x}$. In this case the derivative of $f(x)$ is given by $f'(x) = 1 + e^{-x}$. Now assume $x_0 = 1$.

$$x_1 = x_0 - \frac{x_0 - e^{-x_0}}{1 + e^{-x_0}}$$

Replacing x_0 by 1 we have

$$x_1 = 1 - \frac{1 - e^{-1}}{1 + e^{-1}} = 0.53788$$

Using the same formula, we can compute other terms in the sequence obtaining the following values after 3 more computations:

$$x_2 = 0.56698$$
$$x_3 = 0.56716$$
$$x_4 = 0.56715$$

You may easily check the computations yourself, but let us assume the preceding values are correct. Using Newton's method we are able to arrive at the required accuracy after 4 iterations rather than the 18 interactions required by the iteration method.

Of course, Newton's method does not always converge faster than other algorithms; it actually has a tendency to converge slowly because it introduces the computation of $f'(x)$. For some functions, Newton's method does not converge at all. Consequently, when using Newton's algorithm for computing zeros, the program should have some reasonable maximum number of iterations that it performs, after which it terminates even though a satisfactory zero is not computed. The following FORTRAN program is an implementation of Newton's algorithm and imposes an upper limit of 50 iterations.

FORTRAN PROGRAM

```
      PROGRAM NEWTON
C*    This program computes a real zero of function F(X) using
C*    Newton's algorithm. The derivative of F(X) is denoted by FF(X),
C*    the first estimate of a root is denoted by X0 and the next
C*    approximate zero is denoted by X1. As in previous algorithms,
C*    EPS denotes the measure of accuracy with which the approximate
C*    zero is computed.
C*
```

```
      INTEGER COUNT
      REAL F, FF, X0, X1, EPS
      LOGICAL DONE
      F(X) = (Insert definition of desired function)
      FF(X) = (Insert definition of the derivative of F(X))
      PRINT *, 'ENTER INITIAL ESTIMATE AND ACCURACY DESIRED.'
      READ *, X0, EPS
      DONE = .FALSE.
      COUNT = 0
 10   X1 = X0 - F(X0)/FF(X0)
          IF (ABS(X1-X0) .GT. EPS) THEN
              X0 = X1
              DONE = .FALSE.
              COUNT = COUNT+1
          ELSE
              PRINT *, 'ONE REAL ZERO IS ', X1
              DONE = .TRUE.
          ENDIF
          IF ((.NOT. DONE) .AND. (COUNT .LE. 50)) GO TO 10
          IF ((.NOT. DONE) .AND. (COUNT .GT. 50)) PRINT *,
     +        'NO ACCEPTABLE ZERO FOUND AFTER 50 ITERATIONS.'
      END
```

Secant method. The method we present next uses the slope of the secant line. Given two points, $(x_{i-1}, f(x_{i-1}))$ and $(x_i, f(x_i))$, the slope of the line through these points is given by

$$\frac{f(x_i) - f(x_{i-1})}{x_i - x_{i-1}}$$

Substitute this value in place of the derivative in Newton's formula to obtain

$$x_{i+1} = x_i - \frac{f(x_i)}{\dfrac{f(x_i) - f(x_{i-1})}{x_i - x_{i-1}}}$$

Multiply numerator and denominator of the second term by $x_i - x_{i-1}$, which gives

$$x_{i+1} = x_i - \frac{x_i\, f(x_i) - x_{i-1}\, f(x_i)}{f(x_i) - f(x_{i-1})}$$

Finally, obtain a common denominator for both terms on the right side of the equation. This results in the formula called the *secant method* for finding a real zero of a function $f(x)$:

$$x_{i+1} = \frac{x_{i-1}\, f(x_i) - x_i\, f(x_{i-1})}{f(x_i) - f(x_{i-1})}$$

Although the secant method usually requires more iterations to obtain a satisfactory zero, it takes less computer time because only one function must be evaluated. True, on the first iteration both evaluations must be made, but the value for $f(x_i)$ becomes $f(x_{i-1})$ on subsequent iterations and only one function evaluation is required.

As with Newton's method, there are situations where the sequence of approximate zeros does not converge. So here too provision must be made to terminate iterations after some maximum number. Because the secant method often converges slowly, we choose a larger maximum number of iterations, here 100.

FORTRAN PROGRAM

```
      PROGRAM SECANT
C*    This program computes an approximate real zero for F(X)
C*    using the slope of the secant line through two points on
C*    the graph of F(X) to compute two approximations to such a zero.
C*
C*    VARIABLE DEFINITIONS
C*    X0 is an initial estimate of the zero.
C*    X1 is the next approximation to the zero (given as input
C*        data in the first interaction and computed on all others).
C*    X2 is the next computed approximate zero.
C*    EPS is closeness of approximation to the actual zero.
C*    DONE is a logical variable used to indicate whether or not
C*        a satisfactory zero has been found.
C*    COUNT is the count of iterations performed.
C*
      LOGICAL DONE
      INTEGER COUNT
      REAL X0, X1, X2, EPS, F0, F1
      F(X) = (Insert definition of desired function)
      COUNT = 0
      DONE = .FALSE.
      READ *, X0, X1, EPS, F0, F1
 100  IF (ABS(X1-X0) .GT. EPS) THEN
          DONE = .FALSE.
          F0 = F(X0)
          F1 = F(X1)
          X2 = (X0*F1 - X1*F0) / (F1 - F0)
          COUNT = COUNT+1
      ELSE
          PRINT *, 'THE APPROXIMATE REAL ZERO IS ' , X2
          DONE = .TRUE.
      ENDIF
      IF ((.NOT. DONE) .AND. (COUNT .LE. 100)) GO TO 100
      IF (COUNT .GT. 100) PRINT *, 'NO ACCEPTABLE ZERO FOUND ',
     +    'IN 100 ITERATIONS.'
      END
```

Definite Integrals

The definite integral

$$\int_a^b f(x)\,dx$$

is defined to be the area bounded by the curve $y = f(x)$ and the lines $x = a$, $x = b$, and $y = 0$, as shown in Figure 8.1.

FIGURE 8.1

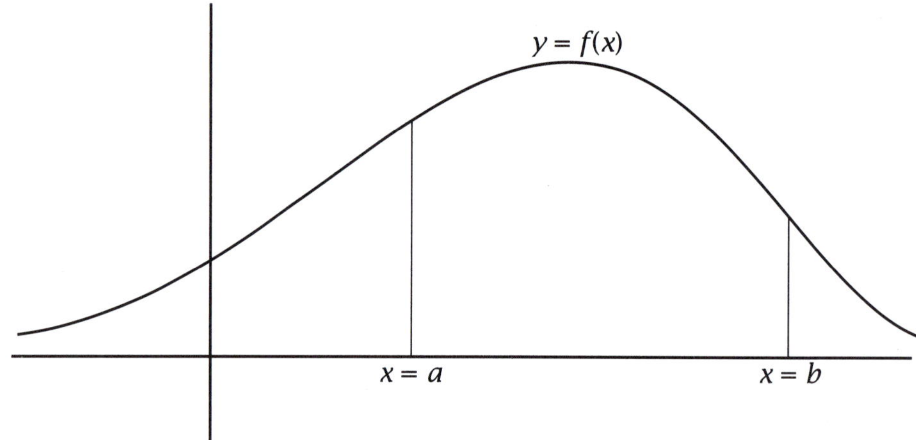

If F(x) is a function whose derivative is $f(x)$ and F(x) is continuous on the closed interval $[a,b]$ then it is true that

$$\int_a^b f(x)\,dx = \mathrm{F(b)} - \mathrm{F(a)}$$

When it is difficult or impossible to determine the exact form of F(x), the value of $F(b) - F(a)$ may be approximated by computing the value of the area bounded by $y = f(x)$, $x = a$, $x = b$, and $y = 0$ using one of the following methods: Trapezoid approximation, the midpoint method, or Simpson's or Boole's rules.

Trapezoid approximation. This method requires that the area bounded by $y = f(x)$, $x = a$, $x = b$, and $y = 0$ be divided into trapezoids each of width h where

$$h = \frac{b - a}{n}$$

where n is an arbitrary positive integer.

It is shown in mathematics that as n becomes large, the sum of the n trapezoids approaches the exact value of the area, which represents the definite integral we want to evaluate.

FIGURE 8.2

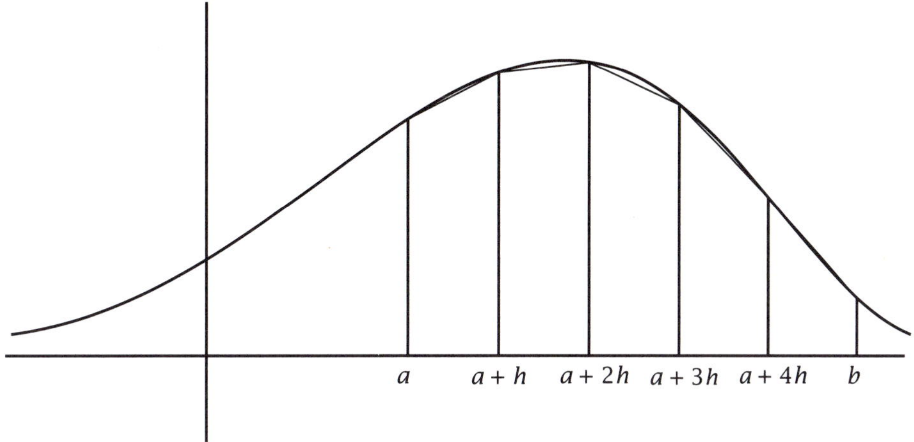

If S_1 is the area of the first trapezoid, S_2 the area of the second trapezoid, and so on with S_n being the area of the nth trapezoid, then

$$\text{Area} = S_1 + S_2 + \ldots + S_n$$

$$\text{where } S_1 = \frac{f(a) + f(a+h)}{2}\, h$$

$$S_2 = \frac{f(a+h) + f(a+2h)}{2}\, h$$

$$\vdots$$

$$S_n = \frac{f(a+(n-1)h) + f(b)}{2}\, h$$

$$\int_a^b f(x)\,dx \approx \frac{h}{2}\,[f(a) + f(a+h) + 2\,f(a+2h) + \ldots + 2\,f(a+(n-1)h) + f(b)]$$

$$\approx h[1/2\; f(a) + f(a+h) + f(a+2h) + \ldots + f(a+(n-1)h) + 1/2\; f(b)]$$

$$\approx \frac{h}{2}\,[f(a) + f(b)] + h\sum_{k=1}^{n-1} f(a+kh)$$

This last formula is what is generally known as the *trapezoidal rule*, from which this method is called the *trapezoid approximation method*.

The larger the number n of trapezoids, the closer the computed approximate integral comes to the true value of the integral. Of course, the larger n is, the greater the number of computations required and the longer it takes to obtain the result.

FORTRAN PROGRAM

```
      PROGRAM TRAPZ
C*    This program reads the values of A, B, and EPS, then computes
C*    the definite integral from A to B of F(X)DX with a measure
C*    of accuracy of EPS using the trapezoidal approximation method.
C*
C*    VARIABLE DEFINITIONS
C*    A is the lower limit of the integral.
C*    B is the upper limit of the integral.
C*    EPS is the measure of accuracy of the approximation.
C*    OLDVAL is the computed value of the integral with N=I.
C*    NEWVAL is the computed value of the integral with N=I+1.
C*    N is the current number of trapezoids approximating the area.
C*
C*    The program terminates when the absolute value of the
C*    difference between OLDVAL and NEWVAL is less than or equal
C*    to the value of EPS.
C*
      REAL A, B, EPS, OLDVAL, NEWVAL, X
      INTEGER N
      PRINT *, 'ENTER LEFT AND RIGHT ENDPOINTS OF INTERVAL'
      PRINT *, 'OF INTEGRATION. ALSO ENTER ACCURACY DESIRED.'
      READ *, A, B, EPS
      N = 2
      OLDVAL = (B-A)*(F(A)+F(B)) / 2
      NEWVAL = INTEGR(A, B, N)
 10   IF (ABS(OLDVAL-NEWVAL) .LE. EPS) GO TO 100
          PRINT *, 'THE INTEGRAL AFTER ',N-1,' ITERATIONS IS ',OLDVAL
          N = N+1
          OLDVAL = NEWVAL
      GO TO 10
 100  PRINT *, 'THE VALUE OF THE INTEGRAL IS ',NEWVAL
      END
C***********************************************************************
      FUNCTION INTEGR (A, B, N)
C*    This function computes the approximation to the integral of
C*    F(X) with limits A and B using the trapezoidal approximation
C*    method. The value B-A is divided into N equally wide trapezoids.
C*
      REAL A, B, H, SUM, X
      INTEGER I, N
      SUM = (F(A)+F(B))/2
      DO 10 I=1, N-1
          SUM = SUM + F(A+I*H)
 10   CONTINUE
      INTEGR = H*SUM
      END
```

```
C**************************************************************************
      FUNCTION F(X)
      REAL X
      F = (Insert definition of desired function)
      END
```

Midpoint method. We may also approximate the area bounded by the graph of $y = f(x)$, $x = a$, $x = b$, and $y = 0$ by computing the midpoint of the distance from a to b, then constructing two rectangles with the base of each equal to $(b - a)/2$, as shown in Figure 8.3

FIGURE 8.3

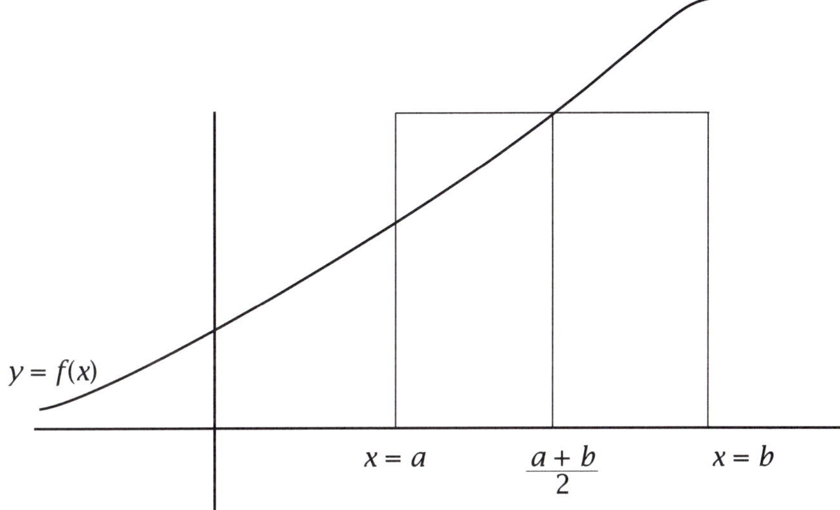

As you can see, the right rectangle underestimates a portion of the area under the curve and the left rectangle overestimates a portion of the area under the curve. The sum of the areas of the two rectangles provides an estimate of the total area. Thus

$$Area = 2\left(\frac{b-a}{2}\right)f\left(\frac{a+b}{2}\right) = (b-a)\,f\left(\frac{a+b}{2}\right)$$

In order to obtain a closer approximation to the bounded area, more rectangles, say n rectangles, may be constructed. Note that we assume n to be an even number. If we let

$$h = \frac{b-a}{n}$$

then we obtain

$$\int_a^b f(x)\,dx = \int_a^{a+h} f(x)\,dx + \int_{a+h}^{a+2h} f(x)\,dx + \ldots + \int_{b-h}^{b} f(x)\,dx$$

Now apply the formula from the preceding page to each of the integrals on the right of the equals sign to obtain the following approximation to the desired integral:

$$\int_a^b f(x)\,dx \approx h\left[f\left(a+\frac{h}{2}\right) + f\left(a+\frac{3h}{2}\right) + \ldots + f\left(a+\frac{(2n-1)h}{2}\right)\right]$$

$$\approx h\sum_{i=1}^{n} f\left(a+\frac{(2i-1)h}{2}\right)$$

As in the trapezoidal approximation method, we start with n=2, then increase n until the change in two successive approximations is less than epsilon.

FORTRAN PROGRAM

```
      PROGRAM MIDPT
C*    This program reads values for A, B, and EPS and computes an
C*    approximation for the integral of F(X)DX with limits of A and B.
C*    Computation terminates when two successive approximations
C*    differ in absolute value by an amount less than or equal to EPS.
C*
C*    VARIABLE DEFINITIONS
C*    A is the lower limit of the integral.
C*    B is the upper limit of the integral.
C*    EPS is the measure of accuracy of the integral approximation.
C*    OLDVAL is the approx. for the integral for some even N.
C*    NEWVAL is the approx. for the integral for N + 2.
C*
      REAL A, B, EPS, OLDVAL, NEWVAL
      INTEGER N
      PRINT *, 'ENTER LEFT & RIGHT ENDPOINTS OF INTERVAL'
      PRINT *, 'OF INTEGRATION. ALSO ENTER ACCURACY DESIRED.'
      READ *, A, B, EPS
      N = 2
      OLDVAL = (B-A/2) * F(A+B/2)
      NEWVAL = INTEGR(A, B, N)
 10   IF (ABS(OLDVAL-NEWVAL) .LE. EPS) GO TO 100
         PRINT *, 'THE ', N1, ' ITERATION RESULT IS ', OLDVAL
         OLDVAL = NEWVAL
         NEWVAL = INTEGR(A, B, N)
      GO TO 10
 100  PRINT *, 'THE VALUE OF THE INTEGRAL IS ', NEWVAL
      END
```

```
C***********************************************************************
      FUNCTION INTEGR(A, B, N)
C*
C*    Computes the approximate value for the integral of F(X) from A to B
C*    using the midpoint method. The number of rectangles starts with 2,
C*    then increases by 2 each iteration until a satisfactory integral
C*    approximation is obtained.
C*
      REAL A, B, H, VALUE
      INTEGER I, N
      H = (B-A)/N
      VALUE = 0
      DO 10 I=1, N
          TEMP = (2*I-1)*(H/2)
          VALUE = VALUE + F(A+TEMP)
10    CONTINUE
      INTEGR = VALUE*H
      END
C***********************************************************************
      REAL FUNCTION F(X)
      F = (Insert definition of desired function)
      END
```

Simpson's rule. Probably the most widely used method of numerical integration is *Simpson's rule for approximating a definite integral.* If the interval of integration is $[a,b]$, then this method requires that we cover the area bounded by the curve $y = f(x)$, $y = 0$, $x = a$, and $x = b$ by an even number $2n$ of equal width rectangles. As in the other approximation methods we compute the width h of each rectangle as follows:

$$h = (b-a)/(2n)$$

Then we can approximate the value of the integral

$$\int_a^b f(x)\ dx$$

by the formula

$$(h/3)\ [f(a) + 4f(a+h) + 2f(a+2h) + 4f(a+3h) + 2f(a+4h) + \ldots + 2f(b-2h) + 4f(b-h) + f(b)]$$

As with the previous methods of numerical integration, the smaller the value of h the more accurate is the approximation of the true value of the integral. Again, the program we present reads an input value for epsilon such that when two successive approximations for the integral, each using different values for $2n$, differ by an amount less than or equal to epsilon, the last approximation is reported as the desired approximation for the value of the integral.

FORTRAN PROGRAM

```
      PROGRAM SIMPSN
C*    This program reads values for A, B, and EPS and computes an
C*    approximation for the integral from A to B of F(X)DX using
C*    Simpson's rule. The program starts with the value for N=1, N=2,
C*    N=3, and so on until the difference between two successive
C*    approximations is less than or equal to EPS.

C*    VARIABLE DEFINITIONS
C*    A is the lower limit of the integral.
C*    B is the upper limit of the integral.
C*    EPS is the desired accuracy.
C*    OLDVAL is the approximated value of the integral when N=K.
C*    NEWVAL is the approximated value of the integral when N=K+1.
C*    H is the computed width of each rectangle.
C*
      REAL A, B, EPS, OLDVAL, NEWVAL, H
      INTEGER N
      READ *, A, B, EPS
      H = (B-A)/2
      OLDVAL = (H/3)*(F(A) + 4*F(A+H) + F(B))
      N = 2
      NEWVAL = INTEGR(A, B, N)
 10   IF (ABS(OLDVAL-NEWVAL) .LE. EPS) GO TO 100
         PRINT *, 'THE INTEGRAL VALUE WHEN N = ', N-1, ' IS ', OLDVAL
         N = N+1
         OLDVAL = NEWVAL
         NEWVAL = INTEGR(A, B, N)
      GO TO 10
 100  PRINT *, 'THE FINAL VALUE OF THE INTEGRAL IS ', NEWVAL
      END
C***********************************************************************
      REAL FUNCTION INTEGR(A, B, N)
C*
C*    This function computes an approximation for the integral
C*    from A to B of F(X)DX using Simpson's rule with H = (B-A)/(2*N).
C*
      REAL A, B, H, VALUE, T1, T2, T3
      INTEGER I, N
      H = (B-A)/(2*N)
      VALUE = 0
      DO 10 I=1, N
         T1 = 2*I-2
         T2 = T1+1
         T3 = T2+1
         VALUE = VALUE + F(A+T1*H) + 4*F(A+T2*H) + F(A+T3*H)
 10   CONTINUE
      INTEGR = (H/3)*VALUE
      END
```

```
C***************************************************************************
      REAL FUNCTION F(X)
      REAL X
      F = (Insert definition of desired function)
      END
```

Boole's rule. *Boole's rule for approximating a definite integral* requires that the interval of integration be divided into $4n$ intervals of equal width h where $h = (b-a)/4n$ and a and b are the lower and upper limits of integration respectively. Boole's rule approximates

$$\int_a^b f(x)\, dx$$

as follows:

$$(2h)/45 \sum_{k=1}^{N} (7f(a + (4k-4)h) + 32f(a + (4k-3)h) + 12f(a + (4k-2)h) + 32f(a + (4k-1)h) + 7f(a + 4kh))$$

Thus, for n=1, Boole's rule becomes

$$(2h/45)\,[7f(a) + 32f(a+h) + 12f(a+2h) + 32f(a+3h) + 7f(b)]$$

where $h = (b-a)/4$.

For n=2, the approximation becomes

$$(2h/45)\,[7f(a) + 32f(a+h) + 12f(a+2h) + 32f(a+3h) + 14f(a+4h) + 32f(a+5h) + 12f(a+6h) + 32f(a+7h) + 7f(b)]$$

where $h = (b-a)/8$

Among the methods for numerically computing an integral, Boole's method converges most rapidly. It also requires the most computing in terms of function evaluation. During each interaction of Boole's method, four different function evaluations are computed; Simpson's method evaluates two different functions during each interaction.

FORTRAN PROGRAM

```
      PROGRAM BOOLE
C*    This program reads values for A, B, and EPS, then computes an
C*    approximate value for the integral from A to B of F(X)DX
C*    using Boole's rule. The program sets the value of N to 1, 2,
C*    3, and so on until two successive approximations are
C*    within EPS of each other. The last value is reported as
C*    the desired approximation to the value of the integral.
C*
```

```
C*    VARIABLE DEFINITIONS
C*    A is the lower limit of the integral.
C*    B is the upper limit of the integral.
C*    EPS is the desired closeness of approximation.
C*    H is the width of each subinterval.
C*    OLDVAL is approximation to the integral when N=K.
C*    NEWVAL is approximation to the integral when N=K+1.
C*
      REAL A, B, EPS, H, OLDVAL, NEWVAL
      INTEGER N
      PRINT *, 'ENTER LEFT AND RIGHT ENDPOINTS OF INTERVAL'
      PRINT *, 'OF INTEGRATION. ALSO ENTER ACCURACY DESIRED.'
      READ *, A, B, EPS
      H = (B-A)/4
      OLDVAL = ((2*H)/45)*(7*F(A) + 32*F(A+H) + 12*F(A+2*H)
     +    + 32*F(A+3*H) + 7*F(B))
      N = 2
      NEWVAL = INTEGR(A, B, N)
 10   IF (ABS(OLDVAL - NEWVAL) .LE. EPS) GO TO 100
          PRINT *, 'WHEN N = ', N-1, ' THE APPROX INTEGRAL = ', OLDVAL
          N = N+1
          OLDVAL = NEWVAL
          NEWVAL = INTEGR(A, B, N)
      GO TO 10
 100  PRINT *, 'THE FINAL APPROXIMATION IS ', NEWVAL
      END
C***************************************************************************
      REAL FUNCTION INTEGR(A, B, N)
C*
      REAL A, B, H, VALUE, T1, T2, T3, T4, T5
      INTEGER I, N
      H = (B-A)/(4*N)
      VALUE = 0
      DO 20 I=1, N
          T1 = 4*I-4
          T2 = T1+1
          T3 = T2+1
          T4 = T3+1
          T5 = T4+1
          VALUE = VALUE + 7*F(A+T1*H) + 32*F(A+T2*H)
     +        +12*F(A+T3*H) + 32*F(A+T4*H) + 7*F(A+T5*H)
 20   CONTINUE
      INTEGR = ((2*H)/45)*VALUE
      END
C***************************************************************************
      REAL FUNCTION F(X)
      REAL X
      F = (Insert definition of desired function)
      END
```

Polynomials

Many of the functions in engineering and scientific applications can be approximated by polynomials through the use of Taylor's series or MacLaurin's series. It is thus worthwhile to consider a method for evaluating a polynomial of degree n in the least amount of time.

Suppose that

$$P_n(x) = a_0 + a_1x + a_2x^2 + \ldots + a_nx^n$$

is a polynomial of degree n. By factoring, it is possible to write

$$P_n(x) = a_0 + x\,(a_1 + x\,(a_2 + \ \ldots\ + x\,(a_{n-1} + xa_n)\ldots)$$

By writing the terms on the right side of the preceding equation in reverse order we obtain

$$P_n(x) = (\ldots(a_nx + a_{n-1})x + a_{n-2})x + \ \ldots\ + a_1)x + a_0$$

For example,

$$P_3(x) = (((a_3x) + a_2)x + a_1)x + a_0$$

Similarly,

$$P_4(x) = ((((a_4x + a_3)x + a_2)x + a_1)x + a_0$$

The preceding is called *Horner's method for evaluating a polynomial.* To implement this method using a computer program, we assume that the coefficients, $a_0, a_1, a_2, \ldots, a_n$ are stored in order in an array A. The following program segment performs the required task:

PROGRAM SEGMENT

```
      P = A(N)
      DO 10 I = N-1, 0, -1
          P = P*X + A(I)
 10   CONTINUE
```

Since the derivative of a polynomial is also a polynomial, Horner's method is equally efficient in evaluating the derivative of a polynomial. If a polynomial $P_n(x)$ is as previously given, then its derivative, $P'_n(x)$ is given by

$$P'_n(x) = (((\ldots(na_nx + (n-1)a_{n-1})x + (n-2)a_{n-2})x + \ \ldots\ + 2a_2)x + a_1)$$

The following FORTRAN program segment computes this derivative. We use the name PPRIME for the derivative.

PROGRAM SEGMENT

```
      PPRIME = N * A(N)
      DO 20 I=N-1, 1, -1
          PPRIME = PPRIME*X + A(I)
 20   CONTINUE
```

FORTRAN PROGRAM

This program incorporates both of the preceding program segments and reads the coefficients of the polynomial. Note that if a term k is missing in the polynomial, it is necessary to enter a coefficient of zero for A(k). For example, if the polynomial is $x^3 - 2x + 1$, the array A has 1, −2, 0, 1 entered as the values to be stored in A(0), A(1), A(2), and A(3), respectively.

```
      PROGRAM POLY
C*    This program reads the coefficients of a polynomial of degree 100
C*    or less and the value of X for which the polynomial is to be
C*    evaluated. Output is the value of the polynomial and its derivative
C*    at the given value for X.
C*
      REAL A(0:100), X, P, PPRIME
      INTEGER N
 5    PRINT *, 'ENTER THE DEGREE N OF THE POLYNOMIAL, 0 < N <= 100.'
      READ *, N
      IF ((N .LT. 1) .OR. (N .GT. 100)) GO TO 5
      PRINT *, 'NOW ENTER THE COEFFICIENTS IN ORDER FROM THE'
      PRINT *, 'CONSTANT TERM TO THE HIGHEST DEGREE TERM.'
      READ *, (A(I), I=0, N)
      PRINT *, 'FINALLY, ENTER THE VALUE OF X FOR WHICH THE'
      PRINT *, 'POLYNOMIAL IS TO BE EVALUATED.'
      READ *, X
      P = A(N)
      PPRIME = N*A(N)
      DO 10 I = N-1, 1, -1
          P = P*X + A(I)
          PPRIME = PPRIME*X + A(I)
10    CONTINUE
      P = P + A(0)
      PRINT *, 'POLYNOMIAL VALUE AT X = ', X, ' IS ', P
      PRINT *, 'VALUE OF THE DERIVATIVE AT X = ', X, ' IS ', PPRIME
      END
```

Interpolation

Interpolation is the process of obtaining values of a function at points for which they are not directly available. In order to help you understand the necessary formulas, we present some introductory concepts from the theory of finite differences.

DEFINITION

First divided difference: Let $f(x)$ be a function and $f(x_i)$ be the value of the function for $x = x_i$. Then

$$f(x_i\, ,\, x_j) = \frac{f(x_i) - f(x_j)}{x_i - x_j}$$

is called the *first divided difference* of $f(x)$ at x and $x_{i,j}$.

Similarly, if $f(x_i, x_j)$ and $f(x_j, x_k)$ are two first divided differences of $f(x)$, then

$$f(x_i, x_j, x_k) = \frac{f(x_i, x_j) - f(x_j, x_k)}{x_i - x_k}$$

is called a second divided difference of $f(x)$.

DEFINITION ***Difference***: Suppose $f(x)$ is a function and

$$x_k = x_0 + kh$$

for $k = \ldots, -2, -1, 0, 1, 2, \ldots$ such that $f(x_k)$ exists and is a unique value for each x_k. Then we define

$$f(x_k) = f(x_{k+1}) - f(x_k)$$

as the *difference* of $f(x)$ at x_k.

Linear interpolation. Now suppose that a function $f(x)$ is evaluated at n points $x_0, x_1, x_2, \ldots, x_n$ and the values obtained for $f(x)$ at these points are $f(x_0), f(x_1), f(x_2), \ldots, f(x_n)$. To compute the approximate value of $f(x)$ for x not equal to x_i for $i = 0, 1, \ldots, n$ and $x_0 < x < x_n$ a method called *interpolation* is often used. In *linear interpolation*, if $x_i < x < x_{i+1}$, $f(x)$ is on the straight line joining $f(x_i)$ and $f(x_{i+1})$. Using the two-point form of the equation of a line gives us

$$f(x) - f(x_i) = \frac{f(x_{i+1}) - f(x_i)}{x_{i+1} - x_i}(x - x_i)$$

from which we can obtain

$$f(x) = f(x_i) + \frac{f(x_{i+1}) - f(x_i)}{x_{i+1} - x_i}(x - x_i)$$

We shall rename the previous form of $f(x)$, $P_1(x)$ to indicate that it was obtained from assuming that $f(x)$ is a linear polynomial between x_{i+1} and x_i.

To illustrate the use of linear interpolation, assume that $f(0) = 3$ and $f(1) = 7$, and that we want to compute $f(0.2)$. Note in this case that $x_i = 0$ and $x_{i+1} = 1$, $f(x_i) = 3$, $f(x_{i+1}) = 7$.

Substituting appropriate values into the formula for $P_1(x)$ we obtain

$$P_1(0.2) = 3 + \frac{7-3}{1-0}(0.2 - 0) = 3 + 4(0.2) = 3 + 0.8 = 3.8$$

Now we are ready to develop a FORTRAN program that reads values for x, x_0, x_1, $f(x_0)$, and $f(x_1)$, then uses linear interpolation to compute $f(x)$. Recall that linear interpolation requires that x_0 and x_1 be distinct values. The following program checks that the user complies with that requirement as well as providing a value for x that is between x_0 and x_1.

Linear interpolation may be used to compute values for $f(x)$ where x is not between x_0 and x_1, but such approximations are not as likely to be good.

FORTRAN PROGRAM

```
      PROGRAM LININT
C*    This program reads the coordinates of 2 points on the graph of
C*    the function F(X) and computes a linear approximation for F
C*    at the provided value of X.
C*
C*    VARIABLE DEFINITIONS
C*    X0 and F0 are coordinates of the first point on F(X).
C*    X1 and F1 are coordinates of the second point on F(X).
C*    X and Y are coordinates of the interpolated point.
C*
      CHARACTER ANS
      REAL X0, X1, F0, F1, X, Y
 5    PRINT *, 'ENTER PAIRS OF POINTS, (X0,F(X0)), (X1,F(X1))'
          READ *, X0, F0, X1, F1
 10       IF (X0 .EQ. X1) THEN
              PRINT *, 'X0 AND X1 MUST BE DISTINCT. ENTER AGAIN.'
              READ *, X0, F0, X1, F1
              GO TO 10
          ENDIF
          PRINT *, 'ENTER A VALUE FOR X BETWEEN ', X0, ' AND ', X1
          READ *, X
 100      IF ((X .LT. X0) .OR. (X .GT. X1)) THEN
              PRINT *, 'X MUST BE BETWEEN ', X0, ' AND ', X1
              PRINT*, 'ENTER ANOTHER X-VALUE.'
              READ *, X
              GO TO 100
          ENDIF
          Y = F0 + ((F1-F0)/(X1-X0))*(X-X1)
          PRINT *, 'THE VALUE OF F(',X, ') IS ', Y
          PRINT *, 'DO YOU WANT TO COMPUTE ANOTHER VALUE FOR F(X)? Y/N'
          READ *, ANS
      IF ((ANS .EQ. 'Y') .OR. (ANS .EQ. 'y'))GO TO 5
      END
```

Quadratic interpolation. Although linear interpolation is the simplest of interpolation formulas, the results it gives may not be as accurate as needed. Even when $f(x)$ is not known at one point, the range of acceptable values for it at that point is generally known. Therefore, if the difference between $P_1(x)$ evaluated at the specified point is outside the range of acceptable values for $f(x)$ at that point, linear interpolation is not accurate enough.

A possibly more accurate approximation for $f(x)$ may be obtained by using *quadratic interpolation*. In this method of approximating $f(x)$ we assume that $f(x)$ is the graph of a quadratic polynomial rather than a straight line between the points $(x_0, f(x_0))$ and $(x_1, f(x_1))$. Consequently, we need to know the coordinates of three points on the graph of $f(x)$ in order to perform quadratic interpolation. The necessary formula is

$$P_2(x) = f(x_0)\,\frac{(x - x_1)\,(x - x_2)}{(x_0-x_1)\,(x_0-x_2)} + f(x_1)\,\frac{(x - x_0)\,(x - x_2)}{(x_1-x_0)\,(x_1-x_2)} + f(x_2)\,\frac{(x - x_0)\,(x - x_1)}{(x_2-x_0)\,(x_2-x_1)}$$

It is essential that none of x_0, x_1, or x_2 be equal, since if they were, one or more denominators in the formula for $P_1(x)$ would be zero.

The program we give is interactive so the user may choose options. For example, given an initial set of values for x_0, $f(x_0)$, x_1, $f(x_1)$, x_2, and $f(x_2)$, the user may provide more than one value of x for which the program is to compute the interpolated value $f(x)$. Or the user may choose to enter a new set of values for x_0, $f(x_0)$, x_1, $f(x_1)$, x_2, and $f(x_2)$ each new value of x. The value of x must in each case be in the range $\min(x_0, x_1, x_2) < x < \max(x_0, x_1, x_2)$ in order to ensure as accurate an interpolated value as possible.

FORTRAN PROGRAM

```
      PROGRAM INTER2
C*    This program expects as input data the coordinates of 3 points
C*    on the graph of a function F(X) as well as a value for X at
C*    which the program is to compute F(X). We use quadratic interpolation.
C*
C*    VARIABLE DEFINITIONS
C*    (X0,F0), (X1,F1), (X2,F2) are coordinates of the 3 points.
C*    X is the point at which F(X) is to be interpolated.
C*    P2 is the interpolated value for F(X).
C*    TEMP0, TEMP1, TEMP2 are storage locations for fractions
C*        ((X-X1)*(X-X2))/((X0-X1)*(X0-X2)), and so on.
C*
      CHARACTER ANS
      REAL X0, F0, X1, F1, X2, F2, TEMP0, TEMP1, TEMP2, P2
 10   PRINT *, 'ENTER PAIRS X0,F0; X1,F1; X2,F2'
      READ *, X0, F0, X1, F1, X2, F2
 25   IF (((X0-X1)*(X0-X2)*(X1-X2)) .EQ. 0) THEN
         PRINT *, 'X0, X1, AND X2 MUST BE DISTINCT. TRY AGAIN.'
         READ *, X0, F0, X1, F1, X2, F2
         GO TO 25
      ENDIF
      PRINT *, 'ENTER THE VALUE FOR X. X SHOULD BE WITHIN'
      PRINT *, 'THE INTERVAL COVERING X0, X1, AND X2.'
      READ *, X
```

```
 20     IF ((X .LT. AMIN(X0,X1,X2)) .OR. (X .GT. AMAX(X0,X1,X2)) THEN
            PRINT *, 'X SHOULD BE GREATER THAN MIN(X0,X1,X2)'
            PRINT *, 'AND LESS THAN MAX(X0,X1,X2). TRY AGAIN.'
            READ *, X
            GO TO 20
        ENDIF
C*
C*      Compute the value of P2(X).
C*
        TEMP0 = ((X-X1)*(X-X2)) / ((X0-X1)*(X0-X2))
        TEMP1 = ((X-X0)*(X-X2)) / ((X1-X0)*(X1-X2))
        TEMP2 = ((X-X0)*(X-X1)) / ((X2-X0)*(X2-X1))
        P2 = F0*TEMP0 + F1*TEMP1 + F2*TEMP2
        PRINT *, 'THE INTERPOLATED FUNCTION VALUE WHEN X = ', X,
     +     ' IS ', P2
        PRINT *, ' DO YOU WANT TO COMPUTE ANOTHER APPROX FOR F(X)? Y/N'
        READ *, ANS
        IF ((ANS .EQ. 'Y') .OR. (ANS .EQ. 'y')) GO TO 10
        END
```

Cubic interpolation. Just as a quadratic polynomial may do a more accurate job of approximating a function than a linear polynomial, so also a *cubic polynomial* may be more accurate than either of them. Four distinct points are required in order to derive a cubic polynomial. Assume the four points are denoted by $(x_0, f(x_0))$, $(x_1, f(x_1))$, $(x_2, f(x_2))$ and $(x_3, f(x_3))$. In this case the formula for the desired cubic polynomial is

$$P_3(x) = f(x_0)\frac{(x-x_1)(x-x_2)(x-x_3)}{(x_0-x_1)(x_0-x_2)(x_0-x_3)} + f(x_1)\frac{(x-x_0)(x-x_2)(x-x_3)}{(x_1-x_0)(x_1-x_2)(x_1-x_3)}$$

$$+ f(x_2)\frac{(x-x_0)(x-x_1)(x-x_3)}{(x_2-x_0)(x_2-x_1)(x_2-x_3)} + f(x_3)\frac{(x-x_0)(x-x_1)(x-x_2)}{(x_3-x_0)(x_3-x_1)(x_3-x_2)}$$

It is required that x_0, x_1, x_2 and x_3 be distinctive values.

As with previous interpolations, cubic interpolation is apt to yield better approximations for the true function values if the value of x for which the interpolation is to be computed is in the range from $\min(x_0, x_1, x_2, x_3)$ to $\max(x_0, x_1, x_2, x_3)$. The cubic interpolation program presents options for its operation and checks the entered value for x to determine if it is in the appropriate range. If the value for x is not in range, the user is requested to enter a new value that is in the range.

FORTRAN PROGRAM

```
      PROGRAM INTER3
C*    This program expects as input data the coordinates of 4 points
C*    on the graph of F(X). These points are designated as
C*    (X0,F(X0)), (X1,F(X1)), (X2,F(X2)), and (X3,F(X3)). Also
C*    required is the value of X at which the function is approximated.
C*    Cubic interpolation is the method used.
C*
C*    VARIABLE DEFINITIONS
C*    ANS is the code entered by the user to select an option.
C*    X0,F0; X1,F1; X2,F2; X3,F3 are coordinates for 4 points on the function.
C*    TEMP0, TEMP1, TEMP2, TEMP3 are quotients used in computations
C*        ((X-X1)*(X-X2)*(X-X3))/((X0-X1)*(X0-X2)*(X0-X3)) and so on.
C*    X is value for which an approximate function value is to be computed.
C*    P3 is interpolated value for the function at the point X.
C*
      CHARACTER ANS
      REAL X0, X1, X2, X3, F0, F1, F2, F3, TEMP0, TEMP1, TEMP2
      REAL TEMP3, P3, X
 10   PRINT *, 'ENTER PAIRS OF VALUES, X0,F0, X1,F1, X2,F2, '
     +    'AND X3,F3, AS THE 4 POINT COORDINATES.'
      PRINT *, 'X0, X1, X2, AND X3 MUST BE DISTINCT VALUES.'
      READ *, X0, F0, X1, F1, X2, F2, X3, F3
C*
C*    Check if X-values entered are distinct.
C*
 15   IF(((X0-X1)*(X0-X2)*(X0-X3)*(X1-X2)*(X1-X3)*(X2-X3)) .EQ. 0) THEN
          PRINT *, 'THE X-VALUES MUST BE DISTINCT. TRY AGAIN.'
          READ *, X0, F0, X1, F1, X2, F2, X3, F3
          GO TO 15
      ENDIF
      PRINT *, 'ENTER THE VALUE OF X AT WHICH THE APPROXIMATION'
      PRINT *, 'IS TO BE COMPUTED. X SHOULD BE WITHIN THE'
      PRINT *, 'INTERVAL COVERING X0, X1, X2, AND X3.'
      READ *, X
 20   IF ((X .LT. AMIN(X0,X1,X2,X3,)) .OR.
     +    (X .GT. AMAX(X0,X1,X2,X3))) THEN
          PRINT *, 'X MUST BE GREATER THAN MIN(X0,X1,X2,X3)'
          PRINT *, 'AND LESS THAN MAX(X0,X1,X2,X3). TRY AGAIN.'
C*        READ *, X
          GO TO 20
      ENDIF
```

```
C*
C*     Compute the interpolated value for F(X).
C*
       TEMP0 = ((X-X1)*(X-X2)*(X-X3)) / ((X0-X1)*(X0-X2)*(X0-X3))
       TEMP1 = ((X-X0)*(X-X2)*(X-X3)) / ((X1-X0)*(X1-X2)*(X1-X3))
       TEMP2 = ((X-X0)*(X-X1)*(X-X3)) / ((X2-X0)*(X2-X1)*(X2-X3))
       TEMP3 = ((X-X0)*(X-X1)*(X-X2)) / ((X3-X0)*(X3-X1)*(X3-X2))
       P3 = F0*TEMP0 + F1*TEMP1 + F2*TEMP2 + F3*TEMP3
       PRINT *, 'THE INTERPOLATED VALUE FOR F(X) IS ', P3,
     +     ' WHEN X IS ',X
       PRINT *, 'DO YOU WANT TO COMPUTE ANOTHER APPROX FOR F(X)? Y/N'
       READ *, ANS
       IF ((ANS .EQ. 'Y') .OR. (ANS .EQ. 'y')) GO TO 10
       END
```

Summary

In this chapter we have discussed some numerical methods for computing values for which exact determinations are either difficult or impossible.

Zeros of a function. Although exact formulas are known for finding zeros of polynomials of degree 1, 2, or 3, this is not the case for polynomials of degree greater than 3. We presented four techniques for computing real zeros of functions and polynomials: The ***bisection*** method, the ***iteration*** method, ***Newton's*** method, and the ***secant*** method.

Definite integrals. Evaluating definite integrals is another task for which exact solutions are not always known, or for which the process is difficult. We presented four techniques by which the definite integral may be computed: ***Trapezoidal approximation***, the ***midpoint*** method, ***Simpson's*** rule, and ***Boole's*** rule

Polynomials. Given a polynomial of any degree, it is always possible to evaluate the polynomial at a specific value of its variable. However, it is important to know how to write an efficient computer program to accomplish this task. We discussed ***Horner's*** method for evaluating a polynomial, a method whose usefulness is repeatedly verified in the fields of science and engineering.

Interpolation. Finally, we presented three methods for computing approximate values of a function $f(x)$ for which coordinates of points on the graph of the function are known and the value of x is specified: ***Linear***, ***quadratic***, and ***cubic*** interpolation. These methods are useful for computing approximations of the function value at points for which the function value is either not available or at which values are difficult to obtain by any means other than numerical approximation.

End of Chapter Exercises

1. Use Newton's methods to find the square root of a number. Note that if x is the square root of A, then $x^2 = A$ and $x^2 - A = 0$. From this we can write $f(x) = x^2 - A$ and $f'(x) = 2x$. These last two equations can be applied directly to Newton's method so that you can obtain a formula for x_{k+1} in terms of x_k that can then be used as the function definition in Newton's method. Use as the original estimate x_0 the value A/2, providing the value of A as input data to the program.

2 Use the function $f(x) = x^3 - A$, where A is a real number, to compute the real cube root of A using Newton's method. Use analysis similar to that used in Exercise 1 to obtain a formula for x_{k+1} in terms of x_k. Use A/3 as the first estimate x_0.

3. Run the program given in this chapter for Newton's method with the following functions:

a. $F(X) = XE^{-X}$, $X_0 = 0.2$, EPS = 0.001

b. $F(X) = 2X^4 - X^2 + 6$, $X_0 = 1.0$, EPS = 0.001

4. Assume that A is a positive real number. Write a program to find a representation for A in the form

$$A = Q \times 2^{2N}$$

where $1/4 \le Q \le 1$ and N is a positive integer. The square root of A can then be written as SQRT(A)=SQRT(Q)*2**N

You should be able to show that if Newton's method is used to compute the square root of A, the iterative formula to use is

$$x_{k+1} = \frac{1}{2} x_k + \frac{A}{2x_k}$$

Use X0 = (2Q + 1)/3 and observe how quickly the sequence of approximations converges to the square root. This algorithm is the one used most often in commercial software for computing square root.

5. Use the secant method to compute a zero for each of the following functions with an accuracy of 0.0001:

a. $f(x) = x^2 - 2x - 1$, $x_0 = 2.6$, $x_1 = 2.5$

b. $f(x) = x^3 - x - 3$, $x_0 = 1.7$, $x_1 = 1.67$

c. $f(x) = x^5 - 2x^2 - 10$, use your own values for x_0 and x_1.

6. Develop a FORTRAN program to compute a zero of a function $f(x)$ using the following formula for iteration:

$$x_{k+1} = x_k - \frac{f(x)}{f'(x_k)} - \frac{f''(x)\,(f(x))^2}{2\,(f'(x_k))^3}$$

This is known as Oliver's method. Compare the speed of convergence of Oliver's method and Newton's method for the following functions:

a. $f(x) = x^2 - 2x - 1,\ x_0 = 2.6$

b. $f(x) = x^3 - x - 3,\ x_0 = 1.7$

c. $f(x) = x^5 - 2x^2 - 10,\ x_0 = 1$

7. Find the quadratic interpolation polynomial, $P_2(x)$ for

$f(x) = x^3 - 3x + 2$ using $x_0 = -1,\ x_1 = 0,\ x_2 = 1$.

8. Use the quadratic interpolation program given in this chapter to obtain approximations for $f(1)$, $f(1.25)$, $f(2)$, $f(2.25)$, and $f(2.5)$. Assume that these points are on the graph of $f(x)$: (0, 5), (1.5, 10), (3, 7).

9. Develop a method and an accompanying FORTRAN program to compute a linear interpolation for a function of two variables, $z = f(x,y)$. Note that a linear equation in two variables is of the form $z = Ax + By + C$, and that you need 3 points to approximate A, B, and C. Assume the following 3 points (x,y,z) are on the graph of $z = f(x,y)$: (2,1,5), (1,3,7), (3,2,4).

10. ***Least squares linear approximation.*** Suppose n points (x_1,y_1), (x_2,y_2), . . . , (x_n,y_n) are given. Then the least squares line $y = Ax + B$ is the line for which

$$D^2 = d_1^{\,2} + d_2^{\,2} + d_3^{\,2} + \ . \ . \ . \ + d_n^{\,2}$$

is the minimum and where $d_i^2 = (Ax_i + B - y_i)^2$. Write a program to compute A and B. The only real problem here is to minimize D^2 with respect to A and B. That is, we must obtain the partial derivatives

$$\frac{\partial D^2}{\partial B} = 2\sum_{i=1}^{n} (Ax_i + B - y_i)$$

$$\frac{\partial D^2}{\partial A} = 2\sum_{i=1}^{n} (Ax_i^{\,2} + Bx_i - x_i\, y_i)$$

Then both of these partial derivatives are set equal to zero, giving

$$\sum_{i=1}^{n} (Ax_i + B - y_i) = 0$$

$$\sum_{i=1}^{n} (Ax_i^{\,2} + Bx_i - x_i\, y_i) = 0$$

Thus, your program should solve these two simultaneous equations in A and B. To make these simultaneous equations somewhat easier to solve, note that they can be written in the following form:

$$\left[\sum_{i=1}^{n} x_i\right] A + nB = \sum_{i=1}^{n} y_i$$

$$\left[\sum_{i=1}^{n} x_i^2\right] A + \left[\sum_{i=1}^{n} x_i\right] B = \sum_{i=1}^{n} x_i\, y_i$$

In these computations you will need the n points, (x_1,y_1), (x_2,y_2), . . . , (x_n,y_n). Provision should be made in your program to read these coordinate values.

11. Revise the program given for the trapezoidal rule to compute the value of the following definite integrals. Use 10 subintervals in your computations.

a. $$\int_1^3 3x^2 \cos x \, dx$$

b. $$\int_0^{10} \frac{x}{1 + x^2} \, dx$$

c. $$\int_0^1 \frac{4}{1 + x^2} \, dx$$

12. ***Midpoint algorithm for an integral.*** The midpoint rule for approximating the value of a definite integral is given by the equation:

$$\int_a^b f(x)\, dx = h \sum_{i=1}^{n} f(a + (i - 1/2)h) \quad \text{where} \quad h = (b - a)/n.$$

Develop a program that implements this algorithm. Provide for reading the limits of integration, the value of n, and the error limit which we have called EPS throughout this chapter.

13. Revise the program for Simpson's rule so that it uses 10 subintervals. Then use it to compute the values of the following definite integrals:

a. $$\int_1^3 3x^2 \cos x \, dx$$

b. $$\int_0^{10} \frac{x}{1 + x^2} \, dx$$

c. $$\int_0^1 \frac{4}{1 + x^2} \, dx$$

Compare these results with those of Exercise 10.

14. ***Sequential trapezoidal rule.*** When the trapezoidal rule is used repeatedly with an increasing number of subintervals, the method is called the sequential trapezoidal rule. The formula is as follows:

$$\int_a^b f(x)\, dx = \frac{h}{2} \sum_{i=1}^{2^j} \left[f(x_{i-1}) + f(x_i)\right]$$

where $h = (b-a)/2^j$ and $x_i = a + h_i$.
Note that $a = x_0 < x_1 < \ldots < x_{j^{2-1}} < x_{2^j} = b$.

Write a program to implement this method of evaluating an integral.

15. Use the program from Exercise 14 to compute

$$\int_0^1 \frac{dx}{1 + x^2}$$

for $j = 2$. This means that $h = (1-0)/2^2 = 1/4$.

Chapter 9

Further Options

Preceding chapters discuss the basic features of FORTRAN that one needs to become an effective programmer. The commonly used properties of FORTRAN have been described; most readers will neither need nor desire further capability. But you may run into special problems or difficult situations that call for extraordinary solutions. For those times, we present in this chapter some useful advanced features.

The style of this chapter is simpler and more direct than in previous chapters. There is sufficient detail to clarify what is being described, but there are fewer examples and a less detailed narrative. Your accumulated knowledge of FORTRAN fills in the gaps, and the brevity of the discussion makes it easier to find quickly what you need.

Type Declaration Statements

These nonexecutable statements designate the structure of data. Most of the type declaration statements have already been introduced; here we discuss some in more detail.

DOUBLE PRECISION. This statement is included in full FORTRAN 77. It causes the data stored in a given variable to have twice as many significant digits as usual—hence the name *double precision*—by using two storage locations rather than one. When a variable has been declared DOUBLE PRECISION, two consecutive locations are packed together to store its value. In a mixed mode expression, double precision is the dominant data type. Double precision variables are always real.

Here is the form of the DOUBLE PRECISION statement:

```
DOUBLE PRECISION V1,V2, . . . ,VN
```

where V1, V2, . . . ,VN represent variable, array, or function subprogram names.

Note that it is also acceptable to use the term DOUBLEPRECISION with no space between the words.

The D format. The D format specification is used for the input and output of double precision values. It has the same general properties and form as the E specification. Its form is

```
DW.D
```

where W represents the total number of spaces in the width of the field being input or output, and
the second D represents the number of decimal positions in the input or output value.

The D format specification produces exactly the same output as the E specification. The only difference is that the D format signals the computer to retrieve the value for X from two adjacent memory locations rather than one.

To designate a double precision constant one uses the same exponential form as for single precision constants, but with the letter D replacing the letter E. Here is an example:

EXAMPLE

```
      DOUBLE PRECISION X
      X = 2.7691234567D9
      WRITE(6,10)X
 10   FORMAT(1X,D15.8)
```

COMPLEX. The COMPLEX statement in full FORTRAN 77 has the form

```
COMPLEX V1,V2, . . . ,VN
```

where V1,V2, . . . ,VN are FORTRAN variable names, including arrays, or function subprogram names.

This statement declares that each variable or function listed is to be treated as a complex value. Each complex value is stored in two adjacent memory locations, each location containing a real number. One of the real numbers is called the *real* part of the complex number, the other the *imaginary* part. For example, if the complex number is Z, where Z = X + *i*Y and *i* = {SQRT(−1)}, then X and Y are the real numbers stored in the two adjacent memory locations set aside for complex variable Z.

Complex value constants are defined by using a pair of parentheses in which are enclosed two real numbers, the first one being the real part of the complex number and the second one being the imaginary part. For example, consider the following program segment:

EXAMPLE 1

```
COMPLEX Z,W
Z=(2,3)
W=(0,3.5)
```

In this case Z is the complex value 2 + *i**3 and W is the complex value 0 + *i**3.5, or simply *i**3.5.

Whenever complex values are processed, one must remember that two real numbers make up each complex number. Thus, two fields must be reserved in input or output operations for each complex value. Consider this example:

EXAMPLE 2

```
      PROGRAM COMPLX
      COMPLEX W,Z,T
      READ 10,W,Z
10    FORMAT(2F10.2,2F10.3)
      T = W + Z
      PRINT 20,W,Z,T
20    FORMAT(1X,F10.2,2X,F10.2)
      END
```

W, Z, and T are all declared COMPLEX, so it makes sense to perform the sum of W and Z, the result of which is also a complex number stored in two adjacent memory locations.

If W = X1 + *i**Y1 and Z = X2 + *i**Y2, then T = W + Z = (X1+X2) + *i**(Y1+Y2) where, of course, the sums X1+X2 and Y1+Y2 are again real numbers, each stored in one of two adjacent memory locations.

Note that in statement 20, two F formats are provided in order to output the two parts of a complex number.

Recall from the study of complex numbers that if Z = X + *i**Y, then the absolute value of Z, denoted by |Z|, is given by $\sqrt{X*X+Y*Y}$. Recall also that if Z1 = X1 + *i**Y1 and Z2 = X2 + *i**Y2, then the product is

$$Z1*Z2 = (X1*X2 - Y1*Y2) + i(X1*Y2 + X2*Y1)$$

All of these arithmetic operations are handled automatically by the FORTRAN compilers when complex data types have been declared.

LOGICAL. The form of the LOGICAL statement is

```
LOGICAL V1,V2, . . . ,VN
```

where V1,V2, . . . ,VN are names of variables, including arrays, or functions.
The only variables that may be stored are the logical values TRUE or FALSE;
similarly, if a function name appears, the value of that function must be either TRUE or FALSE.

The L format. When LOGICAL variables appear in output statements, the L format specification is required:

```
L1
```

where the integer 1 allows one space for the output: T for true or F for false.

EXAMPLE Here is a program example using the LOGICAL statement:

```
      PROGRAM LOGEX
      LOGICAL A, B, C
      A = .TRUE.
      B = .FALSE.
      C = A .OR. B
      PRINT 10, A, B, C
 10   FORMAT (1X,3(2X,L1))
      END
```

A, B, and C are all declared logical variables and logical values are assigned to A and B. Furthermore, the line

```
      C = A .OR. B
```

causes a logical value to be assigned to C. The output of this program is

```
      T F T
```

Note that the L specification in the FORMAT statement at reference number 10 is used for printing logical variables.

Consider now a problem that lends itself nicely to the use of logical variables in the program solution.

Problem 9.1
Using Logical Variables

OBJECTIVE Input a number N and compute N factorial if N is greater than 0 and less than or equal to 15.
If N = 0, output "0!=1".
If N is greater than 15, output "N IS TOO LARGE".
If N is negative, output "N IS NEGATIVE".

SOLUTION To solve this problem, we use four logical variables:

One is set to TRUE if N is greater than 15.
The second is set to TRUE if N is less than zero.
The third is set to TRUE if N=0.

For values of N other than those specified, these three logical variables have the value FALSE.

The fourth logical variable is assigned the value TRUE if any of the first three is TRUE. Thus, this fourth variable is used to determine when N factorial is to be computed.

FORTRAN PROGRAM

```
      PROGRAM LOGIC
      LOGICAL LARGE, NEG, ZERO, BAD
      DATA LARGE, NEG, ZERO/3 * .FALSE./
      INTEGER K, N
C*
      READ*,N
      IF (N .GT. 15) LARGE = .TRUE.
      IF (N .LT. 0) NEG = .TRUE.
      IF (N .EQ. 0) ZERO = .TRUE.
      BAD = LARGE .OR. NEG .OR. ZERO
C***************************************************************************
C*    BAD HAS A VALUE OF FALSE ONLY IF N-FACTORIAL IS TO BE COMPUTED.      *
C***************************************************************************
      IF (.NOT. BAD) THEN
          K=N
          DO 50 I=1,N-1
              K=K*(N-I)
 50       CONTINUE
          PRINT*,N,' FACTORIAL IS ',K
      ELSEIF (LARGE) THEN
          PRINT*,N,' IS TOO LARGE'
      ELSEIF (NEG) THEN
          PRINT*,N,' IS NEGATIVE'
      ELSEIF (ZERO) THEN
          PRINT*,' 0 FACTORIAL IS 1'
      ENDIF
      END
```

The program is executed for N = 20, 15, 7, 0, –12, and 6, with these results:

```
 20 IS TOO LARGE
 15 FACTORIAL IS 2004310016
  7 FACTORIAL IS 5040
  0 FACTORIAL IS 1
-12 IS NEGATIVE
  6 FACTORIAL IS 720
```

This shows how logical variables are conveniently used in a decision making process. Sometimes they improve both the understandability as well as the efficiency of a program.

EQUIVALENCE. The general form of the EQUIVALENCE statement is

```
EQUIVALENCE (V1,V2, . . . ,VN)
```

where V1,V2, . . . ,VN are simple or array variable names all of which use the same memory location.

The EQUIVALENCE statement conserves memory by having variables share a memory location. Let's look at some examples.

EXAMPLE 1

```
REAL A(5),B(10),C,D,E
EQUIVALENCE (B(3),A(2)),(C,D,E)
```

The EQUIVALENCE statement causes B(3) and A(2) to name the same memory location and the other members of the arrays A and B to share locations in order. Since A is an array of 5 locations and B an array of 10 locations, the specification leads to the pairings B(2) and A(1), B(4) and A(3), B(5) and A(4), and B(6) and A(5).

C, D, and E appear in the EQUIVALENCE statement in the same pair of parentheses, so these three names are associated with one memory location.

EXAMPLE 2

```
CHARACTER A*4,B*4,C(2)*3
EQUIVALENCE (A,C(1),(B,C(2))
```

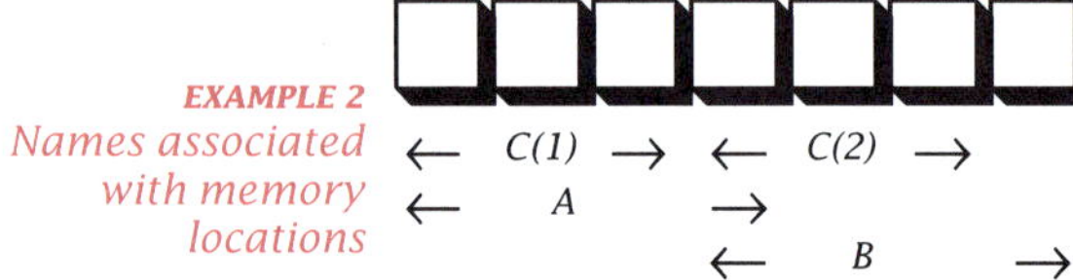

CHARACTER sets aside 4 characters for A and B and 3 for C(1) and C(2).

EQUIVALENCE associates the first character of A and of C(1) with the same memory location and the first character of B and of C(2) with another.

Since C(2) begins in the next location after C(1) and variables A and B are longer, the first character of B actually shares a location with the last character of A.

EXAMPLE 3

```
INTEGER A(2,3),B(6),C(10)
EQUIVALENCE (A(1,1),C(1)),(B(1),C(5)).
```

A and B are arrays of 6 locations each and C is an array of 10 locations.

A(1,1) and C(1) appear in the same parentheses in the EQUIVALENCE statement, so the 6 locations of array A coincide with the first 6 locations of array C.

B(1) and C(5) appear in the same parentheses, so the 6 locations of array B coincide with C(5) through C(10)

EXAMPLE 4 INVALID

```
INTEGER A(3),B
EQUIVALENCE (A(1),B),(A(2),B)
```

This situation is ***invalid.*** B appears with both A(1) and A(2) in the EQUIVALENCE statement, but it is impossible for variables A(1) and A(2) to be identified with the same memory location.

EXAMPLE 5

```
REAL A(2)
DOUBLEPRECISION D
EQUIVALENCE (A(1),D)
```

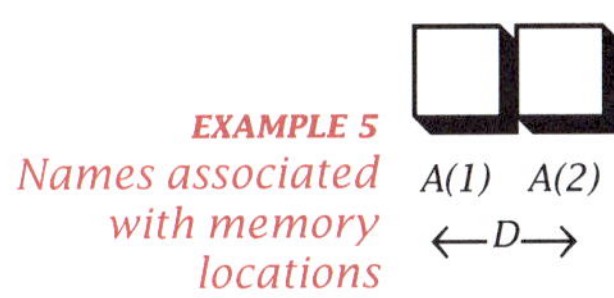

EXAMPLE 5 Names associated with memory locations

The DOUBLE PRECISION variable D occupies 2 computer words and the REAL array A occupies 2 computer words. The EQUIVALENCE statement causes A(1) and the most significant half of D to be stored in the same computer word, leaving A(2) and the least significant half of D in the adjoining word.

EXAMPLE 6 INVALID

```
REAL A(3)
DOUBLEPRECISION D(3)
EQUIVALENCE (A(1),D(1)),(A(2),D(2))
```

This situation is ***invalid.*** Array A occupies 3 adjacent memory locations as defined in the REAL statement. Array D, defined as 3 DOUBLE PRECISION elements, occupies 6 adjacent memory locations. If A(1) is associated with the first location of D(1), the adjacent A(2) cannot be associated with the most significant part of D(2) two locations away.

This assignment of names and memory locations will work if only A(1) and D(1) are made equivalent, deleting the last part of the EQUIVALENCE statement:

EXAMPLE 6 REVISED

```
REAL A(3)
DOUBLEPRECISION D(3)
EQUIVALENCE (A(1),D(1))
```

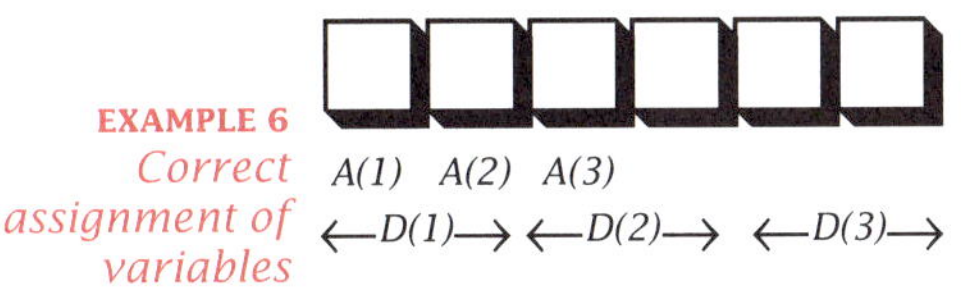

EXAMPLE 6 Correct assignment of variables

Labelled COMMON. In Chapter 7 we discussed briefly the syntax and use of the COMMON statement in making data available among subprograms and calling programs. There we discussed the *unlabelled* or *blank* COMMON statement and suggested that corresponding variables in related COMMON statements should be of the same data type with the same structure—and preferably with the same name.

We now introduce a form that allows us to make blocks of data available to two or more modules, the *labelled* COMMON statement:

```
COMMON /NAME/ V1,V2, . . . ,VN
```

where NAME is any acceptable FORTRAN variable name, called the *common block name*, enclosed by slashes, and
V1,V2, . . . ,VN are the names of single or array variables.

The size of the common block is the number of memory locations specified by the variables to the right of the name plus any additional locations that may become associated through EQUIVALENCE statements.

Uses. This statement allows you to ***identify portions*** of common block statements for use in subprograms instead of having to match the original COMMON statement by inserting dummy data. This advantage will become obvious in the examples.

Also, you may use ***more than one*** statement per program or subprogram; an unlabelled COMMON statement may occur only once in any program or subprogram.

EXAMPLE 1

```
PROGRAM EXAMP1
REAL B,X
INTEGER N
COMMON /A/ X(10),B,N
.
.
.
END
SUBROUTINE SUB 1
REAL X,Y
COMMON /B/ Y(5),X
.
.
.
END
FUNCTION FUNC1(D)
REAL C,X,Y
INTEGER I
COMMON /A/ Y(11),I, /B/ X(5),C
.
.
.
END
```

Here are two named common blocks, A and B.

Block A appears both in the main program EXAMP1, and in the function subprogram FUNC1. In both programs block A has size 12, with the first 11 words REAL and the last word INTEGER.

Block B appears in subroutine SUB1 and in function FUNC1, both times having size 6, all REAL.

Note that though the block name for a given common block must be the same in each subprogram or main program, the variable names may be different in different subprograms—though still of the same data type.

■ *But it is still good programming style to keep the structure and the name of the variables in separate common blocks identical.*

Note in function FUNC1 that more than one named common block may be declared in the same COMMON statement.

EXAMPLE 2

```
PROGRAM EXAMP2
REAL B(7),X,Y
COMMON /AA/ X(5),Y
EQUIVALENCE (B(1),X(1))
.
.
.
END
```

The COMMON statement sets the size of common block AA at 6. But B(1) is associated with X(1) in the EQUIVALENCE statement, and array X is in common block AA. Array B is thus also in block AA, and since the REAL statement dimensions B with 7 words, common block AA is also of size 7.

Combining statements. When you use an EQUIVALENCE statement with a COMMON statement, be cautious about two aspects of their relationship:

1. Variables that appear in two different common blocks must not be associated in an EQUIVALENCE statement.

EXAMPLE 1

```
COMMON /A/ X,Y,Z, /B/ R,S
EQUIVALENCE (X,R)
```

This situation is ***invalid.*** Since X is part of common block A and R is part of common block B, these two variables must not be associated in the EQUIVALENCE statement.

EXAMPLE 2

A related situation appears in the statement

```
COMMON /A/ X,Y,Z, /B/ X,R,S
```

This situation is ***invalid.*** The variable X may *not* appear in two different named common blocks.

2. An EQUIVALENCE statement must not cause a named common block to extend to memory locations preceding the ones specified in the COMMON statement.

EXAMPLE 3

We have seen a combination of REAL and EQUIVALENCE statements cause the common block to extend one memory location *further on* in memory than was specified in the COMMON statement. Such extensions are permitted. But this program segment illustrates an action that is not permitted:

```
COMMON /A/ X(3)
REAL N(4),X
EQUIVALENCE (N(2),X(1))
```

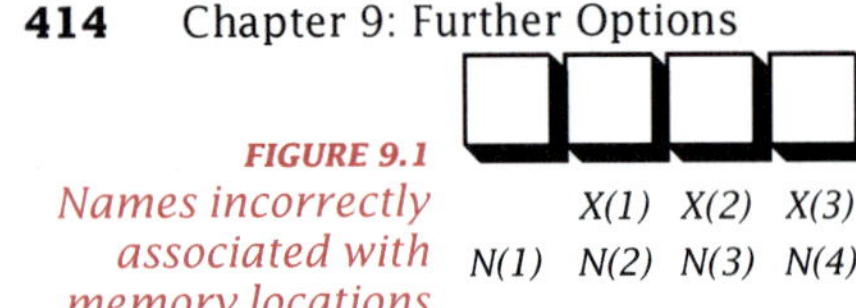

FIGURE 9.1
Names incorrectly associated with memory locations

This situation is ***invalid.*** The EQUIVALENCE association of N(2) and X(1) causes N(1) to precede the specified common block. Such forced extensions of a common block toward the beginning of memory are not permitted.

Size and structure. Though it causes no errors, it is not good programming practice to declare in one program COMMON variables of different size and structure. With COMMON statements, use identical variable array names with identical structures if possible.

The next two examples demonstrate difficulties that arise from combining variables of different sizes and stuctures. Assume default data type declarations based on the first letter of the variable name.

EXAMPLE 1

```
REAL A,B
COMMON A(2,3),B(5),N
.
.
.
CALL SUB5(X)
.
.
.
END
SUBROUTINE SUB5(Y)
REAL X,A
INTEGER NN
COMMON X(10),A,NN
.
.
.
END
SUBROUTINE SUB6
REAL AA
COMMON AA(10)
.
.
.
END
```

This example shows how common memory is shared by the main program and subprograms. Table 9.1 shows the names by which the memory shared in common is known in each subprogram. Notice that the amount of storage set aside in common is whatever is specified by the *largest* number in any of the COMMON statements.

TABLE 9.1 *Names assigned to common storage positions*

Position	*Name in main program*	*Name in SUB5*	*Name in SUB6*
1	A(1,1)	X(1)	AA(1)
2	A(2,1)	X(2)	AA(2)
3	A(1,2)	X(3)	AA(3)
4	A(2,2)	X(4)	AA(4)
5	A(1,3)	X(5)	AA(5)
6	A(2,3)	X(6)	AA(6)
7	B(1)	X(7)	AA(7)
8	B(2)	X(8)	AA(8)
9	B(3)	X(9)	AA(9)
10	B(4)	X(10)	AA(10)
11	B(5)	A	
12	N	NN	

▪ *Although allowed, this method of using different names for common locations is not good programming practice.*

EXAMPLE 2 Here is another program in which COMMON statements, though correct, are not used wisely to achieve an understandable, well-structured program. Sequence numbers on the left are only for reference in the discussion.

```
      PROGRAM EXCOMM
      REAL A(5),B,C,D,X
      COMMON A,B(2,3),C(4),D
      READ*,A,D
      X = FUNC4(0)
      PRINT*,B,X
      CALL SUB7
      PRINT*,A,D
      PRINT*,B,C
      END
C***************************************************************************
C*                           FUNCTION SUBPROGRAM FUNC4                    *
C***************************************************************************
      REAL FUNCTION FUNC4(A)
      INTEGER A,I
      COMMON X(10),D
      I=1
 5    IF (I .GT. 5) GO TO 15
          X(11-I) = X(I)
          I=I+1
          GO TO 5
 15   D = X(9)*2.8
      FUNC4 = X(10)
      RETURN
      END
```

```
26 C***********************************************************************
27 C*                                     SUBROUTINE SUBPROGRAM SUB7                      *
28 C***********************************************************************
29       SUBROUTINE SUB7
30       REAL X,Y
31       COMMON X(3,4),Y(4)
32       X(3,3) = 15
33       X(3,4) = 20
34       I=1
35 10    IF (I .GT. 4) GO TO 20
36          Y(I) = I*I
37          I=I+1
38          GO TO 10
39 20    RETURN
40       END
```

TABLE 9.2 *Names assigned to common storage positions*

Position	*Name in main program*	*Name in FUNC4*	*Name in SUB7*
1	A(1)	X(1)	X(1,1)
2	A(2)	X(2)	X(2,1)
3	A(3)	X(3)	X(3,1)
4	A(4)	X(4)	X(1,2)
5	A(5)	X(5)	X(2,2)
6	B(1,1)	X(6)	X(3,2)
7	B(2,1)	X(7)	X(1,3)
8	B(1,2)	X(8)	X(2,3)
9	B(2,2)	X(9)	X(3,3)
10	B(1,3)	X(10)	X(1,4)
11	B(2,3)	D	X(2,4)
12	C(1)		X(3,4)
13	C(2)		Y(1)
14	C(3)		Y(2)
15	C(4)		Y(3)
16	D		Y(4)

This example clearly shows how the COMMON statement specifies memory locations in a main program and subprograms. Table 9.2 lists the variable names in common memory as interpreted by each module.

Line 4 causes the reading of 6 numbers. First read are the 5 numbers of variable A. Since variable A appears without subscripts in the READ statement, the entire array is read. The sixth number is stored in variable D.

Suppose that when this program is executed the input data provided are 10, 20, 30, 40, 50, 60. After the READ statement is executed, the first 5 words in the common area contain 10, 20, 30, 40, and 50. The sixth word D contains the value 60.

Line 5 calls subprogram FUNC4. Because of the COMMON statement in FUNC4, the values for X(1) through X(5) are 10, 20, 30, 40, and 50. A look at Table 9.2 will help you see why.

Lines 18–20 assign values to X(10) through X(6) that are equal to the values at X(1) through X(5).

Line 22 assigns to D the value equal to the product of X(9) and 2.8. Since X(9) is 20, the same value as X(2), D is 56.

Table 9.3 shows the contents of the computer words in the common area and their names in the main program after line 15 is executed. Note that up to this point, no values have been assigned to words 12–15 of the common area. Word 16 in the common area contains the value 60 from the input data above.

TABLE 9.3 *Names assigned to common storage positions after line 5 is executed*

Position	*Contents*	*Name in main program*	*Name in FUNC4*
1	10.	A(1)	X(1)
2	20.	A(2)	X(2)
3	30.	A(3)	X(3)
4	40.	A(4)	X(4)
5	50.	A(5)	X(5)
6	50.	B(1,1)	X(6)
7	40.	B(2,1)	X(7)
8	30.	B(1,2)	X(8)
9	20.	B(2,2)	X(9)
10	10.	B(1,3)	X(10)
11	56.	B(2,3)	D
12		C(1)	
13		C(2)	
14		C(3)	
15		C(4)	
16	60.	D	

At line 6, output occurs causing the printing of the entire array B and the single variable X. The value in variable X in the main program is FUNC4(0), which is assigned the value of X(10) in the subprogram and therefore equals 10. With no format specified, the output is 5 numbers per line:

```
50.0        40.0        30.0        20.0        10.0
56.0        10.0
```

Line 7 calls subprogram SUB7 into action, which sets X(3,3)=15 in SUB7, computer word 9, and X(3,4)=20 in SUB7, word 12.

Then Y(1) through Y(4) in SUB7 are assigned values equal to the squares of their subscripts. Table 9.4 shows the resulting contents of common memory.

TABLE 9.4 *Names assigned to common storage positions after SUB7 is executed*

Position	*Contents*	*Name in main program*	*Name in FUNC4*	*Name in SUB7*
1	10.	A(1)	X(1)	X(1,1)
2	20.	A(2)	X(2)	X(2,1)
3	30.	A(3)	X(3)	X(3,1)
4	40.	A(4)	X(4)	X(1,2)
5	50.	A(5)	X(5)	X(2,2)
6	50.	B(1,1)	X(6)	X(3,2)
7	40.	B(2,1)	X(7)	X(1,3)
8	30.	B(1,2)	X(8)	X(2,3)
9	20.	B(2,2)	X(9)	X(3,3)
10	10.	B(1,3)	X(10)	X(1,4)
11	56.	B(2,3)	D	X(2,4)
12	20.	C(1)		X(3,4)
13	1.	C(2)		Y(1)
14	4.	C(3)		Y(2)
15	9.	C(4)		Y(3)
16	16.	D		Y(4)

After executing subprogram SUB7, control returns to line 8 of the main program, which causes the printing of entire array A and the simple variable D:

```
10.0        20.0        30.0        40.0        50.0
16.0
```

Next, line 9 causes the output of entire arrays B and C, resulting in

```
50.0        40.0        30.0        15.0        10.0
56.0        20.0         1.0         4.0         9.0
```

Keeping track of names. Before we leave the COMMON statement, let us emphasize that any variables specified in common are available to all program modules in which the COMMON statement appears. However, the variable names associated with memory locations in common may be different in the main program and in each subprogram. The position of a variable in the COMMON list determines the name associated with it in each subprogram. This fact was clearly demonstrated in previous examples.

You probably noticed, however, how difficult it was to keep track of the contents of variables in the common area because COMMON statements were not identical in the main program and subprograms.

- *We strongly urge you to avoid programming like this.*

FORMAT specifications T, TL, and TR. In Chapter 6 we discuss the use of the FORMAT statement with the apostrophe, slash, parentheses, and format specifications I, F, X, A, and H. Earlier in this chapter we discuss the D format for double precision values and L format for logical variables. At this time we present information about format specifications T, TL, and TR.

In some input situations and many output situations it is helpful to be able to move quickly to the right or left before resuming printing or reading. This capability is similar to the tab on an ordinary typewriter, which gives these three format specifications their names. Think of the T specification as meaning *tab*, the TL specification as meaning *tab left*, and the TR specification as meaning *tab right*.

The form of these three specifications is similar:

```
TN     TLN     TRN
```

where N is an integer specifying the number of positions to be moved.

TN moves to position N. Susequent input or output begins in position N.

TLN moves N positions to the left of the current location.

TRN moves N positions to the right of the current location.

EXAMPLE

```
      PRINT 10
 10   FORMAT (T20,'ABC',TL1,'XYZ',T18,'RST',TR23,'OPQ')
```

T20 sets the output device to begin in position 20. The letters ABC are output in positions 20, 21, and 22.

TL1 moves to the left one position from the current position 23, setting the output device to begin in position 22. The letters XYZ are output in positions 22, 23, and 24. Note that this causes X to be printed on top of C.

T18 moves to position 18. The letters RST are output in positions 18, 19, and 20. This causes T to be printed over A.

TR3 moves three positions to the right. The letters OPQ are output in positions 24, 25, and 26. This causes O to be printed over Z.

Data File Processing

Previous discussions of data files introduced only the simple techniques needed to understand what was happening in particular examples. FORTRAN does in fact have sophisticated tools available to process data files. We discuss six of the most useful here.

ENDFILE. Causes the insertion in a file of an *end-of-file* or EOF symbol. The form of the statement is

```
ENDFILE U
```

where U is the logical unit number of the data file.

A single ENDFILE statement may be used to place an EOF symbol on more than one file. For example:

EXAMPLE

```
ENDFILE (U1,U2, . . . ,UN)
```

places an EOF symbol at the end of each of the files with logical unit numbers U1,U2, . . . ,UN. Notice that the list of numbers is in parentheses.

BACKSPACE. Moves the file pointer back one record, so the next reading from the designated file occurs from that earlier record. This allows a record that has already been read to be read again. Here is its form:

```
BACKSPACE U
```

where U is the logical unit number of the data file.

It is possible to backspace on multiple data files with a single BACKSPACE statement. Here is an example:

EXAMPLE

```
BACKSPACE (U1,U2, . . . ,UN)
```

backspaces one record on each of the files with logical unit numbers U1,U2, . . . ,UN. Parentheses are used with multiple unit numbers.

REWIND. Repositions the file pointer to the beginning of the first record in the file. This statement has two forms:

`REWIND U` *or* `REWIND (UNIT=U, ERR=N)`

where U is the logical unit number of the file to be processed, and N is the reference number of the next statement to be executed if an error occurs during the rewind process.

EXAMPLE 1

```
REWIND 4
```

causes the repositioning of the internal pointer to the beginning of the data file associated with logical unit 4.

EXAMPLE 2

```
REWIND (UNIT=4, ERR=50)
```

If an error occurs during rewinding, this statement also specifies that the program will next execute the line with reference number 50.

OPEN. Prepares a file for input or output. Before a data file can be processed, it must be logically connected, or *opened*, using this statement. The form of the OPEN statement is as follows:

```
OPEN (P1,P2, . . . ,P9)
```

where P1,P2, . . . ,P9 refer to the nine parameters below. The first item must be specified; the others are optional.

P1 `UNIT = U`

where U is the logical unit number of the file. This item must be specified first. The designation UNIT = may be omitted.

P2 `IOSAT = I`

where I is an integer variable set to zero by the system if the file is opened without error, and set to a system-dependent positive value if an error is encountered in opening the file.

P3 `FILE = 'Filename'`

where Filename must comply with the rules for naming FORTRAN variables.

P4 `ERR = N`

where N is the reference number of the next statement to be executed if an error occurs in processing the file.

P5 `STATUS = 'XXX'`

where XXX is OLD, NEW, SCRATCH, or UNKNOWN.

P6 `ACCESS = 'XXX'`

where XXX is SEQUENTIAL or DIRECT.

P7 `FORM = 'XXX'`

where XXX is FORMATTED if it is a file containing characters; or UNFORMATTED if it is a binary file.

P8 `RECL = L`

where L is record length.

P9 `BLANK = 'XXX'`

where XXX is NULL or ZERO.

Only the logical unit number of the file being opened and the file name are required, parameters P1 and P3. Every compiler has default values for all the other parameters, so you need not always specify them. But be sure to find out what the default values are for the other seven parameters; do not assume they will be what you expect.

EXAMPLE

```
OPEN (2, FILE='STUDNT', STATUS='OLD')
```

Notice that some parameters are omitted.

The first parameter is always the logical unit number; 2 in this example.

This statement causes a previously existing OLD file called STUDNT on logical unit 2 to be attached to a program and thus available for input or output.

CLOSE. Places an EOF symbol at the end of a file and disconnects the file from the program. The general form is

```
CLOSE (P1,P2,P3,P4)
```

where P1, P2, P3, and P4 are as follows:

P1 `UNIT = U`

where U is the logical unit number of the file. This item must be specified first. The designation UNIT = may be omitted.

P2 `IOSAT = I`

where I is an integer variable set to zero by the system if the file is opened without error, and set to a system-dependent positive value if an error is encountered in opening the file.

P3 `ERR = N`

where N is the reference number of the next statement to be executed if an error occurs in processing the file.

P4 `STATUS = 'XXX'`

where XXX is KEEP if this is an existing file that is to continue existing; or DELETE if this is an existing file that is to cease existing.

The default value is KEEP unless the file was a SCRATCH file previous to the execution of the CLOSE statement, in which case the default value is DELETE.

EXAMPLE 1 `CLOSE (2)`

causes an EOF symbol to be placed at the end of the data file currently identified as logical unit 2. Since no other parameters are specified, system default conditions apply.

EXAMPLE 2 `CLOSE (3, IOSTAT=I, STATUS='DELETE')`

places an EOF symbol at the end of the data file identified as logical unit 3.

Variable I will contain zero if the file was closed without error, otherwise it will contain a positive value.

After the CLOSE has been executed, the file no longer exists because of the DELETE parameter.

INQUIRE. Used to determine information about a data file. The form of the statement is

```
INQUIRE (P1,P2, . . . ,P16)
```

where P1,P2, . . . ,P16 are as follows:

P1 Logical unit number of file. ***This unit number may be replaced by a Filename.***

P2 `IOSTAT = V2`

where V2 is a variable to which the system assigns the value zero if no error occurred during the INQUIRE, and assigns a positive value if an error occurred.
If no error occurred but an EOF condition was encountered, V2 is assigned a negative value.

P3 `ERR = N`

where N is the reference number of the next statement to be executed if an error occurs during the INQUIRE.

P4 `EXIST = V4`

where V4 is a logical variable, TRUE if the file exists, FALSE if it does not exist.

P5 `OPENED = V5`

where V5 is a logical variable, TRUE if the file is currently connected to an input/output unit, FALSE if it is not.

P6 `NUMBER = V6`

where V6 is an integer variable to which the system assigns the logical unit number of the input/output unit to which the file is connected. If no unit us currently connected to the file, V6 is undefined.

P7 `NAMED = V7`

where V7 is a logical variable, TRUE if the file has a name, FALSE if it has not been assigned a name.

P8 `NAME = V8`

where V8 is a character variable to which the system assigns the file name, if any. If the file has no name, V8 remains undefined.

P9 `ACCESS = V9`

where V9 is a character variable, value SEQUENTIAL if the file is connected for sequential access, DIRECT if the file is connected for direct access. If the file is not currently connected, V9 is undefined.

P10 `DIRECT = V10`

where V10 is a character variable, YES if the file is a direct file, NO if it is not, and UNKNOWN if the system cannot determine.

P11 `FORM = V11`

where V11 is a character variable, FORMATTED if the file is a text file, UNFORMATTED if the file is a binary file. If the file is not connected, V11 remains undefined.

P12 `FORMATTED = V12`

where V12 is a character variable, YES if the file is a formatted (text) file, NO if not, and UNKNOWN if the system cannot determine.

P13 `UNFORMATTED = V13`

where V13 is a character variable, YES if the file is an unformatted (binary) file, NO if not, and UNKNOWN if the system cannot determine.

P14 `RECL = V14`

where V14 is an integer variable to which the system assigns the value of the record length if the file is connected for direct access. If the file is not connected or if the connection is not for direct access, V14 remains undefined.

P15 `NEXTREC = V15`

where V15 is an integer variable to which the system assigns the record number of the next record to be read or written. If the file is not connected for direct access or if the record position cannot be determined because of a previous error condition, V15 remains undefined.

P16 `BLANK = V16`

where V16 is a character variable, NULL if null blank control is in effect, ZERO if zero blank control is in effect and the file is connected for formatted input/output. Otherwise, V16 remains undefined.

EXAMPLE 1

```
INQUIRE (UNIT=5, FORM=F, RECL=L)
```

The file associated with logical unit 5 is examined. The variable F is assigned FORMATTED, UNFORMATTED, or UNKNOWN and the variable L the value of the record length in the file.

EXAMPLE 2

```
INQUIRE (2, NAME=N)
```

The file associated with logical unit 2 is examined and variable N assigned the file name, if there is one.

EXAMPLE 3

```
INQUIRE ('EXAMPL', OPENED=S, NUMBER=M)
```

The file named EXAMPL is examined. If it has been opened, variable S is assigned TRUE; otherwise, S is FALSE. Variable M is assigned the logical unit number to which the file is currently connected if it is connected; otherwise M is undefined.

Additional Features

The following special features of full FORTRAN 77 ease certain tasks. Since most of these features are not available in many FORTRAN compilers, be sure to determine the capabilities of your compiler before using them. Full FORTRAN 77 makes available not only the features we are about to consider but also all of those previously mentioned in this book.

System Library Functions for String Processing

Several library functions are available to help in processing character strings. Some of these have been presented in the text in a cursory manner. We discuss the four most frequently used in detail here.

LEN. Determines the number of characters in a character variable or constant. When the argument of LEN is a character variable, the value returned by LEN is always the declared length of the variable.

EXAMPLE

```
L=LEN('JOHN A. PETERSON')
```

results in the integer 16 being stored in L.

INDEX. The integer value of this function is the position in a character string where the first character of a given substring is found. The first argument specifies the string, the second the substring.

EXAMPLE

```
C1='ABCXRSCXRNCX'
C2='CXR'
N=INDEX(C1,C2)
```

results in the integer 3 being stored in variable N because the C of CXR is in position 3 of character string C1.

CHAR. Identifies the character associated with a given integer in a coding sequence. The argument of CHAR may be an integer constant, a variable, or an arithmetic expression.

EXAMPLE 1 For example, assume a coding sequence of 01–26 for the letters of the alphabet, with A as 01 and so on. If the integer 11 is the argument to the function CHAR, the function value is K, letter number 11.

EXAMPLE 2 Here's another example based on that coding sequence:

```
I=4
J=7
C=CHAR(I+J)
PRINT*,C
```

outputs the letter K, the character whose specified code is 11, the sum of 4 and 7.

ICHAR. This function is the inverse of function CHAR. Its argument is a character variable or constant of length 1 and its value is an integer equal to the coding sequence of the character specified by the argument.

EXAMPLE

```
I=ICHAR('G')
PRINT*,I
```

Assume the coding sequence for letters of the alphabet as for CHAR. The code for G is 07, so the output is 7, output without the leading zero.

System Library Functions for Making String Comparisons

Four library functions are available that make it possible to compare character strings *lexically*. To compare lexically is to compare the *internal code* for two character strings according to the given operator and set the library function, which is a logical function, to TRUE or FALSE.

Each function has two arguments that specify the character strings being compared. The first character string is compared to the second, and the value of the function is determined by whether the comparison is correct as stated or not. Remember that the first string is always compared to the second string, never the reverse.

LGT. *Lexically greater than*, with the form

```
LGT(ARG1,ARG2)
```

The value is TRUE if the internal code for the contents of ARG1 is greater than the internal code for the contents of ARG2; otherwise the value is FALSE.

LGE. *Lexically greater than or equal to*, with the form

```
LGE(ARG1,ARG2)
```

The value is TRUE if the internal code for the contents of ARG1 is greater than or equal to the internal code for the contents of ARG2; otherwise the value is FALSE.

LLT. *Lexically less than*, with the form

```
LLT(ARG1,ARG2)
```

The value is TRUE if the internal code for the contents of ARG1 is less than the internal code for the contents of ARG2; otherwise the value is FALSE.

LLE. *Lexically less than or equal to*, with the form

```
LLE(ARG1,ARG2)
```

The value is TRUE if the internal code for the contents of ARG1 is less than or equal to the internal code for the contents of ARG2; otherwise the value is FALSE.

EXAMPLE

Assume that the coding sequence, or *collating sequence*, for the letters of the alphabet is A=1, B=2, . . . , Z=26 and blank=0. Then consider this program segment:

```
STATE1='MINNESOTA'
STATE2='TEXAS'
IF (LLE(STATE1,STATE2)) GO TO 200
```

The internal code for MINNESOTA is 13091414051915200l, clearly more than TEXAS at 2005240119—except that LLE fills TEXAS with blank spaces on the right to make strings of equal length. MINNESOTA thus comes in less, the condition is TRUE, and the program goes to 200.

■ *Numeric blank codes are inserted in the numeric code for the shorter string before the specified comparison takes place.*

The PARAMETER Statement

Sometimes it is useful to be able to name a constant with a symbolic name—*pi*, for example—but have the constant itself operative in the program. FORTRAN 77 accomplishes this using the PARAMETER statement:

```
PARAMETER (NAME1=EXP1,NAME2=EXP2, . . . ,NAMEN=EXPN)
```

where NAME1, NAME2, and so on are acceptable FORTRAN symbolic names, and
EXP1, EXP2, and so on are constants or arithmetic expressions containing only constants.
The type of each symbolic name must correspond to the type of the related constant expression.

EXAMPLE

```
PARAMETER (PI=3.14159, WHRATE=12.7, HEAD='REPORT A')
REAL PI, WHRATE
CHARACTER HEAD*8
```

In any subsequent program statement, whenever the symbol PI is used, the value 3.14159 replaces it. Similarly for WHRATE and 12.7, and HEAD and the character string REPORT A.

■ *When a symbolic name appears in a PARAMETER statement its value may not be modified anywhere in the program.*

Multiple Entries and Returns

We have been assuming that, when a CALL statement is executed, the subroutine called is entered at the first executable statement. Similarly, program control is assumed to return to the calling program at the first executable statement after the CALL statement. This is both the most common and most easily understood form of calling a subprogram and returning to the main program.

However, FORTRAN does allow for alternate entry points into subroutines and alternate return points to the main program. Multiple entry is accomplished through the use of the ENTRY statement, and multiple return points are enabled through the use of the RETURN EXP statement.

RETURN EXP. Causes a return to the calling program at various points depending on the value of EXP. Here is the form:

```
RETURN EXP
```

where EXP is an integer constant or expression referring to the position of a reference number in the associated CALL statement.

When this form of the RETURN statement is used, the CALL statement must contain in the parentheses following the subroutine name as many statement reference numbers as there are RETURN values. Each statement reference number is preceded by an asterisk to distinguish it from an argument.

The value of EXP is not a reference number; it simply refers to the position of the appropriate reference number in the CALL statement. The actual return is to that referenced statement.

EXAMPLE

```
      .
      CALL SUB(N,*100,*150,*200)
      .
100   READ*,A
      .
150   READ*,B
      .
200   READ*,C
      .
      END
      SUBROUTINE SUB(I,*,*,*)
      .
      IF(I.EQ.1)RETURN 1
      .
      IF(I.EQ.2)RETURN 2
      .
      RETURN 3
      .
      END
```

The CALL statement contains 3 reference numbers preceded by asterisks. In the subroutine, argument I provides a means to select from the 3 returns. If I=1, then RETURN 1 is selected and the program returns to line 100. If I=2, return is to statement 150. If I=3, return is to statement 200.

It is not difficult to conceive of situations where this multiple return feature is useful. Here, a completely different variable is input at each of the returns. Similarly, different actions can follow each of the READ statements.

This feature makes it possible to write a program with considerable flexibility while using only one subroutine, although the cost is a program that is less structured, and therefore less understandable.

ENTRY. Enables entry to a subprogram at more than one point. The additional entry points are somewhat restricted: They may not be in the range of a DO loop nor in the range of an IF-THEN-ELSE structure. The general form of this statement follows:

ENTRY NAME (Arguments)

where NAME is the name used to call the subroutine at the alternate point, and
Arguments are any subroutine arguments.

▪ *This feature makes a program very unstructured and the logic difficult to understand. Consequently, we advise against its use.*

EXAMPLE This example illustrates the unstructured nature of a program that uses the multiple entry feature.

```
1         PROGRAM MAIN                          Main program
2         REAL A,X
3         READ*, A
4         CALL SUB(A,*10,*20)
5         A = FUNC(A)
6         GOTO 15
7    10   CALL SUB1(A)
8    15   PRINT*,A
9         STOP
10   20   X = FUNC1(A)
11        PRINT*,X
12        END
13        SUBROUTINE SUB(X,*,*)                 Subroutine SUB
14        X = X*X
15        IF (X .LE. 100) RETURN 1
16        IF (X .GT. 900) RETURN 2
17        ENTRY SUB1(X)
18        X = 3*X
19        RETURN
20        END
21        REAL FUNCTION FUNC(A)                 Function FUNC
22        FUNC = SQRT(A)
23        RETURN
24        ENTRY FUNC1(A)
25        A = SQRT(A)
26        FUNC1 = SQRT(A)
27        RETURN
28        END
```

Run this program with the input data below and determine whether or not the program produces the output shown.

INPUT `10 40 100 -34 0 7 30`

OUT PUT `300 6.32456 10 5.83095 0 147 51.9615`

ANALYSIS The main program is lines 1–12, subroutine SUB is lines 13–20 and function FUNC is lines 21–28.

At line 3 a value is input to A.

Subroutine SUB is entered at line 13 and the value of A, brought into the subroutine as argument X, is squared.

At lines 15 and 16 the squared value is compared with 100, and possibly, depending on its value, with 900. ***If the square of A is less than 100***, return to the main program takes place at reference number 10 (line 7). There subroutine SUB is called again, this time under its new entry name SUB1, and entered at line 17. When line 18 is executed, the value brought into subroutine SUB by the argument X is multiplied by 3 and control returns to the main program at line 8. There the current value of A, now three times the value read in, is output and execution stops.

If at line 15 the square of A, carried into the subroutine as argument X, is ***greater than 100***, then line 16 is executed. The square of A is compared with 900; if it is greater, return to the main program occurs at line 10, statement number 20. At line 10 the function FUNC is called by its alternate entry name of FUNC1 and entry occurs at the alternate entry point, line 24. At line 25 the square root of A is computed, actually A-*squared* because of the action at line 14. Line 26 has a second square root computation. Therefore, when return to the main program occurs at line 11 the value that is output will be the square root of the original value of A input at line 3.

If at line 15 the square of A, brought into the subroutine as argument X, is ***not greater than 900***, lines 17 and 18 are executed and the square of A (argument X) is multiplied by 3. This is followed by a return to the main program at line 5. There, function FUNC is called and argument A, actually now 3 times the square of A originally input, is processed by the square root library function at line 22. Return to the main program is at line 6, which transfers control to line 8, statement number 15, where output takes place and execution stops. The value output at line 8 this time is the square root of 3 times the square of the original value input for A.

Computed GO TO. Next we discuss two ***outmoded*** GO TO statements available in FORTRAN, the computed GO TO and the assigned GO TO. Both of these should be avoided because they contribute to poorly structured programs. We include them only because they appear in some old FORTRAN programs.

The general form of the computed GO TO is

```
GO TO (N1,N2, . . . ,NK),INDEX
```

where N1,N2, . . . ,NK are positive integers that are reference numbers of statements in the program, and
INDEX is a positive integer variable or arithmetic expression not less than 1 nor greater than K. The comma before INDEX is optional in FORTRAN 77 but required by some other FORTRAN compilers.

INDEX specifies one of the reference numbers N1,N2, . . . ,NK by indicating its position in the list. The statement with this reference number is then next to be executed. The usefulness of this structure comes when INDEX is an arithmetic expression. In this case, the GO TO occurs after the indicated computation, and thus the reference number of the line to be executed next depends on the computation of INDEX. This is the origin of the name *computed* GO TO.

Problem 9.2 Updating Stored Files

SITUATION We need a program to retrieve and update eight different data files stored on magnetic disk. These files contain information related to six categories of machinist plus one each for office and maintenance staff. Eight subprograms are already written, one to process the data for each of the files. Assume the following codes:

Category	*Code*	*Category*	*Code*
Apprentice	1	Inspector	5
Journeyman	2	Manager	6
Master	3	Office staff	7
Supervisor	4	Maintenance staff	8

OBJECTIVE Write a program to read a code and from its value select the appropriate subprogram. Assume that if the code is 9 we are to stop.

FORTRAN PROGRAM

```
      PROGRAM MAIN
      INTEGER CODE
10    READ*, CODE
      IF (CODE .EQ. 1) GOTO 100
      IF (CODE .EQ. 2) GOTO 200
      IF (CODE .EQ. 3) GOTO 300
      IF (CODE .EQ. 4) GOTO 400
      IF (CODE .EQ. 5) GOTO 500
      IF (CODE .EQ. 6) GOTO 600
      IF (CODE .EQ. 7) GOTO 700
      IF (CODE .EQ. 8) GOTO 800
      IF (CODE .EQ. 9) GOTO 900
      PRINT*, 'ERROR IN CODE ',CODE
      GOTO 10
100   OPEN (1,FILE='APPR',STATUS='OLD')
      REWIND 1
      CALL SUB1
      GOTO 10
200   OPEN (2,FILE='JOUR',STATUS='OLD')
      REWIND 2
      CALL SUB 2
      GOTO 10
```

```
300  OPEN (3,FILE='MAST',STATUS='OLD')
     REWIND 3
     CALL SUB3
     GOTO 10
400  OPEN (4,FILE='SUPR',STATUS='OLD')
     REWIND 4
     CALL SUB4
     GOTO 10
500  OPEN (5,FILE='INSP',STATUS='OLD')
     REWIND 5
     CALL SUB5
     GOTO 10
600  OPEN (6,FILE='MNGR',STATUS='OLD')
     REWIND 6
     CALL SUB6
     GOTO 10
700  OPEN (7,FILE='OFFC',STATUS='OLD')
     REWIND 7
     CALL SUB7
     GOTO 10
800  OPEN (8,FILE='MNTC',STATUS='OLD')
     REWIND 8
     CALL SUB8
     GOTO 10
900  STOP
     END
```

Subprograms SUB1, SUB2, . . . , SUB8 update the eight data files.

REVISION In order to simplify the program through the use of a computed GO TO statement, replace the first 12 lines of code with these 4 lines:

```
     PROGAM MAIN
     INTEGER CODE
10   READ*, CODE
     GOTO (100, 200, 300, 400, 500, 600, 700, 800, 900) CODE
```

By making this exchange of 4 lines for 12 lines, and leaving the rest of the program unchanged, everything is accomplished as described earlier.

An integer value is input to variable CODE at line 10. Then if CODE=1, the computed GO TO statement causes program control to transfer to line 100. If CODE=2, program control goes to line 200, and so on, for values of CODE up to and including 9.

It is important that CODE not have values outside of the range of integers 1–9 since there are exactly 9 reference numbers listed inside the parentheses of the computed GO TO. If CODE contains a value outside that range, the compiler disregards the computed GO TO statement and control is transferred as if it were a CONTINUE statement.

Not only is the number of program statements reduced by using the computed GO TO, but the resulting program is easier to follow.

Assigned GO TO. Another transfer statement available in FORTRAN providing for a branching situation is the *assigned* GO TO. It gets its name from the fact that its key variable is *assigned* a value using a special ASSIGN statement. There are two forms of the assigned GO TO:

FORM A

```
GO TO NVAR
```

where NVAR is an integer variable previously assigned a value through the ASSIGN statement. The assigned value is a statement reference number; program control transfers to the statement with that reference number.

FORM B

```
GO TO NVAR, (N1,N2,N3, . . . ,NK)
```

where NVAR is assigned a value equal to one of the integer constants N1,N2,N3, . . . ,NK. Program control then transfers to the statement with that reference number.

Here are two program segments using these two forms of the computed GO TO:

EXAMPLE 1

```
ASSIGN 50 TO N
GO TO N
```

In this program segment, N is assigned the value 50, a reference number in the program. When GO TO N is executed, program control transfers to the statement with reference number 50.

EXAMPLE 2

```
       ASSIGN 30 TO IN
       CO TO IN, (10,20,30,40,50)
 10    READ 30,X
 30    FORMAT(A2)
       GO TO 50
 20    READ 100,X
 100   FORMAT(A6)
       GO TO 50
 40    READ*,X
 50    PRINT*,X
```

This example has an error: Statement 30 is a nonexecutable FORMAT statement. It is not possible to transfer control to a nonexecutable statement. This error can be corrected by replacing 30 with the reference number of any executable statement.

The ASSIGN statement may also be used to assign a FORMAT statement number in an input or output statement. This makes it possible to select one FORMAT statement from among several that appear in the program.

EXAMPLE 3 Suppose, for example, that there are 4 FORMAT statements in a program, with reference numbers 60, 70, 80, and 90. The following statements provide the output specified in the FORMAT with reference number 80:

```
ASSIGN 80 TO FRMAT
WRITE (6,FRMAT) NAME,RATE,WAGE
```

Statement Order

The order of executable statements clearly follows the logic of the algorithm designed to solve the problem. The order of nonexecutable statements is dependent on the FORTRAN compiler; for FORTRAN 77 this order is valid for the main program and for all subprograms:

1. PROGRAM, FUNCTION, or SUBROUTINE statement.

   The PROGRAM statement for the main program is optional in FORTRAN 77, though some compilers require it in order to specify input/output devices.
2. PARAMETER statement(s).
3. IMPLICIT statement(s).
4. INTEGER, REAL, COMPLEX, DOUBLE PRECISION, LOGICAL, or CHARACTER statements.
5. DIMENSION, COMMON, or EQUIVALENCE statements.
6. DATA statement(s).
7. Any function statement ***definitions***.
8. ***Executable statements*** in logical order.
9. END statement.

Further Reading

Some features of FORTRAN 77 are omitted from this book. These are all rather sophisticated capabilities most often used by professional programmers with extensive experience in FORTRAN programming. For the reader interested in a complete statement of the features of FORTRAN 77, refer to the publication of the American National Standards Institute (ANSI), *American National Standard Programming Language FORTRAN*, available as publication ANSI X3.9-1978 from ANSI, 1430 Broadway, New York, NY 10018.

Summary

In this chapter we have presented some advanced features that will make FORTRAN 77 an even more powerful programming language for you. Because this chapter already discusses topics in condensed form, our summary simply shows general forms of the statements and programming concepts presented.

We discussed five ***type declaration statements***.

DOUBLE PRECISION V1,V2, . . . ,VN

where V1,V2, . . . ,VN represent variable names or function names.

COMPLEX V1,V2, . . . ,VN

where V1,V2, . . . ,VN represent variable names or function names.

LOGICAL V1,V2, . . . ,VN

where V1,V2, . . . ,VN represent variable names or function names.

EQUIVALENCE (V1,V2, . . . ,VN)

where V1,V2, . . . ,VN represent simple or array variable names.

This conserves memory by allowing a single memory location to be identified by two or more names.

COMMON /NAME/ V1,V2, . . . ,VN

where NAME is the block name and must comply with the usual rules for naming variables, and
V1,V2, . . . ,VN represent variables.

This labelled COMMON statement makes blocks of memory available to two or more program modules.

Three additional ***format specifications*** were presented: T, TL, and TR. All position the output device and are similar to tabs on a typewriter.

We discussed six ***data file processing statements***:

ENDFILE U

where U is the logical unit number of the file on which the end of file mark is to be placed.

BACKSPACE U

where U is the logical unit number of the file to be backspaced one record.

REWIND U *or* **REWIND (UNIT=U, ERR=N)**

where U is the logical unit number of the file to be repositioned at its beginning record, and

N is the reference number of the next statement to be executed if an error occurs during the rewind process.

```
OPEN (P1,P2, . . . ,P9)
```

where P1,P2, . . . ,P9 are the parameters listed in the text.

```
CLOSE (P1,P2,P3,P4)
```

where P1, P2, P3, and P4 are the parameters listed in the text.

```
INQUIRE (P1,P2, . . . ,P16)
```

where P1,P2, . . . ,P16 are the parameters listed in the text.

Some system functions related to the processing of ***character strings*** were discussed. These include the following:

Finding the number of characters in a string using LEN.

Locating the position of occurrence of one character string within a second one using INDEX.

Identifying the character associated with a given code number using CHAR.

Identifying the numeric code for a specified character using ICHAR.

We also discussed system ***functions LGT, LGE, LLT,*** and ***LLE*** for comparing the numeric codes of two characters.

We introduced the ***PARAMETER statement*** to refer to a constant by its symbolic name:

```
PARAMETER (NAME1=EXP1, NAME2=EXP2, . . . ,NAMEN=EXPN)
```

where NAME1, NAME2, . . ., NAMEN are acceptable FORTRAN names and EXP1, EXP2, . . . , EXPN are constants or expressions involving only constants.

The ENTRY and RETURN statements provide more than one entry point to a subprogram or function or more than one return point to the main program.

```
ENTRY NAME (ARG1,ARG2, . . . ,ARGN)
```

where NAME represents the name to be used for calling the subroutine, and
ARG1,ARG2, . . . ,ARGN represent the usual subprogram arguments.

```
RETURN EXP
```

where EXP represents any integer constant or integer arithmetic expression and is used to identify the position in the CALL statement of the reference number to which return is to occur.
In the CALL statement, reference numbers are preceded by asterisks.

End of Chapter Exercises

1. Determine which of the following statements are true and which are false.

a. When using subprograms it is essential that COMMON statements be used so that all program units needing access to the same data will be able to have that access.

b. It is not permissible to use both the DATA statement and COMMON statements in the same program.

c. A variable appearing in a blank COMMON statement cannot be initialized by a DATA statement.

d. Labelled common blocks having the same name must be of the same size.

e. The size of a common block may be legitimately changed by an EQUIVALENCE statement.

f. The IMPLICIT statement will not change the type of a variable whose type is specified by another statement.

g. In order to use a labelled common block in a subprogram it must first have been defined in the main program.

h. There must be no more than one blank common block in a program.

i. To define a blank common block, you simply omit the block name in the COMMON statement.

j. The PARAMETER statement makes it possible to pass information between subprograms and main program.

k. Before you can use any variable in a PARAMETER statement you must assign a value to it.

l. If there is a PARAMETER statement in a program it must precede any DIMENSION statements.

m. An IMPLICIT INTEGER statement cannot be used in the same program as an INTEGER statement.

n. No more than one PARAMETER statement may appear in a program.

o. Variables included in a labelled common block must not be passed as arguments in a subprogram.

p. There is no means of providing for more than one entry point to a subprogram.

q. When a subprogram has been called and has completed its tasks, control always returns to the statement in the calling program immediately following the CALL statement.

r. Variables specified in COMPLEX statements must also be defined as REAL or INTEGER.

s. The statement X=(2, 5, 3, 0) is valid only when X has been specified as a double precision variable.

t. All variables in any given arithmetic expression must be of the same type or else the compiler will say there is an error.

u. If an arithmetic expression includes one complex variable then all variables in that expression must be complex.

v. If an arithmetic expression includes one double precision variable then all variables in that expression must be either double precision or complex.

w. The ENTRY statement makes it possible to enter a subprogram at some point other than the beginning.

x. A statement of the form RETURN N appearing in a subprogram will cause control to return to the statement in the calling program whose reference number is the current value stored in N.

y. The REWIND statement is used to position the internal input/output pointer to the beginning of a data file.

z. The BACKSPACE statement makes it possible to read a record from a data file more than once.

2. Check the following statements or program segments for possible errors in syntax. If a statement is incorrect, make changes in it so it becomes valid.

a. `SUBPROGRAM SUM(X,Y)`

b. `ENTRY X,Y`

c. `ENTRY X(Y)`

d. `FUNCTION F(X)=X*X+1`

e. `SUBROUTINE SUB(X,*,*)`

f. `PARAMETER P1,P2`

g. `ENTRY X(Y,*,*)`

h. `RETURN 2`

i. `CALL SUB(X,10,20)`

j.
```
      COMMON A,B
      DATA A,B/2*0/
```

k.
```
      DIMENSION A(10)
      COMMON /A/B(10)
```

l.
```
      SUBROUTINE SUB
      .
      .
      .
      ENTRY
      .
      .
      .
```

m.
```
      COMMON A(10),B(20)
      EQUIVALENCE (A(1),B(10))
```

n.
```
      COMPLEX X
      READ 10,X,A
 10   FORMAT(F10.2,A6)
```

o.
```
      DOUBLE PRECISION X,Y
      READ*, X,Y
      Z=X+Y
```

p.
```
      DIMENSION Z(10),A(10)
      COMPLEX Z
      READ 10,Z,A
 10   FORMAT(10(F10.2,A1))
```

q.
```
      CALL SUB(X,10)
      SUBROUTINE SUB(Y,*)
      .
      .
      .
      RETURN 10
      .
      .
      .
```

r.
```
      CALL SUB1(X)
      .
      .
      .
      SUBROUTINE SUB(X,Y)
      .
      .
      .
      ENTRY SUB1(Z)
      .
      .
      .
```

3. Describe the output of each of the following programs. Assume the programs are correct and will run without error and assume default data types where necessary.

a.
```
      PROGRAM ONE
      IMPLICIT INTEGER (A-Y)
      READ*,VAR1,VAR2
      Z=(VAR1+VAR2)/2.0
      PRINT VAR1,VAR2,Z
      END
```

Assume input data of 2 and 7.

b.
```
      PROGRAM TWO
      COMMON /A/ B(10)
      DO 10 I=1,10
 10   B(I)=I*I
      CALL SUB
      PRINT*,B
      CALL SUB1
      PRINT*,B
      END
```

```
      SUBROUTINE SUB
      IMPLICIT INTEGER (A-Z)
      COMMON /A/ X(5),Y(5)
      DO 10 I=1,5
 10   X(I)=Y(I)/X(I)
      ENTRY SUB1
      DO 20 I=1,5
 20   Y(I)=Y(I)/X(I)
      RETURN
      END
```

c.

```
      PROGRAM SORTIT
      LOGICAL FLAG
      COMMON A(100)
      FLAG = .TRUE.
      READ*,N
      IF (N .LE. 0 .OR. N .GT. 100) THEN
          PRINT*,'ERROR IN NUMBER OF NUMBERS.'
          FLAG = .FALSE.
      ELSE
          READ*, (A(I),I=1,N)
      ENDIF
      CALL SORT(FLAG,*30,*20)
 20   PRINT*, (A(I),I=1,N)
 30   STOP
      END
      SUBROUTINE SORT(F,*,*)
      LOGICAL F
      COMMON A(100)
      IF (.NOT. F) RETURN 1
      DO 10 I=1,N-1
          K=I
          DO 20 J=I+1,N
              IF (A(K) .GT. A(J)) K = J
 20       CONTINUE
          T=A(I)
          A(I)=A(K)
          A(K)=T
 10   CONTINUE
      RETURN 2
      END
```

Assume the following input data in the order given:

```
8, 3, 5, 10, 2, 12, 9, 6, 5
```

d.

```
      PROGRAM MAT
      INTEGER MATR(20,20)
      COMMON /ONE/ MATR
      DO 20 I=1,20
      CALL ROW(I)
 20   CONTINUE
      PRINT 30,MATR
 30   FORMAT(20A2/)
      END
```

```
      SUBROUTINE ROW(N)
      COMMON /ONE/ MATR(20,20)
      DO 10 J=1,20
 10   MATR(N,J)=N
      RETURN
      END
```

e.

```
      COMPLEX X,Y,Z
      X=(2.5,3)
      Y=X+X
      Z=X+Y
      X=X-Y
      Y=X+Y
      PRINT 10,X,Y,Z
 10   FORMAT (2F10.2)
      D=CABS(X+Y)
      PRINT*,D
      END
```

You may want to refer to the appendix to check the results of library function CABS.

f.

```
      LOGICAL A,B,C
      A = .TRUE.
      B = .FALSE.
      C = .NOT. B
      B = A .OR. B .AND. C
      A = .NOT. (A .OR. B) .AND. (B .OR. .NOT. C)
      C = (A .OR. B .AND. C) .OR. (A .AND. B .OR. C)
      PRINT 10,A,B,C
 10   FORMAT(3L2)
      END
```

4. Identify any syntax errors in the following programs.

a.

```
      PROGRAM MAIN
      ENTRY SUB1
      READ*, A
      CALL SUB(A)
      IF (A .LE. 0) CALL SUB1
      PRINT*, A
      END
      SUBROUTINE SUB(B)
      IF (B .GT. 30 .OR. B .LE. 0) B=0
      IF (B .EQ. 0) RETURN
      DO 10 I=1,100
          B=B/2
          IF (B .GT. 1) GO TO 10
          B=I
          RETURN
 10   CONTINUE
      PRINT*, 'BAD INPUT'
      STOP
      END
```

b.

```
      PROGRAM MAIN
      COMMON /A/ B(3),AB(5)
      DATA B,AB/3*1.,5*2./
      CALL SUB
      PRINT*,B,AB
      END
      SUBROUTINE SUB
      COMMON /A/ X(5),Y(3),Z
      REAL B(5)
      EQUIVALENCE (Y(1),B(1))
      DATA B/2.,1.,2.5,3.5,6.1/
      DO 10 I=1,5
 10   X(I)=B(6-I)
      RETURN
      END
```

c.

```
      PROGRAM MAIN
      X=FUNC1(1)
      Y=FUNC2(1)
      PRINT*,X,Y
      END
      FUNCTION FUNC(X)
      INTEGER X
      ENTRY FUNC1(I)
      FUNC1 = X*I
      RETURN
      ENTRY FUNC2(I)
      FUNC2 = I*I
      RETURN
      END
```

d.

```
      PROGRAM MAIN
      COMPLEX X,Y,Z
      COMMON /A/ X,Y
      READ 10,X,Y
 10   FORMAT(2F10.2)
      CALL SUB
      PRINT 10,X,Y
      Z=FUNC(X,Y)
      PRINT 10,Z
      END
      SUBROUTINE SUB
      COMMON /A/ VAR1,VAR2
      DOUBLE PRECISION VAR1,VAR2
      VAR1=VAR1+VAR2
      VAR2=VAR1-VAR2
      RETURN
      END
      FUNCTION FUNC(X,Y)
      COMPLEX FUNC
      FUNC=CONJ(X+Y)
      RETURN
      END
```

You may want to refer to the appendix to check the purpose of library function CONJ.

■ *For exercises in programming, we suggest that you select exercises from earlier chapters and try to write better programs by using some of the additional* FORTRAN *features described in this chapter.*

Appendix A
Number Systems and Internal Representation of Data

In order to better understand techniques employed by computer designers in the electronic representation of information, we begin by presenting some basic facts about number systems and then discuss the details of representing data inside the computer memory.

Number systems.

Decimal numbers. Consider the decimal number 235. The number 10 is the *base* of the *decimal* number system, and the digits used are the familiar 0, 1, 2, 3, 4, 5, 6, 7, 8, and 9. Using the mathematical definition $b^0 = 1$ for any real number b, we know that

$$235 = 2 \times 100 + 3 \times 10 + 5 \times 1 = 2 \times 10^2 + 3 \times 10^1 + 5 \times 10^0$$

The righthand side of the equation is called the *polynomial form* of the number 235.

Though the digit 2 is the smallest digit in the previous example, 2 represents the greatest portion of 235 because of its position in the number. The position value of a digit is called its *rank*, so

2 has rank 10^2
3 has rank 10^1
5 has rank 10^0

In general, the rank of a decimal number n positions to the left of the decimal point is $10^{(n-1)}$.

For a number with fractional parts, for example 235.718, the rank of 7 is 1/10; of 1, 1/100; and of 8, 1/1000. We can also say that the rank of 7 is $(1/10)^1$, of 1 is $(1/10)^2$, and of 8 is $(1/10)^3$. Note that each move to the right results in a decrease in rank by a factor of 1/10.

We summarize our review of decimal numbers as follows:

1. The base of the decimal number system is the number 10.
2. The rank of a digit in a decimal number is a power of either 10 or 1/10.
3. The rank increases by a power of 10 for each position moved to the left of the decimal point.

4. The rank decreases by a power of 1/10 for each position moved to the right of the decimal point.

Binary numbers. The theory of number systems makes it possible to design number systems with any base. Since the decimal system is the most common, we assume the base is 10 unless noted. As far as possible, we use the decimal digit symbols to represent the digits in other number systems. For example, the *binary* number system uses the digit symbols 0 and 1 and has as its base the decimal number 2. Consider the number 1011.101 from the binary system:

$$1011.101 = 1 \times 2^3 + 0 \times 2^2 + 1 \times 2^1 + 1 \times 2^0 + 1 \times (1/2)^1 + 0 \times (1/2)^2 + 1 \times (1/2)^3$$

From the righthand side of this equation, you see that the rank of digits in the binary system can be powers of either 2 or 1/2.

The binary system summary is similar to that of the decimal system:

1. The base of the binary number system is the decimal number 2.
2. The rank of a digit in a binary number is a power of either 2 or 1/2.
3. The rank increases by a power of 2 for each position moved to the left of the binary point.
4. The rank decreases by a power of 1/2 for each position moved to he right of the binary point.

Octal numbers. Two more number systems are important to computer science, the *octal* system and the *hexadecimal* system. The octal number system has as its base the decimal number 8. The digits in this system are 0, 1, 2, 3, 4, 5, 6, and 7. As an example of an octal number take 156.24. We write

$$156.24 = 1 \times 8^2 + 5 \times 8^1 + 6 \times 8^0 + 2 \times (1/8)^1 + 4 \times (1/8)^2$$

The octal system summary is again similar to that of the decimal system:

1. The base of the octal number system is the decimal number 8.
2. The rank of a digit in an octal number are powers of either 8 or 1/8.
3. The rank increases by a power of 8 for each position moved to the left of the octal point.
4. The rank decreases by a power of 1/8 for each position moved to the right of the octal point.

Hexadecimal numbers. The hexadecimal number system, also referred to as the *hex* system, has as it base the decimal number 16. This number system requires more digit symbols that the decimal system. The symbols most commonly used are 0, 1, 2, 3, 4, 5, 6, 7, 8, 9, A, B, C, D, E, and F. Thus, the first six letters of the alphabet are used as symbols along with the 10 decimal digits. A in hex is 10 in decimal, B is 11, C is 12, and so on through F.

Let's consider the hexadecimal number 5A7.B2.

$$5A7.B2 = 5 \times 16^2 + 10 \times 16^1 + 7 \times 16^0 + 11 \times (1/16)^1 + 2 \times (1/16)^2$$

Note that the hexadecimal number is on the left side while the decimal equivalent is on the right side.

The following statements are true for the hexadecimal system:

1. The base of the hexadecimal number system is the decimal number 16.
2. The rank of a digit in a hexadecimal number are powers of either 16 or 1/16.
3. The rank increases by a power of 16 for each position moved to the left of the hexadecimal point.
4. The rank decreases by a power of 1/16 for each position moved to the right of the hexadecimal point.

Converting numbers. When you read a number in any system other than the decimal system, you cannot use the names for decimal position—'*teen* or *twenty* for the second position, *hundred* to name a number in the third position, and so on. The binary number 1011.1 must be read "one, zero, one, one, point one." The same is true for numbers in other systems.

For anyone planning to do much work with computers, it is important to know how to convert numbers from one system to another, especially from the common decimal system into the binary system used by most computers. As bridges between these two systems we often use the octal or the hexadecimal system. We now discuss some algorithms for converting numbers.

Converting from decimal to another system. There are four steps in the conversion. If we call the decimal integer I and wish to convert to an integer in the number system of base b, we proceed as follows:

1. Set $M = I$.

2. Divide M by the base b, which gives a quotient Q and a remainder R, a digit of the equivalent integer in the new system.
3. If $Q = 0$, the conversion is complete and the equivalent integer is the number obtained by writing the remainders R obtained in step 2 in the order computed from right to left. If Q is zero, stop processing.
4. Set $M = Q$ and go to step 2.

EXAMPLE 1 Convert the decimal integer 2610 to its octal equivalent.

2610/8 = 326, remainder 2
326/8 = 40, remainder 6
40/8 = 5, remainder 0
5/8 = 0, remainder 5

The octal equivalent is 5062.

EXAMPLE 2 Convert the decimal integer 6825 to its hexadecimal equivalent.

6825/16 = 426, remainder 9
426/16 = 26, remainder 10
26/16 = 1, remainder 10
1/16 = 0, remainder 1

The hexadecimal equivalent is 1AA9, with decimal number 10 written A.

Converting a decimal fraction. If we call the decimal fraction F we convert it to its equivalent in a number system of base b using these steps:

1. Multiply F by b and call the result Y. If Y=0, go to step 4. If not, go to step 2.
2. Note the integer part of Y (it may be zero) since it is a digit in the equivalent number.
3. Set F equal to the fractional part of Y (maybe all of Y) and go to step 1.
4. The conversion is complete and the equivalent number is obtained by writing the integer parts of Y from step 2, in the order computed from left to right following a period.

This may never produce Y=0 at step 1. If not, stop the algorithm when as many digits as desired are computed.

EXAMPLE 3 Convert the decimal fraction .2 to its binary equivalent.

$.2 \times 2 = \underline{0}.4$
$.4 \times 2 = \underline{0}.8$
$.8 \times 2 = \underline{1}.6$
$.6 \times 2 = \underline{1}.2$

$.2 \times 2 = \underline{0}.4$
$.4 \times 2 = \underline{0}.8$

Although Y is never zero, we stop at 6 digits and write the result .001100 as the binary fraction equivalent to the decimal fraction .2.

EXAMPLE 4 Convert the decimal number 126.25 to its equivalent octal number.

We convert the integer portion 126 by applying the integer algorithm and the fractional portion by applying the fraction algorithm.

$126/8 = 15$, remainder $\underline{6}$
$15/8 = 1$, remainder $\underline{7}$
$1/8 = 0$, remainder $\underline{1}$

The octal equivalent of 126_{10} is 176_8, where the subscripts indicate the base of the number system. Now we convert the fractional part.

$.25 \times 8 = \underline{2}.0$
$.0 \times 8 = \underline{0}.0$

The octal equivalent of $.25_{10}$ is 2_8. Therefore, $126.25_{10} = 176.2_8$, and the conversion is complete.

Converting from another system to decimal. In converting a number from base b to a decimal system it is perhaps easiest to express the number in its polynomial form then compute the decimal equivalent.

EXAMPLE 5 Convert the binary number 101.01011 into its decimal equivalent. The right side of the equation below is polynomial form.

$$\begin{aligned} 101.01011 &= 1 \times 2^2 + 0 \times 2^1 + 1 \times 2^0 + 0 \times (1/2)^1 + 1 \times (1/2)^2 \\ &\quad + 0 \times (1/2)^3 + 1 \times (1/2)^4 + 1 \times (1/2)^5 \\ &= 4 + 0 + 1 + 0 + .25 + .0625 + .03125 \\ &= 5.34375 \end{aligned}$$

Binary, octal, and hexadecimal numbers. Because the base numbers of these three systems are related to each other as powers of 2, conversions among these systems are relatively easy to perform. Since $8 = 2^3$ and $16 = 2^4$, we can conclude that each position in an octal number has the value of three positions in the binary system. Similarly, each hexadecimal digit has the value of four binary digits.

EXAMPLE 6 $10101.01101_2 = \underline{010}\ \underline{101}.\underline{011}\ \underline{010}_2 = 25.32_8$

Beginning at the binary point, underline groups of 3 binary digits. If the leftmost group does not have 3 digits, leading zeros are added. Similarly, if the rightmost fractional group does not have 3 digits, trailing zeros are added.

Then each group of 3 binary digits is converted into its octal equivalent, keeping its position.

Consider each of the triplets from left to right. Zeros have been added at the left and right to make complete triplets.

$010_2 = 2_8$ $101_2 = 3_8$ $010_2 = 5_8$ $011_2 = 2_8$

Therefore, $10101.01101_2 = 25.32_8$.

To convert an octal number into a binary number, reverse the procedure. Expand each octal digit to its equivalent in 3 binary digits.

EXAMPLE 7 Suppose we convert 25.32_8 into binary equivalent:

```
 2    5 .  3    2
010  101 . 011  010
```

Below each octal digit, write its binary equivalent. By placing the binary point directly below the octal point, we retain the correct positions of integer and fractional digits in the binary number.

We turn next to converting from binary to hexadecimal numbers. Since $2^4 = 16$, we conclude that every group of four binary digits converts to one hexadecimal digit. Here is an example:

EXAMPLE 8 Convert 110101.11_2 to its hexadecimal equivalent.

$$\begin{array}{ccc} 0011 & 0101 & .\ 1100 \\ 3 & 5 & .\ C_{16} \end{array}$$

Add leading and trailing zeros if necessary to create quadruplets of binary digits. Then each quadruplet is converted into its hexadecimal equivalent.

The hexadecimal point keeps the same relative position as the binary point. Recall that the letters A, B, C, D, E, and F are hexadecimal digits equivalent to decimal 10, 11, 12, 13, 14, and 15.

Converting from hexadecimal digit gives rise to four binary digits. Study this example and the procedure should be clear:

EXAMPLE 9

$$\begin{array}{cccc} 3 & D & .\ 9 & F_{16} \\ 0011 & 1101 & .\ 1001 & 1111 \end{array}$$

Numbers inside a computer. Having discussed procedures for converting numbers from one numeration system to another, we are ready to consider the *internal representation* of information in a digital computer. We begin with integers.

Integers. Any information stored in a computer is represented internally in a form logically equivalent to a collection of binary digits. Furthermore, most computers are equipped to store a fixed number of binary digits in each storage unit, called a *word.* Computer word size varies from 12 bits to 64 bits, with 32 bits being a very common word size. Let's assume for this discussion that our computer has a word size of 32 bits.

When a decimal integer is stored in a computer it is converted to its binary equivalent, then stored starting at the right of the computer word. One bit of the word is usually reserved to specify the *sign* of the number, usually the leftmost bit—typically, 0 is positive and 1 is negative.

EXAMPLE The decimal number + 123 is stored like this in a 32-bit word:

00000000000000000000000001111011

The leftmost bit is zero because the number is positive. The number itself is right adjusted in the word, so if you analyze the binary number shown you will see that

$$1111011_2 = 123_{10}$$

Complements of binary numbers. There is another common method of storing negative numbers in computers. It involves the concept of the complement of a number. In the binary system, the complement of a single digit is the opposite digit. Thus, the complement of 0 is 1, and the complement of 1 is 0. Given a binary number x of more than one digit, its complement, denoted by $\overline{x}$, is the number made up of digits such that each one is the complement of its counterpart in x. For example, consider the 16-bit word

$$x = 0000000000101100,$$

then $$\overline{x} = 1111111111010011$$

This form of the complement is called the *ones complement.*

It is easy for the computer to complement a number, so complements are handy ways of doing arithmetic operations. For subtraction, *add* the twos complement of the subtrahend. The *twos complement* of a binary number is the result of adding 1 to its ones complement. That is, given a binary number x, the twos complement is $\overline{x} + 1$.

$$x = 0000000000100101$$
$$\overline{x} = 1111111111011010$$
$$\overline{x}+1 = 1111111111011011$$
$$x+(\overline{x}+1) = 0000000000000000$$ *if 16 bits are allowed*

Since the sum of any number in any system and its negative is 0, it appears that $\overline{x} + 1$ is the negative of x. Thus, the twos complement of the binary number x represents $-x$.

If we use the twos complement to represent negative integers, then the range of values for integers that may be stored is -2^{m-1} to $+2^{m-1} - 1$ where m is the number of bits in a word.

Real numbers. The internal representation of real numbers differs among the various available computers. There are some common features that we shall mention, however, after which we will describe the details of one method employed in some computers.

When representing real numbers, most computers designate certain bits to specify the coefficient and other bits to specify the exponent of the real number. By *coefficient* and *exponent* we mean something very much like .625 and 2, respectively, when 62.5 is represented as $.625 \times 10^2$.

The difference is that in a computer, all numbers are represented as bits. Not only do certain bits specify the coefficient and the exponent, but it is necessary to have one bit specify the sign of the coefficient. Typically, a sign bit of 0 indicates positive while a sign bit of 1 denotes negative.

EXAMPLE In order to show how 62.5 is stored in a 16-bit word, let's suppose the bits are identified 0–15 from right to left. The coefficient is stored in bits 0–7, the exponent in bits 8–13, the sign of the exponent in bit 14, and the sign of the coefficient in bit 15. Figure A.1 shows these assumptions:

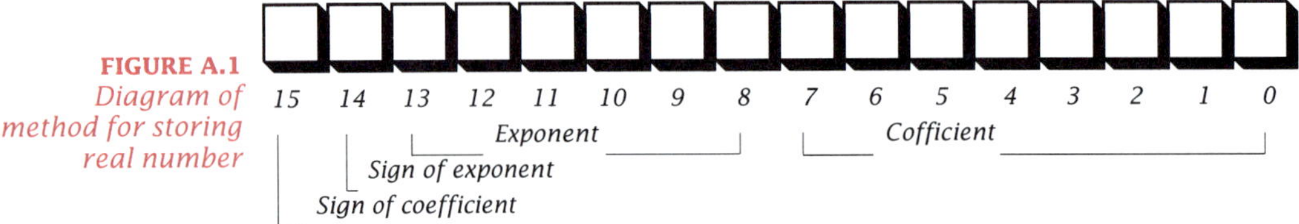

FIGURE A.1 *Diagram of method for storing real number*

Since all internal numbers are binary, convert 62.5_{10} to its binary equivalent. First convert 62:

$$
\begin{aligned}
62/2 &= 31, \text{ remainder } \underline{0}\\
31/2 &= 15, \text{ remainder } \underline{1}\\
15/2 &= 7, \text{ remainder } \underline{1}\\
7/2 &= 3, \text{ remainder } \underline{1}\\
3/2 &= 1, \text{ remainder } \underline{1}\\
1/2 &= 0, \text{ remainder } \underline{1}
\end{aligned}
$$

Therefore, $62_{10} = 111110_2$. Next we convert $.5_{10}$ as follows:

$$.5 \times 2 = 1.0$$

Therefore, $.5_{10} = .1_2$. Now we can write the entire binary equivalent of 62.5 as 111110.1, or $.1111101_2 \times 2^6$, or $.1111101_2 \times 2^{110}$. This last form has both coefficient and exponent in binary form.

Now we insert the coefficient .1111101 in bits 0–7 and the exponent 110 in bits 8–13. Bit 15 is 0 because the coefficient is positive, bit 14 is 0 because the exponent is positive. All other bits are zeros. Figure A.2 shows the result:

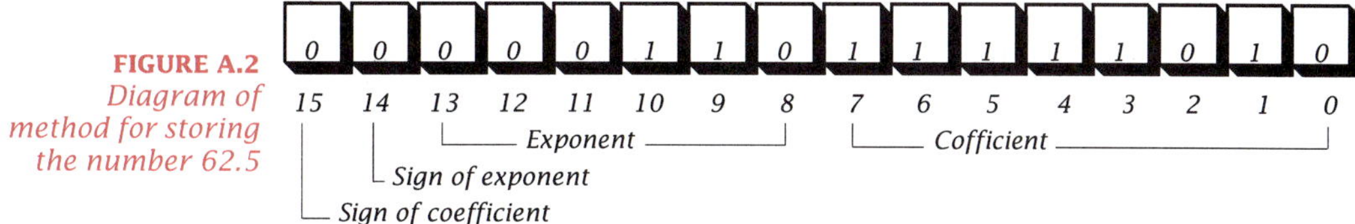

FIGURE A.2 *Diagram of method for storing the number 62.5*

Since the writing of even 16 bits as in Figure A.2 is tedious, internal representations are sometimes written in octal or hexadecimal form. The hexadecimal number for 62.5 is 0 6 F A:

0000	0110	1111	1010
0	6	F	A

Each quadruplet of binary digits is converted to its hexadecimal equivalent.

In this example, we assume that the normal form for the coefficient assumes the binary point at the extreme left end of the coefficient field. However, in most computers the binary point is actually at the extreme *right* of the coefficient field.

This does not change the validity of our method, but it does produce more negative exponents for real numbers. Since the binary point is stored to the right of where it is in the actual number represented, the negative exponent indicates that the binary point must be moved to the left.

Representing character data. Nonnumeric or character data are represented internally as bits arranged according to some coding scheme. Table A.1 shows a standard character set of 63 characters and the code for each character in common coding schemes.

Each of the coding schemes has a particular advantage. ASCII is the acronym for American Standard Code for Information Interchange and is the standard 8-bit code.

EXAMPLE 1 From Table A.1, verify that the internal representation of the word DOGS in a 32-bit word using ASCII code is

0100	0100	0100	1111	0100	0111	0101	0011
4	4	4	F	4	7	5	3

Some computers, like the Cyber series from Control Data Corporation, have words of 60 bits. For these computers it is more efficient to use External BCD code since that 6-bit code allows for the storage of 10 characters per computer word.

EXAMPLE 2 In External BCD, the word COMPUTERS appears as follows:

110 011 100 110 100 100 100 111 010 100 010 011 110 101 101 001 010 010
6 3 4 6 4 4 4 7 2 4 2 3 6 5 5 1 2 2

Verify the result from Table A.1.

TABLE A.1 *Standard character sets for selected characters*

Character	Hexadecimal EBCDIC code	External BCD code	Hexadecimal ASCII code
:	7A	00	3A
A	C1	61	41
B	C2	62	42
C	C3	63	43
D	C4	64	44
E	C5	65	45
F	C6	66	46
G	C7	67	47
H	C8	70	48
I	C9	71	49
J	D1	41	4A
K	D2	42	4B
L	D3	43	4C
M	D4	44	4D
N	D5	45	4E
O	D6	46	4F
P	D7	47	50
Q	D8	50	51
R	D9	51	52
S	E2	22	53
T	E3	23	54
U	E4	24	55
V	E5	25	56
W	E6	26	57
X	E7	27	58
Y	E8	30	59
Z	E9	31	5A
0	F0	12	30
1	F1	01	31
2	F2	02	32
3	F3	03	33
4	F4	04	34
5	F5	05	35
6	F6	06	36
7	F7	07	37
8	F8	10	38
9	F9	11	39
+	4E	60	2B
–	60	40	2D
*	5C	54	2A
/	61	21	2F
(	4D	34	28
)	5D	74	29
$	5B	53	24
=	7E	13	3D
blank	40	20	20
,	6B	33	2C
.	4B	73	2E
#	7B	36	23
[		17	5B
]		32	5D
%	6C	16	25
"	7F	14	22
_	6D	35	5F
!	5A	52	21
&	50	37	26
'	7D	55	27
?	6F	56	3F
<	4C	72	3C
>	6E	57	3E
@	7C	15	40
\	E0	75	5C
^		76	5E
;	5E	77	3B

Appendix B
FORTRAN Library Functions

The following library or intrinsic functions are included as a part of FORTRAN 77. Names preceded with an asterisk are generic; the results computed by the function are the same data type as that of the argument(s). When using functions that convert data from one type specified by the argument(s) to another type specified by the function name, it is your responsibility to provide arguments of the required data type. Data types are listed using the first letter of their name: **R**EAL or floating point, **I**NTEGER, **D**OUBLE PRECISION, **C**OMPLEX ($x+yi$), **C**HARACTER, **L**OGICAL, and **G**ENERIC.

Symbolic name	*Number of arguments*	*Argument data type*	*Result data type*	*Description and limitations*
ABS	1	R	R	Absolute value of $x = x$ if $x \geq 0$, $-x$ if $x<0$.
IABS	1	I	I	Same as for ABS but in integer form.
DABS	1	D	D	Same as for ABS but in double precision.
CABS	1	C	R	CABS(X) = SQRT(REALSQ(X) + IMAGSQ(X)).
*REAL	1	G	R	Converts integer to real.
FLOAT	1	I	R	Converts integer to real.
SNGL	1	D	R	Converts single precision to double precision.
IFIX	1	R	I	Converts real to integer.
AINT	1	R	R	Produces the largest signed integer less than or equal to argument.
INT	1	R	I	Same as for AINT but result is integer.
IDINT	1	D	I	Same as for INT but argument must be double precision.
*MOD	2	I	I	MOD(X,Y) – remainder of X/Y.
AMOD	2	R	R	AMOD(X,Y) = remainder of X/Y.
DMOD	2	D	D	Same as for AMOD but with double precision.
*MAX	2 or more	G	G	Determines the maximum value among its arguments.
AMAX0	2 or more	I	R	Finds the largest of the specified integer arguments and gives real results.
AMAX1	2 or more	R	R	Same as AMAX0 but arguments are real.
MAX0	2 or more	I	I	Same as AMAX0 but result is integer.
MAX1	2 or more	R	I	Same as AMAX0 but arguments are real and result is integer.
DMAX1	2 or more	D	D	Same as AMAX0 but arguments and result are double precision.
*MIN	2 or more	G	G	Determines the minimum value among its arguments.
AMIN0	2 or more	I	R	Finds the smallest of the specified integer arguments and gives real results.
AMIN1	2 or more	R	R	Same as AMIN0 but arguments are real.
MIN0	2 or more	I	I	Same as AMIN0 but result is integer.
MIN1	2 or more	R	I	Same as AMIN0 but arguments are real and result is integer.
DMIN1	2 or more	D	D	Same as AMIN0 but arguments and result are double precision.

Symbolic name	*Number of arguments*	*Argument data type*	*Result data type*	*Description and limitations*
*SIGN	2	R	R	SIGN(X,Y) = sign of Y with |X|.
ISIGN	2	I	I	Same as SIGN but with integers.
DSIGN	2	D	D	Same as SIGN but with double precision values.
*DIM	2	R	R	DIM(X,Y) = X − AMIN1(X,Y).
IDIM	2	I	I	Same as DIM but with integers.
DDIM	2	D	D	Same as DIM but with double precision values.
SNGL	1	D	R	Converts double precision real argument to the most significant single precision.
DBLE	1	R	D	Converts single precision real argument to double precision.
REAL	1	C	R	Produces the real part of a complex argument.
AIMAG	1	C	R	Produces in real form the imaginary part of a complex argument.
CMPLX	1 or 2	R	C	Converts one or two real arguments into complex form.
*EXP	1	R	R	EXP(X)=e^x.
DEXP	1	D	D	Same as EXP in double precision.
CEXP	1	C	C	CEXP(z) = e^x(COS(x) + i * SIN(y)) where $z = x + i * y$, i = SQRT(−1).
*LOG	1	G	G	Produces the natural log of its argument.
ALOG	1	R	R	Produces the natural log of a real, non-negative argument.
DLOG	1	D	D	Same as ALOG in double precision.
CLOG	1	C	C	CLOG(z) = .5*ALOG(x^2+y^2) + i*ATAN(y/x), where $z = x + i*y$.
*ALOG10	1	R	R	Produces the common log of a real, non-negative argument.
DLOG10	1	D	D	Same as ALOG10 in double precision.
*SQRT	1	R	R	Produces the square root of a real argument.
DSQRT	1	D	D	Same as SQRT in double precision.
CSQRT	1	C	C	CSQRT(z) = SQRT(x^2+y^2)(COS(t) + i*SIN(t)) where t=(1/2)*ATAN(y/n) and z=x+iy.
*SIN	1	R	R	Produces the trigonometric sine of a real argument where the argument is in radians.
DSIN	1	D	D	Same as SIN in double precision.
CSIN	1	C	C	CSIN(z) = SIN(x)**cosh*(y) + i*COS(x)**sinh*(y), where z=x+iy
*ASIN	1	R	R	Produces in radians the arcsine of a real argument.
DASIN	1	D	D	Same as ASIN in double precision.
*COS	1	R	R	Produces the trigonometric cosine of a real argument where the argument is in radians.
DCOS	1	D	D	Same as COS in double precision.
CCOS	1	C	C	CCOS(z) = COS(x)**cosh*(y) − i*SIN(x)**sinh*(y) where z=x+iy.
*ACOS	1	R	R	Produces in radians the arccosine of a real argument.
DACOS	1	D	D	Same as ACOS in double precision.
*ATAN	1	R	R	Produces in radians the arctangent of a real argument.
DATAN	1	D	D	Same as ATAN in double precision.
*ATAN2	2	R	R	Produces in radians the arctangent of (X/Y) where Y is not zero.
DATAN2	2	D	D	Same as ATAN2 in double precision.

Symbolic name	Number of arguments	Argument data type	Result data type	Description and limitations
*TANH	1	R	R	Produces the hyperbolic tangent of a real argument.
DTANH	1	D	D	Same as TANH in double precision.
ICHAR	1	CH	I	Converts character code of a character argument to its integer equivalent.
CHAR	1	I	CH	Converts an integer argument to its equivalent character.
LEN	1	CH	I	Produces the length (number of characters) of a character string argument, including blanks.
INDEX	2	CH	I	INDEX(CH1,CH2) = position in character string CH1 where substring CH2 begins.
LGE	2	CH	L	LGE(CH1,CH2) = true or false depending on whether or not the code for CH1 is greater than or equal to the code for CH2.
LGT	2	CH	L	Same as LGE but the comparison is "greater than."
LLE	2	CH	L	Same as LGE but the comparison is "less than or equal."
LLT	2	CH	L	Same as LGE but the comparison is "less than."

The preceding list of library functions includes all those in FORTRAN 77; *other versions of* FORTRAN *have additional functions. Here are five of the most common. Before you use these in a program, check that your system includes them.*

Symbolic name	Number of arguments	Argument data type	Result data type	Description and limitations
RAND	0 or 1	I	R	Argument (if required) determines the starting point of a sequence of pseudo-random numbers uniformly distributed between 0 and 1. A negative argument (if required) causes a different sequence every time.
AND	2 or more	L	L	Produces a result in logical form when the logical AND is performed on two or more arguments.
OR	2 or more	L	L	Produces a result in logical form when the logical OR is performed on two or more arguments.
COMPL	1	L	L	Produces a result in logical form when the logical COMPLEMENT is performed on the argument.
SHIFT	2	R,I	R	SHIFT(X,N) causes a circular shift to the left of N bits in the internal representation of X. SHIFT(X,–N) causes an arithmetic shift to the right of N bits in the internal representation of X.

Many versions of FORTRAN *make available some library subroutine subprograms; here are four of the most common. To use them, insert a* CALL *statement in your program. Before using these in a program, check that your system includes them.*

Subroutine	*Description and limitations*
EXIT	Terminates the program.
DATE	Produces the current date from the computer's internal clock.
IDATE	Produces the year and day of the year as a single 5-digit number YYDDD where YY is the 2-digit year designation and DDD the 3-digit day-of-year.
CLOCK	Produces the time of day as HHMMSS where HH is the 2-digit hour designation, MM the 2-digit minutes, and SS the 2-digit seconds.

Index